WoL 782·421

Libraries, books and more . . .

1 1 JUL 2012 **1 3 MAR 2023**	
W/TON LIBRARY	
4-10-16	

PARALLEL
LIVES

BLONDIE

PARALLEL
LIVES

BLONDIE

DICK PORTER & KRIS NEEDS

OMNIBUS PRESS
London / New York / Paris / Sydney / Copenhagen / Berlin / Madrid / Tokyo

Exclusive Distributors
Music Sales Limited,
14/15 Berners Street,
London, W1T 3LJ.

Music Sales Corporation,
257 Park Avenue South,
New York, NY 10010, USA.

Macmillan Distribution Services,
56 Parkwest Drive
Derrimut, Vic 3030,
Australia.

Every effort has been made to trace the copyright holders of the photographs in this book but one
or two were unreachable. We would be grateful if the photographers concerned would contact us.

Printed in the EU

A catalogue record for this book is available from the British Library.

Visit Omnibus Press on the web at www.omnibuspress.com

Contents

For Donna & Michelle

Introduction

"Maybe we were a reality TV show before there was reality TV," Chris Stein remarked during a phone conversation a couple of years ago. Of course, Chris was referring to Blondie, the group he formed with Deborah Harry five decades ago which, from the least promising of beginnings, clawed a path through the ruins of downtown New York to become a global phenomenon.

Today, Blondie are duly recognised as one of the 20th century's most influential and innovative groups, fronted by the most imitated (though never equalled) female singer of all time. Ignited by the success of 1978's 'Denis', Blondie fired off a salvo of groundbreaking hits that included '(I'm Always Touched By Your) Presence Dear', 'Hanging On The Telephone', 'One Way Or Another', 'Sunday Girl', 'Heart Of Glass', 'Atomic', 'Call Me', 'The Tide Is High' and 'Rapture' – the latter being their homage to Chic, which brought New York's hip hop revolution into the mainstream.

While Debbie's striking beauty made it impossible for her to escape becoming a pin-up in the old-fashioned sense, she saw that it happened on her terms. It quickly became apparent that she was a strong-willed, clever, and culturally articulate woman, who would open the door for successive generations of female singers to seize control of their own destinies. By demonstrating that it was possible to be intelligent *and* beautiful, she lit a path that runs from Madonna to Lady Gaga. Her refusal to be manipulated by any authority but her own established a post-feminist ideal that would inspire women such as Garbage's Shirley Manson, Gwen Stefani and Pink.

Similarly, the fleeting but dynamic riot grrrl movement drew much of its spirit of independence from Debbie.

As the creative dynamo at the pulsing core of Blondie, Debbie and Chris may have been the most vibrantly idiosyncratic partnership to emerge from New York's punk era. But they also faced the challenge of maintaining a relationship amid the incessant pressures of leading a number one group, besieged by business nightmares and inter-band ego wars, and exacerbated by drugs. These and other factors combined to run down Blondie's first phase, with Chris' debilitating illness as the final nail in its coffin.

Happily, Blondie returned in 1998, as Debbie, Chris, Clem Burke and Jimmy Destri topped the charts again with 'Maria'. New members joined the fold to extend the group's legacy and establish them as a popular fixture on the summer festival circuit. Such is the timeless magic of the songs and Debbie's allure that new generations have embraced them, as old-timers look back with affection.

Blondie's story ranks among the most resonant of rock'n'roll tales. On one level, it concerns the love and creativity shared by two unique individuals. However, it is equally about New York, the city that suffused the group with its energy, attitude and excitement. Few other bands are as synonymous with, or evocative of their hometown as Blondie. Even at the peak of their global popularity, Debbie and Chris kept their ears to the New York sidewalk and their feet planted in the disparate scenes flourishing amid the city's underground art epicentre and throughout the parallel club movements of punk, disco and hip hop. In the case of the latter, they were the first white group to trumpet the revolutionary new style, scoring a huge hit with 'Rapture'. For four of their five years at the hub of the media spotlight, Chris and Debbie ensured they regularly appeared on Glenn O'Brien's weekly *TV Party* on cable television.

Outside the steady trickle of much-anticipated new material, Blondie's influence can be found constantly as their songs show up on the soundtracks of TV programmes, movies and ads, and Debbie's pout is always evoked by the latest tousled blonde singer. As she herself now reflects, "Blondie were part of a chain of events, part of the New York scene where we were feeling it and really living it. Blondie did what we did before anyone knew what was happening, and laid a lot of groundwork for other bands. We were probably too early. I think the music industry caught up with us, but they didn't like us when we started. We did feel we were like outsiders breaking into the establishment."

This book is the second of the authors' 'New York Stories' trilogy – our first, *Trash!*, being a 'before, during and after' history of The New York Dolls, whose infamous exploits dovetail with Debbie's life in the early part of this book's narrative.

There is also a personal connection between Blondie, the quintessential New York band, and co-author Kris, who championed them early on when he was editor of *Zigzag* magazine. As Kris tells it:

In recent years, whenever I was called up to write features about life in the eye of the Blondie hurricane or appear in documentaries, the question of a book started being asked again. Working on these projects had already brought me back in touch with Chris and Debbie, who I hadn't spoken to for over 20 years. The conversations with Chris were always a delight, his lazy drawl meandering from Blondie's early days to his Animal Records label – plus, without fail, the inexorably changing face of his beloved New York City. We talked about the need for a book chronicling the New York music scene, even a Blondie biopic, but never a 'Blondie book' – although, when this project was finally underway, Chris just said, "Anything you need".

He had already supplied the best reference I could wish for after I asked him for an intro for a Blondie magazine piece I was writing a couple of years ago:

"I was really fond of Needs in a period where we were regularly savaged by British rock journalists who would appeal to our good graces and come on all friendly like. Kris proved to be a staunch supporter whose moral code was not at odds with his face value. In retrospect, I look back with a degree of fondness at the battles that went on in the press but, at the time, I was glad to have Zigzag provide me with the occasional platform to shoot back from. Kris accompanied us on various forays into the hinterlands of Britain as we lived out our fantasies of Beatle-mania, so I was quite pleased to hear from him again after all this time."

The feeling was mutual. Debbie and Chris's fiercely independent natures have ensured Blondie's enduring legacy. This book tells how it happened.

KRIS NEEDS
DICK PORTER
2012

Chapter One

An American Girl

"The only thing I wanted to be as a teenager was a beatnik. I loved that whole ideal of artists, musicians, writers. It was a choice, a life choice, and it hasn't always been easy."

Debbie Harry

In June 1979, Blondie achieved what was then considered a key signifier that a band had made it in the USA: appearing on the cover of *Rolling Stone*. Journalist Jamie James – subsequently described by Debbie Harry as "a strutting little pompous git" – caught the group on one of the off-days that sometimes occurred during this period, as Blondie's fame exponentially grew while the press seemed regularly reluctant to take them seriously.

In his *Rolling Stone* piece, James was put on the defensive from the start: "I can tell the moment Debbie lays eyes on me that she hates my guts." The fact that it had taken 'Heart Of Glass' hitting number one in the US charts to arouse the magazine's ardour irked Debbie, who asked him why they had shown no interest three years earlier. The hapless writer tried to splice reportage of in-band sniping to his evident lack of empathy with Blondie's music or the scene from which it emerged, bookending his piece with an interview with a woman who likes to be called 'Cag' – Catherine Harry, Debbie's adopted mother.

Until that point, accounts of Debbie's pre-New York past had been restricted to her adoption, her New Jersey school days and vague allusions to mostly unspecified forms of teenage rebellion. James kicked off with Cag's anecdote about Debbie's singing debut – her sixth-grade class had once staged a 'Tom Thumb wedding', featuring one kid as the groom, another as the bride and a third cast in the role of bridesmaid. She also recalled Debbie soloing on the 1912 chart-topping parlour standard and wedding perennial 'I Love You Truly' for the grand finale.

Cag explained what a tight-knit family the Harrys were. "The only Christmas she wasn't here was the time she was on tour in Australia [1977]. She was so depressed, and I was so depressed. She said, 'I'll never be away for Christmas again.' Debbie's a wonderful daughter."

Had Debbie been much of a hit with the boys? "Are you kidding?" Cag erupted, going on to relate the story of how her adopted daughter was approached to enter the high school beauty pageant. "She didn't particularly want to go in; they called her in … She was always beautiful. When she was a baby, my friends used to tell me I should send her picture in to [baby food manufacturer] Gerber's, because she would be picked as one of the Gerber Babies. But I didn't send it in. I didn't believe in her being exploited."

"My mother was offered a contract for me to become a Gerber Baby, but my mother told me there was no way. She wouldn't be a showbiz momma. So maybe that's why it took me so long to get my music together," confirmed Debbie, touching upon the trait that led to her becoming a creative late bloomer.

"She is shy," continued Cag. "When she's not performing – and you must know this – she's quiet, with a very pixie sense of humour. She's not real outgoing or loud. She's sort of retiring … very family-oriented … She's the one that got homesick at camp."

Deborah Ann Harry was born Angela Tremble in Miami, Florida on July 1, 1945. She was adopted at the age of three months by Catherine and her husband Richard, who worked as a salesman of woven clothing labels in Manhattan's fashion district. ("He was very casual about it," Debbie would remember. "He always said that if people want something they're going to buy it.") The family lived in the quintessential small town of Hawthorne, New Jersey, described by Debbie as "a typical suburban commuter kind of town".

Debbie appears to have been an insecure, solitary child, unhappy with the way she was dressed down by a mother who "didn't contemplate a future for me other than marriage". To a degree, this emphasis on conformity sprang from the teachings of the Episcopalian faith, to which the family subscribed. Although this ascetic strain of Protestant Christianity was subsequently abandoned by Debbie (who dismissed it as simply comprising "no incense, no confession" and "good hymns"), she also recognised that it laid the foundation of a broader interest in spirituality. "It teaches you to be real pragmatic. Then you start to wonder about God. Then you just leave the church. A lot of Protestants don't go to church. But it's very social, very community supportive. But I think that G–O–D is like the answer to a formula for creating life. Or some kind of energy or anti-gravity. It's like the answer to an equation and it's become mythical over the years. But at one time we all knew what it was. I don't know when it was exactly, but that was the ancient knowledge. It's become diffused as it was handed down and turned into myth."

While Debbie's insecurities may have stemmed from her adoption, the Harry household (which also included a younger sister, Martha, and a cousin, Bill, who lived with the family) was evidently warm and loving. Although Catherine and Richard were strict, they imposed boundaries on their children in a caring manner.

When Debbie was four years old, her parents broached the idea that she was adopted in the gentlest way possible. "They framed it in a bedtime story about [a child] being chosen," she later revealed. "And then said, 'And that's how we got you.'"

Kids are highly adaptive creatures, and this was certainly true of Debbie. "To me they were just my mum and dad and I was very happy that way." Looking back, she clearly appreciates the pivotal roles that Catherine and Richard played in her development. "The turning point in my life was being adopted and moving to New Jersey. If not I might have stayed in Florida and who knows what could have happened. Maybe I would have worked at Disneyland."

In common with many adoptees, the notion of her biological mother as a mystery figure inspired imaginative childhood speculation. "Not knowing where I came from is a great stimulant to the imagination, and it has always meant I don't take anything for granted," Debbie observed. "One afternoon while we sat in the kitchen drinking coffee my Aunt Helen said I looked like a movie star, which thrilled me and fuelled another secret fantasy about Marilyn Monroe possibly being my natural mother. I always thought I was Marilyn Monroe's kid. I felt physically related and akin to her long before I knew she had been adopted herself … Why Marilyn and not Lana Turner, Carole Lombard, Jayne Mansfield? Maybe it was Marilyn's need for immense doses of demonstrative love that is the common denominator between us. Although that doesn't fit me, because I got loads of love. My parents had to put up with some stupid shit from me like I've always had this sense of destiny, and when I felt I wasn't being appreciated, I'd tell them. 'You'll be sorry you talked to me like this when I'm rich and famous.' They would laugh. At least I kept them entertained."

Rather than becoming mired in feelings of abandonment, Debbie's stable home life and mental agility enabled her to draw positive elements from being adopted. "Having a big question mark about your identity, especially when you're a kid, because you're always trying to figure out who you are anyway, led to this double portion of ambiguity – the great unknown. One of the things I've always felt about not being identified, not knowing exactly what I was supposed to look like or what I was supposed to do, was that I could be whoever I wanted to be. And I really, really wasn't like anybody. I think that's helped me, but it was also difficult at times."

Debbie would subsequently find her biological father, although her birth mother refused any contact when her whereabouts were unearthed in the late eighties. "I found out some personal history. I went to the agency that I was adopted through and I spoke with the representative. She took out all my files, and the files from that period were very, very in-depth – I was adopted right after the war, and people kept good records because there were so many lost loves and so much confusion going on – so many children."

Recounting the circumstances of her birth, Debbie explained, "I think on my father's side, I have seven or eight half brothers and sisters. My father was already married and my mother was not married. She got pregnant and then found out he was married and had all these children. She was heartbroken and she went away, had me and put me up for adoption." To this day, Debbie has no intention of making contact with any paternal siblings from her biological family. "I don't see what purpose it would serve," she asserts. "How would I relate to them?"

In later years, Deborah employed therapy as a means of exploring the emotional impact of being adopted at such an early age. "I think it gave me some fear and some anger, and I didn't know how to separate the two, because I think they are very closely related ... It was a core issue for me and must have happened at a time when I was unable to put it into language, but it was something that I had experienced as an infant. A trauma. So eventually I was able to identify that, and to say, 'Oh, that's what happened,' and to take that by the hand."

Aside from Cag's conventional aspirations for her daughter, economic necessity played a key role in how Debbie dressed. "I was always wearing second-hand clothes. We were really broke then. And my mother wasn't really into pop culture at the time, so it wasn't really driven home to me what the fifties were like.

"I hated the way I looked growing up. I had this blonde hair, pale-blue eyes and these jutting cheekbones. I didn't look like any other kids I grew up with and I felt very uncomfortable about my face. I hated looking in mirrors and I definitely didn't think I was pretty," Debbie later insisted. "When I was a baby I was real pretty, but in between I was a real mess. I was very ugly. I just grew up weird ... My mother always made me get these weird haircuts and I always had to wear clunky shoes and shit. I never thought I was pretty.

"My mother and I never got along in terms of clothing at all. She wanted me to look like I was a preppy WASP from Connecticut – that was good fashion to her, and I sort of loathed it ... I always wanted to wear black and I wanted to wear things that were tough looking. There was a phase where I wanted to wear big flannel shirts and tight pants, and I always wanted to wear my sweaters backwards. I had clear ideas about what I wanted and it really had nothing to do with the times. So my mother and I never agreed."

Looking back on the sartorial conflict that parents and their offspring habitually engage in, Debbie now admits to a greater understanding of her mother's perspective: "I appreciate some of the things she said now; she had some good fundamental rules that she followed. I wanted radical, I wanted sex, I wanted movie stars. But she had very classic ideas and she was right in many respects – that some things would ultimately look better on me; like a tailored line, a simple line, would look better on me than something frilly. I mean, they didn't have any money, she didn't have a great wardrobe or anything; a few pieces.

"When I was a teenager, my father started doing a little bit better, things got a bit easier," reveals Debbie. "When you don't have a lot of dough it gives you a sense of humility and value. But a lot of people come up that way; I'm certainly not bragging about it. Plus my mother and father have very old-fashioned values about loyalty and stayed married for 60 years through thick and thin. It wasn't always great — they had their ups and downs."

Despite initially lacking confidence, Debbie first revealed her voice in the church choir. "There I was, a fat, cherubic soprano getting it on with the Christian Soldiers," she would recount. "I loved singing so much I won the choir's perfect attendance award, a silver cross, truly earned by my parents for getting me to practise every week." She would later make an enthusiastic if limited cheerleader. "I wasn't very good at twirling, actually," she confessed. "I'd get very nervous and I would always drop it. But I think that's why they chose me. They had me there twirling and dropping the baton for the bending over aspect. I was there for the pervert fathers. Looking at my underpants!"

Although Debbie reacted against any kind of preordained suburban destiny, she was never an outright rebel at the high school where she was later described by classmates as "friendly" and "popular". "I feared and hated school passionately," she reflected. "School was like treading water to me. Art classes were my favourites, but painting/drawing wasn't considered important. Having shaken off the fat years I made baton twirler and was voted the prettiest girl in my senior class. Apart from that I didn't have much going for me in high school. I felt everybody was trying to limit what I was before I'd tried anything.

"I was always nervous at school. I liked being in the classroom, learning things. But I couldn't take the tension, having to pass a test. I was terrible at math, although I was quite good at geometry: ratios, envisioning the relationships of lines in space. English and art were my best subjects, but I had no idea of being a writer, or a songwriter, at that point."

As a means of escaping the cloying suburbia of Hawthorne, Deborah would travel to Manhattan to soak up the atmosphere and excitement absent from the quiet streets of her hometown. "I was 12 or 13 years old and on a Saturday morning for 80 cents, I could get a round trip ticket to

New York City. So I would get on a train and I would go into the city and I would walk around the West Village, which was old timey New York with the little streets and I would look in all the theatres and the clubs and the coffee shops, I would look at all the posters and see who was playing – it was very exciting for me."

In common with many teenagers from limited income households, Deborah also took part-time work as a means of raising some spending money. These early forays into the world of employment quickly established the idea that working in the straight world may not be for her. "I had two jobs that I really didn't like. I used to clean this woman's house but that was when I was really young, and then later on when I was in high school I got a job in a redemption centre for S&H green stamps, and that was completely humiliating. The people who came in there and wanted their merchandise were really demanding about it. Maybe they thought they were getting something for nothing and they had to be aggressive about it, but it just seemed that everybody was so mean."

As her worldview expanded, Debbie – who acquired her first serious boyfriend when she was 14 – gravitated toward the social and creative fringes, "I was an outsider in high school," she explained. "I always used to wear black, and I had my hair striped out and I always bleached it different pastel colours. Every time I got in with some people I got disenchanted and I got kicked out or quit, and I had to worry because my mother was always worried about my reputation, and my best friend was a fag. It was raunchy, but it was fun."

"All I remember about high school was how boring it was," recalled Debbie. "I made average and good grades at Hawthorne High School. I was never in any trouble. I was just steady. I was just there … I don't think that anything that I did in school was representative of me. You have to fit into the regime and you get through it." Despite continual pressure to conform, the teenage Debbie had little inclination to toe the line. "I got into a sorority. I had to run around and act a certain way, supply certain things upon command, like gum if they wanted gum. I was offensive to them, so I got canned. But the reason I got kicked out was because of this friend of mine who was really great, really nutty, but they thought he was too horrible. Mostly because he was gay. They said, 'You can't hang around with him.' So I got the axe. The girl that brought up the charges later on married him.

"I must have had 10 or 12 different colours of hair. At first I would use a mix of peroxide and ammonia, stuff that was easy to get. I started with streaks, and then it gradually turned orange. That's when my mother would start to notice. All of a sudden at dinner, she'd say, 'Your hair is different. What did you do?' And I'd just say, 'Oh, I lightened it a little.' My father would go, 'Well, I don't know if I like this, hmmm …' But he liked it on my mother; so it was semi-acceptable. Later, it was turning up platinum."

Her experimental approach to cosmetics also led to Debbie's first experience of life as a self-invented outsider. "I used to come into school covered in beauty marks," she explained. "I looked like I was splattered in mud so the other girls thought I was a little bit weird. And I used to come home for lunch and if my mother wasn't home, I'd whip into her room and start applying stuff all over me. But I was really young.

"I practised putting on makeup a lot. I used to study it carefully and practise everything. I used to sit in front of a mirror and try to make myself look Oriental. I made a lot of mistakes; sometimes I'd walk out of the house looking like a ghoul and not really know it. One time in eighth grade my mother wasn't home; so I went upstairs and started fooling around. When I went back to school after lunch, no one would talk to me. Everybody went to one side of the lounge, and I was all by myself, practically in tears."

Despite these early setbacks, the realisation that Debbie was not quite the ugly duckling she had imagined herself to be dawned upon her, then puberty hit early. "I first became aware of my sexuality when I was about 10 or 11. I think that everybody does, it's surely not extraordinary to me. I had an interesting experience when I was 11: We were on holiday in Cape Cod, and I used to go out with my cousin … walking the holiday streets at night. When we left the house we used to put on lipstick, without our mothers knowing. Well, we picked up these guys, who were much older than us. They followed us back to where we lived and they said, 'OK, we'll pick you up later and we'll go out for a drink.' At 11p.m. that night our mothers had put us in pyjamas and told us to go to bed, when these two guys came knocking at the door. We went down and opened it and you should have seen the faces of these two guys when they saw these two little kids there, without lipstick. It turned out that they were both very famous musicians. They gave us both autographed pictures and stuff. But my parents were really shocked."

Deborah's precocious looks also had the disquieting effect of attracting local weirdos. "I happen to have a sensual nature. And I suppose it comes out in pictures. I've always had that kind of response as a female. I know, because I've always been followed by perverts. Always the sick kind. In public places, flashers. I remember once when I was a child. It was at the zoo, and I was with my mother. This man came over and whipped open his coat. Disgusting."

But as her personal sexuality flourished with hormonal gusto, young Deborah began visiting a pickup drag, known in the local vernacular as 'Cunt Mile', in search of sexual kicks. "I liked to experiment, I think I really enjoyed the darker side – the underside of things," she recounted. "I didn't do a great deal of it, but it was very meaningful for me. I wanted to see a real cross-section, I wasn't content to be a white middle class girl growing up and doing what was expected of her. But it certainly was pretty nice."

Looking to expand her developing horizons, Debbie took to driving with enthusiasm. "It sort of saved me," she asserted. "It's how I got through high school. When things would get too intense I would just get in a car." Now independently mobile, Deborah found that she was drawn to the nearby town of Paterson. "Both my grandmothers lived in Paterson. A lot of people don't believe that there is such a place. In the London *Times* in 1965, there was a piece about William Carlos Williams' poem 'Paterson'. They said that, 'Paterson is an imaginary town in New Jersey which Williams created as his symbol of America.' Thirteen miles outside Newark, and those limey intellectuals thought it was a myth."

Although Deborah had ambitions of travelling around Europe, in 1963 she was enrolled at Centenary College in Hackettstown, New Jersey. "My parents didn't think going to Europe was the right thing to do. I didn't really want to go to school, but I did because I was very submissive. I didn't know what else to do. I really had no idea how to take care of myself. I had been programmed for marriage and a certain degree of higher education. I don't think my parents contemplated a future for me other than marriage. I was marketed for that, I was produced for that. This two years was to finish me off, to perhaps meet someone."

This 'finishing school' (described by Debbie as "a reform school for debutantes") was founded in 1867 by the Newark Conference of the United Methodist Church, becoming a girls' preparatory school in 1910, then a junior college for women in 1940. Debbie's graduation with a Bachelor of Association of Arts degree in 1965 was seen as the last educational step before her stipulated future as a fully domesticated housewife.

While there were several early factors that would prove crucial to the emergence of Debbie's Blondie persona, being one of the biggest stars on the planet would only have been a wild fantasy at this point. As a teenager, her ambitions stretched no further than becoming a beatnik: "It was always my dream to live the bohemian life in New York and have my own apartment and do things. I didn't like suburbia. I always had my own secret, private ideas … I always knew I would be involved in entertainment somehow."

Debbie had enlivened her New Jersey childhood by creating a fantasy world populated by untouchable movie icons. By the time she reached Centenary College, she had developed a fascination with the anti-establishment archetype exemplified by James Dean in *Rebel Without A Cause*. Naturally enough, her concept of glamour at the time was provided by the then-ubiquitous Marilyn Monroe. "She was the most controversial female while I was growing up, so she cast a large aura and I was very interested in that – her charisma. I never really had that thing of dying to be another person; I was in awe of everybody, really. I knew I wanted to be a performer of some sort. I was kinda vague about it but I was good at music."

In terms of adopting such subversive role models in her suburban life, Debbie was inclined to be pragmatic. "It wouldn't get me anywhere to be a rebel, except I'd always be punished and locked in the house. But I always stated what I thought. [My parents] were liberal intellectually and politically. They themselves and how they were weren't liberal. They tried to get me to understand it and I did, but they were firmly entrenched in their way of life. I was just waiting for the time I could do what I wanted to do."

Exposure to jazz and European cinema laid the ground for much of Debbie's aesthetic sensibility. "Some of my biggest influences were Paul Desmond, Dave Brubeck, Cal Tjader, all those freaked-out jazz musicians, I really got into that," she'd recall. Indeed, the first album that Deborah Harry fell in love with was the 1955 compilation *I Like Jazz*, which featured contributions from artists such as Duke Ellington and Dave Brubeck. "I didn't have a lot of money to buy records … so I'd listen to a lot of radio … a little radio where I could have my ear right next to the speaker. In those days DJs could be freaky – the late-late-night DJs were the ones. Funky, soulful stuff, maybe a little bit of rock. What could be better? I was always a radio head."

Deborah Harry's expanding palate of influences was also shaped by the magnetic pull of nearby New York. "When I was a little kid my mother and father used to take me to do the traditional kid things. Radio City shows, the tree at Rockefeller Plaza. New York was always the big fascination and the big Mecca for entertainment, anything that was exotic. My father worked here for more than 25 years. I guess I sort of started taking bus trips to the city when I was in the eighth grade. I would come in to the Village and check out what was going on."

Once she was ensconced at Centenary College, Debbie enrolled in creative writing classes. "I seriously started to write in 1964 … poems. They weren't very good. I used to write little stories." However, being just old enough to remember a time before rock'n'roll, it was this still new music (rather than literature) that ignited her rebellious instincts. "One of the greatest things about it was that it was forbidden," she recalled. "That forced young people to have an identity. You could sort through everybody by who they liked, or whether they liked rock'n'roll at all.

"1959-1965 was a great time to be a rock'n'roll teenager," she reminisced. "Radio was at its peak. Every show was in heavy competition to discover the newest, wildest sound on plastic … The first rock stuff I got into was Frankie Lymon doo-wop during the fifties. Later, my dancing friends and I did the Strand, the Hully Gully, the Swim, the Jump, the Bop, the Watusi and the Twist – kicked off by the Mashed Potato which, when seen for the first time, caused some kind of scandal at school: 'You're dancing like a nigger, girl … You can't do that!' Until that time expressing how the music made you feel hadn't been done."

Like many American teenagers of the era, Debbie could hardly fail to notice The Beatles' impact on the US pop landscape as the band touched down to invade in February 1964. However, rather than being swept away by the prevailing currents of Beatlemania, her artistic sensibility took heed of the dynamics behind the group's rampant popularity. "I learned a lot of things from The Beatles about sassiness. I always thought they were sassy; that was my label for them. Attitude is very important. And I always felt that sex is a cool thing to sell. It's a sure thing."

While John, Paul, George and Ringo enraptured the masses, Debbie fell under the brief supernova spell of New York's girl groups. These provided some living, breathing rebels to identify with and to model her early individuality upon.

11

The 10-storey Brill Building, which got its name from the tailor occupying the ground floor, had dominated New York's entertainment industry in the late fifties. By 1960, however, while it still housed hotshot songwriters Jerry Leiber and Mike Stoller, most on-the-button contemporary music was emanating from the cheaper, funkier Music Building at 1650 Broadway – a maze of cubicles furnished with desks, phones and an upright piano that played host to the hordes of publishers, promoters and songwriters who descended on the city. As the sixties began to swing, those little cubicles began churning out Top 10 hits at a relentless rate – often from those run by Aldon Music, the company started by music biz veteran Al Nevins and hotshot young entrepreneur Don Kirshner, who made the first of many killings in the white teenage market opened up by Dion & The Belmonts with their young singer/songwriter Neil Sedaka. Happening new writing partnerships of the time included Gerry Goffin and Carole King, Barry Mann and lyricist Cynthia Weil (who broke the Brooklyn stranglehold by hailing from a rich Upper West Side Jewish background), Ellie Greenwich and Jeff Barry.

Goffin and King owned the distinction of writing the first number one single for a black all-female group, the wistfully infectious 'Will You Love Me Tomorrow?' by New Jersey's Shirelles, in 1960. This opened the floodgates for the earliest form of girl power.

The girl-group phenomenon spread like wildfire, prodded full-force by another new arrival called Phil Spector – a diminutive record producer who cast a skyscraper shadow over the early sixties New York music scene. Although born in the Bronx in 1939, he had been taken to California by his mother in 1953 after his father committed suicide, learning his studio craft from Gold Star producer Stan Ross and scoring his first hit record in late 1958 with The Teddy Bears' 'To Know Him Is To Love Him' (titled after the inscription on his father's tombstone). Leiber and Stoller's mentor, Lester Sill, then arranged for Spector to come to New York and work with the duo, resulting in the lustrously intoxicating 'Spanish Harlem', a huge hit for Ben E. King in late 1960.

Hailing from Brooklyn, The Crystals were the first group Spector signed to Philles, the label he started with Sill in 1961 (later grasping sole ownership after his partner backed down). Spector set about developing the panoramic 'wall of sound' he applied to the new girl groups, leading the way with The Crystals after their 1961 debut hit, 'There's No Other (Like My Baby)', merely bruised the Top 20.

Vivacious blonde singer–songwriter/producer Ellie Greenwich was another key component in the girl-group phenomenon. Together with husband Jeff Barry, Broadway's pop queen wrote some of the biggest hits for the girl groups, including Spector's Ronettes, The Crystals and several for The Shangri-Las. (In addition to penning several of the hits that fired Debbie's musical passions, more than a decade later Ellie would provide backing vocals for Blondie on 'In The Flesh'.)

Although hailing from Brooklyn, Ellie Greenwich grew up in the affluent Long Island suburb of Levittown, teaching herself piano and composing songs by her early teens. She attended Queens College aged 17 and, in 1958, released her first solo single, 'Silly Isn't It', for RCA under the name Ellie Gaye. She became a Brill Building regular after her piano skills caught the attention of Jerry Leiber while she was waiting for an appointment. Leiber and Stoller allowed her to use their facilities so long as they had first pick of the songs she came up with. Ellie and Jeff Barry married in October 1962, as their songwriting partnership blossomed into a hugely successful exclusive arrangement with Leiber and Stoller's Trio Music.

When Leiber, Stoller and veteran third partner George Goldner started Red Bird Records in 1964, Barry/Greenwich were installed as staff writers and producers, scoring an immediate number one with the Dixie Cups' Spector-produced 'Chapel Of Love'. Ellie's success pricked the ears of her old childhood friend George Morton, who visited her at the Brill Building to the chagrin of husband Jeff, who maliciously asked Morton what he did for a living. Not wanting to lose face, George replied that he wrote hit singles. Barry challenged him to bring one in. Energised by the pressure, the songless Morton took a gamble, booked time at a local studio and invited four girls who had already impressed him at local events: The Shangri-Las (who took their name from a local Chinese restaurant). The Shangri-Las had been formed from friendships between the Weiss and Ganser families who lived in the tough Cambria Heights neighbourhood of South-East Queens. Mary and Liz 'Betty' Weiss and twin sisters Marguerite 'Marge' and Mary Ann Ganser attended the local Andrew Jackson High School. Sharing a mutual love of music, between 1963 and 1964 the four would practise their harmonies, routines and stage presence around the pop songs of the day, soon graduating to playing local teen hops and school dances.

While driving to the demo studio in his Buick, Morton pulled up by a Long Island beach and poured out 'Remember (Walking In The Sand)'.

The seven-minute demo impressed Leiber to the extent that he signed The Shangri-Las to Red Bird for five years in April 1964. After they recorded a more compact version 'Remember' became a summer hit, complemented by the group's bad girl image. This was a new strain of teenage rock'n'roll, delivered from a feminine perspective. Morton's innovative production heightened the song's melodrama via his trademark sound effects, in the form of crashing waves and seagull calls.

Morton was suddenly a studio hotshot, signing to Red Bird as staff producer. He was nicknamed 'Shadow' by George Goldner – after the mysterious pulp magazine character because his whereabouts could never be established. Working more like a movie director, Morton guided The Shangri-Las through two years of worldwide hits and mini-symphonies including 'Leader Of The Pack', 'Give Him A Great Big Kiss', 'I Can Never Go Home Anymore', 'Give Us Your Blessings' and the sepulchral B-side confessional 'Dressed In Black' – a blueprint for future punk generations that could have been written for Debbie Harry.

Red Bird folded in 1966 after Leiber and Stoller had already bowed out, unsettled by Goldner running up significant gambling debts and the dissolution of the Greenwich/Barry marriage two years earlier. The Shangri-Las signed to Mercury, releasing two more singles, 'Sweet Sounds Of Summer' and 'Take The Time', neither of which troubled the charts. The group split, typically ending their run almost penniless and subject to lawsuits that prevented them recording. Mary travelled, and then worked as a secretary in Manhattan while taking college classes. She later went into the architectural industry, then furniture, subsequently running a commercial interiors dealership in the eighties.

Betty had a child and later started her own cosmetics business on Long Island, while Mary died in March 1970, aged 22, after suffering from seizures for some time. The remaining Shangri-Las reunited in 1976, when 'Leader Of The Pack' made the UK Top 10 on reissue. Sadly, Marge would succumb to breast cancer in July 1996, aged 48.

Young Debbie Harry was particularly drawn to the doomed tragic-teen aura of The Shangri-Las (in 1977, Phil Spector would remark that she reminded him of one of the group). They had quickly became one of the greatest, most influential groups of all – thanks largely to the cinematic production of 'Shadow' Morton, whose teenage mini-operas compressed whole storylines into the grooves of a seven-inch single. Spector's monumental creations had been breathtaking, but The Shangri-Las dared to venture where female singers had rarely been before – exploring themes of forbidden love, alienation, teenage loneliness, tragic death (even going so far as to recount the death of an archetypal 'mom' on 'I Can Never Go Home Anymore') and simmering paranoia caused by some ambiguous trauma, on the pseudo-classical 'Past, Present And Future'.

The girl group's black-clad, streetwise image and attitudinal pouts pre-dated punk, captivating Debbie to the extent that a version of the poignant 'Out In The Streets', Mary Weiss's favourite Shangri-Las song, would be tackled at Blondie's first recording session in 1975. The group's epic melodramas, peppered with bad boys in leather jackets who were 'good/ bad but not evil', also influenced other seventies New York acts – including Jayne County, The Ramones and, just before them, The New York Dolls, who lifted the "When I say I'm in love" opening line of 'Give Him A Great Big Kiss' for their 1973 urban melodrama 'Looking For A Kiss', while Dolls guitarist Johnny Thunders would cover the song on his first solo album. (Over in the UK, The Damned used the "Is she really going out with him?" intro from 'Leader Of The Pack' to kick off their debut single, 'New Rose'.)

The girl groups had also consolidated Debbie Harry's growing fixation with nearby New York City, twinkling over the Hudson River. By 1965 it was entering into a cultural revolution, off the back of the 'British invasion' that had taken place the previous year.

Chapter Two

Village Heads

"The drug experience was edifying and illuminating, but the other side is that it was habitual and destroys brain cells. Did I have a drug of choice? Well, I chose a lot of drugs."

Debbie Harry

Without Chris Stein, the Blondie phenomenon would never have ignited on such a global scale or have been so diversely fascinating. He is the one who became Debbie's rock, keeping her positive, offering challenge and excitement, and providing sanctuary. He would be her intensely knowledgeable creative foil as the pair juggled pop culture with underground art and street music, while the world went Blondie-crazy.

Responsible for Blondie hits that include 'Rip Her To Shreds', 'Heart Of Glass', 'Rapture' and 'Dreaming', the Harry/Stein songwriting partnership can be rated alongside Lennon/McCartney, Jagger/Richards or Strummer/Jones. It also followed the classic Broadway hit factory tradition of personal intimacy providing a springboard for dynamic creativity – Barry/Greenwich being one obvious example.

Witnessing the couple together during Blondie's rise and fall between 1977 and 1982 was often touching as they cohabited in their own binary orbit, immune to the external hassles of press criticism, clamouring media and rabid fans. Chris would laugh at Debbie's expeditions from hotels to nearby shops, her famous face disguised behind wigs and shades. In fact they would laugh a lot, whether at the antics of old mutual friends or at the absurdity of it all. Through the first half of Blondie's first phase they would also find solace in each other's company, as they bitterly protested about their management.

Stein was always into comic books, grindhouse movies, extreme pop culture, arcane or obscure musical forms, and the heritage of his home city. He relished the fact that he could now rub shoulders with the likes of William S. Burroughs and Andy Warhol as a fellow artist who, for a time, was more successful or well-known than either of them. Underneath the thick-framed glasses and amiably stoned professorial demeanour lurked a dry humourist, a foraging and sometimes fearless musician, and an outstanding photographer. Stein was loyal to those who showed him support, too – even at the peak of Blondie-mania he would take the time to keep in touch, via regular phone calls and letters, with one of this book's co-authors.

Chris may now have found a new partner and devoted the last few years to fatherhood, but the bond between him and Debbie provides the spark which holds Blondie together even today. He is also among the short but illustrious list of godfathers of what is oft identified as 'New York City's musical melting pot', rising above any 'Disco Sucks' prejudice early on to work with Chic and being one of the first downtown musicians to pick up on the burgeoning hip hop movement emanating from the South Bronx. The disparate roster of the Animal label he ran between 1982 and 1984 established him as one of the few from NY's class of '76 to put his money where his mouth was, projecting a panoply of pioneers and misfits to wider public attention via the reflected glare of Blondie's spotlight.

Christopher Stein was born in Brooklyn on January 5, 1950. His mother, Estelle, was a painter and window designer, while Ben, his dad, was a salesman and frustrated writer who had been a labour organiser and wrote for the radical press in the thirties and forties. "I remember the FBI coming to our house when I was a kid," explained Chris. "And I used to listen to my parents' Leadbelly records, and they had black friends, which was a little unusual at that time."

"Both of them were 'reds'," added Stein. "They had met in the party so my Jewishness was limited. They were more atheistic in their views, and I didn't have a barmitzvah, although of course I had plenty of relatives who were practising. In retrospect, I wish I knew a little more Hebrew. My father used to speak Yiddish with my grandfather quite fluently. I love listening to Lenny Bruce – I admire his ability to make Yiddish sound cool."

Visits from The Man notwithstanding, the Steins ran a typical non-practising Jewish liberal artistic household. His parents chose a gentile name for their son, specifically so that he would not be subjected to antisemitism. "Yeah, that was really bizarre," he reflected. "There are a lot of 'Chris Steins' now if you look it up, but not then. I remember guys saying when I was growing up: 'Oh, that's a weird name for a Jewish boy!'"

Estelle and Ben's relationship was sometimes uncommunicative – Chris has described his mother as "neurotic" and "somewhat controlling", while his father gradually eased himself out of the relationship and eventually moved in with a younger woman. "I remember that we'd go to the Catskills and my mother would basically lock herself in a cabin and paint the whole time. Not that my father was the easiest person to get along with – he had a very sarcastic, Yiddish sense of humour, one that I've inherited. One that is very New York."

An only child, Chris drew his initial musical inspiration directly from his parents; his earliest musical memories are of his mother singing songs from films such as Federico Fellini's 1954 drama *La Strada*. "When I was a kid most of my heroes were 60-year-old black men. All those great blues guys like Muddy Waters and John Lee Hooker." Later, his passion for folk music would intertwine with a liking for newer groups like The Beatles and Stones. "My head paralleled the rise of all these groups when they first came about. I feel really lucky that I was born in 1950 and could see all that stuff."

"I always liked Dylan, the Stones, The Beatles, the usual shit," Chris recounts. "I liked [the Stones] up until 'It's Only Rock 'N' Roll'. I liked Henry Mancini a lot too. And soundtracks. *Dr No* was one of my favourites. And 'Peter Gunn'."

Initially, Chris enjoyed drawing (particularly spacemen) before setting his sights on becoming an Egyptologist. But everything changed after he got his first guitar from his parents when he was 11 years old. "I didn't know you were supposed to press the strings down onto the frets to get different notes. I thought there was one fixed note and that was it," said Chris. His unorthodox approach to the instrument was furthered by early exposure to bluegrass legend Lester Flatt. "When I saw Flatt playing slide I didn't know what it was. I thought he was playing with his thumb so I started playing a lot with my thumb and it took me a year or two to gradually get my fingers round the other side of the neck."

Easily bored, Chris spent countless hours sitting in his room playing guitar and developing an understanding of folk music and the civil rights movement. He was also technically adept and developed a penchant for pulling speakers from discarded televisions and hooking them up to his beat-up record player. These were duly festooned around his room, which was painted a suitably bohemian black. A constant stream of friends dropping by to smoke pot and groove to sounds played at ear-splitting volume caused his mother to brand her son's bedroom 'a den of inequity'. This nascent nonconformity would ensure he fitted in perfectly once he started hitting the West Village.

Like Debbie, Chris loathed school – after attending elementary school PS 199 in Midwood (where he played a leaf in a fourth-grade play: "It was pathetic. I had brown crepe paper all over me"), he moved onto Andries Hudde Junior High, before completing his compulsory education at Midwood High School where he was "traumatised by having to eat in the high school lunchroom", wore steel-rimmed spectacles and generally ignored the teachers. "It was a school for fuck-ups who couldn't fit into the system," observed Chris. "I was always a little off-centre … and when my father died in 1965, I began to become more withdrawn and sullen."

That same year, Chris became the first kid to get thrown out of the school he described as "the last great greaser hangout in Brooklyn" for having long hair. (At the time, there was a test case going on where an excluded pupil sued his school for a similar dismissal; the school nervously invited him back; he refused.) Similarly, his luxurious locks failed to meet with the approval of the local hoods. "We would pass by the pool hall and these gangster types would beat up anyone with long hair," he recounted. "I remember this pair, the Sirico brothers, would call us 'faggots' and try to do us damage."

By the time he was 15, Chris had spent sufficient time practising in his bedroom to unveil his guitar chops before a wider audience. "I floated in and out of a great number of Brooklyn groups, including The Morticians, who rehearsed a great deal but only played one gig … a promotional thing for a local barber — in his shop," he recalled. "I was in a lot of bands. One called Fananganang ... The Morticians, which became The Left Banke. I was in The Millard Fillmore Memorial Lamp Band — we used to play in Washington Square all the time."

The Morticians lined up as Stein on guitar and vocals, Simon Summers (guitar, bass, vocals), Barry Goldman (guitar, bass, vocals) and drummer George Cameron, who left to join he Left Banke and enjoyed a massive hit with 'Walk Away Renee' in September 1966. When the band dissolved that same year, Chris set out in search of new musical kicks. "I spent a lot of those folk-rock days just hanging out in Greenwich Village, playing my guitar in Washington Square and catching glimpses of the big local groups: The [Lovin'] Spoonful, The Magicians ... even saw Jimi Hendrix a couple of times."

"During these years he learned from a cross-section of guitarists from John Fahey and [bluegrass pioneer] Lester Flatt, to the Lovin' Spoonful and Bob Dylan," explained Deborah. "He was going to a private school called Quintano's, but he was still a goof-off."

The Leonard Quintano School For Young Professionals was a *Fame*-style establishment that groomed students for careers in the performing arts and could count the likes of The Shangri-Las' Mary Weiss, future New York Dolls Syl Sylvain and Billy Murcia and Aerosmith's Steven Tyler among its alumni. Tyler subsequently described Quintano's as a "school for fuck-ups like myself where you just had to show up to graduate."

Understandably, the trauma of his father's sudden death had a massive impact on Chris. "He was only in his fifties, but he was a very sensitive man and his inability to release his creativity had put a great strain on him," Debbie later explained. Recalling his dad's gentle nature, Chris observed, "He just generally believed in freedom and peace, that was it really. He died 'cause he was frustrated, being locked into his day-to-day existence, his job ... he was frustrated into an early grave."

Although rock'n'roll provided him with an outlet, Chris would struggle to cope with his bereavement. "My father dying made me a little crazy. I wasn't able to deal with it." The full extent of this would not become apparent for almost four years. In the meantime, Chris continued his informal musical education by hanging out in Greenwich Village.

Despite being airbrushed by the anodyne gentrification blighting much of New York City, Greenwich Village looks structurally much the same as it did in the last century. No buildings rise above mid-storey height, as its streets disregard the 19th-century numbered grid system between Sixth and Ninth Avenues and Houston to 14th. The neighbourhood started out as a wealthy rural hamlet, growing into a proper village within the ever-expanding city, attracting artists, activists, theatre groups and defiant homosexuals early in the 20th century. Speakeasies thrived during Prohibition, before booming jazz and blues clubs moved in. After World War II, 'the Village' attracted artists with its cheap rent and creativity seemed to coruscate through the bars and clubs. The main gathering spot was Washington Square Park, a short walk from Broadway at the foot of Fifth Avenue, its late 19th-century marble arch known as 'the Gateway to the Village'. From the end of World War II, the Sunday afternoon hootenannies where singers exchanged songs were attended by devotees and those who could not get into the clubs, for reasons ranging from age to colour. The Park was the folk scene's open-air epicentre.

Although by the mid-sixties The Beatles had arrived to change the face of American popular music, back in the Village shockwaves were still reverberating after Bob Dylan had used the neighbourhood as a launch pad to fame and fortune. Of course, there was already a thriving folk scene there before he showed up, which he tapped into with his talent to reinterpret and bare-faced cheek. Until Dylan's arrival the Village had been a more insular community, dominated throughout the fifties by venerable overseer Pete Seeger who, after meeting Woody Guthrie in March 1940 at an event in aid of displaced migrant workers, formed the system-lambasting Almanac Singers. By the sixties, clubs and coffeehouses were swelling with troubadours such as Tom Paxton, Phil Ochs and Peter, Paul and Mary (the folk-pop trio handled by Dylan's manager, Albert Grossman), establishing the Village as a music industry boom town.

At the other end of the aural spectrum, The Velvet Underground's assimilation of noise and avant-garde elements embellished Lou Reed's street vignettes. They were a major influence on Chris, who – along with many other aspiring downtown musicians – enjoyed elements of gutter-level danger and narcotics with his rock'n'roll. At a time when many bands were simply 'going psychedelic' with a string of beads and some phasing, The Velvet Underground cleaved an audaciously innovative path. Formed around Reed and John Cale in the latter's Ludlow Street loft, the group resolutely kicked against the zeitgeist; sliding out of New York's sleazy underbelly, they malevolently belched extreme noise terror at a time when flower power was blossoming.

New York City put out totally contrasting signals that, when carried by their emissaries to the West Coast, were almost a declaration of war. It created an East/West schism that would presage the hip hop beefs of the eighties.

After the long-delayed release of *The Velvet Underground And Nico* in March 1967, erstwhile manager Andy Warhol was keen to open a new club to replace the band's previous regular venue, The Dom. He happened on a new space at 420 East 71st Street called The Gymnasium – actually the gym of Sokol Hall, an activity centre serving the Czech and Slovak community. On March 24, the now Nico-less Velvet Underground began a residency at what was promoted as a 'new happening discotheque', continuing each weekend for a month under the banner 'Work Out At The Gymnasium'. The venture closed soon after, mainly on account of sparse attendance levels.

Among those who did show up were Chris's new band, First Crow To The Moon, which also featured Summers and Goldman from The Morticians plus singer Jim Savage, saxophonist Sonny Boy and guitarist Alan Avick (who Stein recalled was "an incredible guitarist but he died young – of leukaemia"). The quintet scored the gig supporting the Velvets through Joey Freeman, a friend of Chris who worked for Warhol. "It was his job to go wake Andy up at his house and stuff," explained Stein. "So one day he said to my band in Brooklyn – it didn't have a name, it was just a blues band – 'Do you want to play with the Velvets?'

"It was pretty late at night by the time we got out of the subway in Manhattan and headed toward The Gymnasium. Walking down the block with our guitars we actually saw some people coming down the street and they said, 'Oh, are you guys the band, because we've been waiting there all night and we couldn't take it any more, we left because they never showed up.' So we said, 'Yeah, we're the band.' We went inside and there was hardly anyone there. Somebody said Andy was supposed to be there, but he was off in the shadows with his entourage, we never saw him. We hung around for a little while and they played records, then we headed up for the stage. It was a big echoey place, we had absolutely no conception of playing a place like this whatsoever, but [Velvets drummer] Maureen Tucker said we could use their equipment. So we plugged into their amps and the amps were all cranked up superloud … The only song I remember doing was 'You Can't Judge A Book By Its Cover'."

"We must have done a few more," Chris later recalled, "but I remember sitting down after a while because the whole thing had gotten me pretty discouraged. Then somebody came over and said, 'Oh Andy likes you, he thinks you're great.' We must have played five or six songs then we just gave up. By that time the rest of the Velvets had arrived. After a while, they started to play and they were like awesomely powerful. I had never expected to experience anything like that before … I was really disappointed that they didn't have Nico, because we thought she was the lead singer, but I distinctly remember the violin and their doing 'Venus In Furs' because a couple of people in dark outfits got up and started doing a slow dance with a chain in between them … There were maybe 30 people there. It was very late, but it was a memorable experience."

Mixing original material with cover versions and sometimes going by the alternate name of The Bootleggers, First Crow To The Moon played venues such as The Crazy Horse on Bleecker Street and Flatbush Terrace in Brooklyn. In addition the group held jam sessions at The Nite Owl on West Third Street, when it closed in the afternoons.

First Crow To The Moon drifted apart; Chris spent 1967's summer of love tripping in San Francisco but, as the lysergic heat subsided, he felt the pull of his hometown, returning to New York before the year was out.

★★★

In comparison with the vibrant chaos of New York, mid-sixties New Jersey was a different world; its open spaces, shopping malls and small-town fastidiousness provided just the kind of environment to stoke a desire to escape among disaffected teenagers. Debbie's trips to Manhattan became increasingly frequent as the lure of glamour and excitement exerted an irresistible pull upon her. "I came from a very provincial atmosphere. Suburbia, New Jersey. Grew up in a small town, in a family that was very small town, and I wanted the world. I really wanted to taste everything," she recalled. "It was always my dream to live the bohemian life in New York …"

Deborah set about finding herself work to support the relocation; her initial stint at a Gift Mart was followed by a job at the BBC's New York office, where she operated the telex machine and learned how to edit tapes for radio broadcasts. To an extent this provided her with the inspiration to begin experimenting with sound. "I hung out with jazz musicians. I met Bob Evans, the piano player. I met a lot of weird people like Tiger Morse, Tally Brown ... They did jazz all the time. It was free, abstract, non-music music. Whenever it became music, it was music. Most of the time, it was noise – percussion, screeching, shit like that. I chatted and yelled and banged stuff and carried on."

Moving into an apartment on St Mark's Place in the East Village, Debbie began to realise her bohemian ambitions by becoming an artist. "I didn't know what else to do," she admitted. "I had no idea how to take care of myself."

"I was curious," she remembered, "I wanted adventure, and to feel and absorb things, and see what was going on. I was on the shy side, but determined to discover who I was. Desperate to, actually. Desperation and obsession are good things. I don't know if I was that intelligent about it. I got myself into uncomfortable situations, but managed to come out the other side. I was shy, but fascinated with the underground, beatniks, strange, fringe people, and I got to meet them, and to study human nature.

"I was really excited to be on my own and to see all the stuff that was going on in New York at the time. I thought it was rather sexy. The early days of rock'n'roll was all counter-culture. It was forbidden – all rather clandestine. Churches forbade it and schools set dress codes."

Ideally placed to explore the full range of cultural developments detonating around her as the sixties climbed towards a creative zenith, Debbie immersed herself in the burgeoning hippie zeitgeist. "I went to the Be-Ins in Central Park. They were great – a lot of crazy people tripped out of their minds, dressed great. That was one thing I liked about hippy nation; everyone was always dressed up. In a way, the sixties in New York were a larger version of what went on at CBGB in the early seventies. You had Sun Ra playing in the park. The Fugs were around town, The Velvet Underground were playing at The Balloon Farm."

Despite Debbie's observation that, "I don't know if it did anything special for me," some of the musical elements of the peace and love scene made an indelible impression. "I'll never forget seeing Janis Joplin with Big Brother

And The Holding Company at the Anderson Theatre in 1967, when she grabbed a bottle of Southern Comfort off the top of the upright piano, took a belt, and went straight into 'Ball And Chain' begging, 'Take my heart.'

"When I saw Janis, I thought, 'Wow, what courage!' She communicated who she was, what she was singing about. It wasn't just a technical experience for her, making notes come out and waving her arms around. She was doing with her body what she felt in those songs."

As with Chris, a yearning to seek out what was fresh and 'happening' in New York drew Debbie to the gravity well of artistic expression generated by Warhol and the Velvets. "The first time I saw them was one of the best shows I have ever seen. I didn't have a clue who they were. I used to go to this place – a big room called The Balloon Farm … which was like a former Ukrainian nursing home, and it was The Velvet Underground playing live with Nico. The stage set and colours were designed by Andy Warhol who was also doing the lights. It was beautiful. Mo Tucker on drums was fucking great. And you could just wander in and watch them."

Such close exposure to the Velvets furnished Deborah with radical new ideas about how female musicians and vocalists could present themselves. "You couldn't help feeling a different sense of time because they created an overpowering fresh environment," she asserts. "Nico could be very quiet. She would stand there, so cool. She would wear this chartreuse jacket, with her long, very blonde hair, standing completely still – 'I'll be your mirror.' She would just do that, with the rest of the Velvets behind her, so dark and menacing. Blondie once did a big festival in Barcelona, one of our earliest shows in front of a large audience, and we shared a little caravan with Nico. She was in there shooting up; 'Wow, Nico shooting up! Cool!' Then she went out and played her songs on the harmonium. She was still gorgeous."

"I was just a baby growing up in the middle of this incredible scene," observed Debbie. "I was on the fringes of that whole Factory thing. I was this shy person who didn't talk very much, just hung out and looked cute and watched everybody. They were all so eccentric and beautiful and flamboyant then. It's funny because – except in certain quarters – people have become so conservative and uniform. It's like cookie-cutters; people are just stamped out. It's so refreshing when someone like you comes along who's exotic or eccentric, whatever you wanna call it."

By 1966, Deborah took her initial steps into performance by joining her first groups. "After I'd moved to New York I was in and out of the Uni

Trio, which was a St Mark's area jazz group, and the Tri-Angels, but nothing came of either of them," she explained. "I was painting then, but beginning to feel music more, so I started painting sound. But sound had to be painted on walls, not canvas, so I decided to move into music, stopped painting, and spent more time in clubs with live music."

In addition to hooking up with these short-lived bands, Debbie also briefly cast her sights toward musical theatre. "I used to buy *Backstage*, which listed open calls for Broadway shows like the one for *Hair*, when thousands of kids showed up and stood on an endless line. I didn't know about agents, and I went to a few of these auditions on full-size stages in Broadway theatres, but I never got further than singing, 'Oh, la-da-da,' before a voice would boom, 'Thank you very much,' out of the dark, and I would trot off, having waited in line a whole day being sweaty and nervous, along with all these showbiz hopefuls. Looking back that scene makes me think of a convention of bag women."

As the year approached its end, Deborah took another step forward by joining her first professional group – the exotically named First National Unaphrenic Church and Bank, where she sang and banged percussion. More of a collective than a band, FNUC&B cloaked abrasive art-school modern jazz in hippie idealism, splitting after their involvement in recording the 1967 album *The Psychedelic Saxophone Of Charlie Nothing*, released on John Fahey's Takoma label after Debbie had left the group. In addition to saxophonist Nothing (otherwise known as Charles Martin Simon), The Unaphrenics included drummer Tox Strohaw, Fuci (who played the triangle and contributed 'screams' and 'yells') and percussionist Sujan Souri. "The First National Unaphrenic Church and Bank had marginally more stability, except that Tox was an escaped convict," Debbie explained. "He was living on an Indian reservation in the Smokie Mountains and we had to smuggle him back to New York with a beard and an assumed name – they were strange days."

In early 1967 Debbie hooked up with Paul Klein, the husband of her high-school friend Wendy Simon, who had noticed her "little nasally voice" and formed a group along with bassist Steve De Philips. Keyboardist Wayne Kirby and woodwind multi-instrumentalist Ida Andrews were recruited fresh from the Julliard performing arts school, before the expanding line-up was rounded out by Peter Britain (lead guitar/vocals) plus percussionists Gil Fields and Anton Karasforth. "So then we had a group of people, who together could play 20 different instruments on stage and create a lot of effects," recounted Klein. "That was the birth of the Willows."

Named after Kenneth Grahame's 1908 classic children's novel, Wind In The Willows were fairly typical of the hippie era's fixation with naivety and nature. "It was pretty awful," Debbie asserted. "That was baroque folk rock. I didn't have anything to do with the music then. I was just a back-up singer." A feature in underground newspaper *World Countdown News* noted, "Debby [sic] Harry, 22, is the second girl in the group. Debby sings lead on several numbers and provides harmony on most of the rest. She plays tamboura, plus kazoo and tambourine."

Although she may have had reservations about the band's sound and image, 'Debby' was very much on message when talking to the paper: "I think that everybody should go beyond the lyrics and whatever we or any group is saying directly, and tune into the overtones of the music. An audience should relax and identify with the overall picture we are trying to paint instead of trying to get inside of our material and interpret our meanings. Instead of concentrating on our music and specific parts of it, people should first sit back and react freely to all of it."

The tragically unnecessary death of Wendy Simon's sister, Beth Ann, alleged to have starved while attempting a macrobiotic diet, indirectly led to Wind In The Willows scoring a manager and record deal. Future *Village Voice* heavyweight Robert Christgau reported on Beth Ann's death and subsequently stuck up a friendship with Klein, who lived on the same Seventh Street block. At Klein's suggestion, Christgau began hanging out with the group with a view to composing a feature about the struggles of a young band in New York. He then brought the group to the attention of another friend, press agent Dominic Sicilia, who in turn introduced them to manager Peter Leeds.

Leeds, who would go on to play a significant part in Debbie and Chris's future, secured the group an album deal with Capitol Records. "It was a sort of folk-rock album. A sweet, saccharine kind of thing. I wasn't really a writer on that," Deborah insisted. "That record is very childlike to me. I didn't have a great deal of input. I was a back-up singer, doing high harmonies with the lead singer. It was his trip. He envisioned himself as this big-daddy folk guy with a teddy bear aspect."

Capitol duly sent its new investment on the road, the group travelling cross-country for gigs in Boston, Los Angeles and San Francisco, giving

Debbie her first taste of life on the road: "I remember one concert before 3,000 people and it was a great rush. I loved it, it was a thrill."

However, neither *Wind In The Willows* (the debut album) nor the band's live excursions set the world aflame and, despite recording a second album, Debbie's dissatisfaction with the group she later described as "a temporary association of convenience" quickly surfaced. "I wasn't turned on by the music any more. I thought we should make certain changes, but Paul [Klein, lead singer] didn't agree, so I told them I was leaving," she explained. "We did a second album that was a little more tasteful – for me, anyway – but it never came out. I have no idea what happened to it."

Although she had enjoyed her experiences of recording and performing, the folk scene hardly evoked the wild outsider spirit that initially excited Deborah's musical creativity. "I was a chirpy, cheery soprano in that group singing back-up and going, 'Oooooooo.' Actually, I loved doing the music, because all I wanted to do was sing, to paint music, you know, but I was just really a sideman in that group and I found it very frustrating and I just lost interest," she observed. "I decided I wanted to do something harder, faster, and more exciting."

Debbie's departure from Wind In The Willows marked the beginning of a half-decade estrangement from performance, during which she enthusiastically embraced the smorgasbord of drugs ubiquitous to the art and music scenes. "I know that the first time I was exposed to pot was in 1964," she confirmed. "All those drugs – LSD, heroin – became a part of my social life. I didn't shut myself off from anything. I really wanted to embrace it all. So I did."

"Drugs was chic," asserted Deborah. "Everybody in New York was fooling around with drugs. That's just what the scene was like. It wasn't like today where everybody knows what the implications are and what the results are. It was just a very small, elitist art world. Up in a loft. 'Look at my pictures! Aren't they neat? Yeah? OK, let's do some drugs to celebrate then.' It was just a fashionable situation. The stockbrokers weren't doing cocaine, only we were doing cocaine. It was just for freaks, and the quantities that are available now weren't available then. It was the sixties, man."

"I think that was when I really went crazy," reflected Debbie. "That's when I was really weird. My boyfriend [Gil Fields] was a drummer. He had been in the band for about a week. He was an unbelievable, high-calibre drummer, a drummer since he was three years old … He died. But – it's unbelievable – he taught me so much about music.

"That's the thing about the sixties; there were all these tragedies. There are still these articles about … people that are – they call them survivors. I don't want to be labelled as that … [But] a lot of people died."

In retrospect, Deborah retains a strong sense of perspective about her pharmaceutical experiences: "I think we're all completely vulnerable to substances. I approached drugs in a way that was as obsessive as the rest of my compulsive behaviour. I went and I did them and did them and did them until I got tired of doing them. I think they were really something I needed. Had I been going to a psychiatrist I think they would have had me on some kind of antidepressants to balance me out a little bit. So I was sort of self-medicating, I guess. It works to a certain point, and then you become victimised by the culture of it, and by the addictive process. Getting high is great, but the other side of that is a real drag."

Aside from the proximity to drugs afforded by a touring band and the fringes of the art scene, Debbie had mainlined herself into the epicentre of New York Babylon by taking a job as a waitress at Max's Kansas City, 213 Park Avenue South. Max's was opened in December 1965 as a club-restaurant by Mickey Ruskin, a Cornell graduate from Jersey City who had previously opened The Tenth Street Coffeehouse, then Les Deux Magots on Ninth Street and artist-musicians' hangout The Ninth Circle on West 10th Street. "I didn't know that Mickey was a junkie at the time," Deborah later revealed. "My boss was a junkie, I was a junkie, everyone was a junkie."

Max's quickly became a hangout for artists, sculptors, musicians, writers, poets, jet-setters and Warhol's riotous gaggle of Factory freaks and superstars. The illustrious list of artists who played the club (often in their early days) included Bruce Springsteen, Aerosmith, Bob Marley, Tim Buckley, Suicide, Tom Waits, Odetta, Gram Parsons and the ubiquitous Velvet Underground – who played their last shows with Lou Reed there in 1970. After becoming a kind of glam-rock epicentre in 1973 – regularly attracting the likes of David Bowie, Iggy Pop, The New York Dolls and the cream of New York's groupie subculture – it closed the following year but would re-open in 1975, to play a part in Blondie's early career as a live band.

"The first incarnation of Max's was heavy duty. That's not a phrase I like to use, but it clearly defines what was going on," recalled Debbie. "All Hollywood came. The photographers, sculptors and artists were all at the bar, in the front, while the back room was full of the Andy Warhol crowd, the late night people and musicians. Who did I serve? You name 'em. Who's the actor who was *Our Man Flint*? James Coburn! He was so gorgeous. Stevie Winwood, Jefferson Airplane, Jimi Hendrix. Then there was Andy with all of his nutty superstars ... Max's was a perfect place to work. You were a fly on the wall. You could be as visible, or as invisible, as you wanted to be. I could meet people and talk to them – or not. I was just the waitress.

"I was too stubborn to, you know, get some guy to pay my rent, I figured that was more work than for me just to get another job. So working at Max's Kansas City was great, I got to meet everybody, see all these fabulous people."

"I was basically a kid and I'd be serving dinner to Janis Joplin," beamed Deborah. "My shift was from 4.00 to midnight or I'd get the later shift from 7.30 to closing. The people who came in at 7.30 for dinner were working people and then, little by little, the people who wandered in got freakier and freakier. I loved Warhol and that whole crowd. I used to go in the back room and wait on Gerard Malanga, the superstars – Jane Forth, Ultra Violet, Viva, this one, that one. It was staggering. Just so delicious and fun."

Despite Debbie's excitement at waiting tables for the glitterati, the slightly soiled glamour of Max's notorious back room had provided a hip veneer to what could often be a tough working environment. "I used to cry a lot then generally," she admitted. "It wasn't just them, they just triggered it off. They were very frustrating people to wait on. The only one I got friendly with was [musician/dancer/actor] Eric Emerson and he was friendly with everybody, especially girls. I made it with Eric in a phone booth upstairs. One time only."

The emotional rollercoaster that Deborah experienced was in no small way accentuated by her narcotic intake. However, filmmaker Emile de Antonio provided the young waitress with some sage advice.

"During the sixties I was still unsure of exactly who I was, which made it difficult to deal with other people and kept me out of whack in relation to myself as well,' she observed. "This was debilitating and painful. In *Popism*, his history of the sixties, Andy Warhol says Emile de Antonio encouraged him before he was discovered. Emile was the first person to give me encouragement too. He's a remarkable, wonderful maniac. We talked about my problems and I said I thought it would take me two years to work them all out. Emile replied that it would take more like eight. I was horrified by his thinking. I was such a nerd and got pissed as hell, but he was right."

Another of Max's back-room habitués was Leee Black Childers, a photographer subsequently hired as vice president of Bowie's Mainman organisation who later went on to manage Johnny Thunders' post-New York Dolls band, The Heartbreakers. Leee remembers Deborah as a fresh face amongst the glamorous wolves that prowled the club. "As I recall, she would waitress in the back room – you didn't make much in tips, because everybody was pretty broke, but at least you got to be in the back room! She was very pretty and everybody was always hitting on her. She always had ambitions of performing."

For Debbie, serving food to chemically unbalanced hipsters provided some much-needed fringe benefits: "I met all the stars and served them their steaks. Most of them were so stoned they couldn't eat and still gave me five dollar tips. I'd wrap up the steaks and take them home."

Debbie's waitressing stint ended after eight months, when she ran off to San Francisco with a millionaire – enjoying the luxury of his mansion for a month, before getting bored and returning to New York. It was another teenage girl's fantasy fulfilled. "He was just a 'run of the mill' millionaire but it seemed like a good idea at the time," she explains. "It was something I'd always wanted to do."

Like Deborah Harry, Chris Stein had returned to Manhattan following his tripped-out summer in San Francisco. "I think I got my first apartment in like 1969 or 1970," he recalled. "First Avenue and First Street. The funeral home was still there. And then the bathhouse was like the first gay bathhouse in the city." However, without the focus of a band to bring him out of his private world he became increasingly reclusive, as delayed shock from his father's death combined with regular LSD consumption to propel him toward a mental breakdown, which would see him committed to Belleville Hospital Centre, a New Jersey psychiatric institution, for several months. Chris considered his incarceration to be just an occupational hazard for acidheads: "Flipping out was the norm. Everyone I knew would do their stint in the nuthouse at some point or another."

On his release, Chris then faced the draft board which was calling him up as a potential conscript for the Vietnam conflict. "I told them to check off everything, that I was a drug addict, gay, whatever," he revealed. Fortunately, this gambit ensured that he failed the medical, leaving him free to head to Woodstock to enjoy the last rays of hippie sunlight.

As a means of providing himself with some direction, Chris also enrolled in a photography course at the New York School of Visual Arts. "Photography is easy to pursue because I'm already set up to do that," he asserted. "And I went to art school and studied graphics too, so I'm just utilising what's at my disposal. My mother was a beatnik painter; I've been around artists all my life."

Chapter Three

Brave New Babylon

"The New York Dolls were great attitude. If nothing else, they were a great attitude."

Johnny Thunders

M ost depictions of New York City during the 20th century opened with the most famous skyline in the world and worked their way down. The city was well established as the port where hopeful immigrants arrived; the capital of capitalism; the prototype for the modern metropolis. It was a place where people came to change their lives, to realise their previously stifled artistic leanings and, hopefully, to make their fortunes.

But, as the sixties turned into the seventies, the Big Apple entered an economic downward spiral that would render it bankrupt by the middle of the decade. As immigration quotas expanded nearly half a million people arrived from Latin America and the Caribbean, coinciding with a substantial 'white flight' to the suburbs. Unemployment soared and, as thousands of city employees were dismissed, the parks became overgrown mugging fields; the subway system regularly broke down; libraries were closed; rather than being paved with gold, the streets were generally caked in grime and uncollected garbage. With fewer police on the beat, drug supermarkets did a roaring trade and crime raged so fiercely that the city would take decades to shake off its reputation as one of America's scariest urban dystopias. As Alan Vega, vocalist of Suicide, recalls, "New York was collapsing."

"Economically, it was just a whole different world. It really was like living in Beirut," asserted Debbie. "It wasn't all peace and love," she added, perhaps superfluously. "Racially and economically, there was a lot of separation. The Lower East Side was a dangerous place to live, although I liked it there. You had these great Russian, Ukrainian and Spanish restaurants, where you could eat well and cheaply."

As has often been the case, societal impoverishment gave rise to an upsurge in grass-roots creativity. New York would spawn several epochal musical movements in the space of a decade, including low-rent glam, Bowery punk and its angular aftershock. All were initially made possible through the dirt-cheap rents that facilitated an influx of artists and musicians willing to put up with the squalor and danger. The Cast Iron District (later renamed SoHo – South of Houston – and TriBeCa – Triangle Below Canal Street) had become an abandoned ghost town full of lofts and warehouses. Further East, the area around the Bowery was also eerily vacant, while parts of Alphabet City looked like London after the Blitz. Many of these abandoned spaces provided a fertile spawning ground for alternative strains of creativity.

Much of this activity was described as 'underground'. The term had been coined by New York's *Village Voice*, 'the world's first underground newspaper', established in 1955, but the phrase did not enter the popular consciousness until around 1964 – following a wave of films, publications and plays. The counterculture hijacked it as the perfect catch-all banner for alternative creativity, and in the immediate post-sixties years, 'underground' came to mean a loosely defined anti-authoritarianism striving for self-expression, far-out drug experiences, sexual freedom and, ultimately, an alternative society.

For Deborah Harry, these winds of societal change initially blew at a distance. After returning from her brief Californian sojourn, she found work as a Bunny Girl at the notorious Playboy Club. Recalling why she took the job, Debbie explained, "I think it was because of this man that my mother and father knew, Mr Whipple – like the [supermarket] commercial – except he was different, real handsome; I always had a big crush on him. He was a businessman who used to travel a lot, wild and exciting; he used to flirt with me a little, and I would *die* because he was so handsome. He was a *Playboy* subscriber and raved about the clubs – that was where I first heard about them. I always had it in the back of my mind. I did it for the money."

"I didn't consider it a profession," Debbie later added. "A lot of the women there believed that, though. They were into it for the huge income. Those girls made some dough. The drink prices were high, and the percentages were good for the Bunnys. I did OK. I only stayed there for seven or eight months. I was getting to the point where I was getting into the big showrooms, where the girls would clean up. In those days, you came away with $1,500 cash on a weekend.

"There were girls there who started their own businesses from what they made; girls were making from $300–$500 a night. Cash! You had 35 people per show to wait on; sometimes you'd be carrying a double-stacked tray … A man watching a girl in a little costume with her tits hanging out, struggling with a tray among 500 people, he thinks, 'Holy shit! How did she do that?' It's no big deal to give her a tip."

The gig as a Bunny paid well enough to finance Deborah's continuing narcotics consumption. "I was stoned most of the time," she'd explain. "I wanted the money. It was a goal and something I had always had held in front of me in my younger life. When you're younger, you have idyllic dreams of things to do. I did it and it's not so good. It's pretty disgusting work."

"You had to maintain a level of appearance," she later recalled. "You'd had to go through the inspection line before you went to work. They felt they had some kind of ownership thing, that they could call you and expect you to drop everything and work. It was actually really quite offensive."

Despite the need to finance her habit, Debbie had no ambition to appear as a *Playboy* model. "I was too thin at the time. I don't think I was *Playboy* magazine material. I mean, yeah, I looked cute. But they weren't looking for that. They wanted someone a little more sexual.

"It was definitely interesting, but it was a short-lived occupation. I got such massive publicity out of doing it. But I never met Hugh Hefner until Blondie took off."

Ultimately, the nine months that Deborah spent working as a Bunny Girl would be the final phase of the drug-enhanced dislocation she'd felt since leaving Wind In The Willows. "I did junk for about three years," she admitted. "I couldn't stand the surroundings. I like the drug. I like the high, there's nothing better, but I can't stand the scene. You have to deal with extortionists. For a while, I had this dealer living in my house on 107th and Manhattan Avenue and I nearly went berserk. That really finished me on the whole trip. These 40-year-old guys with guns and infections all over their bodies. I don't think they ever went to the bathroom. I just quit. At the same time, I met this doctor on Central Park South who gave vitamin shots with amphetamine and I started doing that instead. And that was like bouncing off and going in another direction."

Although fuelled by speed, this new direction provided Debbie with the sense of self she'd been lacking. "I stopped doing junk and I didn't need the money as much. In a way, I used drugs to stimulate myself or control my state of mind to help me get through a rough, emotional time in my life. When I felt a little more secure, I was ready to go on as a person without any help, assured of what I was."

Like many people who seek to establish who they actually *are*, Debbie returned to what had motivated and, to a degree, defined her as a younger woman: her ambition to perform. "I wanted music that popped and as a Bunny I was losing my hop. I just wanted out. I moved to a $75-a-month studio apartment, but eventually the real estate broker who handled the building came around and said I could stay there for no rent whatsoever if I made it with him on a regular basis. I thought, 'Oh shit! I'm not going to get involved with this.' So, burned out but determined to regain my strength, I packed everything and moved upstate to live outside Woodstock in Phoenicia with my pregnant girlfriend."

Having extracted herself from the drugs culture, Debbie continued her self-examination in a less chaotic environment. "I wanted to learn self-hypnosis," she revealed. "I thought if I learned some kind of technique, a physical technique or a mental technique, that would be able to support me if I ever felt I needed to take drugs – so that I could get out of this rat race. But then I got into the psychoanalytic rat race – and that was another one! I mean, that was taking as much time and money as the other thing had; so I had to get out of that, too."

After four months Deborah also got out of Phoenicia, returning to the family home in Hawthorne. "It took me some time to readjust. I got the old blow-ups and put on a lot of weight," she explained. "By the time I left Phoenicia in 1970 you couldn't tell the difference between me and my pregnant girlfriend."

As her parents both held day jobs, Debbie had an abundance of time for introspection. "The idea of doing music haunted me every day," she recalled. "I said to my family, 'I think about doing this every single day.' My mother never said not to do it, she just said, 'Be practical.' I worked in a health spa in Paramus teaching exercises.

"I did make-up and facials and I fooled around with hair, but I could only really do trims. I've ruined some people. I cut my sister's hair once and she wanted to kill me. I don't blame her; she looked like a lampshade."

In 1971, Debbie helped her parents move to Cooperstown, in upstate New York, where her mother ran a gift shop. Keen to re-establish her independence after a year back in the nest, she scored a rented room from a truck driver, situated underneath the George Washington Bridge on the Jersey side of the Hudson River in Fort Lee. She then fell into a relationship with a young car salesman, who helped Deborah relocate to a new apartment, although the new couple spent the bulk of their time at his place. "Suddenly I was all set for a new life again with my job and my boyfriend," she recounted. "The job was a bust, but that wasn't all. We discovered we weren't meant for each other, and I moved back into my own apartment. I went to cosmetician school, and started a job in a friend's beauty salon in Jersey. My ex kept calling me in the middle of the night – possessiveness was a major reason we broke up – to make sure I was home alone."

Both Debbie Harry and Chris Stein had experienced the birth pangs and growing pains of the sixties underground movement at close quarters, but were too young and unworldly to be anything more than peripheral contributors. Their trajectories had often taken them into one another's social orbit, but had always narrowly missed the eye contact that would eventually ignite their relationship – and give birth to Blondie.

It would require another subcultural upheaval to bring the two of them together and unleash their creative personalities.

The scene which sprang up around The New York Dolls at the Mercer Arts Centre was one of those rare, magical instances when a random collision of unique personalities hits the same place at exactly the right moment. The soiled glamour personified by the Dolls and their exotic followers was inextricably linked to the Warhol crowd – who'd been behaving this way for years in the back room of Max's – and, in terms of shattering taboos, the gay scene – which had remained underground for decades.

The brief blooms of liberty in the second half of the sixties garlanded the path for the outrageous sartorial styles and behaviour that became almost the norm by the mid-seventies. Although not quite the milestone in gay liberation/disco history that it's often credited as, the 1969 Stonewall riots had played a key role in broadening New York's horizons.

Despite the lifting of laws against serving alcohol to homosexuals in 1967, the Stonewall Inn remained a target for homophobic police looking to hassle the clientele. It was also one of many Mob-controlled Village venues which owed its unhindered existence to a weekly payout handed over to the police. When this failed to happen during the week that culminated in the riots of June 17, 1969, the bar was raided and the more flamboyant drag queens herded into meat wagons. However, rather than disperse meekly, the bar's patrons retaliated with bottles and other missiles. This conflict continued across several nights, becoming symbolic of the new age of gay liberation – although gay bars would continue to be raided for years. As renowned disco commentator Vince Aletti put it, "Stonewall was more mythological than real."

In time Blondie would be accepted by the disco crowd, with Debbie becoming an enduring gay icon. Subsequent to Stonewall, many of the characters around the downtown scene (many of whom would find a new focal point at the Mercer Arts Centre) saw the riots as a turning point that provided militant motivation to their chosen lifestyles. Now the gay underground came into the open, with discos like The Sanctuary providing a countercultural nexus similar to that which had hovered around Andy Warhol and The Factory.

In terms of personal freedom, the early seventies can be viewed as benefitting from the social upheavals of the previous decade – although, in New York, the tide of tolerance would meet banks of resistance once the Dolls appeared. As influential as The Velvet Underground, the Dolls embodied the incoming zeitgeist in a city that had lost the momentum established in the sixties. Greenwich Village's status as a trail-blazing, folk-oriented cultural hub, traversed by busker Chris Stein, had deteriorated to a kind of post-Dylan tourist trail soundtracked by drab singer-songwriters. As for rock, although Bleecker Street now boasted a freak-friendly bar called Nobody's, many major venues had closed by the turn of the decade (including Steve Paul's Scene and The Electric Circus at the old Dom on St Mark's and Fillmore East).

Where Hendrix had once ejected solar flares of virtuosity into the New York night, now legions of lesser talents bored their ever-dwindling audiences with sonic masturbation. The city needed a return to rock'n'roll basics, spliced to a pioneer spirit of loud exhibitionism and decadence.

Enter The New York Dolls. By taking the flamboyant sass of Jagger/Richard(s) to the outrageous extremes of raw, dirty, rock'n'roll, the Dolls set the agenda for the seventies. Uncontrollably rebellious and fuelled by almost every known mind-altering substance, the gender-bending quintet cut a swath across America, Europe and Japan, leaving a trail of destruction in their wake. Five years later, the rest of the world would still be trying to catch up.

In addition to being the five-man rock'n'roll Babylon that defined glitter rock and laid the foundations for punk, the Dolls exerted an irresistible pull upon hip young New Yorkers desperate for new kicks. Chris Stein – who first noticed the omnisexual quintet leering out from a flyer at the School of Visual Arts – found their louche appeal impossible to ignore. "I just saw it going on and it just seemed like a cool thing," he recalled.

By 1972, Chris had abandoned his earnest folk inclinations as his freak antennae homed in on the possibilities of the nascent glitter scene. "I used to be Alice Cooper a lot. I used to wear make-up all the time. You go through periods with archetypes. If you wear make-up people think you look like Alice Cooper," he recalled. "I used to wear eye make-up every day and I'd have people looking at me and completely freaking out. I mean, I thought that was my role in life – to make people crazy on the subway. It's part of the psychology of wanting to be different."

The Dolls were billed to perform at the Mercer Arts Center, an extension built onto the former Grand Central Hotel (then the Broadway Central Hotel). Once notorious as a gangster hangout in the previous century, by now it was little more than a flophouse. The Centre, however, had been the dream of air-conditioning millionaire Seymour Kaback – who loved the theatre and wanted to build the perfect complex to realise his cultural aspirations. He'd acquired the old building and divided it up into smaller performance areas named after famous figures such as George Bernard

Shaw and Oscar Wilde. There was a jazz lounge, a cinema for art-house movies, a room for Theatre of Cruelty performances (such as Arrabal's *And They Put Handcuffs On The Flowers*) and a bar in the foyer.

"It was a renovated place," recalled latter-day Dolls drummer Jerry Nolan. "It was a cross between Victorian-looking design and a really spacey modern *Clockwork Orange* type of place, yet it had some of the old things still left, like chandeliers in certain parts of the walls. It was a great combination of old Victorian and modern."

Although it was the outsider allure of the Dolls that drew Chris to The Mercer, it was that night's opening act — Eric Emerson & The Magic Tramps — that initially ignited his enthusiasm. Familiar to Debbie from their encounters at Max's, Emerson would also play a pivotal role in Chris' musical development.

Born in New Jersey in 1945, Eric had been sent to ballet school by his mother and was later spotted by Warhol dancing at The Dom in April 1966. He subsequently appeared in *Chelsea Girls*, Warhol's split-screen movie centred around 23rd Street's Chelsea Hotel, becoming a Factory stalwart and later appearing in *Lonesome Cowboys*, *San Diego Surf* and *Heat*. Emerson came to wider attention on account of the use of his image on the back cover of The Velvet Underground's debut album. In need of money he attempted to sue, which resulted in his face being obscured by a sticker before a new edition airbrushed him out entirely.

Eric travelled to Los Angeles at the invitation of an experimental rock group called Messiah — house band for a Sunset Boulevard club called Temple Of The Rainbow — whose guitarist, Young Blood, he met during the filming of *Lonesome Cowboys*. Messiah were steered by drummer Sesu Coleman and violinist Larry Chaplan, but only began writing songs after Emerson joined. In early 1971 he suggested they relocate to Warhol-world in New York. Upon arrival, Mickey Ruskin gave the group (now renamed The Magic Tramps) the key to the upstairs room at Max's — unused since The Velvet Underground played their shows there the previous year. The group were immediately embraced by the Warhol crowd, contributing musical backing to Jackie Curtis's horror movie-dialogued show *Vain Victory*, with Emerson dancing from head to toe in glitter alongside Ondine, Holly Woodlawn and Candy Darling. (A 1975 production of the play also featured Debbie Harry in the role of chorus girl Juicy Lucy.)

After gaining a reputation via their Friday-night residency at Max's, The Magic Tramps were offered a gig at the Mercer Arts Center by jazz pianist Michael Tschudin and also played Warhol events with the likes of Jackie Curtis and Geri Miller. The Tramps helped renovate the Mercer, converting the ballrooms into theatres in exchange for rehearsal space. They were the first rock band to play at the venue, participating in an art-video event with Tschudin. By the time the Mercer officially opened in November 1971, the Tramps were playing nightly cabaret sets with him in The Blue Room.

In June 1972, The New York Dolls started their epoch-making Tuesday-night residency at the 200-capacity Oscar Wilde Room. Johnny Thunders famously quipped, "They didn't want us at the Mercer Arts Center until they counted the bar receipts." Electro-punk pioneers Suicide also barged their way into a residency. Despite wildly differing attitudes to music and drugs, they bonded with the Dolls. "The Mercer was an incredible place," recalls Suicide's Martin Rev. "The Dolls played, then people would have to come through our room to leave. We were the next generation, living through the realities of war and bringing the war onto the stage. An expressionistic thing. You'd see the Dolls' audiences dressed up in polka dots and colours. A party scene, it was wonderful."

"Everything came out of glam rock," Chris would later assert. "Suicide predated The New York Dolls, and the scene was very exciting."

Stein and Emerson hit it off immediately Chris – who had arranged for The Magic Tramps to play at the School of Visual Arts Christmas party – scored a gig as the band's roadie, before graduating to intermittent bass and guitar duties, while Eric moved into Chris's apartment on First Avenue and First Street. "Chris and Eric were the only freaks in the building, which was full of lower income families," remembered Debbie. "Everybody thought they were horrible and was terrified the freaks were gonna rape their daughters. Eric didn't help relations with the neighbours by rushing out and screaming in the halls at 4a.m. or coming round to the back of the building in the middle of the night and yelling, 'Throw down my drugs! They're in the drawer!' ... Things got progressively worse. The neighbours hated them, the super was freaking, and Eric was a maniac, although Chris loved living with him because he brought constant excitement into the apartment."

Although he had many endearing traits, living with Emerson's lunatic lifestyle was not always straightforward. "Eric was a Warhol Star – one of the originals – he was clever, charming, talented, and had a huge ego fuelled by the hundreds of people who wanted to have sex with him," explains his partner Elda Gentile. "And he did accommodate them with pleasure. I was only 18, still living at home and naive as can be, and whenever I was in the city he showered all his attention on me. We were madly in love. It wasn't until after I left home that I became aware that you get the whole package and you have to take the whole package – there is no choosing which part of him to accept or not accept. That package came with an open relationship that I didn't know I was in for, masses of free drugs along with nights of social and creative experiences and experiments."

Like Chris, Debbie had no reservations about the Dolls, taking to the band with enthusiasm and making regular trips to the Mercer to catch them live. "She used to come by in her little blue car from New Jersey," recalled Elda. "Ride around with us, and party with the boys." Deborah was particularly taken with Dolls frontman David Johansen, with whom she enjoyed a brief tryst: "I was crazy about David. I thought David was the hot stuff! But I was friends with them all, I liked the original drummer, Billy Murcia, but then I became friends with Jerry [Nolan], and Jerry used to play in an early incarnation of Blondie."

One particular ride with the Dolls led to Debbie almost being busted in her father's Chrysler. "In the car, I had about 14 of the skinniest people you have ever seen with big hair and platform shoes," she explained. "I had The New York Dolls and their girlfriends in full regalia. We got pulled over on the Taconic Parkway. It was outrageous. The cop looked in the window and saw that there were about six of us in the front seat. He said, 'Oh, my God! I can't believe it!' Then, he just drove away. He didn't want to deal with it. He must have thought we were a clown club from the circus."

The scene at the Mercer Arts Center came to an unexpected and dramatic end when the building collapsed on August 3, 1973. "The centre was integrally linked to the Broadway Central hotel, which had a glorious history but had now become a crumbling structure occupied by welfare recipients," Debbie explains. "It was so old and decrepit from years of people pissing on the floor and throwing up in the corner that it just caved in." The collapse of the building's walls coincided with a Magic Tramps rehearsal. "The band left practice and their equipment and ran," recalled Elda. "They could see across Broadway. They ran for their lives."

As Debbie was to discover, disintegrating buildings were not the only life-threatening hazard facing New York's groovy young things. One night she had a narrow escape from a man she believes was subsequently convicted serial rapist/killer Ted Bundy.

"It was late at night and I was trying to get across Houston Street from the Lower East Side to 7th Avenue. For some reason there were no cabs and I was wearing these big platform shoes. This car kept circling round and round, this guy was calling out, 'Come on, I'll give you a ride.' Finally, I gave in and got in the car. I realised I'd made a big mistake. For one, it was very hot in the car, and the windows rolled up nearly to the top. The guy had a white shirt and he was very good looking. Then I realised this guy had the worst BO I have ever smelt. Then I looked over at the door to crank down the window and saw there was no door handle, no crank. I cast my eyes around and saw that the car had been gutted. There was nothing in there. The hairs on the back of my neck stood up, so I stuck my arm out through the crack in the window and managed to open the door from the outside. I was so lucky."

"At the time I didn't know anything about Ted Bundy," Deborah later reflected. "I just thought, 'Thank God I got away from that asshole,' and I just carried on – and years later, after he was executed, I got on a flight and picked up a *Newsweek*, and I'm reading this story, and it says 'Modus Operandi', and it describes how he looked, the inside of his cars, and the hair on the back of my neck once again went out, and I said, 'Oh my God, that was Ted Bundy.'"

"I've been debunked, actually, by those people that debunk you, or whatever," adds Debbie, speaking nearly 40 years after the encounter. "They say he wasn't in New York at that time, but I think they're really wrong, because he had escaped and was travelling down the East Coast. I think that nobody has ever really investigated that. I didn't know until later who it was. It was pretty scary."

Outside of her sometimes fraught relationship with Eric Emerson (with whom she produced a son named Branch), Elda Gentile had formed a girl group named Pure Garbage with Warhol 'superstar' Holly Woodlawn (herself an ersatz girl/drag queen) and David Johansen's girlfriend, Diane. "They never did any real gigs as far as I know, but they were well-known on the scene," recounted Debbie. "I heard about the group and wanted to join, but by the time I got in touch with Elda they'd split up."

Keen to get back into performing, Debbie remained in contact with Elda. "I had been thinking about doing something in music ever since I had stopped doing folk rock," she explained. "So I went to see Elda and she said she knew another girl with a fabulous voice, so we called her up, her name was Roseanne, and the three of us got together as The Stillettoes. That's how I got back into the music business. I had nothing left to lose and everything to gain. Singing has always been an obsession with me. I would wake up every morning with one thought haunting me, knowing that if I didn't try I would never forgive myself. I knew I had a voice but it was somewhere south of my chin at the time. I knew that trying to satisfy this obsession was the only thing I could do to make me feel right."

Speaking in 2011, Elda recalls the group's genesis: "In 1973, when I had Holly Woodlawn's Pure Garbage, I sold my Andy Warhol Cow (which was signed 'To Elda From Andy') for $3,000 to have the funds to rent a loft in the flower district to live and rehearse in. Our show at Reno Sweeney's, a cabaret club in the West Village, was fantastic. Holly was offered training to develop a cabaret show and I encouraged her to accept the offer. In hindsight I am happy I did, as Holly still performs at underground film festivals and events. Cutting her loose was a gift to her.

"I had made a deal with [transgender performer] Jayne County to allow her PA system to remain in my loft in exchange for free rehearsal time and that allowed me to put together The Stillettoes. Jayne invited a guest singer to rehearse one day. Her name was Rosie Trapani, aka Rosie Ross. I was nuts about Rosie and her great big blues voice and told her about my plan to create a three-girl act that, with original material, would define itself with a modern attitude. I had written songs about having sex in public places, living with men who wore make-up and high heel shoes, and even one about the real Dracula — Vlad Tepes, a connection in reality not yet known about in general in the USA. (I was an assistant art teacher for a special program at the Cloisters, a medieval museum which is a part of the Metropolitan Museum of Art, and it was in their library that I discovered this information.)

"All my lyrics were tongue-in-cheek humour. Rosie drew her material from existing songs but I felt with time we could write for her. With Debbie it was the same – she covered songs but didn't write. I met Debbie when I was living with Sylvain Sylvain [of the Dolls] in 1971. I saw her in 1973, waitressing at Max's one night, and also invited her to join. I took her number and told her all I needed to find were musicians."

Although Deborah was delighted to be in a group where she had some say about both image and sound, her parents were less enthusiastic. "They didn't understand it at all and they really tried to convince me that I was wandering off into the world of God knows what. They were kind of right, because I was taking a gamble with my life. But I don't think they really had a clue. They weren't musicians or artists in any way and I don't think they understood that certain part of me, because they didn't have it in them."

Irrespective of parental disapproval, Debbie knew exactly what sort of group she wanted The Stillettoes to be. "I wanted a combination of the aggressive Shangri-Las rock and the round, solid vocals of an R&B girl group, and the overall idea was to be both entertaining and danceable."

Named by Elda, The Stillettoes were backed by guitarists Tommy and Jimmy Wynbrandt – who would later join cult New York power-pop band The Miamis. "Musicians were hard to come by as they all wanted to be in boy bands and wear make-up and platform shoes like the Dolls," Elda recounts. "But Tommy and Jimmy said they would help, Timothy Jackson took on the drumming and my old friend Alter Ego, who started Pure Garbage, played bass. Debbie had called me, eager to move forward. There are a lot of aspects to a do-it-yourself project and it was my project so I didn't mind making all the necessary investments into it. For Debbie and Rosie it was a turnkey operation – they just had to show up, be happy and perform. Easier said than done."

Underground theatre/film director Tony Ingrassia was signed up to choreograph the group. "He worked on the songs with us, concentrating on a mood, projecting a mood through a song, [and devising] stage tricks to give us a cohesive look. He and Elda used to fight about the image. It was her concept," Deborah explained. "We used to work our butts off, and sing for hours until our throats were raw. It was incredible; it was just like going to school. He was real intense about it. I still have to respect him for that. I would get mad at him, but it was stimulating to get that mad."

"Ingrassia promised that if I let him stage The Stillettoes, he would get us on the [Bowie/Spiders From Mars guitarist] Mick Ronson tour," says Elda. "He also was a good acting teacher and I thought it would help

Debbie and Rosie with their stage presence — I had already gone through it. Method acting techniques open people up and Tony made Debbie and Rosie cry a lot."

"Elda wanted to make us a campy, kitsch materialisation of the *True Confessions* heart-throb garbage girl who's fucked and abandoned, widowed or unmarried; Rosie was into rhythm and blues soul music," Deborah remembered. "Rock dancing was non-existent. Disco was just starting to get a real hold on people."

By the time that The Stillettoes made their live debut in October 1973, Rosie Ross had quit the group after Ingrassia stopped directing them and had been replaced by Amanda Jones, who was recruited by Elda. "We played at the Boburn Tavern on 28th Street; it was just a shitty little dive where they took the legs off the pool table to use it as a stage," recalled Debbie." We didn't think we'd get much of a crowd, but the place was jammed; by the next week, David and Angie Bowie were pulling up in their limousine. We had New York by the balls! There was nothing going on in those days."

"Elda and Holly Woodlawn had the loft upstairs, so they asked the owner if they could perform in the pool room at the back," Chris explained. "It was an anonymous little bar but in those days people were always inventing places to play."

"Holly did the lighting, holding a spotlight with a red gel while standing on the bar," recalls Elda. "We had a great turnout. Being related to Eric Emerson meant that everyone in Downtown New York would know about the gig. It seemed like The Stillettoes were off to a great start."

"I loved The Stillettoes," enthused Leee Black Childers. "They were very influenced by those underground plays and musicals that we did. The people who wrote the plays weren't songwriters, so they did old tunes and put new words to them. The words were often outrageously dirty — 'Thalidomide Baby' and stuff like that. The Stillettoes played a mixture of old tunes and show tunes, but with an outrageous twist. They would go from dirty songs to pop songs. The band was a good training ground for Debbie Harry. Debbie was very nervous about being able to sing. She also didn't think she was pretty."

"It was such fun," beamed Debbie. "The Stillettoes were only ever watched by drunks and low-lifes in sleazy bars and we made no money, but it was fun. That whole early seventies period was fun. Sometimes I miss those times. The New York Dolls were fabulous fun. That whole period, I don't know, there were just a bunch of nice bands then, elegant glitter bands with big platform shoes and big everything. It was great … We were campy. We used to have a song called 'Narcissisma' … We did 'Goldfinger', too … And then we had a song called 'Rouge' which was written by Alice Ghostley who was a very odd comedienne – she was on *Bewitched* and she was always the fucked-up, crazy witch aunt."

"The best song was called 'Dracula, What Did You Do To My Mother?'" asserted Elda. "We wore green crosses and skull eyeglasses that we bought on 42nd Street. It was great."

"Everybody was there in bell-bottom pants," added Deborah. "We did a couple of shows. Then the girls were there in tight pants and minis. They had *scoured* the second-hand stores."

Regardless of whatever qualities were on display, The Stillettoes' second gig at the Boburn Tavern would be significant in enabling Chris and Debbie to finally meet. "Elda would invite people while she was out socialising and that's actually how I heard about it," remembered Chris. "At the time I was dating this girl called Elvira, who used to be the girlfriend of Billy Murcia – the drummer from the Dolls. We went out for about nine months – she had a little daughter I really liked. Anyway, Elda had invited her to the show, so I went too."

"He came there with Eric Emerson and Elda. She used to go with Eric. He was sitting in the shadows yet I could feel his piercing gaze upon me throughout the whole show," explained Deborah. "I really couldn't see his face clearly because he was sitting in such a way that his head was [facing] backwards … All I could see was this sort of glow, and I don't know if it was [fate] or it was just sort of apparent that we were supposed to connect up. I know that sounds kind of ridiculous, but I delivered the whole show to him. I couldn't look anywhere else."

Debbie later spoke of feeling an immediate "psychic connection" with Chris, while her future partner admitted, "I was flabbergasted. I was impressed and knocked out by her." Unsurprisingly, the two hit it off. "He was very magnetic to me. He has such beautiful eyes. And I love dark hair on men," purred Deborah. "It's very easy to be friends with Chris, because he's really a lovely guy. He's a weird combination of a very sophisticated mind and very childlike behaviour. It's totally endearing. I was always smitten by those elements of his personality."

"I probably saw in her what a lot of people saw later on, but I got there first," surmised Chris.

Their personal relationship would soon blossom, but first Debbie asked Chris to join the group. "I discovered he was a musician, and one of the other Stillettoes knew him, and we asked him to join our backing band. That was Chris. We fitted from the start."

Chapter Four

East Side Story

"The Bowery was a drab, ugly and unsavoury place, but it was good enough for rock'n'rollers. The people who frequented CBGB's didn't seem to mind staggering drunks and stepping over a few bodies."

Hilly Kristal

Although Chris and Debbie felt an immediate attraction to each other, their personal relationship developed at a slower rate than their creative alliance. With their prime focus set upon reconfiguring The Stillettoes, the couple would regularly stroll between their respective apartments, plotting the band's next move and hatching song ideas.

In addition to drawing them closer together, al fresco brainstorming amid New York's concrete canyons infused their songs with the essence of the city. "I've always felt the environment one lives in has an effect on what one does, and this was certainly proved true in the initial stages of my collaboration with Chris," observed Deborah. "I was walking to his house one day when I started working up a song called 'Platinum Blonde'. By the time I got there I had the lyrics and melody so we started fooling around with it right away. Movement, like walking, driving or listening to the bump, spin, hiss of the laundromat or motors has always been an inspiration for lyrics."

The nascent Stein–Harry relationship developed at a natural, unpressured pace. "Chris and I hadn't become lovers yet, but through working together we'd become friends," Debbie explained. "He knew I was nervous that my past would catch up with me. The all-night phone calls continued, so he said I could stay at his apartment if I would feel safer. However, after a while the Jersey car salesman came to his senses. I think he felt bad about what he'd done."

"Debbie had some so-called ex-boyfriend who was harassing her," confirms Elda. "So there were times she would call and cancel at the last minute. It was freaking us all out, especially Chris. So Tony and Rosie found an apartment for her in their building on the West Side. Chris and the band packed her up in the dead of night and moved her. The ex-boyfriend would call threatening me if I didn't tell him where Debbie was. He was one scary guy."

Chris' laid-back nature, and his understanding of the psychological impact of possessive ex-boyfriends and overenthusiastic chemical consumption, enabled the couple to gradually grow together. "When he saw Debbie, he had the hots for her, like, *unbelievably*," asserts Elda. "I was even a little surprised that she went for it. Let's just say that he was very, very smart the way he handled her. I knew he wanted her body, soul and spirit, but he played it very cool to get her. He nurtured all her insecurities. See, everybody loved Debbie because she had this Marilyn-Monroe-in-the-gutter quality, but she was very insecure, and a little bit paranoid."

"I think it was about three months before we were actually intimate," Chris recalled. "I think we just had a meeting of the minds," added Deborah. "Maybe it's because we've both got such accepting natures and we have a lot of room for a lot of different kinds of people and different dispositions and things like that. We both have a temper, though."

"I'm an independent person, and I've survived quite well being independent," asserted Debbie. "I don't need a man for support in that way. I need a partner, I need someone who wants to share the kinds of things that I enjoy doing, and that is willing to have a woman who's strong. A lot of men don't want to have a strong woman – but a lot do. It probably has to do with intelligence. I like somebody with a good sense of humour."

Chris' openness, his sense of humour and respect for Debbie gradually chipped away at her reluctance to become involved. The couple opted to cohabit at Thompson Street, with Chris subletting his apartment to Tommy Erdelyi – who would shortly become known as Tommy Ramone, The Ramones' drum titan.

Irrespective of being closer to the West Side, Chris found there was no escaping the harsh realities of the New York streets. "It was totally fucking *Mean Streets* there," he recounts. "It was exactly what's in the film with all the fucking social clubs and stuff like that. Eventually we were sort of blacklisted in the neighbourhood because we were just too weird. What happened was I was waiting for Debbie to come home one day and I was downstairs and I had super-long hair and used to wear fucking make-up and all this shit, so everybody thought we were completely weird but we still got along with the super of the building and all the people and stuff. I was waiting for Debbie to come home, and across the street is a bunch of the neighbourhood guys kicking the shit out of this black guy – just for the hell of it ... And I'm just observing this and I hear a voice going, 'No, no! Stop! Call the police!' And it's fucking Debbie who has just arrived on the scene from visiting her parents, and after that we were ostracised."

Despite Deborah's connection to Chris, it was actually Elda that asked him to join The Stillettoes. Setting aside his loose arrangement with The Magic Tramps, he agreed to play full-time partly on account of his attraction to Debbie. Chris took over on guitar, with Elda recruiting Fred Smith as bassist and a friend from the Boburn tavern, Billy O'Connor, as the band's latest drummer. "I met Chris when he was a bass player for Eric Emerson. He would go down on his knees and everything; he was really different as a bass player than he is as a guitarist," observed Debbie. "I thought he was marvellous. But I think it fits him better intellectually to play a guitar than bass."

"We didn't really know what we were doing when we started," Deborah later explained. "We did some Tina Turner songs and a few Rolling Stones songs. We weren't that good. We were just learning. All we wanted to do was songs that had a hook in them, that were danceable, because up to that point everybody was watching these long guitar solos and good old boys singing about 'the road' and it didn't relate to our urban experience at all. It was just Middle America music and we were sick of it."

The band's musical inexperience was matched by the poverty of their urban experience. "We had absolutely no equipment when we started out. We were terrible," Debbie asserted. "Chris had a little tiny amp thing that was terribly noisy. The police radio never stopped coming through. Everyone was responsible for their own mix so it was all, 'Your amp is on 10 so mine's going on 10, too, dammit! Let's watch the singer bleed; I'm putting my amp on 11! See the singer bleed through the nose!' But, oh God, seriously, those were fun days at the beginning, before we got famous and all that shit. We were just disreputable and funky and sleazy and smelly in every way. We were jerks. We were the underdogs."

By late spring 1974, the retooled Stillettoes were confident enough to set their mixture of high camp and late glam before small sections of the public. "Chris calls [The Stillettoes] the last of the glitter groups. It was a sort of campy Shangri-Las/Supremes-type of girl trio," recounts Debbie. "We had a lot of fun but we weren't too musical. The record companies at that time were not interested."

At a time when pretentious progressive opuses such as Pink Floyd's *Dark Side Of The Moon* were selling by the truckload, the fading glam scene still came closest to any form of rock'n'roll dynamism. "It was all glitter bands," declared ex-Stillettoes bassist Fred Smith. "That's what was happening. It was a lot of fun. It was exciting. There were all these groups forming on the Lower East Side. There was CBGB's and Club 82 opening. There was something happening. It was more fun than music. The Stillettoes, like most of the other groups, were probably more into presentation than music, but the girls wrote a few good songs."

Situated on Fourth Street and Second Avenue, Club 82 had been one of Manhattan's most glamorous drag venues between the forties and late sixties, playing host to successive waves of female impersonators. Latterly, 82 had lost some of its transgressive allure once such establishments could operate openly, but still employed a team of lesbians to maintain order at the door. "It was run by this lesbian woman – called Tommy – who was gorgeous and ran it like a brick shithouse," recalls New York Dolls guitarist Syl Sylvain who, with the rest of the 'Lipstick Killers' (as the Dolls were sometimes known to the glitter cognoscenti), had opened the venue for live rock'n'roll in full drag. "It looked all tropical. The Copacabana goes gay, if you will. The centre of it was the actual stage, like a square. Completely around the stage was the bar. We would hang down there. The prostitutes were on 10th Street and after their work hours they would go down to Club 82 and drink down there. They would have like drag shows and do performances."

For a short time, the club filled the countercultural void left by the collapse of the Mercer Arts Center and provided The Stillettoes with a venue for a handful of their early gigs, one of which was attended by Who drummer, Keith Moon. Also at this June 1974 show was a representative from Albert Grossman's Bearsville Records who offered the girls, but not the boys, a recording deal. They demurred.

The same gig also afforded The Stillettoes their first mention in the UK press, as *Melody Maker's* Chris Charlesworth reviewed the show, observing that "some of the songs were well worth putting on vinyl", while an accompanying image depicted "a cuddly platinum blonde named Debbi". Charlesworth, who was the inky paper's New York correspondent, was tipped off about The Stillettoes by photographer Bob Gruen. "He knew I was interested in checking out some rock'n'roll action amongst unsigned acts downtown and there was a band that he thought I might like. 'There's this singer, a blonde girl, looks just like Marilyn Monroe,' he said on the phone. 'Check her out, man, you won't believe it.'"

Charlesworth headed down to Club 82. "It was an old-style dyke bar with mirrors everywhere," he recalls. "I think it was famous in its day as an all-female gay hangout but now fallen on hard times, and the girls who worked it, all of them of a certain age with short crops and dressed in dark men's suits with buttoned-up shirts and ties, figured that a bit of rock'n'roll might keep the creditors at bay. For a while it was a sort of sister club to CBGB's, never as well known but fun all the same, brighter too with more of a party atmosphere. So on this night I paid my $3 on the door and went inside, bought a beer and found Bob by the stage, camera at the ready.

"The Stillettoes turned out to be a trio, backed by a four-piece, who took their cue from the girl groups of the pre-Beatles sixties. There was a black girl, a redhead and a blonde who was the leader, and Bob was right: she wore a clingy, low-cut, full-length satin fifties ball gown in gold that flattered her figure and she was a dead ringer for Marilyn, with platinum hair, a lovely smile and strawberry lips. Their set was under-rehearsed and short – everybody's was down there – and afterwards Bob took me backstage to meet her."

Charlesworth thus became the first – but certainly not the last – British music writer to be enchanted by Deborah Harry. "She just shimmered," he continues. "Her eyes sparkled and when she smiled I just melted. She was cool, committed and she knew her pop too. I was certainly intimidated by her but I tried not to show it and somehow managed to talk to her about this and that while Bob took some more pictures."

At this stage Deborah was working in a New Jersey beauty parlour. "She told me she wanted to be a singer but she had a daytime job," says Charlesworth. "She said she hoped some day to get into the music business full-time. I told her I'd stay in touch and she gave me the phone number of the beauty parlour. Bob took some more pictures, and I went away and in a week or two included my little interview with her in a generic piece I wrote for *MM* about several New York bands like The Stillettoes, Television, The Harlots Of 42nd Street and a few more. I'd sent over Bob's pictures and, naturally enough since she was a vision of loveliness, the subs' desk in London chose to illustrate the feature with one of Bob's big pictures of The Stillettoes' lead singer, taken on the night of my interview."

A week later Charlesworth called Debbie at the beauty parlour where she worked and told her that her picture was in *Melody Maker*. "She was very excited about this. It was evidently the first time she'd ever had her picture in a magazine, or so she told me, and she seemed desperate to get her hands on a copy. A night or two later she drove up to my apartment on East 78th Street in an old green banger with bench seats and I gave her three copies of the magazine and we went out and had a Japanese meal together on the West Side. I don't think she'd ever been to a Japanese restaurant before so I introduced her to sushi and tempura and sake, which she loved. She told me that The Stillettoes were breaking up and she was forming a new band with her boyfriend, Chris Stein, their guitarist. I took note of this and mentioned it in my next New York news column. When she dropped me off at my place after midnight I pulled her towards me across the bench seat, kissed her on the lips and invited her inside, but I was too late – she'd already met another Chris."

Charlesworth stayed in touch with Debbie and, on June 14, 1974, took her to see The Who at Madison Square Garden, the final night of a four-night run. "We had a great view, close by the stage but looking down on John's side," he recalls. "Funnily enough, I don't think she was that impressed. They smashed up lots of gear at the end and maybe she was thinking what a waste it all was."

After the show he brought Debbie backstage to meet the group. "In the dressing room Roger Daltrey tried to put the make on her. He said something like, 'Fuckin' 'ell, Chris, that bird looks just like fuckin' Marilyn Monroe!' and Keith Moon was showing an interest too. She didn't respond to either of their advances – which didn't please Roger, whose strike rate in this department was always very high. She spent the rest of the evening with me, taking in an after-show party at a roller-dome where we danced a lot and Bob Gruen, ever on my trail, took more photographs, including several of us together. I still have them."

A few weeks later, Debbie called Chris Charlesworth and asked him to meet her and Chris Stein at Max's Kansas City. "Upstairs in the bar they told me more about their plans for the new band, and asked me whether I'd be interested in managing them. I was astounded, incredibly flattered, but I declined. I knew very little about management in those days and didn't think I was up to the job. In any case, I was having far too much fun being *Melody Maker's* man in America. I think they thought it would be cool to have a British music writer as their manager and they were probably right, but I wasn't the right one. I did recommend some managers I knew but, as far as I am aware, none of them took them up on it, fools that they were."

At the time of The Stillettoes' initial mention in *Melody Maker*, gender-bending Jayne County – who had appeared in Warhol's stage show *Pork* and subsequently been hired by Bowie manager Tony DeFries' Mainman organisation – was fronting outrageous groups such as Queen Elizabeth And The Backstreet Boys (then as Wayne County). S/he was one of the select few who caught The Stillettoes at Club 82 and considers the venue to be "the predecessor of CBGB's".

In the late summer of 1974 Club 82 would stop booking live bands, leaving the ailing Max's Kansas City and the recently opened CBGB's as the most accessible venues for New York's glitter underground. Situated at 315 Bowery, opposite the dead end of Bleecker Street, the latter premises had been taken over in 1969 by Hilly Kristal, who previously managed the Village Vanguard Jazz Club on Seventh Avenue, before opening a country music bar on 13th Street. The initials stood for 'Country, Bluegrass and Blues', with the appended 'OMFUG' as an acronym for 'Other Music For Uplifting Gormandizers'. Kristal initially decided to convert the space from a biker bar to a steel-guitar-and-checked-shirt establishment, but there was not enough country in town. He would also discover that finding gormandisers to uplift was similarly difficult. "But what happened was, first of all there weren't really enough people to make it work," Kristal explained, "enough things to keep it going day after day here on the Bowery, which was a little bit different to how it is now; it was a mess."

The bar's tawdry location added to its chaotic sense of excitement. In 1974 the Bowery/Lower East Side was still considered dangerous, to the point of being a no-go area for the more timid. The club was dark, narrow and illuminated inside by neon beer signs. Next door was the Palace Hotel, one of the city's flophouses and a major haven for the then-ubiquitous Bowery bums. The club's entrance reeked of vagrant's piss, a fragrance that tended to follow you inside.

For years the Bowery had been the quintessential Skid Row populated by derelicts, as immortalised by Lionel Rogosin's 1956 film *On The Bowery* — a fly-at-the-bottom-of-the-glass view of what, for the first half of the 20th century, had been the happening drag for vaudeville and burlesque entertainment. The film's bleak picture of bums, alcoholics and hustling ne'er-do-wells was brutally raw and still accurate by the time CBGB's opened for business. Before this there had been the *Bowery Boys* B-movies, which ran for 15 years from the mid-forties and set their streetwise Lower East Side heroes against authority figures, cops and mobsters. But for most of the sixties, with much of the cultural action going on in Greenwich Village and further East, around St Mark's Place and the Lower East Side, the Bowery had been left to rot along with its itinerant inhabitants.

Eric Emerson had been friendly with the local Hells Angels chapter whose clubhouse opened in 1969, opposite the local men's shelter on East Third Street. He was on his way home with drummer Sesu Coleman when they stopped off at 315 Bowery; although Kristal had his country bar on West 13th Street, he lived at this address. Within a two-block radius of Hilly's on the bowery were six flophouses holding about 2,000 alcoholics, junkies, social rejects, discarded Vietnam veterans and former inmates of prisons or mental institutions. Traversing the Bowery involved stepping over unconscious bodies, who were easy prey for muggers ('jack rollers', as they were known) when comatose. Hilly was looking to promote live music, so Emerson and Coleman offered to play as they had at the Mercer. The Magic Tramps helped build the stage and performed at the venue's grand opening on October 19, 1972.

In December 1973 Hilly renamed the bar CBGB's. Wayne County and Queen Elizabeth were the first band to play the new club. "I played CBGB's four whole months before Television," asserts Wayne/Jayne. "It was for a crowd of Hells Angels. They used to hang out there a lot before it became cool and The Ramones and Patti Smith started playing there. In fact, I'm the one who told Dee Dee Ramone about CBGB's. He was complaining about there being so few places to play in New York City ..."

"In April, Tom [Verlaine] and I were walking down from his house ... and we passed this place, which the owner, Hilly Kristal, was outside fixing up," Television guitarist Richard Lloyd recalled. "We asked if maybe we could play there and he told us he was going to call the place Country Blue Grass and Blues. So we said, 'Yes, we play stuff like that ...' He gave us a gig, so we got a whole bunch of friends down and convinced him to give us every Sunday for a month."

"There were all these kids and they had no place to play their own rock music," observed Kristal. "They weren't interested in sixties rock, they weren't interested in folk or anything. They were interested in their thing, what they had to say." Hilly Kristal provided a crucial outlet at a time when new, different, or just plain bad groups had nowhere else to go in the city. "They played in their lofts and basements, there were a couple of places they could play once or twice a week, but nobody would let them play their own music most of the time," he added. "So, when I saw this, I just kinda let them play, and then because there were so many of them I said, 'There's a change in the policy; the only way to play here is you have to do your own music.' And that started people coming around, I mean not customers too much but the musicians ... Everybody wanted to do their own music. Some of it was terrible, and others worse than terrible, but it was interesting."

Not many attended Television's first show; half of them were friends who got in free (admission was a dollar) and no one had money to buy drinks. Josh Feigenbaum wrote a review in *SoHo Weekly News* about one of these early gigs, in which he describes the group as "loud, out of tune and pretentious as hell". Patti Smith and her guitarist Lenny Kaye attended minimalist prog-rockers Television's third week, with Kaye recognising that a new 'other' scene was gestating. "The first few times Television played I didn't like what they were doing," recalled Kristal. "I let them play because some of these bands were just interesting. Their music didn't quite make sense at the beginning, but soon after, when they got it together, they did."

In addition to initiating the ripped-and-spiked look that served as the sartorial template for UK punk 18 months later, Television bassist Richard Hell was going out with Elda. "She said, 'I heard this bunch of guys and they dress like old men and they're very funny and they play in this weird bar downtown,'" Chris explained. "And we asked them where they were playing and they said, 'CBGB's.'"

Hell told Debbie and Chris about the bar's new policy of allowing unknown local bands to perform on specific nights. On May 12, 1974, the penultimate night of Television's residency, The Stillettoes made their CBGB's debut as the support act. Aside from Elda's personal connection to the headliners, Chris also had some history with vocalist/lead guitarist Tom Verlaine, having previously been asked to join a germinal version of the group: "[Verlaine] called me up and asked me for a bass player. Actually my friend and I used to make fun of him because when he first came to New York he had shoulder-length hair and he had all these hippy love songs, which he used to play acoustically, and we used to take the piss out of him basically. He called me up looking for a bass player, but by that time I was already doing something with Debbie."

"When I decided to try and put a band together," Verlaine countered, "one of the guitar players turned out to be Chris Stein and he came and heard a few songs and played guitar and said, 'This stuff's too fast, I don't like this stuff. It's not commercial enough.' He could play it though."

The Stillettoes supported Television at two subsequent May CBGB's gigs, and although these events – viewed through the prism of almost 40 years – are now seen as significant, the less than salubrious environs of Hilly's Bowery bar scarcely encouraged any sense of history in the making. "CB's was just like going into somebody's crummy basement," remembered Chris. "There were big stuffed easy chairs and Hilly had these dogs that would crap all around. It was all very funky."

"CBGB's braved the world of music, and we braved the smell of urine to go there," cracked Leee Black Childers. "There was a pipe that came out of the wall, out came a rat, and it ran right across the floor. There were stories based on those kind of places, that when you were sitting on the toilet, the rats would also swim up. If you chose the rock'n'roll lifestyle, that's part of it."

"It was real disgusting. Every night you just had to watch where you walked. Dead dogs, vomit, urgh," insisted Debbie. "It was so small and intimate. Unimportant, basically. Maybe that is kind of important about that – that it wasn't important. There was no value to it. We all had our private fantasies and obsessions, and we just did it for the sake of doing it, with no agenda … I mean, everybody wanted to make a living and make money and be superstars, it was all within our own little brains, because there was no evidence of any of that ever happening."

In the months before the music press latched onto CBGB's, it was difficult to imagine that the bar would develop any kind of cachet. "We would play for whoever was in the bar – which was just a handful of bums and bikers at the start – and Hilly's wife would tell everyone to turn it down," recounts Deborah. "You'd get a couple of beers and then we'd owe them money. I'm serious. There was no money involved. The CBGB's guys were just happy to have somebody in there making some noise."

"It was sort of like going to music college in a way," she mused. "Not only did we get to play, but we got to play in front of an audience – even if they were completely drunk or stoned, it didn't matter."

"[CBGB's] was the kind of place where you felt you could do anything you wanted, because it was so trashed to begin with," enthused Elda. "Here was a sense of freedom in that venue. Hilly ... was like a fatherly figure. And he was very nurturing."

Despite the relatively small number of customers coming in off the Bowery, CBGB's enabled The Stillettoes to develop a reputation. "The whole act became more gaudy and tacky and the press started coming around," Debbie recalled. "I had a black Morticia dress, a gold Day-Glo cross, gold lamé dresses, stupid wigs, a goldfish bowl with a goldfish in it called 'Mr Jaws'. I was developing the Blondie character. She wasn't quite there yet, but she was on her way."

Aside from the odd original such as 'Platinum Blonde', the bulk of The Stillettoes' set was campy covers of songs such as Labelle's 'Lady Marmalade', Jean Knight's 'Mr Big Stuff' and The Shangri-Las' 'Out In The Streets' – which Blondie would revisit almost a quarter of a century later, on their *No Exit* album. "I like everything up to 1971, practically," Chris asserts. "I really like all the girl groups from the early sixties. From the late sixties, I like R&B, black music, lots of different things, too numerous to mention. The obvious things on the surface are The Shangri-Las and The Crystals, Supremes, Lou Reed."

Gentle murmurs of interest about the group travelled as far as the ears of Marty Thau – at that time managing The New York Dolls, who were just about to release *Too Much Too Soon,* the second and final album recorded by the quintet's classic line-up. He was particularly struck by Debbie: "When I first saw her, I was amazed at how beautiful she was. But she was very quiet, and later on I learned from her that that was during the period of time when she was very frightened and paranoid about a lot of things. Like she phrased it, at one point she was just there but she couldn't speak to anybody, she was too fragile. Later, word got back to me that she was a singer in The Stillettoes, and they were very good. I never saw them perform, but I did get a lot of feedback from people who said, 'Hey, Debbie has this group and can sing and she's really beautiful. This group should really be caught to see if there's anything that could be done with them.' But I was involved full time with the Dolls."

"When I first signed the Dolls, I invited The Stillettoes up to my house out in the country, just to spend a nice social day together," Marty recalls. "They all poured into Debbie's beat-up old Camaro, drove up there and we spent that day at my house ... They left, and then about an hour later I get a phone call from them that they were waylaid because the battery went out on the car. So I had to shoot down there with my car and fire up their battery. They somehow ended up at a pool hall, shooting pool with a bunch of rednecks. That's when I first met Debbie."

Although the gigs supporting Television in May and June allowed The Stillettoes to get noticed, their future direction would cause the band to split after the June 12 show at Club 82. "There was too much catfighting going on," said Chris. "It didn't seem the right kind of thing." The crux of the dispute was Deborah's desire to have the band develop musically whereas Elda wanted a more theatrical direction. As Jimmy Wyndbrandt observed, there were, "pretty much irreconcilable differences between Debbie and Elda. They were getting kinda successful even though they hadn't played very much – a three-girl thing hadn't happened in a long time. They broke up, I believe, because of rivalries; everybody had different ideas of where it was going. Chris and Debbie were already thinking about what they wanted to do musically and Elda's very into theatrics."

"I was running out of funds. No one was contributing and Tony [Ingrassia] thought as a single mother I should get a job to carry the project," Elda recalls. "Instead of going in the direction of original material I was told that Debbie and Rosie can now choose their cover songs. We were turning into a disco band! So we had a meeting at Tony's house. Not one of them supported my point of view – forget the tour and forget Tony. Debbie and Chris just sat there in silence. So I quit my own band."

"Three girls trying to get along together is hard enough without worrying about whose ego is going to be on top," asserted Debbie. "Elda wanted a certain person to manage us, and I didn't like the idea of someone saying, 'This is your manager, sign this.' I said I wanted to do my own thing again and I left."

Naturally enough, given Debbie's focus on the musical aspects and her relationship with Chris, the musicians followed her through the exit. "When I split from The Stillettoes and decided that I wanted to do less shtick and more music, I dropped a lot of the more obvious theatrical things," she recounted. "We really didn't have any exact ideas about what we were going to do. But we got to a point in The Stillettoes where we were getting some notoriety, and some following and some press, and then we started not getting along on business and artistic points after a while and we broke off on our own."

It resulted in the formation of a short-lived new group, Angel And The Snake, which featured Harry, Stein, Smith and O'Connor, later joined by two backing singers known simply as Julie and Jackie – the latter of whom worked with Debbie at the newly opened White's Pub on Wall Street.

The reconfigured band made their debut at a near-empty CBGB's in mid-August, supported by The Ramones. "We knew Tommy [Erdelyi] from the Mercer Arts Center," recounted Chris. "One night, we saw him at the 82 Club, and he said, 'I have this band called The Ramones, we don't know where to play, where do you guys play?' So I figured he was playing with Puerto Ricans or something, with a Spanish name …"

"The guy who did The Ramones' artwork, Arturo Vega, used to come to CBGB's wearing a Mexican wrestling mask; for six months he was known only as 'the guy in the mask'," Chris recalled. "The guy from The Screamers, Tomata Du Plenty, Gorilla Rose, and Fayette Hauser, who's the sister of one of the guys in Manhattan Transfer, used to have this weird drag cabaret, and us and The Ramones used to open up for them. Everybody was very supportive; only when the attention came did rivalries start."

After a second CBGB's gig as Angel And The Snake a fortnight later, the band ditched their new name. "1974 was the non-period of punk," insisted Deborah. "Television, The Ramones and us, either as Angel And The Snake or with no name, were just playing around." This 'non-period' saw Debbie and Chris develop their songwriting partnership as a succession of singers and players drifted in and out of the group. "It didn't happen in the early days because we weren't formed musically and we seemed always to be in a state of flux," observed Chris. "I don't think any of the bands were really doing too much at that period. All the bands were fucking around, not really getting anywhere."

First to join was guitarist Ivan Kral, who arrived in October but lasted just three months before departing to hook up with Patti Smith's band in January 1975. "Ivan just got bored," explained Debbie. "There was no publicity, no attention focused on anyone. Ivan was working at the Bleecker Street Cinema and he was always moving. He moved about three times in those three months."

That same month, Jackie and Julie were ousted in favour of Tish and Snooky Bellomo, who would later go on to open the Manic Panic boutique and sing with the notorious Sic Fucks. "I met them through these guys Gorilla and Tomata," Deborah explained. "They used to do comedy skits at CBGB's, things like 'Babs the Stunt Girl' or 'Savage Voodoo Nuns'. Tish and Snooky were in some of the crazier shows."

"That's when we were 'Blondie And The Banzai Babies'. Tish and Snooky sang back-up with us, on and off for over a year and a half," Debbie later elaborated. "We were a dance band but, to tell the truth, we were so bad that to call us a garage band, to call us a band, was a great compliment. We were a gutter band; 'sewer band' is a closer description. We weren't getting any reviews, didn't have any support from any record company, Chris' guitar cost $40, he didn't even have an amplifier, and our drummer couldn't make up his mind whether he wanted to be a drummer or a doctor."

"It seemed like they really didn't have any drive, but obviously they did," reflected Tish. "It seemed like the whole time [I was] in the band they didn't have any idea what they were doing."

"Debbie decided we should be a disco dance band," added Snooky. "She got us a job playing Brandy's Too, an Upper East Side singles place, two long sets a night. The crowd was half friends, who came up to hang out, and half the sleazy singles crowd. They didn't understand a thing, missed lots of the lyrics – like one song that we did called 'Funky Anus'."

"The Ramones came to open for us," continued Tish. "But they started out with 'Sniffin' Glue', and the management asked them to leave. The Tuff Darts walked out in a huff when management told 'em they were too loud."

"We were having a good time and weren't really too career-orientated at the time," rationalised Chris.

Anya Phillips, who met Debbie while they were both working the bar at White's Pub and would become one of the vocalist's closest friends, was among the few who caught the group during this period of instability. "At that time there would be maybe five people in the place. I don't think they even had a cover or admission at the door yet. It was really, really empty. The Ramones opened for Angel And The Snake ... they knew they were changing the name to Blondie and adding two girl back-up singers ... Debbie wore turquoise blue stretch leotard tops and red stockings and she used to do this song called 'Platinum Blonde', where she had this ratty wig and this sort of beat up dress; she'd come on stage and start singing, 'I wanna be a platinum blonde,' and rip off the wig and platinum dress. Chris used to come to the pub to pick her up after work every day. He had long hair and blue eye-shadow and used to wear these leather chaps.

"They hadn't been going together all that long, I think just a few months at that point, but they were really in love," added Anya. "By around October or November [1974] Jackie was singing in the band with another girl named Julie, and all three of them were blonde, so I guess that was the idea of Blondie."

"Julie and Jackie sang back-up for a while, then we took the name Blondie," confirmed Deborah. "I remember it fit together really well, because all three of us were blondes. Then right before our first gig, Jackie dyed her hair dark brown. That didn't work out."

Like much of their early songwriting, the name for Chris and Debbie's unstable band drew directly from the New York streets. "The street noise was, 'Hey, Blondie! Hey, Blondie!' I'm like, 'Jesus ...' Because we were trying to think of a band name and there it was, right in front of me,' recalled Debbie. "Blondie was a comic coming to life ... the idea of a drawing coming to life and stepping on to a stage had a terrific shrillness about it ... I wanted to create this character who was primarily having fun." (When truck drivers and construction workers shouted, "Hey Blondie!", they unconsciously referenced a vintage newspaper 'funny'/comic strip of that title that had entered the popular consciousness.)

After two gigs at CBGB's supporting Television in January 1975 and another pair of shows in support of The Miamis at the turn of the month, the group might not have been any nearer to establishing a settled line-up or image. But at least they now had a name that would stick.

Chapter Five

New York Rockers

"We were working against great odds. We didn't have any money, yet we pursued and persisted. We were tenacious. We kept working the angles, scraping by."

Debbie Harry

As the Bowery began to thaw after another bitter winter, Debbie and Chris' aspirations for their newly named band were in a state of flux. Although 1975 would prove a pivotal year for Blondie, initially the group's personnel, direction and image were so uncertain that their new name was the only concrete element. "We were experimenting a lot," Deborah explained. "Usually, bands have just one style, but we were trying out lots of different styles of music. So it took us longer. That's the only thing I can put it down to. When you look at The Ramones, they do their style of song and they've focused it and perfected it. We were doing lots of things, so they took longer to perfect."

"We worked a lot and just hoped that something would develop," bassist Fred Smith recalled. "We were a little erratic, you know. We had this drummer who kept passing out, he'd just collapse."

Billy O'Connor's nodding out was symptomatic of his uncertainty as to whether he actually wanted to be a professional musician. By March he reached a decision to quit the band and pursue a career in law. With no obvious replacements immediately available, the group placed an advertisement in *The Village Voice*: 'Freak Energy Rock Drummer Wanted'.

Over 40 would-be energetic freaks responded and auditions were duly held. "Most of the guys who came in were schrumpy-looking schlumps in fringe jackets without the fringe. We had to throw some of them out of the room," recounted Debbie. "When Chris and I first discussed putting a band together, we said we didn't want sidemen. We didn't want people just to be a blank wall that could be painted on. We wanted personalities; we wanted features and felt that that was an intrinsic thing about a band. We felt that all the bands that we really liked had characters that stood out on their own."

One of the last aspirants to pass through the midtown rehearsal room was Clement Burke, a 20-year old from Bayonne, New Jersey, who had been orbiting the scene around Club 82 and CBGB's in recent months. "I knew Debbie and Chris were looking for a drummer so I went along to an audition," said Clem. "We sat around for the whole time and we had a lot of common interests in music and the arts, people like Burroughs and The MC5 and The Velvet Underground, but also The Ronettes and bubblegum rock. We went on to play a couple of songs."

"We auditioned 40 drummers in two days and Clem was the last one to come in," Deborah remembers. "He was very experienced. He'd been in bands since he was about 14 years old or something. He was famous in New Jersey and the surrounding towns where he played." In addition to being an accomplished drummer, Clem's sartorial style – he showed up wearing a red US Navy shirt based on one previously sported by The Who's Keith Moon, and what Debbie later described as "fancy shoes" – identified sixties anglophile influences a galaxy removed from the procession of Grand Funk-obsessed hair farmers who preceded him. "We liked him immediately because he was one of the very best players, but more importantly he had a charismatic quality," asserted Deborah. "Clem was definitely what we were looking for ... Keith Moon, the biggest influence on his playing, style and outlook, fitted right in with the rock greats Chris and I emulated."

"The first time I met Debbie I was completely drawn to her charisma. She was undoubtedly a star, a diamond in the rough, a tremendously charismatic person. I had already liked girl group stuff, Shangri-Las, Ronettes; I was already tuned into that. And for me she was of that ilk," remembered Clem. "My whole thing was that I wanted to find my Marc Bolan, or my David Bowie or Mick Jagger. I wanted to find somebody with that much potential.

They had some interesting songs and they were doing original music, and I wanted to play original music. I wasn't very much interested in being a club band."

In addition to empathy with Debbie's broad concept, Clem quickly adapted to Chris' maverick energy. "He had this Alice Cooper fixation at the time. He was really creative on guitar, but he'd present an idea, and you'd have to work with him."

Born in Bayonne on November 24, 1954, Clement Anthony Bozewski grew up in a highly musical environment. "My dad was a society drummer and there were drums around the house. I think the first record that hit me was probably 'Wipeout' by The Surfaris, which is kind of appropriate, and then The Beatles records," he recalled. "I tried to play the guitar but I'm left-handed and all my friends were right-handed so they couldn't show me the chords so I started playing the drums. I was about 14."

Following in his father's rhythmic footsteps, Clem enrolled in the local drum and bugle corps and his grammar school orchestra, both of which helped his endurance and technique, before forming a series of rock'n'roll bands. "It was a good way to meet girls," he grinned. "I had a band my first two years of high school and another band my second two years. We would win Battle of the Bands, and there was this DJ in New York, Bruce Morrow, who had this show called *Cousin Brucie's Big Break* where everyone sent in music. I think we recorded on a mono reel-to-reel tape recorder, and you sent that in and if you got selected, he played it on the radio and then you got to go into the recording studio. We were selected and we won and we went to ABC studios and recorded. That was my first recording session."

As a result of their success in Morrow's contest, Clem's band, Total Environment, got to play at Carnegie Hall. "We had a light show, the whole thing," he recalled. "So I was always in bands at the time. I was in an art rock band and we played a high school assembly and we did 'Peaches en Regalia', the Frank Zappa tune, with full-on band and vibes, timpani, keyboards. I think we went into 'Willie The Pimp' by Captain Beefheart after that."

Although interested in the experimentalism epitomised by Zappa and Beefheart, Clem's passion for reductive rock'n'roll led him to seek out like-minded accomplices for a new band, Sweet Revenge. "I was a big New York Dolls fan and a big fan of David Bowie, Roxy Music, Cockney Rebel, The Sweet, T.Rex," he explained. "Basically, the friends I knew who were into Zappa and Beefheart didn't like that stuff at all. So I found people along the way who were into it."

After a couple of gigs at Club 82 with Sweet Revenge, Clem began hanging out at CBGB's. "Everyone cut their hair and started wearing leather jackets," he recounted. "There were no punks at CBGB's – it was more like bohemian, outcast type of people. It was like a clubhouse for beatniks with about 100 people. I was like 18 years old, just a kid on the streets of New York and by that time we got a storefront on the Lower East Side where we would crash in."

Within four weeks of auditioning for Blondie, Clem would make his live debut at CBGB's. However, in keeping with the group's inability to maintain a settled line-up, it was also Fred Smith's final appearance with the group. "I had an intuition with Fred," Deborah revealed. "He was really unhappy at the beginning of the month. At the end of the month, we had a gig at CBGB and we played terrible the first set. I didn't know what had happened, but during the break between sets, Fred had told Chris he was quitting to join Television. Our next set was worse. We had played a long time with Fred. We were struck dumb by the whole thing, by the whole movement against us. I may be paranoid, but I think that whole clique wanted to destroy us."

"Verlaine and Patti were lurking around in the shadows," added Chris. "We had three nights with The Marbles, but I think we ended up cancelling the last two because everything was falling apart."

Photographer Roberta Bayley, who subsequently shot many iconic images of Blondie and other CBGB's bands, was working the club's door at the time of Smith's sudden departure. "Fred Smith made the big error of his life when he quit Blondie to join Television," she insisted. "But at that point, Television was the one tipped for big, big success. Blondie was the worst band in the city – they were just a joke. Everybody liked them personally but they didn't really have it together on a musical level."

"They were very shaky but I saw they had potential," Marty Thau recalls. "I thought the songs were great, but then I also thought that Suicide could be a hit-making group!"

ove at the pier – Blondie, New York City 1976: (L-R) Jimmy Destri, Clem Burke, Debbie Harry, Gary Valentine, Chris Stein.
OB GRUEN

Strumming brunette Debbie in 1968, during her tenure with Wind In The Willows. GETTY IMAGES

Fronted by Elda Gentile, Debbie and Rosie Ross, The Stillettoes represented a mix 'n' match extension to the girl group canon. BOB GRUEN

The Stillettoes in full flight at CBGBs, June 24, 1974 (L-R): Elda Gentile, Fred Smith, Rosie Ross, Billy O'Connor, Debbie Harry, Chris Stein. BOB GRUEN

ish and Snookie (far left) back Debbie in the short lived Angel And The Snakes as Chris (far right) works the Alice Cooper look.
OB GRUEN

p on the roof; Blondie 1976 (L-R): Gary Valentine, Chris Stein, Debbie Harry, Jimmy Destri, Clem Burke CHRIS WALTER/WIREIMAGE

Jimmy Destri takes centre stage as Blondie fill the cramped confines of CBGBs in 1977. BOB GRUEN

The heart of Blondie – Chris and Debbie cuddle up at Max's Kansas City. ROBERTA BAYLEY/REDFERNS

Producer Richard Gottehrer and rockabilly powerhouse Robert Gordon flank Chris backstage at Max's, June 11, 1977. EBET ROBERTS/REDFERNS

ebbie and Chris frozen in concentration at CBGBs, 1977. ROBERTA BAYLEY/REDFERNS

)on't do it, Gary" – Valentine and Harry blow up Television, Hammersmith Odeon, May 1977. RICHARD E. AARON/REDFERNS

Blondie backstage at the Whisky A Go Go, West Hollywood, 1977. CHRIS WALTER/WIREIMAGE

Joey Ramone and David Johansen inspect Debbie's manicure for a *Punk* magazine photo-shoot, watched by Joan Jett. ROBERTA BAYLEY/
REDFERNS

un-time with Iggy and Debbie; Toronto, March 1977. BOB GRUEN

Blondie's controversial former manager Peter Leeds. BOB GRUEN

he first stirrings of Blondie-mania; Dunstable Civic Hall, March 2, 1978. PAUL SLATTERY

On the road, USA, 1979 (L-R): Clem Burke, Jimmy Destri, Nigel Harrison, Chris Stein, Debbie Harry (front): Frank Infante. ROBERT BAYLEY/REDFERNS

"I saw Blondie perform at CBGB's in 1975 with some people from The Factory," author and Warhol associate Victor Bockris remembers. "I wasn't really into what they were doing back then. The girl group influences, the last vestiges of glam rock falling away from Chris Stein's eyes. They were particularly awkward and uncoordinated that night. I remember Debbie beginning to take something off then stopping in the midst of it as if asking the audience, 'Should I?' People at my table were saying how much they liked her and what a pity it was that she was so unsure of herself. But it was just this human quality – almost the reverse of punk – that drew me to her."

Fred's exit undermined any sense of progress and sent Blondie's collective spirits into a nosedive. Debbie considered auditioning for pop outfits and even learned some of the material that Rufus siren Chaka Khan was then filling dancefloors with. "I felt hopeless and sometimes perhaps hapless but I never felt intimidated," she recalled. "People would come up to me and say, 'You know you should join a cover band and work out in Jersey,' and they would insult the shit out of me. But I stuck with my own thing. I had Chris, actually. Chris was terrific."

Chris made what he later described as a "half-hearted effort" to hook up with the newly formed Heartbreakers, and, despite having only played one gig with Blondie, Clem tried out for Patti Smith's band. Unwisely, he opted to hold his audition at Blondie's midtown rehearsal room and was spotted by Debbie, adding to a sense of growing animosity that had begun to infect the scene.

"Patti helped coerce [Fred] away from us, helped take Fred over to the other side," declared Chris. "Everything on the CBGB's scene was [co-operative] until the tension started being brought upon us and then it got very competitive immediately. For the first two years it was really very communal. I remember playing with all [Television's] equipment – using their guitars and amps. For some reason we had to do a show and we didn't bring any equipment."

As if to add to the general sense of despondency, on May 28, 1975 Eric Emerson's full-tilt life came to an abrupt end when his body was found near the West Side Highway, next to his motorcycle. His death was apparently a hit and run. Eric had been living with Barbara Winter, former wife of multi-instrumentalist Edgar Winter.

"We were sitting around the house just after we woke up when Barbara called with the bad news," Deborah recounted. "He had been a good friend and inspiration to so many people. We didn't quite understand what had happened, but we went up to a party/wake held for him and saw a lot of people from the earlier glitter days. Eric's death definitely marked an end to the glitter period. We still miss him."

Remembering her former partner, Elda Gentile observes, "When Eric got up in the morning, it was like watching a child awake to a new day. He never woke up ragged or worn out by his extreme life. Every day was new and full of possibility to him. He loved life and was very much ahead of his time artistically. Eric was the love of my life, the father of my son Branch and grandpa of my three beautiful grandchildren.

"I saw Debbie and Chris about two months later at CBGB's. I wasn't singing – I was sewing on Saint Mark's Place to try to survive and raise my son. Debbie and Chris offered their condolences and said if there was ever anything they could do to help me and Branch they would."

Ultimately, it was their new drummer's drive and enthusiasm that pulled Blondie around. "Clem, whom we barely knew at the time, called up asking, 'Are you going to do something or not? I think you should at least try'," explained Debbie. "Chris said, 'Well, we have to get a bass player, it's practically like starting over.' I was still working at [White's] but we didn't want to talk about bands for a while. We were fed up and embarrassed with everything."

Having reassessed his priorities in the wake of Fred's decampment and his abortive audition for The Patti Smith Group, Clem resolved to give Blondie his best shot. "We had a common ground in liking The Velvet Underground, Iggy Pop, The Ronettes, The Shangri-Las," he declared. "I didn't have to be educated by anyone as to what the aesthetic of this band was going to be."

"Clem was the glue that actually held it all together, even when it came to working in the studio later," remarks Craig Leon, who would go on to play a significant role in shaping Blondie's studio sound. "He was also the guy that had the real sense of rock'n'roll fandom. He would be looking at pictures of The Who, figuring out how he should stand in a photo! He was always reading all these *Tiger Beat* magazines, all of that. He brought a lot of that element into Blondie. But Blondie was very ramshackle in the beginning."

"[Clem] was really out to work," admitted Debbie. "After the thing with Fred happened, he pushed us really hard. He kept it going." Clem's first move was to go back to his East 10th Street base and return with roommate and old school friend Gary Valentine to fill the bassist vacancy. "He brought over a bass player, who was known for being a poet in school. They went to high school together; he had never been in a band," she recalls. "[Clem] got us rehearsing again and began to bring a bunch of his friends from Bayonne around. Gary Valentine was the ringleader of these kids and pretty soon he started playing bass. If Clem was the Keith Moon of Bayonne, Gary had to be the Bob Dylan. He was super handsome and everybody in Bayonne knew Clem and Gary had to be in a rock group."

"When Clem first told us that he was playing in a band in the city … I wanted to know more about it and asked the usual questions," remembered Gary. "'Well, they're really campy,' Clem said. 'Debbie, the singer, is great. Really sexy, and her voice is terrific. The guitarist's kind of a nut though. He has really weird ideas about how to play. And Fred the bass player's good. The music's sort of like what The Shangri-Las would have been like if they were drag queens.'"

"When Fred Smith quit Blondie to join Television, Clem suggested I might be able to play bass," said Valentine. "He took me to a midtown loft on 37th, near Eighth Avenue with all the hookers outside. We jammed on the Stones' 'Live With Me' for about an hour, smoked grass and just kept playing. At the end they said, 'This is fine.' I was in."

"He wasn't really a bass player at all," explained Clem. "He was a poet and could play piano a little. I brought him to meet Chris and Debbie, and he played one of his songs on the piano and was in the band. Then he quickly learned bass."

Born Gary Lachman on Christmas Eve, 1955, Valentine (who assumed his stage name on joining Blondie as it "seemed like an appropriate name for a teen idol") had fled Bayonne after he caused his 16-year-old girlfriend, Zelda, to fall pregnant in 1974. "Her parents had me arrested for statutory rape," he revealed. "So I left home and moved to Manhattan, which was strictly illegal because it was breaking probation, and that's when I met Clem again."

After moving into the 10th Street storefront opened up by a friend named Crash, Gary began hanging out at CBGB's and accompanied Clem to his audition for Patti Smith's band. Valentine would later emphasise his poverty during this period, claiming he was "living on the streets in Manhattan in the middle of 1975", an assertion Chris Stein later rejected: "Gary never had to starve. He wanted to starve. He wanted to have the image of being a starving artist. He loved that. He was a really good-looking young guy and chicks were lining up to take him home and feed him. He was just intrigued by the idea."

Valentine moved into Chris and Debbie's Thompson Street apartment and began rehearsing with the band, while still reporting to his probation officer in New Jersey on a weekly basis.

By the summer of 1975, Television manager Terry Ork had taken charge of booking arrangements at CBGB's. "Television and Patti Smith's enthusiastic championing of 'art' created a rarefied and slightly stifling atmosphere," observed Gary. "Ork's datebook often seemed too crowded to allow space for Patti's sole serious female competitor. For the first month or so of my tenure, we were *personae non gratae* at CBGB."

Although this marginalisation temporarily excluded Blondie from the epicentre of the new scene, Max's Kansas City had by then been reopened by new owner Tommy Dean, who, after considering turning the venue into a disco engaged Peter Crowley – formerly responsible for booking acts into a 23rd Street gay bar called Mother's – to hire bands. It was at Max's, as well as venues such as Mother's, Brandy's and the Performance Studio on East 23rd Street (where The Ramones had debuted in 1974) that Blondie's new line-up received its initial exposure.

SoHo Weekly News journalist and later *Rock Marketplace* editor Alan Betrock was an early champion of Blondie, and would feature the band in the premiere issue of his *New York Rocker* magazine. Interested in managing the group, he offered to finance the recording of a demo. "Blondie were a real good recording band," he later declared. "I brought a couple of people to see them and I was really hurt and upset, because they just couldn't play live – they'd stop in the middle of a song and start over again, the amps would go out, the guitar would go out, strings would break and they wouldn't have extra ones. I decided that the thing to do for them was just to make a tape and not bring people down to see them."

"I was playing about a month when we did those," said Gary. "He wanted to manage. 'Let's make a demo!' And so he brought us into a studio out on Long Island, someone's garage, basically. It wasn't anything fancy, but it was great, I hadn't done anything like that."

Beginning on June 13, 1975, the quartet of Chris, Debbie, Clem and Gary laid down demo versions of five tracks, a cover of The Shangri-Las' 'Out In The Streets' and four originals: 'Thin Line', 'Puerto Rico', 'Platinum Blonde' and 'Once I Had A Love (The Disco Song)' – the latter being prototype for 'Heart Of Glass', cut at Chris' suggestion toward the end of the sessions. Engineered by Kevin Kelly and produced by Betrock and the band, all songs were recorded in one or two takes. Debbie's overdubbed three-part harmonies on The Shangri-Las' song are eerily effective, displaying an early feel for the studio born out of her love of girl-group productions. "We hadn't recorded anything and we wanted to hear what we sounded like on tape, and have a fairly decent quality demo to play for people," said Debbie. "I was the only one who had recorded before."

"We went to somebody's basement somewhere in Queens," recalled Clem. "It was like no one actually knew where they were going. I'm not sure how we got there; it must have been in Debbie's Camaro. No one really knew what we were gonna do. I remember playing piano on 'Platinum Blonde', and we all thought it sounded great."

"It was so hot and humid that we couldn't keep anything in tune," Deborah remembered. "It was like being under water. Plus there was no sound in the room, no acoustics. I think that if those things were mixed properly they would be a little better. The proportions are a little bit whacked out."

Although Betrock thought the demo "sounded fine", a combination of his other interests and lack of confidence in Blondie's ability to play their songs live curtailed his involvement with the group. "They just weren't that experienced, they weren't that together, they didn't have any money and their equipment was always breaking down," he declared. "[Debbie] was not all that comfortable. And I called her once and said, 'Well, look: I'm working with you and The Marbles and The Marbles can play live and I can't do both of you guys, so I'm gonna work with them.'"

"I don't think Blondie even had it together to have a manager of any kind," recalls Craig Leon. "Alan Betrock was running around with the demos that nobody was interested in. Their first demo was very unimpressive."

"Alan started out interested in managing us, but he started *New York Rocker* and dropped interest because we had personnel shifts and a few problems," explains Debbie. "We had no money and he didn't want to invest his own beyond a certain point, and that's what a band needs initially – someone who can invest a couple of thousand dollars and get their equipment straight, make a demo and present them. That has to be done. It didn't happen for us, and no one had any fucking money so he dropped us and picked up a group called The Marbles ... We were always asking Betrock for the [demo] tape, we said we'd buy it. He wasn't doing anything with it but he didn't want to let it go, 'cos he obviously had plans for it."

These plans reached fruition four years later, when Betrock released the demos as a limited edition EP on coloured vinyl. "I made him swear he'd never release 'The Disco Song', but it got out and he's responsible," Chris reveals.

"He spent about $500 doing these five songs so we offered him the money plus a couple of hundred for his effort and devotion, and helping us out and getting it done. He said, 'Don't worry, I'm not going to do anything with it, it's for me.' Then he went and did a mix. Believe me, it's much different," adds Debbie. "One thing we've learned is we can hardly trust anybody," Chris concludes. "It's very disillusioning."

Any feelings of disappointment at being unable to secure financial backing were tempered by a thawing of the freeze on Blondie appearing at CBGB's. The streamlined quartet debuted at the Bowery bar on July 4, 1975, supporting The Ramones. Shortly afterwards, courtesy of an artist-cum-magician named Eduardo Benton, Debbie and Chris found themselves a new home that would function as band headquarters, situated just three blocks from Hilly Kristal's club. The liquor store below was also the nexus of local wino activity.

"One time Clem and Chris went out to the store and rushed back in yelling, 'Hey! There's a dead bum outside!' He was frozen in the snow," remembered Debbie. "Somebody had seen him walking around with no shoes on earlier in the day. His eyes were open, he had a little white beard, and he had turned blue. Everybody ran into the street to look at the frozen bum until an ambulance came to scrape him up."

"We had the first floor, Eduardo lived on the second and, for the first few months the third floor was empty," elaborated Deborah. "The Bowery was unheated funk, but the space was heaven. There was enough room for me and Chris to live, rehearse and run the complex business of booking Blondie."

"A famous philosopher's girlfriend, who was a very nice lady in great shape, with the Lauren Bacall look, had originally let Eduardo have this great space, and she asked us to move in when she moved out," Debbie explained. "But about a month or so after we moved in he started a downhill slide. He would go into a false biker number, which involved not washing for days and sleeping in a piss-soaked bag with his boyfriend, Alex. He worshipped piss and would piss into beer bottles, leaving half-full ones all over his floor.

"The cats, who moved from Thompson Street to the Bowery with us, were the first to suss out Eduardo's number. They just ran up to his floor and pissed and shit all over his drawings and paintings ... He was gone, but he was definitely an inspiration. He evidently inspired the cats too, but in their case only to greater heights of shitting and pissing. His floor of the house was basically a toilet."

The loft was also apparently haunted. "There was an entrance that came up from street level, a narrow long staircase that was very dark, and at the top of the staircase there was a flat wall with a doorway in it and Chris decided to paint this wall black ... there was a loud knocking and he saw a little boy," Deborah insisted. "[I] flashed on a little kid," confirmed Chris. "It was more like a feeling than actually seeing. It was more a presence."

Despite such unexplained occurrences, Chris and Debbie found practical matters more onerous "We all almost got killed one night," Chris declared. "The whole place cost us $350 a month 'cos there was no heat at night and there was only one bathroom. I used to have to go down about eight in the morning to get the boiler going, then it would start up and go the whole day until they would close the liquor store at six, then there would be no heat until the next morning. Well, one night the flame in the boiler went out and all the gas just got pumped up through the radiators, and when Debbie and I woke up we had black soot around our nostrils."

"Electricity, fire and water gave us the most trouble," added Deborah. "The pipes were always bursting, the fuses were always blowing in the middle of rehearsals, the place was dirty and it smelt terrible, so environmentally speaking we had it covered."

Regardless of the absence of any mod cons, the Bowery loft was capacious enough to provide Blondie with a rehearsal space, office and crash pad. "We did all the rehearsing in our loft, so everybody sort of hung out there a lot, but we – Chris and I – were really the only ones that lived there," Debbie explained. "Everyone had sort of committed at this stage and we put all our time into the band. We had a verbal agreement that we were doing this and we tried very hard to take all the elements of each member of the band and represent those elements musically. It wasn't just Chris' ideas of what music should be and what we were influenced by; it was clearly a composite of all of us."

Another of Chris and Debbie's new neighbours was aspiring fashion designer Stephen Sprouse, who would become one of the couple's closest friends and play a significant role in shaping Debbie's visual image. "He was living on the third or fourth floor," she recounted. "I don't know how he lived up there – there was no heat."

"I had all these stray cats that'd come up onto my floor," said Sprouse. "I'd wake up in the morning and there I'd see Deb, a few feet away from me, giving cat food to these strays. And that's essentially how we met."

"There were backyards that made a courtyard, and all these alley cats were interbreeding," added Deborah. "Hundreds and hundreds. I don't know if they ate rats or whatever, but they were tough, all scarred, one eye hanging out. One ear. We'd see these raging battles."

With Blondie on a budget described by Debbie as "half a shoestring", Sprouse became a vital element in creating a cohesive image. "Steve had some stuff because he had worked for Halston and he knew all these models and elegant women," she explained. "He'd been dressing them, and he had a few pieces left over from that. He liked the idea that we dressed sixties, which was basically out of necessity."

Although constant rehearsals at their Bowery loft knitted Blondie into a far tighter unit, the group were still perceived as the poor relations of a scene beginning to attract interest from record labels and the music press. As A&R representatives circled Television, Patti Smith and The Ramones, there was no evidence of anyone wanting to sign Blondie.

The press seemed less than excited by the band and one particular round-up of the New York scene, from *New Musical Express* stalwart Charles Shaar Murray, dismissed Debbie as, "This cute little bundle of platinum hair with a voice like a squeaky bath toy and quite the cruddiest garage-type garage band I've seen since the last band *I* was in (and that band was a fuzz-box *pretentioso* blues band. This one is just cruddy).

"She has what could politely be described as a somewhat suspect sense of pitch, but her charm lies in the fact that she's a kid who's pretending desperately hard to be a star and who's aware of it. Which is why it works at all (apart from on account of she's so gosh-darned cute, gol-ding it); because her act has that home-made-ish quality.

"Sadly, Blondie will never be a star simply because she ain't good enough, but for the time being I hope she's having fun. Whatever her actual age, though, she's spiritually a part of the Great American Nymphet Tradition."

Such criticisms were particularly hard on Deborah, still struggling with her confidence and searching for a viable stage persona. "We were not well-prepared musically," she admitted. "We were experimenting, and our shows were confusing. There were times when I felt, 'Oh, what's the point? It's just too scary.' Everyone else was getting record deals and great press, and Blondie was at the bottom of the heap. But I had a great friend in Chris, who just went, 'Ah, come on, just keep going. Something's gotta give.' We didn't have a clue what we were doing. The whole thing was a crap-shoot. But CBGB's was fine. We played there for seven months, every weekend. It was our vaudeville, where we got it together."

"No-one took them seriously, myself included, because musically they were very, very ramshackle," Craig Leon remembers. "They were one of two bands who had great song ideas. It could have been either one that I ended up working with at the time. The other one was The Miamis; they were great songwriters but, again, the playing was so all over the shop. Nobody wanted to know Blondie, mainly because they weren't that great live. That's the bottom line. Quite honestly, if I was in a band, I don't know if I would have picked them as my opening act either, back in those days."

But Chris' positivity in the face of this lack of interest proved well-founded. The final piece in the Blondie jigsaw was put in place shortly after Murray's caustic comments saw print on November 8, 1975, as the band expanded to a quintet with the addition of keyboard player Jimmy Destri. "We did a lot of shows as a four-piece where Chris and Clem and I would back up Debbie, in little dives, where you'd set up a guitar amp and a mike on the floor in the bar and play," Gary Valentine recalled. "If we each came out with $5 at the end of the night, that was fine. That meant a cheese sandwich, some potato crisps and breakfast tomorrow, but it was clear that the sound wasn't strong enough."

"We decided we needed a piano player. Through a band called The Fast and a girl called Donna, we got Jimmy Destri," Chris explained. "We wanted a piano, and he had this junky old organ. We didn't know about an organ, especially a Hammond, but he brought it and we ended up using it. It's funny how that was a big turnabout. That became a distinctive part of our sound, because we worked with what we had."

"Jimmy had played with Milk 'N' Cookies for about two weeks right before they went to England to make their album for Island," added Debbie. "But after he had learned all the material, just before they left for London, [vocalist] Justin [Strauss] said, 'You can't come.' Jimmy got a full-time job and went back to school and that's where we found him."

"I remember Jimmy Destri coming to me before he joined Blondie and asking me who should he join, because Talking Heads were interested in him too," Thau reveals. "I said, 'No man, they're not your type of people. Your people really are with Blondie.' I thought Talking Heads were maybe more sophisticated or more elitist. He was just some kid from Brooklyn, so I don't think it would have been a good match up. I thought it was some good advice telling him to go with Blondie."

Born James Mollica on April 15, 1954, Brooklyn boy Destri attended the local John Jay and New Utrecht high schools and got into music through his uncle. "My mother's youngest brother was the drummer for a late fifties/early sixties rock band called Joey Dee And The Starliters who had a hit record in America. They were on *The Dick Clark Show* and I saw my Uncle Joe on TV and said, 'That's what I want to do!' He was a one-hit wonder, had one song then went into construction and every time I said I wanted to go into music he said, 'Don't do it!' But I disobeyed."

Raised on Beatles and Stones records, Jimmy's first venture into rock'n'roll was the Anglopop-infused Knickers, which boasted the guitar stylings of future *Trouser Press* editor Ira Robbins alongside the magazine's singles reviewer, Jim Green, on bass, but managed only two gigs during its year-long existence. "Before I joined Blondie, I was just in Brooklyn with my Revox," he explained. "I went to art school for two years after high school, just like every other musician on earth … I was looking for a gig, any kind of gig, and I began hanging around CBGB's, Max's, and the other clubs in the area. I became friends with Debbie and Chris … They were just starting to form Blondie, not knowing where to go, or who to play with. We had a vibe going as friends; I never even mentioned I could play anything. I think my sister told Debbie, 'You know, he plays piano.' And I said, 'But I don't have one. I have this natty old organ and I can fill in on bass if you need that.' There were no auditions; we just got in a studio and it clicked. They asked me if I had any tunes. I had two tunes, Gary Valentine had two, and they had six, so we had an album's worth of material."

Jimmy made his Blondie debut at Mother's in November 1975. "Everybody was out of tune but we had fun playing together; it just clicked," said Deborah. "We were still a mess, but we were getting more and more excited about playing together."

Soon after Jimmy joined, Blondie were banned from CBGB's for a couple of months after Hilly Kristal overbooked one of their nights. "Hilly had booked a couple of extra bands that he was putting on ahead of us," explained bassist Gary. "I told him what I thought of that, very loudly. I don't remember now if we played that night or not, but I was angry enough at Hilly to piss him off and he told us that he wouldn't book us again." Instead, they started playing venues such as Monty Python's, situated just over the street from Hudson's Army & Navy Store on the corner of the red-light area at 13th Street and Third Avenue.

Early the following month, Clem departed for England to visit a girlfriend studying at Oxford and check out what was happening on the London music scene. At the time that equated with 'pub rock', as the following year's punk explosion was still a distant rumble. He was particularly struck by the sharp image and barely restrained aggression of scene heavyweights Dr Feelgood. "If there's one group that must take credit for giving direction to the New York scene, it must be the Feelgoods," he declared. "I'd originally seen them in London and brought their album back with me, and the fact that a band like the Feelgoods could pack Hammersmith Odeon, make it onto record and then into the charts gave many New York bands faith in what they were doing."

In Clem's absence, the remaining quartet hunkered down in the loft and honed their musical chops. "During the six weeks he was away we rehearsed and wrote new songs, hoping he would be back in time for us to do a New Year's show," said Debbie. Clem did not return until January, however, so the band continued to practise with the intention of making a return to CBGB's that following month.

With Clem, Jimmy and Gary now all fully integrated into the group, Blondie were at last underpinned by a solid line-up and constant practice. However, the incestuous CBGB's scene was becoming increasingly bitchy and their emphasis on the poppier end of the musical spectrum ensured they were regarded as little more than lightweight froth.

"There were a lot of little cliques in those days," asserted Craig Leon. "These were all people running around thinking they were French Symbolists, and here comes Blondie, who are really like true punks and actually much more the mass-media future band than any of the others. In a way, some of those CBGB's bands might have been the dead end of progressive rock'n'roll. Not a lot of people really see that."

"Patti Smith was down on me because she was very competitive, that was her nature," observed Debbie. "She has a very masculine and intellectual approach to music and performing. I don't want to do that. I played a chorus girl, Juicy Lucy, in Jackie Curtis' *Vain Victory* and I found that I liked music better because it's not as intellectual as acting. Rock'n'roll is a real masculine business and I think it's time girls did something in it. I don't want to sound like a libber, but I want to do something to make people change the way they think and act towards girls. Janis Joplin did that, but she had to sacrifice herself. Every time she went out on stage, she had to bleed for the audience. I don't feel like I have to sacrifice myself."

Although Deborah always denied that she held any animosity toward Patti Smith, her largesse was not reciprocated. "Patti wouldn't even want Debbie on the same bill," insisted Jimmy.

"The truth is that CBGB's was like any other gig," Deborah asserted. "Some nights were good. Some were not so good. The room is difficult to play. It's long, and the stage is small. But its ambience and reputation, the way people liked to go there – those are the things that made it happen. It wasn't a venue. It was a feeling. The real value of CBGB's was that you were left alone. Hilly Kristal left you free to play, to do what you wanted. CBGB's was a place for freedom and creativity, experiment and experience. You did your own thing and brought your own audience."

"I guess you could say it was like our version of the Cavern Club," mused Clem. "The thing about CBs was that we were allowed to develop in public. We weren't particularly good when we first started, but we were writing and performing and we were able to do it in front of people, which I think might be a better way to learn how to do it. I'm not really big on people staying in their houses and practising all the time and never feeling as though they're really good enough to play out. I think it's really counter-productive if you want to be a professional musician. There's a lot more to it than how proficient you are as a musician – it has a lot to do with presentation, not being nervous in front of audiences and all that. I think people get more worried about being junior [jazz virtuoso] Dave Weckl, instead of really getting out there and just doing it."

"New York punk was the exact opposite of its image," contends Victor Bockris, on the other hand. "Everybody loved each other and welcomed you into the fold because, like the volunteers at the Alamo, there were so few of them and they were outnumbered. The secret about New York is that it always had an extraordinarily nurturing art community. If you stood up and did something noticeable they would make a point of letting you know how much they liked it and you. And Debbie, perhaps as much as or more than anybody in that scene, was wrapped up in the arms of New York.

"The other secret is the humour that glued together the disparate elements of the New York underground. Chris was a very funny man. I found myself constantly on the verge of exploding into big fat laughter every time I saw him. He used to goof on the ongoing comedy that surrounded us on the Bowery."

"People tend to look back and say great bands were playing there," summarised photographer Bob Gruen. "No, the bands that were playing there *got* great later on. Having had the place to be bad, they got good."

It can be argued that Blondie 'got good' on Valentine's Day, 1976, as their first widely recognised line-up made its maiden appearance in front of the hard-to-impress hipsters and curious thrill-seekers. "I think that was clearly the starting point for us," recalled Debbie. "The show was fun, we got a great response and I felt good about all the work we had done. It was clearly a great departure and next step up for us. We were moving into a bigger world."

Chapter Six

Crossing The Thin Line

"Debbie was an American ponytail girl as seen through the lens of Roger Vadim; Barbarella on speed, or something like that."

Iggy Pop

Although he had passed on the opportunity to manage Blondie, Alan Betrock's enthusiasm was sufficient for him to feature them in the first issue of his bimonthly *New York Rocker*, which hit the streets in February 1976. Betrock felt the CBGB's scene deserved its own press to focus, publicise and even unify the broad spectrum of artists operating around the Bowery bar. In addition to a Blondie interview embellished with a photograph of Debbie sprawling across the four boys, the broadsheet paper ran Television on its cover and features on The Ramones, Talking Heads, Patti Smith, Milk 'N' Cookies and Wayne County, plus a piece on The Heartbreakers by their soon-to-be ex-bassist Richard Hell, under his 'Theresa Stern' pseudonym, and a hand-drawn map of the 'stars'' homes.

The interview, by Jimmy and Tommy Wynbrandt, took place at "Blondie's new communal headquarters on the Bowery", described as their "fortress of solitude ... a military outpost ... geared for war; an all-out assault on New York City." The feature details their Valentine's Day CBGB's set list; opening with 'Man Overboard' before continuing with 'Die Young, Stay Pretty', 'Little Girl Lies' and 'He Sure Works Hard (At Loving Me)'. "[Debbie's] voice coddles, teases, provokes. The audience is hooked now. The band hits a seventh and goes into the finale, 'I Wanna Be A Platinum Blonde', Debbie's tribute to Clairol. 'Ooh, I hope I get laid,' she sings, pleading with the fates. Men are weeping. The show ends."

This overwrought report notes for the first time the effect that Debbie's emergent Blondie persona had on male sections of the audience. "I remember going to see Debbie at CBs at this time," said Elda Gentile. "I think she'd discovered that Blondie identity and was able to run with her." Indeed, just as Betrock's paper first recognised her as the most strikingly photogenic face of the new scene, so the vocalist's hitherto shaky confidence began to solidify. "I was quite nervous about doing shows back then. I think as a person I do have a confident nature and an optimistic nature. As for going on stage I always felt that anything could happen, technical problems whatever, that used to weigh on me," she recalled. "I used to over-sing just so I could hear myself."

Debbie found that being pushed to the front of the stage as a lone lead carried far greater pressure than simply being one third of a vocal trio. "On my own I had to put out more than ever," she observed. "Every time we go on stage, I try to do something different. It's like a process of elimination; something works and we keep it, it doesn't work and we throw it out."

"At the beginning, I tried to incorporate a lot of different girls I knew as well as my own experiences into Blondie. I tried to make her a resilient creature who could bounce back and had a never-say-die, what-the-hell attitude. She was sparkling and adventurous, she liked having fun, liked having sex and was tender and sensitive at the same time. I tried to envisage her like a cartoon character because all the members of the band saw Blondie that way."

As significant as Betrock's more orthodox music journalism, the launch of the resolutely lowbrow *Punk* fanzine in January 1976 also provided CBGB's with coverage that reached as far as Europe. It also established a collective noun for a scene whose participants often had very little musical common ground. "*Punk* had a boorish wit a few notches below that of its mentor, *Mad*," asserted Gary. "It was also highly selective. Where *New York Rocker* covered *all* the music coming out of CBGB's and Max's, *Punk* specialised in a fanatically narrow canon of hard core punk bands; The Ramones, Richard Hell, The Dead Boys and The Dictators. These last two were latecomers to the scene. Like [editor John] Holmstrom and [writer Legs] McNeil, both flirted with a nasty brand of right-wing sensibility. Also like Holmstrom and McNeil, they were into getting very fucked up and acting stupid."

Via its deliberately dumb contents, *Punk* enabled Chris to promote Debbie's public persona by supplying photographs of her – wearing just a guitar and a pout in some, or her soon-to-become-iconic ripped Vultures T-shirt and little else. Before punk rock had even got off the ground, the movement had its 'Punkmate of the Month' – not only guaranteeing Patti Smith's feminist ire but boosting both Deborah's impact and her self-esteem.

Two weeks after Jimmy Destri's live debut at CBGB's, the new Blondie line-up made their first appearance at Max's Kansas City. Although the gig itself was unremarkable, Clem and Gary barely made it, having been busted by a zealous off-duty cop who spotted them smoking pot on the street two nights earlier. Along with their eccentric landlord Eduardo Benton, the band's rhythm section spent an uncomfortable chilly night in the Tombs on Centre Street. "We slept on wooden benches," recalled Valentine. "You couldn't lay in one position for more than 10 minutes. If you wanted a pillow you had to take off your coat. If you took off your coat, you froze." Fortunately, when their case was finally heard only hours before the band were due to go on stage at Max's, the cop admitted he had failed to identify himself as a policeman and the trio were duly released.

The band's next appearance at Max's was far less fraught. Blondie became the surprise hit of the venue's Easter Festival, held across the weekend of April 17-18, also featuring Wayne County, Pere Ubu, Suicide, The Heartbreakers and The Ramones – the latter having played with Blondie at Phase V in New Jersey nine days earlier. *New York Rocker*'s Lisa Persky declared that Blondie – who included her bass-playing boyfriend – had "finally hatched", adding, "Another band's incubation period has ended, and the award for the loveliest Easter Egg goes to Blondie … all of Blondie did much to convince us that they are now deserving of more concrete recognition than they have so far received."

Also among those impressed was producer Craig Leon, who previously worked for Sire Records and had been following events in the New York microcosm with growing interest. "Television were starting to become a big deal with Terry Ork," he recalls. "They were actually the big thing, if there was a big thing. They were the one that 50 or 60 people talked about rather than three or four. I first saw Blondie at CBGB's or one of those other clubs. I'd seen them around and heard them. I'd loved Debbie's presence and her voice always captured me. Fred was out of the band and Gary Valentine was in before they actually started sounding reasonable. I paid attention to them because they had elements of all the sixties stuff that I really loved too, the Phil Spector stuff and The Shangri-Las."

Craig was put in direct contact with Blondie by Hilly Kristal. "One day at the bar at CBGB's, he said, 'Do you want to produce an album for me of everyone that's playing live in the club? We're gonna have a festival, I'll get an engineer with a truck and you and the engineer can produce this record, and go through all the material.'"

Along with engineer Kim King – who previously played guitar with Theremin-infused psychedelic group Lothar And The Hand People – Leon sat in a truck outside Hilly's bar and recorded the festival, which also featured John Cale, Patti Smith, Television and The Ramones. "This is the legendary lost album. This really does exist," asserts Craig. "It's a true story; everybody was recorded during this time. I think it was over a whole month almost, a couple of weeks certainly; five or six bands a night at least. The tape was rolling on all of it. This was the documentation of that scene right at the time when it creatively peaked. In the end, this became the *Live At CBGB's* album. Hilly never got any paper and they were all getting signed.

"New York was very vicious then. Everybody was cut-throat. Everybody's going, 'I don't want to be lumped in with them,' regardless of what they say now. Talking Heads would say, 'Well, I don't want to be seen as being in the same scene as Blondie.' Patti Smith and Debbie didn't want to be in the same room together; just all this kind of infighting crap. The whole idea of a *Live At CBGB's* album was kind of anathema to all these bands who were seeing themselves becoming the new thing, like The Ramones thought they were the new Bay City Rollers. Television thought they were the new Grateful Dead. They were like, 'We don't know anything about this underground community; we're us.' They all tried to *not* have their stuff released on the *Live At CBGB's* album. They consciously said no – they were all signing to different labels. So the only ones that actually got released on the little album that Hilly put up himself were those other bands. It was crap, because all the good bands were not released. Hilly kind of shrugged his shoulders and was bitter. He was never really bitter about anything, but he'd given these bands their break and now they didn't want to be associated with his club because of all the other bands that were there. The story was that Hilly supposedly 'lost' the tapes, which isn't true because we actually took the tapes out of CBGB's and mixed them in studios around New York. I remember doing Talking Heads at Plaza or Electric Ladyland. Those tapes have never been found.

"Basically, I saw the *Live At CBGB's* album as documenting the bands like a Harry Smith or Alan Lomax project, a field recording of what was happening on the streets of New York in 1976. I actually saw that as a very important bunch of recordings, if you had the whole thing still intact, rather than what came out. Now it's like when they find a book of The Bible or the Dead Sea scrolls and some pages are missing! All the pages are missing from what that document should have been. It would have been the Smithsonian version. I knew enough about musicology to know this was an important era. It was, to me, the end of an era, more than the beginning of it; the intellectual takeover, or the elitist intellectual bohemian takeover, of rock'n'roll before it became too corporate for its own good. I was quite happy: 'Yeah, I'll record all this stuff.'

"Kim and I were recording everybody. Hilly gave Blondie a five or six o'clock in the afternoon slot or something, an 'OK – let's get 'em in and out' kind of thing. We were going to record Blondie then we were going to go for dinner down in Chinatown. It might not have been five or six because any time before 11 was early then! But there was nobody in the club and we recorded all of Blondie's set."

At that time Craig had only recently joined Instant Records in partnership with Marty Thau – who had been impressed by The Stillettoes two years earlier – and Richard Gottehrer. A former member of garage band The Strangeloves (of 'Night Time' and 'I Want Candy' fame), Gottehrer had also co-written 'Sorrow' for The Merseybeats (covered by Bowie on *Pinups*), co-written and produced 'My Boyfriend's Back' for The Crystals and produced 'Hang On Sloopy' for The McCoys, who he also discovered.

"Craig and I became good friends when we discovered that we had similar tastes in music and also people, which was an important part of it as well," Marty Thau recalls. Almost every night we would meet at about 11 o'clock, then go to CBGB's and clock all the different groups that were playing there. We would occasionally go over to Max's, but we always felt it was old and, from the Warhol days, kind of washed-up to a degree. They would put on some good acts who only played there because of the pay cheque, not that they felt it had an impact on their career. CBGB's was what it was all about.

"I was trying to reach Seymour Stein and found it impossible to contact him, so I thought, 'Oh, I know Richard Gottehrer.' I didn't know he had split from Stein and become an independent producer on his own, so I contacted him and we got into a discussion about what was going on downtown. He said, 'That sounds amazing, I thought it was maybe just a downtown hype, but it sounds real. Let's go check it out together.' So we met and went downtown and Richard immediately fell in love with what he saw, and understood. Shortly afterwards, we formed Instant Records and hired Craig Leon to come aboard. Then it was the three of us.

"Then we thought, 'Who should we sign? Who would be the best group to sign?' We unanimously agreed it was Blondie. Who else was there? There were other groups but Blondie seemed like the most possible mainstream group; the acceptable face of 'new wave', as they really weren't punk.

"Debbie kept coming into the truck when me and Kim were recording this and listening back to stuff," continues Leon. "Richie was there too and we were just goofing around. She turned around and said to him, 'Would you produce my band?' Richie said, 'I'm in a partnership with Craig and Marty,' which she knew, because Marty was hustling to be their manager and she wasn't dumb by any long shot. It basically transpired that I would go do my arranging thing with them and Richie would produce a single.

"Marty was always a champion of Blondie, and quite honestly both Richie and I thought he was out of his mind! We knew that Debbie was good looking, but you've got to remember that, at that time, it was almost unheard of for an assertive female to be a frontperson. It was a very hard sell, and she wasn't like a hippie chick ... well, she was a hippie chick originally; she's on the cover of *Look* magazine with the Volkswagen going to Woodstock with the flower on her face. The thing is, she didn't fit that image.

"The band's playing was really slovenly and they were really ramshackle-looking. Nobody really took them seriously, but Marty said they were going to be the only band that really makes it out of CBGB's. He said they were gonna be the biggest thing ever. He had that same vision about The New York Dolls, who were equally ramshackle and could barely get through a song. He wasn't so right about The New York Dolls, except they became very influential, but he was quite right about Blondie. Nothing that could show what they were gonna do as songwriters was really evident back then.

If it was, it was in such a rudimentary form that you wouldn't know it. But Marty was always pushing that one.

"I thought she was obviously very beautiful and there was talent within the group, but they sure couldn't play," Thau asserted. "But they had very good musical ideas; it was obvious that they had a sense of arrangement, and colour, and drama, and build. As a frontperson I liked her, but a lot of people thought she was kind of awkward and self-conscious. I didn't include this in my evaluation, it didn't turn me off because I thought she was such a case study to watch."

"It was really Marty Thau, I think, who should have the credit, because he's the one that got Gottehrer and Craig Leon to come down and see us," recalled Chris.

Regardless of initial reservations, Gottehrer soon found Blondie's naïve zest to be infectious. "I remember going to a rehearsal and watching them play and grinning from ear to ear. These were people that had great songs and were playing arrangements almost beyond their means. The execution wasn't perfect, but it had so much spirit. So that got me interested."

"Richard came to our rehearsal to audition us for the album," recalled Clem. "He was blown away that we had 20-30 songs, because nobody [else] could play."

"I could see immediately that the songs were great but that they weren't quite ready to execute them yet," qualified Gottehrer. "They were doing musical things within the songs that two years later all came together – a lot of them were on the *Parallel Lines* album. At the time, their ideas almost exceeded their ability to play them. In the case of the Blondies, their genius and their originality came from their own heads and almost from their *inability* to execute things, just from their desire to experiment."

Having recently produced The Ramones' landmark debut album at Plaza Sound Studios in Manhattan, Craig Leon took Gottehrer and Blondie to the cavernous thirties-style space previously used to record big bands in the early days of radio. "I did a lot of arranging, rearranging and restructuring of material," explains Craig. "I had already done a massive amount of restructuring on The Ramones, getting them to end and begin at the same time! There's not a lot you can do with The Ramones, just a lot of layering and texturing on that album we did, but it's all purposefully subtle. But with Blondie I did a lot of structural work on the songs and arranging in demo form, trying to get the songs to be more recordable. A lot of these bands weren't really recordable at the beginning. Blondie was definitely one of those."

Two songs were recorded with a view to a single: 'X Offender' and 'In The Sun'. Written by Debbie and Gary toward the end of 1975, 'X Offender' lyrically conflates Valentine's experience of being charged with statutory rape with Debbie's sensuously spoken introduction, suggesting the song is the tale of a hooker who falls for the cop who arrested her. "I wrote 'X Offender'," asserted Gary. "The tune came to me one night in Max's Kansas City, and I went back and played it for Debbie and she came up with the lyrics. She turned it into the story of my problems with the law. It became our theme song and we would close shows with it."

"I love to sing about love and sex," Debbie declared. "It's the most popular thing, but I think that some of my twists in the theme are good. Like on 'X Offender,' the first thing that came out on the record that's about a legal thing actually is about how you define what a sex crime is. It's from the woman's point of view. Everybody thinks it's about a hooker but it's not. It's about a young boy who makes love, and it's like a crime of innocence. He becomes tagged for five years of his life as a rapist because he makes a 16-year-old girl pregnant and he's charged with statutory rape."

Debbie's introduction, written by Gottehrer, referenced the doomed romanticism of the sixties girl groups while Jimmy Destri's fairground Farfisa and Clem Burke's Spector-style big beat enhanced the sense of homage. Swapping places, Gary Valentine's 'Born To Run' riffage and Chris' driving bassline imbued the song with a contemporary attack that placed 'X Offender' squarely within the same postmodern canon as The Ramones' 'You're Gonna Kill That Girl'. The whole confection was spectacularly adorned by a confident and assertive vocal performance from Deborah.

"I think 'X Offender' is the best thing we've ever done," insisted Clem in 1981. "It's so compressed and tinny and so Spectoresque. It's almost like an art piece. 'X Offender' totally amazed everybody, because they didn't know what to expect from us and it was a total production, not just the live sound at CBGB's."

"We did a lot of rehearsals at their loft and then a lot of preliminary recording at Bell Studios, which was this great old studio, which became part of a lot of their work, not just the first album," Leon explains. "It was the studio where Shadow Morton did The Shangri-Las and The Four Seasons did all their hits. It was a very funky but cool-sounding place. The night manager there was prone to letting bands from downtown come in for 10 bucks under the table, then you could use the studio all night from midnight to six o'clock in the morning or something. We would just record there constantly, all the time. That gradually shaped into the material for the first Blondie album. I did a lot of stuff there with Blondie; basically, routining and taping all of it, also with Mink DeVille and Richard Hell And The Voidoids. A lot of this was all going on at the same time."

In recording two versions of 'X Offender' that respectively appeared as a single and on the eponymous *Blondie* debut, Craig found the process straightforward. "It's pretty much the same recording but two different mixes. There's the one with double-tracking vocals, the very Beatley, echoey kind of vocal which, with Debbie, got a kind of nice, whispery kind of sound as well. The later version is the album mix, which is much tamer. I was running around all over the place while the album was being made, also doing Richard Hell And The Voidoids wherever they were."

Rather than release a single under their new Instant imprint, Gottehrer, Leon and Thau began shopping around for a deal for the group. "Nobody would sign Blondie," recounts Craig. "Richie was running around with all his contacts and I took them into people who'd offered me a job, including Columbia Records, which is the most corporate thing in the world! It was another one like Suicide: 'Excuse me sir, there's the door there!' But in any case, nobody wanted to sign them and had every excuse why they wouldn't sign them: 'Girls don't work out front,' 'She's too old,' every A&R trick in the book not to want to sign them. We played it to the guy at Atlantic who was putting together Foreigner at the time. He said, 'I'll eat my hat if that ever sells anywhere, I'll resign, that's the worst piece of crap I've ever heard!' Just total vitriol. For the man who went on to put together things like Foreigner, of course it was horrible crap. He was the origin of everything rock'n'roll became that we all grew to hate!

"Finally Richie was able to go to an old friend of his named Larry Uttal, who originally had a label called Bell Records [no connection with Bell Studios], who'd had The Syndicate Of Sound and Ronnie And The Daytonas. Larry had sold Bell to a conglomerate which became Arista Records and started his own label called Private Stock. It would have been fitting because Blondie was the band everybody thought was least likely to succeed and Private Stock was the label that was least likely to. They had to have been the worst crap label. Back in those days there were all these places where, if you really needed money for the weekend and you wanted to buy some weed or go out to dinner with your girlfriend, you could nick a bunch of promos and go down and sell 'em. If you had to exist on Private Stock, you couldn't buy a hotdog! You could bring in 100 clean copies and you'd probably get a nickel, as opposed to a couple of Ramones promos and your evening was set. The best thing they had was the very watered down Frankie Valli & The Four Seasons. He was one of the owners of the label. They made a lot of money though. I think they were the first with this Simon Cowell-type crossover junk. They had a guy from New Jersey called Peter Lemongello – very sappy middle-of-the-road, Barry Manilow-type things. Private Stock must have sold millions without it going on the charts. He was huge."

"Nobody was interested in Blondie," asserts Marty. "There were always various comments like, 'She looks great and the band suck,' or, 'The band's great but she's too sweet,' or whatever. They were silly, uninformed comments but the reality was that we couldn't get a label to sign them. But I knew Howard Rosen, who was the head of promotion at Private Stock, because his grandfather and my father had been in business together years before, so in a sense I knew a lot about his family history. He was doing a very good job at this little label, although the style of music they were into was removed from Blondie. But I figured any label that will get the music out there will be rewarded because there'll be such a buzz on it that they wouldn't know what hit them. So I went to Howard's house and played him 'X Offender' and he said, 'If Bruce Springsteen can have a hit with "Born To Run" this could be a hit.' That's a bit of a stretch but I'm not gonna comment. We struck up a deal with Private Stock but with the proviso they had to schedule or guarantee an album, and all the budget that goes with it, within 30 days or Blondie would be free from their contract. Sure enough, when 'X Offender' came out there was an immediate buzz on it. We had reviewers calling for copies and they didn't know what hit them at Private Stock and immediately picked up the option. All of a sudden Blondie had an album, when nobody would touch them.

"People criticise Private Stock and they deserve some criticism in the respect that they weren't really naturally married to this kind of music and, in many respects, did not have a clue what to do with it. But it ended well because Chrysalis, who were smart enough to recognise what was going on, arranged to purchase the contract. That's the true story behind the whole thing. Nobody was attached from Instant's point of view to Private Stock, but they performed a very needed function: they got a record out there."

The only minor quibble with the two-single Private Stock deal was the label's insistence that the debut 45 be retitled. "They made me change the name," Deborah explained. "That song was supposed to be called 'Sex Offender'. But renaming the song turned out all right. It was the first of a big trend of things beginning with the letter 'X'." Concerned that being called 'Blondie' would cause confusion between the band's identity and her own, Debbie also toyed with the idea of renaming the group 'Hitler's Dog' – archly referencing the fact that the Fuhrer's sheepdog was named Blondie. "The label would have dropped us," she observed. "I loved that name, though. It's really funny, isn't it?"

"I personally like 'X Offender' better because it adds some double meaning to it," asserts Chris. "But when you think about it, did 'Satisfaction' get played on the radio?"

Released on June 17, 1976, 'X Offender' was a turning point for Blondie. "People realised we could actually make a good record," recalled Clem. "Initially, when we were playing at CBGB's, we may not have been the greatest live band, but we were experimenting with different ways of presenting ourselves. Making the record was the thing for us. We always wanted to have hit records. We didn't really want to be underground. We wanted success on our own terms."

"It was definitely a sixties sound," added Gary. "It was sort of an anthem, and got us the record deal. It defined what Blondie was about; we were getting more and more poppish."

"Blondie were sort of the exception to the CBGB's rule in that they were actually a very good-looking group," said Mary Thau. "They were young and they were happy and positive, and their songs were loaded with hooks. They were really the pop dream."

For Blondie, who had been dismissed as the lightweight runt of the CBGB's litter, there was satisfaction to be derived from hearing the single booming out of the bar's jukebox. "That was more important than hearing it on the radio," beamed Clem. "I remember walking into CBGB's when it was crowded and the song came on. It was phenomenal that someone had actually paid to hear the song."

More paid to come and see Blondie over three nights across June 17–19, as the quintet delivered their most assured live performances to date. "We played in tune, we didn't flub, we had a stage presence, and it worked," recalled Gary. "We went from being a band that would open for anybody to packing CBGB's." Private Stock president Larry Uttal was among those impressed by the gigs: "I was very turned on by the sound of her voice. She had that early sixties sound that was becoming popular again. She reminded me of Rosie And The Originals," he claimed, referencing the doo-wop quartet who scored a number five hit with 'Angel Baby' in 1960.

Just as Marty Thau had anticipated, Uttal recommended that the label take up its option to have the band record an album. After Frankie Valli showed up to check out the group's show, the deal was rubberstamped. "He came to see us at CBGB's," says Debbie. "A limo – on the Bowery? Fuck!" Blondie naïvely signed the contract without getting legal advice, much to their later regret. "We were ignorant and couldn't afford a lawyer," Debbie would recall. "We were still considered the band least likely to succeed."

Before recording the album, Blondie played a series of gigs throughout July 1976. In addition to further shows at CBGB's and out-of-town sets at the Stone Pony in Asbury Park, New Jersey, and the Rathskeller, Boston, the group also appeared alongside The Heartbreakers and The Fast at Max's, where they found they could now charge $200 for the weekend.

Despite now being a signed band with a single behind them, Debbie remained cautious about Blondie's potential. "I was always consciously observing and appreciating things, but as far as having visions of success we've been realistic. [Chris and I] both have a tendency to play things down, so as not to build ourselves up and get disappointed and there was no feeling that we were going to be successful at the time. Everybody thought we might make it as big as the Dolls."

The group were also captured on film by director Amos Poe – who would subsequently feature Deborah in *Unmade Beds*, his reworking of Jean Luc Godard's 1959 *nouvelle vague* classic *Breathless*. For *Blank Generation*, Poe's document of the CBGB's scene, he filmed the group in and around their loft headquarters. "Amos came to the loft and shot us clowning around like The Beatles in *A Hard Day's Night*," remembered Gary. "Our segment ended with 'the boys' pushing Debbie's Camaro up the Bowery."

Sadly, the group were compelled to abandon the loft after Eduardo flipped completely and threw them out. "We'd gotten too serious for him with our daily rehearsals and business meetings," explained Debbie who, along with Chris, moved into the top floor of a brownstone on 17th Street, between

Sixth and Seventh Avenue. Gary would shack up with his girlfriend, Lisa Persky.

In August and September Blondie recorded their debut album, produced by Gottehrer and Leon at Plaza Sound Studios. Craig referred to his classical background for "recurring motifs and counter-melodies" as the band worked from noon until one or two in the morning six days a week, then around the clock as the deadline loomed.

As with most debut albums, it captured their already honed live set. "*Blondie* was basically done live, with the four musicians playing," explained Clem. "The playing is pretty straight," added Debbie. "The only overdubs are one or two keyboard parts and a couple of other lines. We're less nervous now and have a better rapport with one another. The more you do something, the better you get. Now I'm so much more secure about what's happening with the music that I can get off more on the performing."

"To tell you the truth, I never even knew if Deborah could sing until we went in to make the record," Jimmy Destri admitted. "I could never hear her on the equipment we had to use on stage."

"I always knew the songs were pretty well sussed," said Burke. "There was a nucleus of maybe 15 or 16 at the time, and there was also the taste we all had in cover songs. I didn't know too many people in my group of friends who really liked The Shangri-Las or The Velvet Underground. They were all in their bedrooms trying to be the next Jimmy Page. There was a specific vision we had that not many people had at the time."

"There was still a lot of stuff left over from previous incarnations Chris and Debbie had had – some old glam stuff and campy sort of things," remarked Valentine. "My influences were British Invasion, Velvet Underground and, later, Television. Jimmy's were similar and Clem's a walking rock'n'roll encyclopaedia, so we decided to go in that direction, and that's when we became very identifiable."

"Clem's influence was the perfect counterpunch to Chris' artier side, and that was really a driving force," commented Jimmy. "It was actually part of the thing that kept me there. Because I walked in with this vision of my own – you know, 'Here are my songs, and this is what I want to do.' And it was Clem who sort of took me aside. Otherwise Chris and I would have banged heads from day one."

Despite having a direction and a repertoire of material upon which to draw, Blondie had very limited studio experience. "They were shambolic," recounted Marty Thau. "But through that you'd start hearing this great kind of re-creation of the Shangri-Las mentality, mutated with all these other things. So I got to thinking, 'Well, I kinda know what they're going for; there's this little Herman's Hermits guitar thing here, and it's coming from all these different sources.' Then it hit me why they had never come across on tape, because that really had to be channelled into, like, 'Let's take the best bits of all these ideas and make it so you can actually hear them one at a time!'"

"The concept of that first album was based on the personality Blondie brought to the subject matter," explained Deborah. "When you listen to the whole thing you notice a predominant theme of violence and gunfire. I don't think there's a song without a reference to someone getting shot, stabbed, degraded, or insulted. It's prime-time television on record."

So far as Thau was concerned, much of the credit for Blondie's distillation of pop-cultural influences on vinyl belonged to Craig Leon. "Richard Gottehrer was in the studio and thought he was in charge, but it was really Craig who was the backbone of the whole thing."

Indeed, contrary to the sleeve credits, Leon mixed the whole album. "When it went over to Chrysalis, all of a sudden the 'Craig Leon' disappeared," he reveals. "But I was much more involved with them than one might think. I never cared about stuff like that and was very free with credits – much to my chagrin now. I was a musician and part of the underground scene, so I thought people should get credit for what they do; hence Tommy Ramone gets an associate producer credit on that first album for coming up with the concept, which now gets turned into that he's the producer of the album, which he's never claimed.

"Richie was this kind of executive vibe producer. He's exactly like the Brill Building producer that he was. He'd be the guy that would show up and everybody would be rehearsing and trying to get a guitar in tune and refine that thing, 'Chris you should play bass and Gary should play guitar,' things like that, which happened a lot. Then he'd show up and say, 'Hey, we really need a tambourine here,' and start beating on a tambourine and jumping all round the studio and just vibing everybody up. That was Richie's forte."

"I always thought Richard Gottehrer was a very good producer," offered Jimmy. "He maybe wasn't as strong and committal with us as he should have been, or as Mike Chapman was later. But he was always very good, always has a great sound and he makes great records, fun records. Very entertaining records. He's basically a nice guy. He wasn't tough enough to get into the pain and misery of being here."

Certainly, Gottehrer found directing the band's raw energy a challenge. As a means of adding some further experience to the company, he recruited former girl-group songwriter Ellie Greenwich and her backing singers to provide additional vocals for 'Man Overboard' and 'In The Flesh'. "They really weren't very good, and I was looking for more of a voice," observed Ellie of her limited role. "But little did I know!"

"We had always been trying to contact Ellie," Chris recalls. "We had tried to contact her a couple of years previously when we did a demo with Alan Betrock. We did 'Out In The Streets', which is one of her songs. She'd got it but couldn't do it because I guess she was busy with her other affairs and stuff. Our producer was friends with her from the old days and she was happy to do it. We were really happy to have her come into it. It was great. She's a really nice person."

"On both those songs they worked it out in the studio, but Debbie really conducted it," he explained around that time. "Those are the two girls that Ellie works with all the time. She lives right over on 57th Street. She was very sweet, and she did it really slick. Gottehrer got about three versions of 'Man Overboard' and 10 versions of 'In The Flesh'. I tried to get some of them off him, but he probably threw them out."

"He made so many mixes of 'In The Flesh' it was just crazy," added Debbie. "'Man Overboard' was supposed to have a Latin sound, and I think Richard gave it more of a girl-group sound."

"There was this big Las Vegas sound and this little minimal band sound," continued Chris. "Ran the gamut. The one that's on the record is sort of in between."

"We went through a lot of their material and chose the ones that appear on the album," recounted Gottehrer. "For the most part the arrangements are theirs. They have a terrific awareness of what they're about and what their music is about. I think it's a great record – I think their style, sense of humour, their meaning comes through from the first note to the last."

Ultimately, 11 tracks were selected for inclusion. A reworking of 'X Offender' stated the band's intent for a set that featured other extremely danceable uptempo numbers such as 'Little Girl Lies', the bitchy 'Rip Her To Shreds' and 'Kung Fu Girls'. These were interspersed with songs drawn from other regions of the group's influences: the surf-toned 'In The Sun', 'Attack Of The Giant Ants' (complete with horror-show sound effects) and 'In The Flesh' – a memorable teen ballad inspired by Debbie's crush on David Johansen, which would become Blondie's second single.

Much of the implied bitchiness is delivered with Debbie's tongue lodged firmly in her cheek, "'Rip Her To Shreds' is a combination of personalities," she explains. "It can't be pinned down on one person because it wasn't about just one person. And I would have to include myself amongst them. That song was very self-deprecating – it was scathing about some other creature, but it was scathing about myself as well. It's a take-off about the whole bitchiness thing. We can all be a bitch every now and again."

Blondie celebrated completing the album with a party in the studio attended by The Ramones, The Miamis, Richard Hell and assorted hangers-on. "From the point of view of what a record is," observed Richard Gottehrer, "it's something that's got a life about it, I could feel the record living … I just thought the songs were outrageous, and I think with a sense of humour and fun about it all. The interesting thing is the first album's a bit out of tune, and just the way it goes together makes an interesting noise, an interesting sound. That's what I think the charm of it is, too. It's almost like listening to the early Bob Dylan records when he first went electric. You know, those overtones are as important as the notes people are playing. That's what we caught there."

"There's a great difference to what they sound like on the album and what they actually sounded like," observes Craig Leon. "That's why they had to eventually get the other two guys in the band. They didn't have the greatest equipment in the world, even at that stage. They were broke. I don't think they made any money from the Private Stock deal and if they did it was only a couple of thousand dollars between all of them."

"I think the strongest art comes from the strongest people, not the weakest ones," Debbie declared. "I didn't think I was strong enough at one time, but I do now."

With *Blondie* the album in the can, Blondie the group returned to Max's for the latest of their landmark 1976 performances. Although time spent in the studio had assisted the group's musical development and collective confidence, their visual image could only be honed before a live audience. In keeping with their stripped-down, sixties-driven sound, Blondie had hit upon an unfussy postmodern take on classic rock'n'roll styling.

"The only way to make everybody look good and cool was to go to second-hand stores and get really tight things, little suits with the narrow lapels, small-collared suits which nobody was wearing," explained Deborah. "The reason we got these clothes is because they were what we could afford at first. I was always raving in the early days about straight leg pants. Bell-bottoms used to really make me crazy because they'd 'swoosh' and get in the way and I was always falling down in them."

"There was this shop right down the street from Blondie, a Jewish used clothing salesman who only had black suits and black leather jackets for sale really cheap for the Bowery bums," recalls Craig Leon. "That's why everybody was wearing black leather jackets and black suits on the Bowery! That's where they all bought their clothes, myself included, because it was a lot of fun. That was the only shop they could afford to buy clothes in."

"We never did any sort of deliberate thing," clarified Chris. "Just certain style elements that we thought worked."

With the four guys kitted out in tight jackets and straight trousers, the smart musicians presented a largely monochrome background upon which their frontwoman could be projected. At Max's, Debbie walked on stage in a striking zebra-striped mini-dress that generated admiration and desire in equal measure. The impact of the dress, fashioned from a discarded pillowcase by Stephen Sprouse after Eduardo fished it out of the garbage, was enhanced immeasurably by photographer Bob Gruen capturing the show on film. "I walked on stage in the zebra dress ... and the audience went wild," recounted Debbie. "It was the first time that this had happened to us, and that picture by Bob Gruen has been around the world a million times. After that gig, we began to gain some balance, whatever we did now somebody was there to approve."

The following month saw the release of 'In The Flesh' as the second single for Private Stock. Backed with 'Man Overboard', the swoonsome track was earmarked early on as a potential seven-inch. "'In the Flesh' was intended as a single, because Gottehrer put a lot of work into it, with back-up singers and all that stuff," said Clem. Although, like 'X Offender', the disc made little impact outside the New York scene, in Australia it provided Blondie with far wider international exposure and a surprise hit.

"The video of 'X Offender' was supposed to have been shown on an Australian TV show, *Countdown*," explained Burke. "But when the tape came on it was 'In The Flesh'. Everyone rushed out and said they wanted 'In The Flesh', so 'In The Flesh' became a number one hit in Australia. It created huge problems when we finally got to Australia, because the people that were tuned to such things knew we were a New York underground punk rock group from the depths of the Bowery. But then the other half of the audience expected a band that played light pop ballads."

With the album scheduled by Private Stock for December, Blondie continued developing their live act with gigs at the Cuando Gym on Seventh Avenue (where they took the stage at 2.30a.m. and made such an impression that everyone assumed they were the headline act – leaving genuine headliners The Dictators with no audience), Max's (with Tuff Darts) and CBGB's. Reflecting on the Cuando Gym show, Debbie recalled, "That was the first time I felt really good after playing. Super heaven. Perhaps it was because that was the first real stage we played on … Afterwards The Dictators and the promoters were pissed off with us."

When *Blondie* hit the shelves six weeks later, it was Debbie's turn to be annoyed. Although the group were moderately happy with the album, particularly as it was recorded after they'd been together for only nine months and still had much to learn, the way their label chose to market it became another matter entirely. "Private Stock put out this infamous photo of Debbie in a see-through blouse, which was not the character of the band," recounted Gary. "She did sexy stuff on stage but it was tongue-in-cheek, very camp. That pissed us off, and I don't think she even liked that picture very much."

Debbie – who had been assured that the shot would not be used 'uncropped' – was horrified by use of the picture, describing it as a "fiasco … [which] insulted the band considerably". Chris recalls she was "very pissed off", adding himself, "It's not selling us in the right way."

Like the vexatious image of the vocalist, the album's sleeve was shot by Shig Ikeida, who produced an image of the band lined up diagonally, dressed largely in black and white, with Debbie to the fore. "For the album photo session I remember we all got loaded," recalled Valentine. "I was drinking White Russians, one after another, and I'm absolutely plastered in that photograph. It's amazing that it came out such a real good cover."

Former Wind In The Willows manager Peter Leeds had re-established contact with Deborah though Richard Gottehrer, who had played *Blondie* for him. "I thought it would be *avant garde*-y," said Leeds. "Then I got to

Richard's house and heard the first album and it was, you know, the sixties, the organ, what have you, and I just fell down, I loved it so much."

Suitably enthused, Leeds began making overtures toward the band with a view to taking them under his managerial wing. He too recalled the furore caused by Private Stock's cynical marketing. "This poster came out and they just hit the roof. I remember they were in my apartment on 75th Street *screaming* about this poster ... That particular poster, as far as she was concerned, was not sex but sleaze. And she hated it. It was not the revealingness [sic] of it, it was the attitude she hated. And not beautiful, you know, not classy."

This kind of prurient promotion would play a part in establishing the myth that Blondie were some kind of musical burlesque, with Debbie prone to stripping or taking the stage without panties. "I've never taken anything off," she explains. "I've only ripped up outer garments in an effort to articulate a song. Rip it to shreds − it's just little movements and campy gestures, I've never done any porno rock'n'roll."

Jody Uttal, Private Stock's director of publicity, later told *Rolling Stone*, "At the time, it was really the only way we had to market them." More accustomed to selling MOR and novelty records, the label had little idea of how to promote something new. But, as Debbie reflects in retrospect, "Maybe tomorrow's music is what we're doing today."

"We had to do what we felt," recalls Chris. "We couldn't be writing 'Rock'N'Roll Baby' because that would have been virtually impossible. It would have been easy but we just would have felt compromised with ourselves, which isn't the right way to feel about art."

"Look at it this way, from a business point of view, I didn't know anybody in the business and Chris didn't know anybody," adds Deborah. "If we were gonna try and do AM radio songs, I would never get a band together and struggle and struggle and struggle for no money, playing dates uptown in club circuits where you would have to play everybody else's music and be AOR and from there try to get a record contract, it would be foolish, so the natural course is to do something that's personal and fresh."

More happily, *Blondie* was greeted by largely favourable reviews. The *New York Times'* John Rockwell confessed that, when he'd seen the band the previous spring, he'd found the music "crude", declaring that Debbie's singing was "tensely off-pitch and even her tough hussy-strutting looked timorous and unsure." With the album before him, he modified his opinion:

"It turns out to be a most appealing disk debut indeed. Miss Harry sings with a pretty, graceful assurance, the band plays spiffily and the songs themselves are full of clever pop twists and arrangements – not so much punk rock, more a kind of progressive pop."

The *SoHo Weekly News* observed that *Blondie* "shows a depth that will surprise the legions of sceptics … there's a Ronettes-style fifties flavour, that rapid-fire surfin' sixties sound, and a uniqueness in lyric and interpretation that's all Blondie. I stand impressed."

Similarly, *The Village Voice* homed in on the "pastiche of sixties rock moves", concluding, "what makes Blondie's first set more than just a fanzine mentality collection of 10-year-old styles by 25-year-old diehards is that it consistently conveys the same energetic conviction in its dumbness as the original punk rockers, yet like, say, The New York Dolls, the group are implicitly intelligent enough not to ram their understanding of earlier rock'n'roll down your throat. Like The Ramones, they have both drive and a sense of humour … you've got what rock'n'roll has always really stood for: the sort of unselfconscious fun that transcends both scenes and generic restrictions."

At the end of a year that saw Blondie establish a settled line-up, record their first two singles and an album and develop into an exciting live act, the band played their biggest show so far – an open-air New Year's Eve concert amid the snow, sleet and slush of Central Park's Bethesda Fountain, organised by the New York Department of Parks. Two thousand hardy souls braved the bitter cold to catch Blondie's set. At the stroke of midnight, the group launched into Booker T And The MGs' 'Time Is Tight' as five men in eight-foot high 'Hands of Time' costumes capered around them. Debbie later described the experience as "one of those moments that is Xeroxed on my brain".

The gig was comparatively profitable, with Blondie receiving a fee of $500. "It was one of the first times we ever got paid," announced Chris. It also established a tradition for Debbie. "I have a rule," she explained. "I always work on New Year's Eve. I don't care where I do it, whether it's a club or a bar or a big stage, it doesn't matter. I just have to work because I always feel it's symbolic for me for the next year."

The year 1977 thundered in with an intensive run of shows, including gigs supporting John Cale at My Father's Place in Roslyn, Long Island and three shows at Max's – one of which was billed as a 'Big Party For Blondie' and featured support from The Cramps.

Throughout January Peter Leeds continued to pursue his interest in managing Blondie. Although the band were aware they were reaching the stage where it would be impractical for them to organise their own shows and the dispute with Private Stock over Debbie's picture was unresolved, they remained uncommitted to anyone else fighting their corner. Having failed to gain the band's trust despite assurances that, if they engaged him as manager, they would be free to leave at any time, Leeds made a decisive move. With legendary KROQ DJ Rodney Bingenheimer heavily featuring cuts from the album on his West Coast radio show, the impresario booked Blondie into a run of concerts in Los Angeles.

"I didn't trust him from the moment I saw him," insisted Gary Valentine. "Nobody asked him to, but he set up some gigs for us in LA and flew us out. At the Whiskey he came backstage and said he didn't think we should be doing a song I'd written called 'Euphony'. I said, 'Hang on – you're not our musical director.' From that moment I'm sure he wanted me out."

In addition to setting up the week's residency at the Whisky, Leeds arranged for Blondie to stay at the Montclair Dunes Hotel, where they would play a show at the hotel disco as a means of paying their board. On February 9, the night the group were set to make their West Coast debut supporting soft-rocker Tom Petty, Leeds summoned Blondie to his hotel room and set a contract before them. "I knew that there was going to be a heavy industry crowd, and I was determined that before they were on stage, I was going to have that paper signed," he explained. "I just called them to my room and I wasn't letting them out of there."

"He took us to his hotel, the Sunset Marquis, and says, 'I want you to sign this contract,'" recalled Valentine. "It was like a 10-year thing, and either we signed or he was going back to New York without us."

"It was a pretty standard management deal," declared Leeds. "It was five years. I guaranteed them $3 million in the five years, and if they made the three million there were options. My cut was 20 percent. A real standard management contract: 12 pages with lots of lawyer mumbo-jumbo."

Still uncertain, the band argued the wisdom of accepting the deal but eventually signed. "Blondie were very serious," Marty Thau recounts. "They had no money. They came to us and said, 'Give us $1500 and you can manage us.' I was lucky to feed myself! I turned to Richard Gottehrer and he said, 'No, I don't want to be in the management business.' So I dropped that and they ended up with Peter Leeds. I didn't personally care for him; he was not the friendliest person or the warmest person."

Despite misgivings about signing a contract, Blondie's first experience of playing in Los Angeles was overwhelmingly positive. "LA was really inspirational to us," announced Clem. "We didn't really know what to expect and it was kind of a beginning for us. Everyone in LA was walking around with shag haircuts and velvet jackets; they're still into glitter. Then slowly but surely people started coming to our gigs in skinny ties and everything."

"I hadn't really been outside New York that much," remarked Gary. "The second time we played [in April 1977], people were wearing skinny ties and mod suits. We definitely had an influence. That was adolescent rock heaven. We were staying in Beverly Hills, running up incredible tabs, doing all the things you do when you're 20, and somebody says, 'OK, you're a rock star now.'"

Chris was excited about making an impact on what was an almost horizontally laid-back scene. "We've conquered New York," he grinned. "We just beat The Ramones' record at Max's by $10. But we realise it's like starting all over here. It's like the first step on a new ladder."

As the buzz around Blondie's Whiskey residency grew, elements of the local rock aristocracy swung by to check them out – memorably including Phil Spector. "He came to our show with an 'In The Flesh' button – one of Private Stock's promotional ideas – pinned to his jacket," Valentine recounted. "He was wrapped in a long black cape, wore impenetrable sunglasses and was accompanied by a bodyguard ... He made everyone else leave the dressing room and launched into a long and meandering monologue, peppered with remarks like, 'Who the hell do you think you're talking to?' whenever one of us wanted to say something ... He wouldn't let us leave and had his bodyguard stand in front of the door. Later he invited Chris and Debbie to his house to talk about producing our next record. He wouldn't let them leave there, either."

"I think Phil expresses interest in people that he likes, that he can see something of himself in, 'cos he also expressed some interest in The Ramones," says Deborah. "I think it's a very high form of flattery, but I don't know if he was really into producing us. I think he has a direct pattern; he wouldn't want to deviate that much. I think he's interested in doing his own material. We went to his fortress, his hacienda. It's not really alone, it's in a very crowded neighbourhood. It's very close to Sunset Strip, but it's surrounded by a wall; a big house with dogs and lions outside. He did a real interesting thing with Leonard Cohen that he played us, and Dylan. He got Leonard Cohen singing rock'n'roll, which is strange."

As the *LA Times'* Robert Hilburn described Blondie as "sleaze rock" and "a flashy version of The Shangri-Las meet Lou Reed with lead singer Debbie Harry playing both roles", news reached the group that they had been invited to support Iggy Pop on his 'comeback' tour – also featuring David Bowie as part of the former Stooge's backing band. Unsurprisingly, the band's new management readily agreed. "The second week we were in LA we got the word we were going on tour with Iggy, so instead of just one week in LA we ended up spending three months on the road," explained Clem. "We got word that we were going to do the Iggy tour and we were totally floored. This was just coming from playing clubs twice a month in New York. David Bowie had heard our album while he was in Berlin and wanted us to do the tour."

"It was great," confirms Chris. "They were real gentlemen to work with, very polite. They're real professionals, into the idea of a whole show with a first act. We were treated very well."

After some enthusiastically received shows at Mabuhay Gardens in San Francisco, Blondie returned to New York for a pair of sold-out gigs at Max's on March 10-11. Immediately after, the weary group climbed into a mobile trailer and set out for Montreal – the site of the initial concert of the Iggy tour.

"It was perfect. Bowie was involved, so it was well organised," enthused Clem. "The first day I met Iggy we both had on the same Beatle boots, so we had something in common right from the start. The first day he and Bowie came into the dressing room and introduced themselves." Burke would nominate meeting Bowie as one of the highlights of his career. "It was a great thrill. He accepted us as working musicians on a professional level. He liked us, so the relationship was really easy. Bowie was really interested in Jimmy as a keyboard player because Jimmy has a Polymoog. He'd come to our soundchecks and give Debbie hints on what to do on stage. He was really willing to help."

"We'd been warned not to pester him in the dressing room," grinned Debbie. "But he came and talked to us."

The respect and admiration between two rock legends and the upcoming young band was mutual – and, to a degree, salacious. Not known for his sexual reticence, Iggy took a keen interest in Deborah. "Bowie and I both tried to hit on her backstage," he revealed. "We didn't get anywhere, but she was always very smooth about that. It was always, 'Hey, well, maybe another time when Chris isn't around.' Always very cool about it."

For her part, although Debbie admitted to being flattered, she saw it as part of a light-hearted tease. "It was a lot of fun. They're two really great stars, musicians and writers that I've always admired. The whole thing was mind-blowing to be on tour with them in the first place. And to have flirtations with guys like that was just the icing on the cake."

After more than a month traversing North America, Blondie completed their run of concerts supporting Iggy at the San Diego Civic Centre on April 15. Before heading back to New York, the group played another week at the Whisky-A-Go-Go where they brought the tour to a suitably chaotic finale. "We wound up having this big jam," remembered Clem. "We did 'Anarchy In The UK' with Joan Jett [then of The Runaways, on guitar] and 'I Wanna Be Your Dog' with Rodney Bingenheimer playing keyboards … I was singing lead and Debbie was my dog – I had her on a chain. It was total chaos."

Although the rest of the band saw the value of letting off a little steam at the end of their first major tour, Gary took a less light-hearted perspective. "It all collapsed into sheer noise, but everyone involved thought it was great fun," he recounted. "All I could think was that this really wasn't what I had in mind when I thought about being in a band."

"After three months on the road you go crazy," rationalised Clem. "We were invited to this party in San Francisco with The Tubes. Jimmy, Gary, this girl and myself got there late. We went up to the door and the guy wouldn't let us in because it was too crowded. We told him that we had been invited but he wouldn't let us in. I kicked the door and he started chasing me. Jimmy walked up to the door – it had these big plate glass windows – and stuck his foot through one of the windows. They were going to put a contract out on me because some mobster owned the house, but Bowie paid for the window and got Jimmy off the hook."

Disinclined toward the more lunatic on-the-road antics, Debbie viewed the tour as providing some hugely beneficial experiences. "That was the first time I could go back and forth [on stage] without bumping into the bass player. Iggy had a fucking great band on that tour ... I only saw Iggy throw one hamburger the whole time. He's a pretty intense fellow, but he was very sweet-natured with me. He hung out more with the other guys in Blondie, though. I was with Chris. We were a couple, and we were happy. We loved music and doing shows. Sometimes we'd go out afterwards. A lot of times we didn't. We'd go back to the hotel and fuck a lot. We were lucky."

Chapter Seven

Flying Over With Bombs

"For all people know, we could have just been put together by Peter Leeds, hired and popped out of a can."

Debbie Harry

After they had kicked up impressive little clouds of enthusiasm on both coasts and made their first sorties into the great American interior and Canada, rave reviews for *Blondie* in UK mags *Zigzag* and *Sounds* pointed the way forward for the anglophile group. The Ramones' landmark incursion into Britain the previous year had raised interest in the CBGB's scene and Warners, keen to capitalise on English press approval for the recently released *Marquee Moon*, booked Television into a tour of Britain's finest drafty town halls and crumbling old cinemas. In order to complete a 'New York' package, a deal was struck with Television's manager, Jane Friedman, for Blondie to provide support. "Both bands happened to be in the country at the same time and the tour was just flung together," said Chris.

After arriving at Heathrow Airport on May 17, 1977 and being booked into a shabby Kensington hotel by Peter Leeds where, according to Gary, "even the phones didn't work", the band made their British debut with a warm-up gig in Bournemouth three days later. "We headlined over a band called Squeeze," recalled Clem. "That was really great, the audience was really spurring us on. Debbie almost got dragged out into the audience. Everybody was going crazy. We got all psyched up."

The tour proper started on May 22 at the notoriously tough Glasgow Apollo, formerly Green's Playhouse, where the following year Suicide would be assailed by a hail of beer-laden missiles when they opened for The Clash. "When we arrived at the Apollo for our soundcheck, we got our first indication that this tour was not going to be as pleasant as our one with Iggy," Valentine explained. "All of our equipment was pushed into a tiny space at the front of the stage. [Tom] Verlaine had decided that we were to work within this restricted area. Our brief encounters with him made it clear that he wasn't particularly happy to have us on his tour."

Although the two groups had often shared bills and audiences in New York, in Britain there was an evident division between the demographics each band was attracting, "It's a whole different thing in England," Clem observed. "The kids consider us a dance band or a pop band, which is what we always try to be. They consider Television a Grateful Dead type of thing. Nothing against them or anything, but the people that got into Television were wearing plaid shirts, long hair and beards, and smoking joints, rocking back and forth in their seats. The people that came to see us were kids with skinny ties rushing up to the front, trying to jump up on stage. It was a weird mixture."

"The New York punk scene was very diverse compared to the English scene. The British punk scene was a lot narrower," Chris later remarked. "The Clash and The Pistols and 999 and Sham 69 and all these bands were a lot closer to each other than Talking Heads and Television and us."

"We were under the impression that it was going to be equal billing, but it wasn't," added Burke. "It was bad because the audience was really mixed; half of Television's audience didn't want to know about us and half of our audience didn't want to see them. It split down the middle."

In Glasgow Blondie opened with 'Kung Fu Girls', with Debbie doing her Bruce Lee high-kick routine. The band piled through first-album songs and newer numbers earmarked for the next, including '(I'm Always Touched By Your) Presence, Dear'. A few bars into 'X Offender' Debbie stopped the song, bellowing "Wait a minute!", then, "Aww fuck!" They started again, then Chris flung his instrument into the drum kit as they stalked off, obviously unhappy.

Sound problems would become a persistent bone of contention. When they struck the band could get moody, fighting on stage or storming off. That night, as with others on the tour, the malfunctioning equipment could be blamed on 'support band syndrome', which often leaves groups without a soundcheck and with sound engineers who were more concerned with reading the paper than helping a support act who are not paying their wages.

The tour continued around the country before reaching London's Hammersmith Odeon. By this time Blondie had tightened up their show considerably; Debbie dressed to kill in a black leotard ensemble and gave a performance that went for the throat. The quintet also extended their tradition of well-chosen encores by performing Ronnie And The Daytonas' 'Little GTO', Martha And The Vandellas' 'Heart Wave' and The New York Dolls' 'Jet Boy'.

"It was very different in terms of audiences. In America audiences were still very bohemian and a little bit coffee shop, but in the UK it was much more physical," declared Chris. "The English are really traditional rockers, really wild," asserted Debbie. "They get up and go crazy. A constant shouting and leaping and swaying. The audiences [in the US] are generally tamer. We always get encores in the States. That's not the problem. It's the general attitude, the general response. Appreciation is expressed differently here."

"I was beginning to find English kids somewhat more literate and sophisticated than Americans," Deborah stated. "They clock everything and were catching all the nuances in the phrasing of the music and words I was singing. They appreciated our act right away, making Britain Blondie's second home. We always had the mod thing as a reference point, and it was always something we followed and took inspiration from. That's probably one of the reasons why and how we took off in the UK, as it was an aesthetic that was identifiable and British people could understand."

Aside from the cultural differences, Blondie also had to adapt to the partisan UK music press. Understandably, the bulk of the ink went to headliners Television. What irked Blondie was the tendency to lionise Verlaine's post-progressive noodling while dismissing their material as lightweight fluff. The prevalent attitude among the 'serious' journalists seemed to be that Blondie were OK for a laugh but Television were furthering the advancement of rock; their attitude was mired in the previous generation's values, failing to grasp the incoming wave.

The media's notion that Blondie's association with 'punk rock' should have some kind of serious message at its core worked against the group's apolitical nature. "If we're saying anything, we're saying have fun," declared Valentine.

"We're a little disappointed that the press is misinterpreting us … They did it to us in the States and it took a while to catch on," said Debbie. "The thing is we've been getting really good responses," added Chris. "If we were getting bottles thrown at us and stuff it would be a different story, they'd be right, but we've got an encore every single show."

"Yeah, we get encores every single show and the press writes us up and puts us down. It's really unbelievable," continued Deborah. "The audiences were really much more wild, slamming and pogoing and all that stuff – much more physical … they have a tribal behaviour that doesn't really exist in this country. Because the ethnology [in the US] is so mixed, people feel sort of isolated. The English culture doesn't punish these people for being eccentric, whereas over here it's a little bit different."

The media coverage also placed the emphasis of publicity squarely on Deborah's shoulders. "The danger is that Debbie could become over-exploited and that could hurt the group," warned Jimmy. "We could turn into a European joke band if we're not careful, and one thing we don't want is to become a second-rate Abba."

"The difference in the media's attitude to a boy or a girl on stage infuriates me," said Debbie. "If a band full of men is on stage and an audience of girls are screaming at them then everything is as it should be … but if it's a girl on stage, then suddenly everything is cheap. Reaction to me has to be cheap because I'm a girl and they're not used to that. If it was The Bay City Rollers up there then everything would be cool."

If there was an ideology of sexual equality emanating from some sections of the punk movement, then much of the press and the ubiquitous 'show us yer tits' element of the audience failed to grasp it. "At first there was considerable indifference to us, and then a considerable amount of resistance – resistance and fear – to me as a female singer," explained Debbie. "To me, the idea of presenting a strong female singer had finally found its time – that it was inevitable. I felt a lot of female singers were always being victimised or used, and that a lot of their lyrics reflected that. And I remember thinking how much I liked the blues of Janis Joplin or Billie Holiday, but how I really did not want to portray that sort of woman – the sort who was always going to get her ass kicked by love or whatever."

In addition to this kind of embedded sexism, Private Stock was an enthusiastic subscriber to the fact that sex sells. If the media chose to focus on Blondie's photogenic vocalist, the label was hardly about to object. "After the press picked us up, the record company didn't care who played bass. Debbie was what they wanted," opined Gary. "We can't go to the press and say, 'Hey, you have to give us a printed picture of the whole band, not just Debbie.' They'd say, 'Oh, we won't use your picture at all.'"

It can be argued that, for a new band hoping to make an impact in a foreign country, any kind of press is good press. Indeed, Jimmy took a pragmatic view of the media focus on Deborah. "If The Rolling Stones were called 'The Big Lips' after Mick Jagger, it'd still be the same unit of energy. It's just like identifying with the singer and she's the focal point. It's worth the occasional slagging from the press that the band are just her backing musicians, which we know personally is not true. After a while the press will realise there's something else here."

More positively, Debbie's strong feminine archetype had what would be described today as an 'empowering' effect on Blondie's female fans. "So many girls come up to me and say, 'Great, keep going, do it.' ... I'm not making enemies of girls, I'm making fans of girls."

As she would later reflect, however, any band can easily become an arena for competitive egos and Deborah became keenly aware of the divisive effect any over-emphasis on her could have. "There were times when I thought it was terrifically unfair to the guys. We tried to make things more equal, like dividing up interviews. But I knew sex was part of the mechanics of promotion. And it was working. I always wondered if anybody was actually listening to what we were doing musically."

The key to managing the media focus on Debbie would be to ensure that, so far as was possible, if sex was going to sell Blondie then it would be on Blondie's terms. "I wasn't just the product of a producer. I was my own product," she later asserted. "I was working very hard to be a good performer, a good singer and to write interesting things. To have that overshadowed by one's looks can be a little bit damaging. But I never paid much attention to criticism unless it was constructive and I could put it to good use. Why would I want to listen to someone else's opinion when I knew what I wanted to do?"

The last night of the UK tour took place at Bristol's Colston Hall on May 31. There was a minibus running from the office of punk fanzine *Sniffin'*

Glue. Among those hitching a ride were the *Glue's* Mark Perry and Danny Baker, plus (representing *Zigzag*) a boggle-eyed Kris Needs:

I'd been introduced to Chris and Debbie by Zigzag founder Pete Frame, who'd taken me to meet them at their cheap Kensington Hotel after the Hammersmith Odeon gig. The couple had retired to bed but surprisingly let us in, Debbie protecting her modesty with a sheet while Chris sat reading a Marvel comic. Instantly friendly, they had invited me to the Bristol gig in three days' time.

At Colston Hall, Blondie seemed to be winning over the seated punks and hippies alike, with their stellar cover of The Doors' 'Moonlight Drive'. Debbie is pretty in pink, almost preppie-style with skinny tie and pony-tail, bouncing around and high-kicking into first-album songs like the rabble-rousing 'Kung Fu Girls', 'Shark In Jet's Clothing', 'Rip Her To Shreds' and their new Iggy tribute, 'Detroit 442'. It's enough to secure an encore, which Gary Valentine struggles to make after taking a wrong turn without his glasses and plunging several feet off the stage. To his embarrassment he lands right in front of the beer-and-speed-fuelled London press contingent. He gets a cheer for regaining his composure and playing through the encore of 'Little GTO'. After Blondie's sun zoom spark, self-appointed headliners Television seem sedately self-indulgent.

The first meeting with Blondie as a group went well enough to say that we hit it off. Being the last night of the tour, the mood is celebratory and silly, especially the boys, Clem Burke wearing the complimentary food, attaching slices of bread to his leather jacket as Chris puns, "It's inbredible!" The Blondie boys are friendly enough and boisterous in that US-band-on-the-road manner. Jimmy and Clem spar with wisecracks, while Gary Valentine seems more serious, although no less approachable. Although all participants contribute essentially to the sound, it's Debbie's striking high profile and Chris's ingenious strategies which are already attracting all the attention. At this vital career stage, where other groups would spotlight their best assets, Blondie do the opposite, almost downplaying the most striking star to appear since Ziggy Stardust in order to maintain internal harmony. I can sense the underlying concern and paranoia when I'm repeatedly asked if we're using a photograph of the whole band as main image with the Zigzag piece. Rumblings will occur whenever Debbie gets a solo cover shot throughout the next five years.

Here's Debbie in the flesh. On first impressions, it's easy to be disarmed by her amazing face and unearthly gaze. In conversation, her voice can take on a mellifluous sing-song quality running a gamut of razor-sharp street tones, New Jersey holler or silken-toned honey angel, tempered with a playful, slightly warped sense of humour. I later find out she's naturally quite shy and reserved until she gets to know someone. Chris is her pillar and spiritual counterpart who loves to expound with dry wit on anything from conspiracy theories to comic books. Debbie and Chris obviously understand classic pop, but their boundless thirst for the new is also evident.

Before taking the stage, Debbie talked about the Blondie name: "We decided to use the name Blondie and then keep it because it had received some publicity. It's an easy name to remember and sort of descriptive. It just happened to work out to be a good name but most of the time people imply it's too feminine and pretty. Then I get tagged with it, but it's really a five-piece thing.

"I've been stuck with blonde hair for three years but I'm getting tired of it. You get tired of bleaching your hair out. I've always had different coloured hair, but to try to stop it now ..."

Realising this might be somewhat untimely, Debbie steels herself back to the mission in hand and issues a prophetic warning before bounding onstage. "We're coming back! We'll be back London! We're flying over with bombs!"

In those times of punky makeovers in the UK, old-fashioned beauty was mocked and eschewed in favour of anti-glamour shock tactics by the likes of Siouxsie, Poly Styrene, Gaye Advert and The Slits. Blondie initially had a difficult task, often dismissed as lightweight music fronted by the kind of bedroom wall pin-up that punk was supposed to eradicate. The previous year, Debbie had declared, "I want to do something to make people change the way they think and act towards girls." Blondie's visit showed they were all still fighting for the cause. Ultimately, she would be the most subversive of all: a sex symbol with brains from New York's underground on *Top Of The Pops*.

Despite her pre-gig enthusiasm in Bristol, Debbie later reflected on the experience of being treated badly by Television and misrepresented by the UK press. "We were really low on the totem pole. Television were already thought of as being real substantial musicians, and they really were technically better than us. We had to learn on the job. They really marketed us as a pop band and the guys started wearing the skinny ties and stuff. I was sort of nervous about it all. I always wished I had somebody to talk to, a mentor, who could explain what was going on. Someone just to say, 'Oh, you'll get used to it.' We didn't understand the business at all. Chris wasn't a businessman. Sometimes he'd sort of say, 'Oh, shut the fuck up.' I felt like I was tied to the bow of ship. Thrust out. I felt like a projectile or something."

The most positive element of the tour by far was the reaction of those who came specifically to see Blondie. "We went out, and the audience reaction was great for us. And that was the first indication that maybe somebody else gets this," remembered Jimmy. "It's the ultimate dream to tour in the UK," beamed Clem. "It pretty much lived up to my expectations. We're looking forward to going back. This time we'll headline and get someone appropriate to support us."

After a short run of European dates supporting Television in early June, Blondie returned to New York and almost immediately got down to the job of recording a second album. Once again, the disc would be recorded at Plaza Sound with Richard Gottehrer producing, although both Craig Leon and Marty Thau had by now moved on. "Though I kept in touch with Blondie I moved out of New York and the New York scene for all intents and purposes," explains Craig. "I was on my own and no longer working with Richard Gottehrer even though we still had a great relationship, which continues to this day."

"I got an offer to form my own label, which was always my hope and dream," says Marty. "So there I had someone saying, 'Yeah, we'll finance you,' so I sold my interest in Blondie to Richard and formed Red Star Records, went from there and signed Suicide and The Real Kids, and eventually put out music by The Fleshtones, Richard Hell, Martin Rev and even some other music I had by the Dolls.

"We were all kind of naïve in a sense, back then. I was very idealistic. I never believed how cut-throat it could be. I found out from some of the people who I regarded so tremendously. I didn't expect Blondie to be as big as they became, but I did expect them to become popular in varying degrees. It really was a pleasant surprise to see them go where they went to. They must have sold about 60 million records. They became probably the world's biggest-selling popular new-wave recording artists of that era. A lot of it had to do with Chris; Chris was very visionary. He really stuck with it and got the ideas together correctly."

The classic second album problems – insufficient written material, differing creative agendas and a greater sense of the commercial pressures – ensured that the making of *Plastic Letters* was a far more fraught experience than recording *Blondie*. "*Plastic Letters* was a very dark album," intoned Jimmy. "Plaza Sound was a dark studio … Radio City was closing."

More than anything, Blondie needed a hit – or, if not, some kind of signature tune to propel the band into the public consciousness. Perhaps surprisingly, it came along with relative ease. Debbie suggested reworking Randy And The Rainbows' 1963 hit 'Denise' from a female perspective. "We did 'Denis' because we had it on a K-Tel compilation – *44 Golden Oldies* or something – and we thought it was a great song," she explained. "I thought if we played a song that had been popular, the DJs would finally listen to us. It turned out to be a monster in England and France. I didn't know this beforehand but St. Denis is the patron saint of France. Psychic choice."

Deborah's prescience extended to improvising a verse in slightly shaky French – a decision that not only rendered a good cover version transcendent, but also survived later attempts to correct her Gallic grammar. "The arrangement and the sound were more like a band playing in the echo-driven 'wall of sound' style by The Crystals and Ronettes," Gottehrer observed. "What made it totally unique, though, was that in the middle she burst into French. Her phrasing and accent aside, it felt great and sounded amazing. Another example of the band's innovative qualities."

Aside from 'Denis', the remaining dozen cuts selected for inclusion on *Plastic Letters* were all original compositions. The credits for these songs were spread around the four songwriting members of the group, the bulk shared between Jimmy and Chris. "On that second record it was hard for me to grasp the point that they were trying to make," remembered Gottehrer. "There were conflicts in general about just which songs to do, almost like, 'We gotta do a few of Jimmy's songs, a few of our songs.'"

This resulted in a diverse range of material, driven for the most part by Stein's ever-growing palate of influences and Destri's experimentation with synthesizers. "I wrote six songs on *Plastic Letters*, and not one has a groove that's similar to the others," Jimmy later remarked. "'No Imagination' is directly inspired by Lou Reed's 'Lady Day' – you know, nightclub decadence. The whole album is like a portfolio of illustrations from a graphic artist. A lot of good songs on there – for Chris it was a stepping stone into what he would finally lock into *Parallel Lines*."

Deborah co-wrote the appropriately energetic (given the title) 'I'm On E' with Chris and the self-explanatory 'I Didn't Have The Nerve To Say

No' with Jimmy, as well as being solely responsible for the vacation romance vibe of 'Love At The Pier'. "This was the first time I worked up the lyrics after hearing the music — which is a much better way to write songs," she observed. This left '(I'm Always Touched By Your) Presence, Dear' as Gary Valentine's only contribution to *Plastic Letters*.

By the time the band returned from Europe it was becoming apparent that Valentine was dissatisfied. He had been working on a list of beefs since the recording of *Blondie*, during which his twinkling, bittersweet song 'Scenery' had been rejected. "I felt that Debbie did a lax vocal, because she wasn't into it," he claimed. "Maybe she didn't want two songs by me on the album. As long as I stayed where they thought I should be, it would be all right, but I wanted more."

On stage, Gary's energetic antics constantly left him out of step with his less bounding bandmates — particularly when he came close to hooking Debbie's eye out with his Rickenbacker machine head (an incident that compelled him to switch to a short-scale bass). "Jimmy got annoyed with me in LA because of all my jumping around. He said it could knock the tuning off on his synthesizer, but I think he just didn't like me trying to draw so much attention to myself. So he picked up my Rickenbacker bass and threw it right across the stage. By the end of that tour, I knew I wanted to quit, so when we got home, and this was pretty naive of me, I told them that because of the tension, the fighting and everything, I thought I should leave after the second album."

"I didn't expect Gary Valentine to be playing on this record," said Deborah. "I didn't think he had wanted to be in the group any more for at least half a year before. I think he had a lot of ideas about what he wanted to do and he felt Blondie was holding him back."

"We couldn't get along on a number of things. It was a mutual thing. Gary was going to leave after the first tour but it dragged out a bit," Jimmy explained. By July 4, things had evidently dragged on quite long enough. By announcing his intentions to leave, Gary had guaranteed himself a creative backseat on *Plastic Letters*. "I wanted my own band, I wanted to play guitar more, I wanted to sing," he said. "At the end of the show, I would switch off. I didn't want to take away from Chris playing guitar. I just thought, 'Why not?'"

Although Valentine subsequently claimed that he quit the band, the truth is that he never got around to it. Peter Leeds pushed the bassist before he could jump. "I think Chris and Debbie had decided they didn't want anybody in the band who wasn't 100 per cent committed but they couldn't tell me, so they got Leeds to do it. I think he was more than pleased," insisted Gary.

Their former manager categorically denies this. "They wouldn't have let me throw him out if I had asked them. He was too much of a long-time friend of Clem's ... He didn't understand why he wasn't as important as Deborah Harry. So I fired him and then I told the band."

Leeds was at least correct in figuring that Clem, in particular, would be less than delighted. "I felt sort of bad about Gary leaving," explained Burke. "I quit the band right after he left, sort of threw a tantrum. I felt at wits' end a bit on *Plastic Letters*, not having a bass player and losing a friend at the same time, and being so new to it all."

Given that he was a key facet in controlling the band's (often dysfunctional) internal affairs, it was fortunate that Clem soon reconsidered and returned to the fold. "The weird thing about Chris and Debbie was, they always needed a scapegoat," he revealed. "I spent a lot of time trying to keep people in the band. Somebody was always on the outs."

For Chris, such manufactured stresses were simply part of the creative dynamic. "Tension is not a bad thing. To me, it's equal to excitement. If there's no tension, there's no excitement," he declared. "The music wouldn't be half as good without the tension," agreed Jimmy. "It's good to have Chris come up with a brilliant song, and my unspoken reaction is, 'Motherfucker! I gotta do something better!' – and vice versa. It gets you off your ass and makes you work hard, especially when there are people in the group who are as smart as you are. It would be a lot easier for ourselves if we were a very laid-back, commune-type group, but we're not – and it makes our music better."

In the short term, Gary's dismissal – which initially led him to follow his girlfriend Lisa to Los Angeles, where he formed power pop trio The Know – meant that Blondie were missing a bassist halfway through recording their second album. Although Chris picked up the four-string slack on 'Fan Mail', 'Denis', and 'Youth Nabbed As Sniper', it was only a temporary solution that could never work live. To fill the gap, Clem recruited another of his Jersey pals, Frank Infante. "Joining Blondie was such a surprise," declared Frank, "they just asked me if I'd play on the record. I played [rhythm] guitar on a lot of the songs too."

Born on November 15, 1951, Frank was already a local legend for his part in World War III, an MC5-type band that hardly ever played without some kind of hassle going down. "All these social misfits would come out, and the cops, too," he recalled. "We were loud, into 'the revolution', but the songs were good. There'd be trouble whenever we played, because we were down on everything." The height of World War III's five-year career had been a stint supporting Aerosmith in 1971.

"I always liked music, even when I was a kid. My mother and father used to play records a lot. I was 13 when I got a guitar, and then I got a bass because I liked the bass a lot. At that time I used to buy music sheets. But they weren't the same key as the record, so I gave up on that. The way George Harrison would play a song wasn't like how it was written on the sheet. To me the best way to learn to play the guitar is to first learn the chords from a chord book. Then just jam along to records and stuff."

Nicknamed 'The Freak' on account of his deathly pallor, Frank's first group was a rhythm and blues covers combo called The Rogues. From there he graduated through a series of Jersey power-chord bands including The End, Rocks and, finally, World War III – where he first encountered Clem, who was playing with Sweet Revenge at the time. A devotee of Keith Richards and Johnny Thunders, Infante soon developed a down-and-dirty, no frills approach to playing guitar. "I like straight-ahead rock, that feeling of power," he declared. "Ultimately the thing is to get to a really primitive point, like the natives in Africa who just beat themselves into a trance, captured by the rhythm. Drums are the main thing."

Although Blondie's sound was decidedly more pop-orientated than anything Frank had been used to, he found he was drawn to the group's lack of orthodoxy. "They were just having fun. 'Blondie has more fun' – that was a slogan. It wasn't a serious muso thing, the energy was there, and the songs were there. Before I joined, the bands I was in were trying to be more musical," he observed. "Rock'n'roll isn't music, it's an attitude. You can play the wrong note and it can be the right note."

With Infante on board as 'guest', Blondie resumed work on *Plastic Letters*. The tensions within the group that bubbled to the surface during Gary's dismissal and Clem's short-lived departure gave the album a darker aspect than its predecessor. Jimmy's synth-driven sound produced an electronic coldness, while Chris' 'I'm On E' ploughed a decidedly existential furrow. "'I'm On E' was about running out of gas – being empty," explained Stein.

"The second record was more of a transitional experience," remarked Clem. "I was pissed that [Gary] left. I brought Frank into the fold, but it wasn't really a unit. I remember doing the photo session, going, 'Somebody's missing.'"

Irrespective of any resentful undercurrents, Blondie's very nature ensured that *Plastic Letters* emerged as anything but downbeat. Aside from immediately accessible slices of edgy pop such as 'Denis' and '(I'm Always Touched By Your) Presence, Dear', 'Contact In Red Square', 'I Didn't Have The Nerve To Say No' and 'Detroit 442' ensured there was plenty of energy on offer.

"Blondie records have always had an assortment of styles," explains Debbie. "For example, there was a song on *Plastic Letters* called 'Cautious Lip' [featuring lyrics by Ronnie Toast, a close friend of Chris and Debbie's who previously supplied stream-of-consciousness sleeve notes for *Blondie*] that explored our appreciation of the late sixties jam bands."

In keeping with his broad spectrum of musical tastes, Chris saw Blondie as being wholly inclusive, about "bringing all people together. I think it's dangerous always to have an 'out' group, the way punk alienated itself from other music."

As they had already discovered in Britain, the band's apolitical nature could sometimes be taken a bit too seriously by the press. While the group were aiming for a wide appeal, they were self-conscious about addressing the issues of the day. "When we talk about things like the environment, people are just gonna say, 'They're full of shit. They're just saying this as a cop-out, to protect themselves,'" opined Stein. "And yet those people who accuse us of copping out, what are they doing? Nothing. They just sit there."

Richard Gottehrer's uncertainty about the overall direction on *Plastic Letters* led him to adopt a simple approach to unify such a diverse set of songs. "His idea of production was to put handclaps on it. He wasn't real precise, he was more into creating a mood," observed Clem.

"That was another trip," agreed Frank. "His approach was, 'You do four takes, and pick the one you like.'"

In retrospect, Burke remains appreciative of Gottehrer's work. "I think that album's really good; Richard Gottehrer's a really good producer. Those early albums hold up to this day," he declared. "The ultimate thing would have been for Bowie and Spector to produce us together. I was thinking maybe they'd kill each other because they're both such egotists. That'd be fantastic."

With *Plastic Letters* in the can, Blondie returned to the road during September and October 1977 for their first gigs since Gary Valentine had been sacked. After shows at CBGB's and My Father's Place in Roslyn, NY, the band headed west for a run of gigs at The Old Waldorf in San Francisco, Huntington Beach, CA, and a week's residency at The Whisky in LA. Arranged by Peter Leeds, these were the first in a series of tours where the manager would work his band non-stop for a solid six months.

"Instead of going right to LA for those gigs with Frank on bass, we should have stayed in New York and got a good player, figured out what we were gonna do, or gone to LA to get somebody instead of having to do gigs right away," Deborah asserted. "We had never had a period of time when we weren't booked or didn't have something to do, where we weren't under pressure to come up with product or have an obligation to fulfil. Our manager … put us on the road before we had a chance to regroup, as it were — reorganise the band. That threw us totally off balance for about two years."

Although competent, Frank's bass technique was not sufficient to secure him a full-time spot in Blondie. While in Los Angeles, Leeds sounded out Nigel Harrison, previously a member of British sleaze/glam outfit, Silverhead.

"I sort of met the Blondies in LA at the Whisky, then met them officially when I flew into New York," Nigel recalled. "I got in at seven in the morning; it was cold and rainy. Peter Leeds called me and the band met and we all went down to this cold, damp, scuzzy rehearsal hall and I just threw myself into it." With a European tour looming in just over a month, he learned two albums' worth of material in two days and did enough at the audition to land the bassist gig, with Frank retained as Blondie's full-time rhythm guitarist.

Hailing from Stockport in Cheshire, Harrison was 26 years old when he joined the group. In addition to being Blondie's only English member, he brought with him a relative wealth of professional experience. Having sent off for a mail-order guitar when he was 12 and received a bass, Nigel settled for four strings, formed a group called The Musketeers with some teenage friends and graduated through a series of blues-infused beat combos, including Aylesbury band The Farm and The Smokey Rice Blues Band. Relocating to Abbey Road in London, Harrison found that proximity to one of the world's most famous recording studios didn't necessarily guarantee access to a rock'n'roll lifestyle.

"I used to wash dishes and search the ads in the back of *Melody Maker*. I called up about anything – 'Topless Go-Go Dancers for Zurich Wanted' – anything to get out! So there was this ad which was meant to read, 'Erotic Relaxed Musicians Wanted,' but read, 'Erotic Relaxers Wanted.' So I called and subsequently joined Michael Des Barres and Silverhead. They gave me £25 a week and I was extremely happy. Andrew Lloyd Webber and Tim Rice of *Jesus Christ Superstar* managed us for a month and then we went with Deep Purple's management and Purple Records. We did a first album in 1972 and toured the US with Deep Purple."

When Silverhead broke up in 1974 after their second album, *16 And Savaged*, Nigel remained in Los Angeles, hanging out on Sunset Strip with the likes of Rodney Bingenheimer and notorious impresario Kim Fowley, while playing with keyboardist Ray Manzarek's post-Doors project, Nite City. Having first heard Blondie's 'X Offender' on Bingenheimer's radio show, he was introduced to Leeds and the group by his friend Toby Mamis, who was working as Blondie's publicist. "Toby thought I'd be right for the band but felt odd about pulling me away from Ray Manzarek. I'd been with Ray since September of 1974 and he was very good to me."

Although *Plastic Letters* was initially conceived with a view to being released on Private Stock, Peter Leeds had other ideas. Blondie's spring tour of the UK had opened their manager's eyes to breaking the band in Europe and he was keen to establish a British record label as a commercial beachhead. To this end he set his sights on Chrysalis Records, an English imprint set up in 1969 through a licensing deal between Island Records and the label's founders, Chris Wright and Terry Ellis. "[Terry Ellis] had been Jethro Tull's manager and I knew he would relate to management, and … I knew that Europe would be vital," said Leeds.

To attract Ellis' attention, Leeds hit on the approach of sending packages of press cuttings to the label boss' home address. It aroused Ellis' curiosity enough to have him enquire about the group and, on discovering they had scored a hit in Australia with 'In The Flesh', he got in touch with Leeds who brought him over to catch Blondie at CBGB's. Although Leeds kept Ellis from talking to the band, he was sufficiently impressed to pursue his interest. All Leeds then needed to do was to extract Blondie from their Private Stock deal.

"I'm in a meeting with Larry Uttal and I say, 'We're not going to make any money together, the band isn't going to be a success here, I want to buy the band's contract out,'" asserted Peter Leeds. "So Larry says, 'It's not for sale,' and I say, 'Everything is for sale, it's just a question of price.' He says, 'OK, I want a million dollars.' And I say, 'Larry, we're not talking about fucking Led Zeppelin for Christ sakes! They sold no records and no concert tickets – what are you holding on to?' So he says he needs the weekend to think about it. On Monday he says, 'OK, $400,000.'"

Leeds raised $500,000 to buy Blondie out of their contract – $100,000 went to Richard Gottehrer for his piece of the band, with the remainder paid to Private Stock. "You know I made a little history when I made the Blondie deal," he claimed. "When in the history of rock'n'roll music did somebody lay down $500,000 to buy the recording rights to a group that had sold 14 records?" He then broke the news to those it affected most.

"It all got totally done behind closed doors," remembered Clem. "I can't say enough about Richard, because he really helped us, but he had us tied up, basically. And we were $500,000 in debt, instantly."

After an all-night session with a series of lawyers, the band finally signed with Chrysalis then immediately blew off steam by getting high and trashing the office. "We were up on this high-rise, 12 floors up, literally trapped in this room, and Jimmy said, 'Here's the phones! Let's call England, let's call France!' Contracts were flying back and forth," recounted Debbie. "I think the sun came up when the deal was done – it was the most cathartic experience for us."

For Blondie, being signed to Chrysalis represented a big deal and, consequently, bigger commercial pressures. This became evident almost immediately, as Debbie was compelled to accompany Peter Leeds on a short promotional tour of Australia at the end of October, while the rest of the band stayed home and bedded in their new personnel ahead of a European tour to coincide with the UK single release of 'Rip Her To Shreds'.

Like Private Stock, Chrysalis wasted little time in exploiting Debbie's image for promotional purposes, captioning tour advertisements with the distasteful, 'Wouldn't you like to rip her to shreds?'

"I was furious when I saw that," she asserted. "That's the problem of art and commerce. We came from the New York City underground. We were trying hard to be artists. We didn't have any idea about merchandising or marketing. The whole thing was a complete, gigantic shock and smack in the face. Everything was horrible – we're losing our identity."

Flying to London from Australia to hook up with the band in time to film a clip for future Factory Records founder Tony Wilson's *So It Goes* TV show on November 7, it was a wonder Deborah even had time to notice the press campaign. After two days at the Montcalm, Marble Arch, Debbie and Chris moved to the Royal Garden Hotel on Kensington High Street, joined on November 5 by the rest of the band. They played their first gig with the new line-up at the famous Aylesbury Friars club, with those bombs strongly in evidence.

In something of a twist, Nigel's first gig with Blondie was on November 12 at Friars, previously his local. "It was ironic," he said later, "Hollywood to New York to Friars!" Priced at £1.75, 1,200 or so tickets sold briskly, promoted in the club's local record shop.

It also turned out to be a landmark night for Blondie, headlining to a full house of fans who, although containing a gaggle of gobbing punks who'd read in the papers that this was how they were supposed to behave, went deliriously apeshit, spurring the New Yorkers to storm the place after then-unknown support band XTC.

Debbie sported a see-through black blouse, black leather trousers and boots, animatedly interacting with one of the most devotional crowds she had encountered. The band were tight and energised as they charged through songs from the first two albums: 'X Offender', 'In The Sun', a sumptuously soaring 'In The Flesh', 'Kidnapper', 'Man Overboard' and an encore of The Runaways' 'I Love Playing With Fire' a sublime masterstroke.

Afterwards, the band duly celebrated the tour launching so triumphantly, with Kris Needs joining in enthusiastically and getting caught in a drunken clinch with Debbie by his missus of the time – who he wouldn't be married to for much longer. "Both of us were pretty euphoric, as it was Blondie's first headline UK show to be greeted with a hint of the mania to come. Debbie liked to flirt and, like many, I was fairly besotted – but, it has to be stressed, I always had the utmost respect for Chris and their relationship."

After dates in Coventry and at the Finsbury Park Rainbow, Blondie played a similarly short run of dates in Paris, Amsterdam and Munich before jet-lagged Debbie made a return trip to Australia for a tour that kicked off with what she described as an "hallucinogenic" opener in Perth on November 29.

"The first time we came out was really weird, because what we were doing was not really commonplace," Chris recounted. "When we used to play, it felt like an exam. Those were the days when ankle-length floral dresses were in, and we didn't really fit in. I remember that the mayor of Perth turned up to our show, and then he never came backstage."

Supported by domestic chartsters The Ferrets, Blondie tracked their way across the huge country, visiting all the major cities, plus smaller urban centres such as Wagga Wagga and Wollongong. Generally, the audiences were a mixture of teenyboppers who seized upon 'In The Flesh', and hipper teenagers who had heard the album. The group themselves found the five-week Australian sojourn gruelling and dull, the only refreshments on the recreational menu being Fosters lager, very weak weed or heroin – Chris sharing Debbie's on-off infatuation with the drug. It concluded at the resort setting of Great Keppel Island, nine miles off the Central Queensland coast.

A brief visit to Bangkok for a quartet of concerts at the turn of the year saw the group play for a total of 8,000 people. "I think we were the second rock group to play there since the end of the war," remembered Deborah. "They got a PA that was really great. And they had about 50 or 75 men setting up the PA and it took them three days because they had never done it before. There were hundreds of wires and every time there was a mistake they had to totally disconnect the system and start over since none of the wires were marked."

"They'd never seen a rock group before. Whole families came to see us; old men in turbans with babies in their arms! They seemed to like it though," recalls Clem, before recounting how an Australian member of the road crew's party piece involved biting the heads off of live cockroaches, then washing them down with a refreshing bottle of urine and exclaiming, "Hmm, good piss this, mate." The group were similarly impressed by Thailand's nuclear-strength weed, which was available for five pence a stick.

Next, the sextet flew another 2,500 miles to Japan on January 5, 1978. Starting five days later, six shows in Osaka, Tokyo and Nagoya were followed by another flight back to London for a one-off gig at the intimate Dingwalls club in London on January 24. "We went around the world and I really didn't know what to expect," observed Frank, who was dazed but happy to be along for the ride. "With Blondie everything is show business. I was always against show business but everything is show business. But playing the guitar comes first. Everything else, like pictures and interviews, is secondary. Playing is a feeling, a lifestyle. I'm not a model and I don't want to take over the world."

"To tie in with the release of *Plastic Letters*, I had decided to give Blondie their first *Zigzag* cover," says Kris Needs. "Chris furnished me with several transparencies from the famous zebra-striped jungle dress session, which he had also used to land Debbie the '*Creem* Dream' spot in the irreverent Michigan-based rock magazine [it dubbed her a 'sweet, young flaxen-haired muffette' in the playfully salacious caption]."

As 1978 dawned there was a sea change in the British music scene, as punk charged up a cliché-ridden cul-de-sac and major labels wrenched dry the udders of a happening new trend. When this all proved too extreme, they found a watered-down derivative in the form of 'power pop'. Blondie had been playing powerful pop music for a few years now, but the most career-stifling thing that could have happened would be for them to become identified with the 'power pop pioneers' tag already hampering San Francisco's beautifully crazed Flamin' Groovies. The worst aspect of the phenomenon was that herds of no-hopers who had been sporting spike-tops and leathers the previous year began taking their best suits to the cleaners and donning skinny ties, while digging out their dad's copy of *Meet The Beatles*. For many labels, power pop represented an innocent, smartly dressed antithesis of punk's antiestablishment rhetoric and seemed (wrongly, as it transpired) that it would be far easier to market to the masses. It was like heading back to 1974's post-glitter/pre-punk limbo with more energy and straight trousers.

Still marginalised by their identification with punk rock in the US, Blondie returned to the UK at just the right time. They had not changed their image or their music, except that the latter had got tighter. They were also in a different league to either punk or power pop: a New York pop band with experimental tendencies and a love of pop music which could be funky but chic, or even downright dangerous.

Chrysalis' campaign for its new signing involved lining up cover features in three out of the four music weeklies. It was decided that a whole raft of promotional action would be kick-started at the Dingwalls showcase, packed with media, music-biz bigwigs and celebrity liggers, who would be sufficiently smitten to stoke a huge buzz ahead of Blondie's first headlining UK tour.

Unfortunately, the odds were stacked against Blondie from the start, as Chris battled a temperature of 104 on account of the flu he'd picked up in Japan. Once on stage, the band fought to be heard properly over the newly hired PA system (manned by a new sound man who'd been working with Kiss) and the group was exhausted from months on the road. All told, not the perfect conditions in which to face a crowd largely composed of the jaded and cynical.

The plan was for co-author Kris to spend the day of the Dingwalls gig with Blondie, grabbing interviews at opportune moments:

Needless to say, this went out of the window from the moment I arrived at an empty club at 2.30 p.m. They were supposed to be winding up the sound check at three, which was when we would have a chat. Eventually, Clem and Jimmy arrive, apologising profusely while explaining about Chris' flu, which was currently being held at bay with the aid of a monster vitamin B12 shot from a doctor. Will they blow out the show? "No, he says he'll do it," says Clem.

The rest of the band arrive: Frank Infante, Nigel Harrison, finally Debbie, dressed against the January freeze in a big, black leather coat ("Do you know anyone who wants to buy it? I can't stand the sleeves"), scarf and woolly hat pulled down over her face. Roadies are still scampering about and tweaking while the group waits … and waits, although Clem tries out his new drum kit with a dazzling barrage of breakneck paradiddles. Huddled in one of the bar-room chairs, Debbie talks about how happy she is with Plastic Letters and the more enjoyable aspects of the tour.

It was only just over six months since I'd first met Blondie when they'd first visited Britain with Television, but they were already in a far more positive place with the prospect of real success in the world beyond the nightmare brewing within Dingwalls. Blondie had liked the coverage I'd given them in Zigzag ("You're the only one we trust!") and my well-intentioned antics at Friars had seemed to break what was left of any ice.

The soundcheck actually didn't start until 7.00 pm, and then when the band clambered on they were greeted by deafening feedback. "That's just what I needed to clear my head," rumbled Debbie. They soldier through album tracks until the sound borders on reasonable, then head back in cars to the Royal Garden Hotel, where the group are unamused to find they've been asked individually to settle their hotel bills, obviously by Peter Leeds. Even writing at the time, I noted, "A hint?"

While the band members take off to shower and eat, Debbie says that Chris wants to talk, so I accompany her to their room, where we arrive to find him propped up in bed, still feeling rough, although his fever has broken. "I'll just wear shades and be cool," he declares.

While Debbie has a bath and gets ready for the gig, Chris shows me his portfolio of photos which will show up in Zigzag or, later, Victor Bockris's book, Making Tracks. We talk about the album and power pop, none of which I'm recording – but this is more of an easy chat anyway. Meanwhile, Debbie potters about, settling on her Dingwalls-friendly outfit of faded denim and gold boots. She's worried she's catching Chris's flu so plans to bring the brandy bottle with her for company. As we're getting ready to leave, Debbie shows me her trumpet. I never knew! "Oh, I just blast through it and make a noise at the end of 'Cautious Lip'," she says, before turning heads in reception as she sashays past the assembled string quartet in a black leather coat with trumpet and brandy bottle in hand.

Dingwalls is packed with press and assorted hangers-on, plus a few fans jostling for space down the front. Soon, Blondie take the stage, tune up and hurtle into 'X Offender'. The volume is ear-shattering in the tight space, easily capable of filling Wembley Arena. The sound man thankfully realises this and levels are adjusted, but Blondie didn't really want to do this gig in the first place, the feedback squeals stoking a gathering onstage tension.

The set is drawn from the two albums, plus a crunching version of The Stones' 'My Obsession', Chris hanging on beneath his shades, sometimes supporting himself on one of the pillars that are annoyingly peppered through the venue. It occurred to me again how adept Blondie are at choosing cover versions, their stratospheric treatment of the Doors' 'Moonlight Drive' narrowly missing the new album. Even through the morass of feedback squalls, it's plain to see how much tighter and more confident the band has got. While the fans at the front relish being this close to Debbie in the flesh, not caring about the music's painful grind, many of the journalists have headed for the bar by the end. The band knows this and the dam breaks after the first encore, 'Youth Nabbed As Sniper'. Clem dives straight into whatever the next song is: a tad too early for the rest of the band, who are still tuning up. Chris pulls him up, so Clem storms off, trashing his kit and shoving Jimmy on the way. "Er, goodnight," says a bemused Debbie. Backstage, there's much shouting, even fisticuffs as the ruckus spills into the outside courtyard, requiring intervention from the venue's bouncers.

Not a good night, later described by Debbie as "a disaster" – a textbook case of on-the-road pressure cooker tensions catalysed by problems over which the band has no control. All the same, something special was obviously going on here, the band now ranked among my favourite people and I concluded the Zigzag feature with, "Blondie are gonna be huge ... and it's written in Plastic Letters."

As January 1978 reached its frigid end, Peter Leeds' exhausting itinerary once again sent Blondie zigzagging across Europe, starting with two gigs in the Netherlands. "By the time we hit the Paradiso in Amsterdam we were playing with manic enthusiasm," recalled Debbie. "We were so ragged and exhausted, but those were some of the most exciting gigs we ever did." After shows in Belgium, France, Austria, and Germany, the tour reached a temporary halt in Stockholm on February 20.

While the band had been on the road, Chrysalis had reissued *Blondie* in December and then released *Plastic Letters* on February 4. The disc came in a sleeve that features the four full-time members of the group at the time of recording and shows Debbie sitting on a police car in a pink dress designed by Anya Phillips. It had been the second attempt at capturing a suitable cover image after the band's new label baulked at the results of an initial session. "I made this dress out of gaffer tape and a pillow case," said Deborah. "It was the way that I looked then – not that unusual. We did a photo-session like that for the cover of *Plastic Letters* and the record company completely rejected it."

The album drew equivocal critical comment from *Trouser Press*'s Ira Robbins, who encapsulated much of the mixed press response by identifying Debbie as "a stronger and more capable vocalist" and praising Chris, Jimmy and Clem's playing, but observing that the disc was "more competent than memorable. The slower the song, the less room there is for Debbie to be at her frolicsome best."

Despite mixed receptions, the disc managed the respectable chart positions of number 10 in the UK, and 72 in the US, as well as Top 40 placings in Germany and Sweden. In part, the album was catapulted to these heights by the massive success of 'Denis', which reached number two in Britain and saw the group make its debut on *Top Of The Pops*, bringing them to the attention of the mainstream British public for the first time. "You'd pretend to record your backing track, and they already had this multi-track recorder," Clem recalled. "I remember the English Musicians' Union guy in the control room; 'Can't you guys stomp in time a little more?'"

"Unshackling myself from my *Zigzag* desk, I went along and have rarely seen the band so excited," says Kris, "especially Clem, who knew too well that he was appearing on the same show that would have hosted so many of his heroes."

Still adapting to her new status as a prime-time pop phenomenon, Debbie found she was now instantly recognisable. "It's really funny, most of the time, going out – the punks, the kids, they're OK. It's people like shopkeepers and stuff like that – they have a different attitude, they have a tendency to yell obscene things at me. More so than before."

Clem, on the other hand, was already thinking about Blondie's next move. "I think it's bad to get trapped into an image as well," he deadpanned. "Maybe now we should all grow our hair long again."

Chapter Eight

Wrapped Like Candy

"We are trying to do what The Beatles did. The Beatles had gigantic mass appeal. They created an identity for a lot of young kids. They created a huge diversity in music. Granted, they had a longer span. Our thing is a lot more compact in a shorter time."

Chris Stein

In England, fate seemed to be smiling on Blondie as they took to the road as a hit band. At Blackburn's King George's Hall on February 23, 1978, they steamed into their set after a plea from one of the crew to "stop gobbing". 'Denis' was introduced as "the one that got us on TV tonight". For the first time, Blondie were playing to a crowd largely drawn by their one hit.

Supported by power-poppers Advertising, the tour continued on to Dunstable's Queensway Hall on March 2. The spherical venue was ahead of its time, with good acoustics. Backstage, the mood was in marked contrast to Dingwalls, the band's road weariness overshadowed by the kind of ebullience generated by a hit single and enthusiastic audiences. Debbie's pout was now recognisable from a growing amount of official and unofficial merchandise, and the sold-out crowd went suitably bananas.

"Growing up in England and knowing the power of *Top Of The Pops* – we were playing a gig in Dunstable and people had seen *Top Of The Pops* and gone out to the gig and it was just mania," recalled Nigel.

"There were some situations where Debbie would just go, 'Jimmy, get me out of here,' and I'd just whisk her out, because people were all over her," Destri added.

Three days later Blondie broke their run of below-par London shows at the Chalk Farm Roundhouse, which your co-author Kris attended in the company of Motörhead's Lemmy – who was itching to meet Debbie. Introductions were duly made and mutual admiration established.

In 1978 the Roundhouse was already in need of the makeover it would receive just over a quarter of a century later, but it was still the funkiest venue in town, water-filled potholes near the rudimentary bar and all. It was packed and this time the equipment functioned perfectly, sparking an energised romp which many felt marked the turning point of Blondie's fortunes live. Debbie, in particular, rose to the occasion, taking the stage dressed in white with a tiny skirt and knee protectors. She was commanding, effervescent and communicative with the crowd, rather than dodging the yelps of "Get 'em off!"

This time reviews were mainly positive, praising Blondie's "vast potential" and "real stage presence". However, 1978 was still the year that crystallised their loathing of the mainstream UK press. Perhaps the pivotal event was a visit from a *Daily Mail* journalist who arrived to 'hang out' with the group.

As Nigel remarked, "What those bastards have done to Debbie is disgusting. She's been kicked in the face. There was this guy from the *Daily Mail*. He stayed with us for two fucking days. He was around before gig, after gig and we made ourselves available to him. He kept on saying what a great group piece he was gonna write. It was just three fucking paragraphs on how fucked up Debbie was without her make-up. I don't know what she'd do to him if she saw him now. That was the last straw as far as she's concerned. You can't trust these bastards. She was really straight and honest with him and look what he does."

The portrayal of Chris and Debbie's relationship also veered toward offensive. "They talk about Chris as some sort of Svengali, and Debbie as somebody who doesn't have brains enough to see through it. It hurts me to see my friends put down," said Jimmy.

"The press has always tried to write Debbie off by calling me her Svengali. It's just another snidely sexist attitude. We've always helped each other out. It's never been a manipulative-type situation," stated Chris.

"That's just sexist shit," agreed Deborah. "That's people not wanting to admit that a woman can be powerful without a man telling her what to do. We've always shared things equally, complemented each other, when it comes to making decisions and so on."

"I'm concerned about the racial issue, which is very heavy," asserted Stein. "It's heavy to me, for one thing, because I've always kept my Jewish name and there've been associations, colouring me as money-grubbing and stuff like that, and that's definitely related to the fact that I didn't change my name to an Anglo name back in 1974 when I was supposed to. Because the mentality that says you have to have that kind of name is definitely there in the rock establishment, just as the racism and sexism that exist everywhere else exist in rock'n'roll."

Blondie were also routinely tossed around by the British music press. If one weekly had been behind the first album then the second was panned, and it was the same with gig reviews – although *Sounds* resolutely stuck to its campaign of featuring the band (particularly Debbie) at every opportunity.

After six long months on the road, Blondie finally returned to New York three days after the British tour had wrapped up at the University of Kent on March 6. Although the gigging, promotion and – most crucially – the huge success of 'Denis' had raised the band's profile and brought them a steadily growing legion of fans, it all came at a price – they were exhausted and broke. "It meant you were in debt for $750,000, but I had a great time," said Clem, acknowledging the amount accrued from the terms of their contract with Peter Leeds and Chrysalis, offset expenses and advances.

Leeds had organised the punishing tour schedule that saw them bouncing back and forth between England and Australia, then England and Europe – made worse for Debbie by the promotional tour of Australia ahead of the first tranche of UK gigs. The band were on wages of $125 a week, operating with a minimal road crew, and any enquiries about how their tour income and record sales were impacting on their debt were evaded.

As Deborah reflected, "It didn't help that our manager told all the boys they could all be replaced. We're out on the road doing a world tour with two roadies, and he flies in and drops that bombshell."

Leeds had identified Debbie as the marketable element of the band and evidently believed treating the rest of the group as hired help served to keep them in line. This was particularly insulting to Chris, who had been the creative powerhouse behind Blondie since its inception. And Leeds, of course, had his own side to the story.

"All of the band was pissed because of the attention that was focused on Debbie," he claimed. "I had long talks with them – 'Don't you understand, she's the ticket?' None of them appreciated how second rate they were without her … She was the ticket."

Leeds sought to separate Debbie from the group, with another promotional tour aimed at securing airplay from stations nervous about broadcasting anything from the punk movement. "We were supposed to have a month off, then go do some stuff on the West Coast and start our next album," Deborah explains. "Everybody but me got a month off – I had to go out and do a promo tour all over the United States. I was flipped out 'cos I was really tired – but forced into doing this tour, which was really necessary at the time. So I did it; I made a compromise and I did it for two or three weeks. I was underweight and exhausted, so I put my foot down and directed my demands to the company: I said I would have Chris on the road with me, and no one else except one of the people from the record company as a liaison, and that's the only way that I would do it."

Once Debbie returned home with Chris, they were greeted by Leeds' latest managerial wheeze – T-shirts emblazoned with the legend, 'Blondie Is A Group'. If it had been devised as a genuine statement of unity, it was based on shaky logic: refuting the idea of separation between Debbie and the rest of the band by drawing attention to that very fact. Either way, the band hated it.

With Debbie and Chris back from their three-week round of meeting and greeting, it wasn't long before Leeds had the band back on the road for a short sequence of West Coast dates, beginning at the Starwood Club in Los Angeles on April 25. Four days earlier, '(I'm Always Touched By Your) Presence, Dear' had been issued as a single in the UK, where it reached number 10 despite the song having been available on *Plastic Letters* for over two months. This delighted Clem: "I put in a lot of work on that. It was a fitting swan song for Gary," the departed bassist who'd written the song.

While in Los Angeles Blondie hooked up with producer Mike Chapman, whom they had first encountered the previous year. "I went to the Whisky

A Go Go to see them in early 1977, and I couldn't believe what I saw," he recalled. "I was so knocked out with this band, I was dying of laughter – they were funny, they were intense, they were very, very much a part of what was brand new in music, so I saw them three nights in a row. I took my wife the second night, and she agreed they were incredible. I had Smokie over here at the time recording, and I was hanging out with the Smokies one night when the Blondies were in town, and we ran into Clem and Jimmy from Blondie one night. I told them I'd love to make records with them one day, if there was a chance, and they said they thought that would be a good idea."

"I think he'd have the right idea about what to do with us. I like working with Richard but I think, if we were going to continue making records, I don't know if I'd want to use the same producer continuously. It would be a different slant on things to work with Mike Chapman," reflected Clem. "Mike was a songwriter – I mean, he wrote [The Sweet's] 'Little Willy,' one of the most bubblegum songs of all time. He appreciated a lot of qualities that other people didn't really appreciate."

Australian-born Chapman had relocated to London in 1967 and, after a spell with psychedelic pop quartet Tangerine Peel, formed a songwriting partnership with Nicky Chinn, whom he met while working as a waiter at A-list nightspot Tramp. The duo got in touch with RAK Records supremo Mickie Most and were invited to his office, to show what they had. After rapidly passing on the first four songs Chinn-Chapman had played him, Most declared the fifth a hit. He was right – the song, 'Tom Tom Turnaround', made the UK Top Five for Australian popsters New World, initiating an unprecedented run of chart success for the 'Chinnichap' songwriting-production duo, which included hits for The Sweet, Mud, Suzi Quatro, The Arrows and Smokie. By 1975, with his relationship with Chinn deteriorating, Chapman had moved to Los Angeles where he continued to write and produce.

Given Chapman's mutual admiration society with Clem and Jimmy and his commercial track record, it was hardly surprising that, upon return to Los Angeles, Peter Leeds sought him out. "That's when Terry Ellis from Chrysalis, and their then manager … sent a little note over to me, which said that if there was ever any intention of changing producers – their current producer was Richard Gottehrer – that I would be the first person considered," Chapman recalled. "It all happened very quickly. I was in the dressing room and met Debbie, and next thing I knew, I was sent to New York to meet with Debbie and Chris, and they terrified me.

"They lived in a world I knew nothing about ... They were New York. I was LA. They thought I'd been sent to destroy their music," explained Chapman. "I sat down in this little hotel room in New York with the two of them, and Debbie didn't say a word. She just stared at me. It was three o'clock in the morning, and I said, 'I've come up here to talk about the possibility of producing you.' I didn't want to force myself on them, and Debbie was just sitting there going, 'Yeah, yeah, is that right?' Chris eventually said that they were sort of interested, but it was a really horrible atmosphere, and I didn't know what to say."

"We didn't know him," explained Debbie. "We only knew him by reputation." Fortunately, the frosty atmosphere slowly thawed as she and Chris played Mike some of their new material. "In the next half hour I heard one creative and beautiful song idea after another. The embryos of a musical masterpiece. My life with Blondie had begun. For better or worse."

The impact of early versions of 'Sunday Girl' and 'Heart Of Glass' left Mike Chapman too embarrassed to tell Chris and Debbie he had considered offering them 'Some Girls', a track he wrote with Nicky Chinn that would provide a hit for bubblegum fifties revivalists Racey in 1979. "The sort of success that Blondie requires has to come from within the group, from their songs, their attitude," he conceded. "I don't write Blondie-styled songs, and I wasn't gonna shove my songs down their throats."

Instead, Mike offered to help arrange the band's new songs with a view to potentially producing their third album. This proved acceptable and rehearsal sessions began shortly after. "At the first rehearsal, we worked on 'Heart Of Glass'," recounted Chapman. "This proved to be a blessing and a huge step forward in cementing our relationship. It was a great idea that needed to be put into the right shape to find a home on American radio playlists. Since both Debbie and Chris were intrigued by the current disco avalanche that was sweeping the country, we decided to go there with the arrangement. Walking down the street after rehearsal, Debbie caught up with me, sort of smiled and said, 'I really like what you did with "Heart Of Glass".' The ice had started to melt."

In June 1978, Blondie entered the Record Plant in New York to record what would become *Parallel Lines* with Mike Chapman. "On *Parallel Lines*, I was given the responsibility by Terry Ellis to put this band at the top of the charts," explained the producer. "He knew they could achieve that and I knew it, too, but I also knew that, given how they were when I began working with them, it might never happen. Terry said, 'Can you do it, Mike?' and I said, 'Yes, I can.' He said, 'OK, I'm going to leave you alone. You've got six months.' So I had to go in there and knock this band into shape."

Although the process would take just six weeks, the group were unprepared for Chapman's determination to run a tight ship. "They didn't know what had hit them. I basically went in there like Adolf Hitler and said, 'You are going to make a great record, and that means you're going to start playing better.'"

"Everybody was excited about working with Mike Chapman but nobody was prepared for it," said Chris. "Gottehrer is very relaxed and was interested in capturing inspired moments rather than personifying a performance or making a hybrid performance. Mike's theory is that if you can do something once, you can do it again better. He would make us do things over and over again until we got up to his standards. And nobody was prepared for that."

"He definitely drove us nuts at the beginning, because we weren't into stuff like that," declared Frank. "He was really into getting the timing right, even the guitar parts. I'd do it over and over to get it pretty precise. The basic tracks were always me, Clem and Nigel."

"I love their first LP; the arrangements and ideas were great, but it was badly put together," remarked Chapman. "Initially I was nervous because I didn't know if I could better record what they'd done before, but still keep it fresh. It was a hard album to make because nobody was used to the discipline I require when I make an album. In the past they'd record and it'd be, 'I guess that's OK.' It took lots of energy to get the tracks down and make them better than OK. I'm glad I did it."

"It probably was a bit tense at first," mused Clem. "But I think that was the idea – actually going professional. With Mike it was very intense. Our first two albums weren't done with the idea of making hit records; they were just playing, almost free-form. But then the idea with Mike was to make a hit album. *Parallel Lines* was the hardest we had yet worked on an album."

141

"Everybody was really concentrating, trying to make a good record," Deborah added. "Mike worked us really hard. I don't think Clem was ready for it. Gottehrer let him get away with murder, so to speak, but Mike was Mr Perfection. Clem was real surprised; he really worked on that record."

Although Chapman felt that Burke was "a gifted drummer but he was totally out of control," it was Nigel Harrison, experiencing his first taste of recording with Blondie, who initially took exception to the producer's exactitude. "Nigel Harrison and I got off on entirely the wrong foot. During the basic track recording of 'Heart Of Glass' I rode him so hard that he threatened to take me apart piece by piece if I didn't back off," confessed Mike.

"He drove us to insanity at times," explained Nigel, who gradually came to understand his attitude and admitted, "I could never understand what a record producer was meant to do until I met Chapman."

Equally, Jimmy Destri – initially so vexed by Chapman that he threw a $50,000 synthesizer at him – gradually came to see Mike's involvement as part of a generally positive vibe. "The first time we all had a strong belief that Blondie could work was just before *Parallel Lines*. We were changing producers, changing labels, money was being poured into us – people in the industry started to believe in Blondie. We'd had a couple of hits in England, and that gave us the belief that if we could do it there – we have the right producer now, and he was thinking the same thing. So it was an initial concentration on the part of Mike Chapman and us to break America."

Although the standards of musicianship on *Blondie* and *Plastic Letters* are inferior to that of *Parallel Lines*, it's inaccurate to simply credit Chapman and ignore the developments that had taken place within the band in the year since they entered Plaza Sound to record their last full-length set. Given that much of the bass guitar on *Plastic Letters* was supplied either by Chris – who had settled on guitar as his main instrument – or Frank – who'd hardly had time to acquaint himself with the material he was asked to record, having Nigel on board made a significant difference. Additionally, Infante had now been in the band for around a year, allowing him to find a space for his rhythm work within the overall framework. Blondie had improved technically before Chapman got to grips with their new material, itself containing some of the best songs the group would ever write.

"I was on the road with Blondie for six months, all around the world, before we recorded *Parallel Lines*, so musically we were real tight," Nigel Harrison asserted.

"I really love and respect [Chapman], but he has a crazy view of things and he still presents the whole picture as if we were a bunch of wild, out of control maniacs that he was roping into whatever," added Chris. "I saw *him* learning stuff as we were doing it. He did stuff with us that I'm sure he had never done before. I know he was inventing things as he went along."

Previously, Blondie's albums were afforded a sense of unity by Debbie's distinctive vocal style and little else. Although the group were known for Jimmy's fairground Farfisa and Clem's drum fills, for every song that confirmed any kind of signature sound there was one that did not. This was due in part to Chris' restless experimentalism and search for new sounds, but also because the songwriting was spread around the group. While both of these dynamics remained firmly in place on *Parallel Lines* (the bulk of the credits shared between Chris and Debbie, with Jimmy contributing two numbers and Frank and Nigel one each), one of Chapman's key contributions was a veneer of cohesion across a set that included some of Blondie's most radical material to date.

Built upon a funky disco foundation, 'Heart Of Glass' was the most obvious example of this sonic radicalism despite its long-time inclusion on the band's set list, having originally been written at Thompson Street back in 1975. "Chris always wanted to do disco songs. He's a Dadaist," declared Jimmy. "We're running through this new wave/I hate disco/punk rock scene, and Chris wants to do 'Disco Inferno' and 'Love To Love You Baby'. We used to do 'Heart Of Glass' to upset people. It was his idea to bring it back, but as a funky song."

"We would like to combine a certain degree of experimentation with mass appeal, like that Donna Summer song, 'I Feel Love'," explained Chris. "It was a big hit and the thing to me is very experimental and was probably a real chancy thing for them to put out, not knowing that everybody would accept something that was completely electronic like that."

"When we did it, it wasn't cool in our social set to play disco, but we did it because we wanted to be uncool," said Debbie. "It was based around a Roland Rhythm Machine and the backing took over 10 hours to get down. We spent three hours just getting the bass drum. It was the hardest song to do on the album and took us the longest in studio hours."

When Chris and Jimmy had returned from one of their 47th Street shopping trips clutching the newly-introduced Roland CR-78 drum machine, they were thinking more of exploring Kraftwerk terrain, especially as the machine also boasted a trigger-pulse mechanism which could be hooked up to a synthesizer. Embracing such new technologies created specific obstacles, such as how to manually achieve a mechanically syncopated drumbeat.

"The original arrangement of 'Heart Of Glass' – as on the Betrock demos – had doubles on the hi-hat cymbals, a more straight-ahead disco beat," recalls Chris. "When we recorded it for *Parallel Lines* we were really into Kraftwerk, and we wanted to make it more electronic. We weren't thinking disco as we were doing it; we thought it was more electro-European." It required getting the most organic of drummers to play in a wholly synthetic manner. "Clem had this attitude that he was Keith Moon and just wanted to play every drum all of the time. My first challenge was to get him to play in time. It was a real challenge to convince them that the early demo of 'Heart Of Glass' was out of tune and out of time."

"Clem used to have a heart attack and be forced to play it. It was so funny, him having to sit there and play 'dugga-dugga-dugga'. But it worked! Because it was so hokey and so disgusting that it really wasn't a disco record," chuckled Debbie.

"Jimmy had that Kraftwerk synthesizer, by that time, he had a cheap Roland synth," said Burke. "There's a weird 6/8 [time signature] skip in the middle – that was Mike's idea."

"It took us maybe four or five days and it's all done manually," remembers Chris. "It's all completely pieced together. The bass drum took three hours. All those guitar parts took, you know, four hours just going 'digga-digga-digga-digga'. Because every 16th note was in time with the rhythm machine. That was the foundation of the whole thing … The first thing that was on the track was the little rhythm machine that you hear in the beginning, and the synthesizer just playing 'bugga-bugga-bugga-bugga'. Everything else was built on top of that. It was punched in, you know, and stuff. But everything is in real time. There's no looping. There's no anything. So every time you hear something it's the only time it's there."

Deborah's vocals were added last. The song's title would give rise to the notion that the song was somehow based on the strangely cerebral 1976 Herzog film of the same name. "I came in with the 'heart of glass' phrase and that was one of the last things of the lyrics," explained Chris. "And I really wasn't aware of the film at all at that point."

Written entirely by Chris, the ethereal incandescence of 'Fade Away And Radiate' represents another departure from any supposed Blondie template. "'Fade Away And Radiate' had been lying around since the first album," he revealed. "We used to do the exact same arrangement, except I did a modified version of the solo. [Prog-rock heavyweight] Robert Fripp [who had recently recorded 'Heroes' with Bowie] came up to us at the Palladium in New York, one of the first times we played there, and said he liked us. We hit it off and he ended up putting his guitar licks on the song. We had it all finished, but we were so excited to have him do it."

In addition to Fripp's glacial guitar contributions, the song features portentous electronica and drums, its intense-but-delicate vocal indicating how Debbie had gained strength and honed her technique. "It was difficult for me," she explained at the time. "The first two albums, with Richard, I would do three and four major vocals in a day, and all the harmony parts and back-ups. I would never do more than three takes on a lead vocal. I would try to go through the whole song, not just verse by verse. With Mike it's much more careful, and I'm much more discerning about it myself. Now I usually do two leads in a day, and sometimes a few harmony parts. When you sing, you go for the timing, the phrasing. You go for the note, for correctness. And then you have to go for the attitude. So there's three things you have to get all at once. The note-for-note things I take for granted, because either you hit it or you don't, and if you don't you just do it over. But the most important thing is the attitude. Sometimes if you put a lot of feeling into a note, it's bent − and it doesn't matter, because it makes it."

Chris Stein's other solo songwriting credit on *Parallel Lines* is 'Sunday Girl', a slice of infectious pop that would subsequently top the UK chart. He also co-wrote the retro-futuristic 'Pretty Baby' with Debbie, who hit upon lyrics based loosely around her impressions of the young actress Brooke Shields (who had recently starred in a controversial film of the same name) at almost the last minute. "It's scary when it's getting time for you to sing and you don't have lyrics written. With 'Pretty Baby' I was saying, 'Oh God, what am I gonna write, what am I gonna write?' The night before I had to record the vocal I finally got an idea."

For Nigel the track should have been a sure-fire hit, although it was never released as a single: "I listen to songs like 'Pretty Baby' and it sounds to me like it's got all the ambience, and the magic of the first take. But it wasn't."

Lyrically based on her unpleasant experience of being pursued by a possessive ex-boyfriend, 'One Way Or Another' sees Debbie's growling vocal underpinned by Nigel's driving melody. "My original music for 'One Way Or Another' was this psychedelic, Ventures-like futuristic surf song gone wrong," he explained. "Jimmy really liked this piece of music, and we would play it while on the road. Then Debbie picked up on it; she came up with the 'getcha-getcha-getcha's. The ending, where it gets crazy, was Chapman's idea."

Aside from the moody and unsettling '11:59', Jimmy Destri teamed up with Chris and Debbie to write the anthemic 'Picture This' – the only time that the trio would collaborate on a song. "'Picture This' is basically my verse music, Chris' chorus music and Debbie's lyrics," said Jimmy. "We all had little pieces of one another's songs, just throwing in bits. I always write with the band in mind."

"I was so excited that in 'Picture This' I rhymed 'solid' with 'wallet'," teased Debbie. "I said, 'Wow. Things are happening now!'" The valedictory 'Just Go Away', which she also wrote, was chosen to close *Parallel Lines* with the same engaging cattiness that infused 'Rip Her To Shreds' with such street-level zest. "The lyrics, which were always third person transsexual anyway, are improving all the time," Deborah added. "I was always a Walter Mitty character and that whole romantic detachment is beginning to show in the songs."

Frank Infante's maiden contribution to the Blondie canon was the slight 'I Know But I Don't Know', which, the rhythm guitarist recalled, "Came out whole. I just sat down with a tape recorder and started to say words and then I started to sing them and play guitar. What does it all mean? It doesn't mean anything … You take whatever you want out of it."

Album opener 'Hanging On The Telephone' and the overdriven 'Will Anything Happen' were both penned by Jack Lee, latterly of Los Angeles power-pop trio The Nerves. "Jeff Pierce from the Gun Club was a fan of ours. He sent our manager a cassette of 'Hanging On The Telephone' by The Nerves, Jack Lee's band," recounted Deborah. "We were playing it in the back of a taxicab in Tokyo, and the taxi driver started tapping his hand on the steering wheel. When we came back to the US, we found that The Nerves weren't together any more and we said, 'Gee, we should record this.'"

Added Frank, "He just came down to the studio in a taxi, and he had those two songs – I haven't heard anything since, but I don't think that he has any complaints."

The only conventionally sourced cover version on the album was an upbeat interpretation of Buddy Holly's 1957 cut 'I'm Gonna Love You Too', which had surprisingly failed to chart when originally issued as a single on Coral Records.

"The end of that album was the whole group sleeping on the floor of the Record Plant at about six o'clock in the morning, and waking up to see Mike and his engineer at the time, Peter Coleman, walking out of the room and bitching about having to carry these 24-track tapes back to LA," recalled Clem. "It was just like, 'Bye – We'll see ya.' We all went back to sleep on the floor, and Mike and Peter left."

After a week of mixing, Debbie was able to reflect on the finished article. "I think it's a firmer statement of our principles because what we've always done is a wide variety of pop music. *Parallel Lines* is a *better* Blondie. *Better* songs. *Better* playing. *Better* singing."

Chapman agreed, "That's what Blondie's all about … I didn't make a punk album or a new wave album with Blondie. I made a pop album. If the radio stations would only forget this evil word 'punk'. It's modern rock'n'roll."

"The stigma of the word 'punk' is something that could not be absorbed into today's American culture as representing anything remotely positive," added Chris. "And that's one of the things that held Blondie back for so long."

Named after an unfinished set of lyrics Debbie had composed ("about communication, characterisation, and the eventual meeting of different influences"), *Parallel Lines* emerged as a more accessible album than its predecessors, but was still wholly in keeping with the group's musical ethos. "What we want to do is to get as many people interested in Blondie as possible so we can show them what we really believe. Not exactly any means to an end, but we'll use as many hooks as possible to get an audience and then show them what we really want to do," Jimmy explained.

"The new album is very definable, normal stuff," said Chris. "We had a few ideas that Chapman didn't want to go on … spacier parts that were left off the final mix. Everyone asks if we're selling out by going commercial, but I view it as a challenge to try to produce something that has mass appeal.

To me it's more a challenge to try and write hit songs than to do something esoteric."

"I happen to think that *Parallel Lines* is a safe album in some ways, and because of that a lot of people are going to accuse us of selling out even more. I think that the album will have more mass appeal, but I still don't think we have abandoned our principles," asserted Deborah. "The only thing that might not be better about it is that it's not as adventurous in terms of our original stance, but maybe our next thing will be a further step in terms of adventure."

On the theme of mass appeal, Chris declared, "I'd like to be like a more real Bay City Rollers, because The Bay City Rollers are so appalling. They're all right, they make good music, but their image ... everybody knows they're not really clean-cut, they're a bunch of punks and run around like maniacs probably. They chase little girls and all that, everybody knows that. It'd be nice to be accessible to that many people. We aim at little kids, we're hopeful. Look what happened to the whole hippy generation, they're all tore up by Madison Avenue, they all got jobs, computer programmers and shit, these are all the same people who were running around being radical, right now they're all trying to buy real estate saying 'We're all part of the system now.' Which is in a sense what we're doing, we're all working in the system but we're trying to get our creative juices out."

However, the system – embodied in the form of Chrysalis Records – was initially less than enthusiastic about how Blondie released their creative juices. "*Parallel Lines* was rejected by our record company," revealed Debbie. "We had established ourselves as doing punk-pop with touches of salsa, meringue, mustard, whatever you could spread around liberally, and they got along with that. Then when we got to the third record, they rejected it. Turned it down – flat. They had a listening session with their executives and they said, 'No. You've got to do it over. Fix it.'"

Chapman intervened to persuade the company the album was indeed the disc full of hit singles it would prove to be. "Mike really had to bat for us with this record," said Deborah. As if to underline the alarming extent of their incomprehension, Chrysalis passed over 'Heart Of Glass', 'Sunday Girl' and 'Hanging On The Telephone' and opted to issue 'I'm Gonna Love You Too' to trail the album in the US – its logic being that the recent release of *The Buddy Holly Story*, starring Gary Busey in the title role, would trigger a Holly revival that never actually materialised on the streets. The single bombed. "I really don't think we have to dilute what Blondie is to crack America," mused Destri. "I think we just have to plan what singles we release over there, and continue as we are without changing."

In the UK, 'Picture This' was the first single lifted from *Parallel Lines*. Issued on August 12, it rose to number 12 in the chart, scoring the band another *Top Of The Pops* appearance.

While the band was in London, the Mirandy Gallery hosted an exhibition of Chris' photographic document of the group's first three years: *Blondie In Camera*. Kris Needs was there:

The event had been astutely leaked to their ever-swelling fan network, meaning hundreds of teenage boys and girls clamouring outside the venue, noses pressed against the glass as the elite press corps guzzle the free booze, occasionally giving the pictures a cursory glance. When Blondie are sighted, the horde scream. When Clem starts hurling 'blonde vinyl' copies of 'Picture This', they jostle and howl. The drummer is getting quite miffed, especially as it's like a Turkish bath in the small gallery. Meanwhile, Debbie is being shunted around from camera to camera, executive to executive. "Debbie, I'd like you to meet … One over here please … Can you purse your lips?" All while being bugged by tabloid journalists and their endless questions about having kids. From my vantage point at the far end with Chris, I suggest wheeling her around in a trolley, Supermarket Sweep-style. "Oh, don't give 'em that idea!" she wails. When we attempt to flee the joint by dashing through the baying mob to a waiting limo, fans leap on the car, paw at the windows and shriek. Not for the first time, The Beatles' Hard Day's Night is mentioned. This was the actual point where we agreed that Blondiemania had indeed arrived, in a fashion not seen since the Fab Four. The nation had a new pin-up and a fresh perfect pop outfit that could finally transcend the narrow confines of punk rock.

A complete contrast comes two days later when I'm invited to witness Blondie work up the new album's songs in a pokey rehearsal room in Victoria. When I arrive, Debbie is still away doing more interviews so the boys are practising, tonight focusing on '11:59' and 'Hanging On The Telephone'. The cursed phrase 'Blondie Is A Group' takes on new resonance; this lot are skin-tight, energised and having a ball. Debbie walks in wearing shades, says nothing and walks out again. She's shattered after another gruelling day of repetitive, anodyne questions, taking time to settle into her bunker sealed from the outside world where she can finally get on with the music. The relentless schedules have not eased for her since before the world tour. For all this hard graft she's being rewarded by mushrooming success, but still broke. By now, I can recognise when she's numbed by schedules. Sometimes I see trying to cheer her up as necessary, or else best leave something or someone else to snap her out of it. Tonight her mood is lightened by recounting a room-shaking Chris Stein fart waking her in the middle of the night. "It nearly blew me out the bed!" She starts giggling. Then Debbie perches on a stool and sings '11:59' like an angel. After hearing the song this way it becomes one of my favourite tracks on the album, that haunting refrain of "Today could be the end of me / It's 11:59 and I want to stay alive," ringing around my head. Why, what happens at midnight? It's as mysterious as any Shangri-Las song.

In retrospect, sitting in a little room as Blondie hone their 1978 set is once-in-a-lifetime stuff, just observing the group at work, passing ideas, laughing frequently (often at my expense). As a 'typical English fan' I'm asked to judge if Buddy Holly's 'I'm Gonna Love You Too' should make the set; two minutes later I gibber to the affirmative. But I'm still concerned about Debbie, who seems to be feeling the strain. We talk about her punishing daily schedule. I remark that she's only human. "I know, but sometimes I forget that myself." Over the coming weekend, Blondie polish their set on a Fulham sound stage, including encores of Iggy's 'Funtime' and T. Rex's 'Get It On'. It's the same place where I saw Mott The Hoople rehearse with Mick Ronson four years earlier, just before they split. Tonight, it sounds like a rebirth, Blondie bringing the tight work ethos drummed in by Chapman to their live set and the big stage.

The final bone of contention to be resolved ahead of *Parallel Lines'* release on September 8, 1978 was the sleeve. The final front image, which depicts a cheery band lined up behind an ashen-faced Debbie standing defiantly with hands on hips, had been rejected by the group but put forward by Peter Leeds. It underlined the feeling that Leeds viewed Blondie as his employees, adding to the list of collective grievances the band was now harbouring against him.

In July, while *Parallel Lines* was being prepared for release, Blondie set out on a support tour with fading sixties heavyweights The Kinks, enabling Clem to encounter one of his boyhood influences. "It was great touring with them, we were going down good, getting encores," he enthuses. "It was great meeting Ray Davies. He wanted to put Debbie in a movie.

"on't use the smiling shot" – Outtake from Roberta Bayley's *Parallel Lines* cover shoot. ROBERTA BAYLEY/REDFERNS

Chris sports one of 'those' t-shirts as he chats to Clem, 1978. ROBERTA BAYLEY/REDFERNS

Debbie on stage at Dingwalls in London, 1979. DENIS O REGAN/
GETTY IMAGES

Punk's greatest pin-up: Debbie in shorts and thigh-high
boots, fronting Blondie at King George's Hall in Blackburn on
February 23, 1978. KEVIN CUMMINS/GETTY IMAGES

oking with gas - Chris and Debbie fool around in their kitchen. ALLEN TANNENBAUM

wasn't like this with Mud!" – Debbie checks on producer Mike Chapman's pulse during the *Parallel Lines* sessions.
BERTA BAYLEY/REDFERNS

A cheap holiday? Frank and Debbie at the Berlin Wall, 1978. COURESTY CHRIS STEIN

The icon adorned by the image – running through new material at CBGBs. STEPHANIE CHERNIKOWSKI/GETTY IMAGES

w York royalty at the Studio 54 launch for Debbie's 1979 appearance on the cover of Andy Warhol's *Interview* magazine (L-R): rna Luft, Jerry Hall, Warhol, Debbie, Truman Capote, jewellry designer Paloma Picasso. ALLEN TANNENBAUM

home turf – Jimmy Destri captured mid set in Central Park.
3ERTA BAYLEY/REDFERNS

Bassist Nigel Harrison – An Englishman In New York.
ROBERTA BAYLEY/REDFERNS

The least likely band lays its golden eggs… Blondie with Chrysalis executives Terry Ellis and Arthur Cookson. ALLEN TANNENBAUM

Blondie pack out their modest hotel room in 1979. VIRGINIA TURBETT/REDFERNS

Smiling Frank 'The Freak' Infante rehearsing ahead of a US ur. ROBERTA BAYLEY/REDFERNS

The long hair and make-up may have been long gone, but Chris' devotion to Alice Cooper endured. ROBERTA BAYLEY/REDFERNS

at Loaf and Debbie compare stares during the 1980 filming of *Roadie*. UNITED ARTISTS/KOBAL COLLECTION

Ripping it to shreds – Debbie the iconic siren in 1977. SHEILA ROCK

Remember the *Preservation* albums? He wants to make a film of that and he wants Debbie to be in it. But I don't know if it'll happen." (It didn't.)

Three weeks later, the group travelled to Europe for a run of shows with The Buzzcocks that finished in Rotterdam the night before the album was due to hit the stores. The group arrived in London just as the weekly 'inkies' were passing judgement on the disc.

In *Melody Maker*, Harry Doherty opened up by observing that "Blondie's third album seems designed to cater for two distinct requirements: a) to satisfy the near-hysterical cries for the pure pop of the band's debut album; and b) to consolidate their popularity with the hard-rock audience that helped chart the second set, *Plastic Letters*." He went on to praise Chapman's production (despite expressing reservations about how he felt the producer restrained Debbie's vocals) and seemed particularly taken with 'Fade Away And Radiate', concluding, "Having subjected the album to intense scrutiny (i.e. I've had a tape for a couple of weeks and played it nightly), I'm of the opinion that the compromise between the first and second album is a healthy one and should ideally serve to confirm Blondie's importance in the present and future."

In *Sounds*, Sandy Robertson appeared to experience some kind of epiphany. "I just decided there is no such thing as Art Rock; all there are is different levels of commerciality," he wrote. Unlike Doherty, Robertson dismissed 'Fade Away' as "one moment of token experimentation", but managed to force out a more positive, "Still, the Blondie magic remains in evidence. That thin but captivating voice, the shuffling drum beat that resembles nothing so much as someone falling downstairs with a pile of suitcases, the punchy guitars."

On tour, the group discovered their European schedule had been changed from that agreed in New York. The issue came to a head when Chris telephoned Peter Leeds, who said he was too busy to tell Blondie of the changes. "He was still treating us like kids. He knew we weren't that dumb but he couldn't bring himself to treat us as equals," Stein stated. After Blondie's New York lawyer told the band it was written in their contract that they didn't have to pay Leeds' travelling expenses on tour, they made sure that this was so. "That tour was pretty sleazy. Our backdrops and rugs were stolen," recalls Chris. "Again, we never saw a cent."

Half a dozen gigs in England were bookended by sold-out shows at Hammersmith Odeon, the first of which gave Clem the opportunity to pay homage to Keith Moon, who had died two nights earlier. "I went downstairs in the hotel and all the British tabloids had the headline 'Keith Moon Is Dead', so that day became kind of a dream sequence for me. We played the Hammersmith Odeon and I wanted to get some gasoline and an axe to use on the drums and no one would give them to me. So I threw my whole drum kit in the audience, not wanting them back, because I wanted to sacrifice them for Keith. And the roadies went and got them back, which I was upset about. It was a real emotional time for me because he had meant so much to me."

Reviewing the Hammersmith gig, Sandy Robertson railed against what he perceived as Chapman's dilution of the group's sound: "An added bonus that comes with seeing Blondie live is that you get to hear just how fine their new songs really are when stripped of the emasculating Mike Chapman identikit production that robs the *Parallel Lines* album of any claims it may have had to rock authority. Stuff like '11.59' and 'Pretty Baby' stands right up there alongside the earlier efforts such as 'X Offender' and 'Kung Fu Girls'."

As the group had discovered on their previous visits, the UK music press was notoriously difficult to satisfy. As Chrysalis' publicity machine ensured more copy than ever before, Blondie found that they were compelled to justify what they were doing and why they were doing it.

"On the whole the English press has been very good to us; the music press," adds Debbie. "The legitimate press is another matter. Straight people. They're kind of strange. I mean, it's sort of exciting to actually get into the equivalent of the *Daily News* or the *Enquirer*. But the music press has been really good to us, even though some of them are cunts."

"The music press is good but you get so wrapped up in it you start thinking it's for real, but it's all just a fucking big cosmic joke and they know it," Chris elaborated. "But you get here and everybody starts reading the papers every day. In America no one knocks themselves out to get the papers ... I don't think the English press is gonna affect what happens to Blondie one way or the other, except for the fact that they affect the fans. Lenny Kaye said the English press had affected Television and were instrumental in their break-up. I certainly don't think they could have that much effect on us. It's constructive, because I think we have to go into a different direction from just being a plain old pop band myself, and I think people telling you that is good."

"We're more than just a plain old pop band. I think we have more idea what we're doing," asserted Clem. "All this stuff for me is like I'm totally living out my ideal. My utopia is *this*, believe it or not. All my dreams come true is actually all this so it really makes me feel good to see people writing reviews about us, to actually say, 'Well, the drummer played off beat there,' or, 'Debbie's hair was out of place that night.' That makes me feel so great that they actually take notice. It really makes me feel that we've achieved something if they can actually take the time out to write about this and that."

Accepting that some of the ambivalent reviews for *Parallel Lines* were indicative of the band in a transitional state, Debbie observed, "Now we're sort of at an in-between stage, commercially and artistically. We're at a stage where we are what we are, and we've been clearly defined, and there is a market for us, right? So we're taking steps in our direction, you know. We're moving on, we're doing things, but we're doing things that people can identify. We're not taking a total turn from what we've been classified as. But, like, the next things that we do, we could very well do a total turnaround."

By now the group were finding the media's emphasis on Deborah's looks truly tiresome. "Debbie gets slagged off just because she's a fucking idol and people look up to her," insists Chris. "That's why she gets slagged off 'cos they have to tear her down 'cos it's like obligatory, you know."

"I didn't create the situation," said Debbie. "My face seems to sell. I can't help that. When you come to watch a group play, you normally watch the vocalist, unless you have a mad infatuation for the drummer. You want to know what I really wish? I wish I got more money for it, that's what I wish. There are all these posters out, and there's only one of them that I get money from."

"But the thing is, there's two sides to it," remarked Jimmy. "I probably would never have had music published as early as I did if it wasn't for Debbie's charisma. Debbie's charisma is helping me get 'Picture This', a song I co-wrote, up into the charts. There's two sides to the coin – people ask isn't it really hard working with Debbie Harry, people never ask isn't it nice, isn't it good – which it is. We have a star, we're glad to have a star, but you must remember we would never have got as far if the representation within ourselves had been stifled – which it's never been. The thing that makes Blondie albums good – which they are – is the fact that they are six people."

"It was never really a nuisance," affirmed Clem. "If you're a drummer, you have to accept a lot of things. The drummer's only as good as the people he's working with. I needed Debbie, and I accepted that. I was never going to be successful on my own."

"Most of those bad reviews are based on some dumb sexuality," Chris asserted. "Debbie is the victim of a lot of reverse sexism ... And it's quite obvious to me that a lot of critics' attitudes are based on this 'How can she do this? How can she go out and expose herself to all these men?'"

"Me getting all the attention may invite the charge of cheap sensationalism, but you've got to do things like that. I'm not that much of an art freak that I'm going to say 'No. No. My art, my art.' This is the business, it's business-art so you have to use everything you've got to your advantage. It would just be foolish for us to ignore it," said Deborah. "This funny thing is that at one time, according to the standards of the day, when we were an art-rock group everybody put us down and said we were a garage band because we were screwed up and funky. And when we got good, we got slick, we got some tight professional touches, and now people say we're not art-rock, we're just commercial crap."

In the end, the band took the view that the British press were often simply fulfilling a need to fill space, "Nigel, being English, explained this to me and it's such a simple thing – the fact that the press over there is a weekly thing, they have to constantly change their views to keep their readers interested," recalled Chris. "What I found, over there, is that whatever the one paper says the other's always gonna say the opposite."

Irrespective of anything that was being written, a sizeable proportion of the nation's youth had decided Blondie were for them. The English gigs had sold out some weeks in advance and the group were received with enthusiasm at times bordering on hysteria. While Chris could celebrate "venturing into the hinterlands of Britain as we lived out our fantasies of Beatle-mania", the upbeat mood was dampened by the deteriorating management situation. It must have been even worse than it looked as, when Kris Needs asked Debbie to look back on her 1978, she cited it as "the most disruptive transitional period for us":

Arriving in Manchester on the afternoon of September 14, I turn up at the Britannia Hotel, first finding Chris and Debbie's room, getting an update on the tour, before we join the rest of Blondie gathered in a room in their stage gear watching themselves on Top Of The Pops. An hour later the same six are sitting in a Manchester Free Trade Hall dressing room waiting for that 90 minutes which starts around nine. Debbie usually seems to start the day quiet and withdrawn, gradually loosening up towards the gig. In every city the kids have had their tickets for weeks, Debbie's face pouting from a thousand lapels every night. Manchester erupts as the group start their instrumental theme before Debbie appears, yells "Surf's Up!" and they're off with 'In The Sun', followed in rapid succession by 'X Offender' and songs from all three albums, energy levels stoked by the rabid crowd climbing on shoulders, throwing gifts ranging from sweets to the odd item of underwear. 'Fade Away' is the big set-piece, Clem and Jimmy starting the cliff-hanging intro with the lights down, until Debbie returns in mirrored gown and shades, sending blinding white light beams at the crowd to stunning effect. She drops the gown for the home stretch rock-out, which powers through 'Pretty Baby', 'Youth Nabbed As Sniper', 'I'm On E', 'One Way Or Another', 'A Shark In Jet's Clothing' (wherein the band are individually introduced) and 'Kung Fu Girls'.

The nightly pattern seems to be initial excitement at The Presence which gives way to pure, unbridled ecstasy as the lengthy set builds to its euphoric climax. Blondie stage invaders are hilarious, leaping up, kissing Debbie, raising arms in triumph then jumping back into the melee. She now expertly teases and stokes the fervour, touching out-stretched hands, dancing sporadically and high kicking with pillow-fight aggression. Meanwhile, Clem Burke's head-shaking drum acrobatics leave little doubt as to who's the natural successor to the recently deceased Keith Moon. 'Denis' brings the house down, while tonight's encores are 'Rip Her To Shreds', 'Attack Of The Giant Ants' (with on-the-road fan Eddie Duggan unable to make a scheduled appearance in an ant-suit because he can't get the head on), T. Rex's 'Get It On', and 'Jet Boy' for their New York roots. Unbelievably, Blondie aren't very happy afterwards, due to some equipment problems and a couple of goofs, but they're in a minority.

Then comes the getaway, when sheer survival becomes the uppermost concern. Outside, there's a relentless hollering chorus of "Blondieee … Debbieee" as several hundred teenage fans clamour around the Apollo's stage door, strangely reminiscent of an eerie swarm of bees. I stand next to Debbie in the small backstage entrance, waiting for the right moment to hop just a few feet onto the coach. Getting the nod from the tour manager who places himself as a human shield, Debbie pulls down her baseball cap, looks at me and smiles. "You ready? Here goes." It's just yards between door and coach but seems more as we run a gauntlet of grabbing hands, one whipping the cap off Debbie's head, much to her annoyance as it had her Jilted John badge on it. The three-minute drive to the Britannia Hotel seems accompanied by most of the crowd, banging on the coach, pulling at the door, always howling. Predictably, many simply race the coach back to the hotel and we have to do it all over again. I ask Debbie if it's like this every night. "Oh, last night was much worse!"

In the hotel bar, the touring party turn in after a swift night-cap, leaving Clem, Jimmy and me deciding to venture to Manchester's Russell Club to check out The Yachts, whose Stiff-released single Clem is a fan of. Their Farfisa-topped sixties-influenced power-pop sounds like a Debbie-less early Blondie. Jimmy is delighted, declaring, "He's got exactly the same model I have!"

Next morning sees a bleary-eyed journey to Birmingham, the in-coach listening including Siouxsie And The Banshees and Dave Edmunds. The Birmingham City Hall soundcheck sees one of those storm-in-a-teacup Blondie arguments, often seemingly there to release the pressure. An hour later it's like it never happened, but the conflicts can feel awkward for those not directly involved. Debbie's been given a yellow T-shirt with an ape on it by one of the stage-door autograph hunters, so tonight her colour is yellow; from mini and T-shirt to socks and tights. Confronting another sold-out crowd, Blondie are initially perplexed as to why they remain seated throughout the first part of their set. The group is obviously on form tonight and know it but, puzzlingly, the audience stay in their seats, nobody dancing, or even standing. Despite increasingly animated antics from the group, such as Debbie trying to turn 'Denis' into a chant of "Ali! Ali" in homage to that night's heavyweight bout between Muhammad Ali and Leon Spinks, watching from the wings it's not hard to notice concerned glances shooting between a group who thrive on audience feedback.

A sortie around the hall reveals a hefty squad of white-jacketed security men heavy-handedly enforcing signs in the foyer warning that the show will be stopped if anyone stands while the main act is on. The crowd is obviously straining at the leash, needing just one word or sign from their leaders, who are oblivious to these restrictions. A "Come on" from Frank and Debbie's beckoning wave during 'Youth Nabbed As Sniper' bursts the levee, the hall rising to its feet as one before rushing forward like a human tsunami. It's so sudden the bow-ties are caught unawares and powerless as the front of stage no-man's-land becomes a sea of outstretched hands and delirious upturned faces. After nearly an hour of being suppressed the crowd are simply going mental.

"That's better," smiles Debbie, *as the band kick into 'One Way Or Another' for a home stretch climaxing with riotous encores of 'Get it On' and 'Jet Boy', Clem striding through his drum kit to hurl his snare into the crowd, Nigel Harrison hitting himself painfully in the eye with his bass, Jimmy humping his keyboards and Chris actually basking in the phlegm raining down from the punks.*

Afterwards in the dressing room is a total contrast to last night, the euphoric band relieved they weren't the cause of a hall full of seat-bound arses. They got through with handicaps too: Debbie's voice was in a fragile state throughout ("I just had to maintain control"), while Nigel's bass-in-the-eye injury looked painful. "This gig tonight was really weird; you saw what happened. The audience was sitting down through the whole first half of the set and we didn't know it was because of the security," says Chris. *"Everybody said that it kept running through their minds that they'd read the press and thought we stunk! There was such a rush when everybody ran up to the front, it was like doing three gigs at once. Really amazing."*

"It surprised us 'cos we didn't think they were getting off on it. It was really weird. Scary," adds Debbie.

Meanwhile, the huge "Blondieee" chant enveloping the transformed hall continues out into New Street, where our police-escorted tour coach is forced to part a roadblock crowd of hundreds, Moses-style. Complete pandemonium erupts when Debbie appears at the coach door and lobs her bouquet out of a window.

Tonight's breakthrough confirmed again how Blondiemania has hit the UK, transcending punk, new wave or any genre; one of those wonderful occasions when a band knows, in a moment of stunning clarity, that it's cracked it and things will never be the same again. Although building all year, it took the craziness of September 1978's tour to demonstrate that, after two years of hard graft and harder knocks, they'd taken the UK on a bigger scale than they or anyone could have dreamed of. The world had a new superstar in the old-fashioned sense; an enigmatic, Monroe-style figure with attitude fronting a fervently innovative punk-pop group.

The Blondiemania phenomenon was clearly evident when the group arrived for a signing session at Our Price records on Kensington High Street. The unprecedented scenes of mass hysteria around the store provided Blondie with a surprise as cathartic as it was unexpected. "They expected maybe a few hundred people and two thousand people showed up at Kensington High Street; they had to block off the road and everything. Fantastic," beamed Debbie.

"That was kind of knowing you'd arrived, when that was going on," recounted Nigel, who temporarily found himself on the wrong side of the closing bus doors as Blondie fled the hysteria. "Because it wasn't fake – it wasn't a couple of hundred people, it was thousands of people."

"It's nice to go in a record store and create scenes in public because I've always tried to create scenes in public and Debbie has too," Chris asserted. "We always did outrageous things, so now we're doing it on a mass level."

Chapter Nine

You Always Pay

"In New York City there's a dog that lives in an alley with a lot of fleas and he gets more money for the tour than the band."

Chris Stein

In October 1978, Chris and Debbie returned home from a string of European gigs – concentrating on Germany, but also taking Blondie over the border into Switzerland and France – to resolve some nagging issues. First of all they moved home, taking over a penthouse on West 58th Street that had previously belonged to actress and singer Lillian Roth, a Paramount starlet during the thirties. "Everybody thinks we're millionaires but royalties take a long time to come through. When you come to New York you can see our spacious penthouse apartment ... The building is falling apart. Everybody keeps reading in the papers that we live in this luxury penthouse but it's just an old crummy apartment," declared Chris.

"You can see the peeling paint with the leaking roof and the mould on the walls," added Deborah. "But we love it, it's home."

"My uncle had to co-sign the lease," said Chris. "Then my mother took that over and then I couldn't get it back. The fucking agency wouldn't give it to me, of course, because I would've had to have lived there for two years. Which I didn't."

Exasperated by Peter Leeds' relentless tour schedules and minimal wage payments, Chris and Debbie had decided he had to go. The couple met with business manager Bert Padell and lawyer Marty Silfen, who advised them to renegotiate their contract. However, Leeds refused to relinquish control, leaving them no option but to instruct his business partner, Edward Massey, that there was no way that any working relationship could continue.

It soon became apparent that extracting the group from their manager's control was not going to be a cheap or easy process. After Padell and Silfen had unsuccessfully examined the contract between manager and band to see if the matter could be resolved, Chris observed, "It's horrendous. It's like all the stuff your old grandmother told you. Shep Gordon, a friend of ours, told us, 'You shouldn't spend all your money on a real expensive straitjacket,' which I think is a great truth of this business."

As negotiations ensued the band could do nothing except carry on playing gigs, while Chrysalis plucked singles from *Parallel Lines*. Issued at the end of October, 'Hanging On The Telephone' sold relatively poorly in the US but rose to number five in the UK chart. "Things take longer to catch on here," explained Debbie when asked about the band's failure to crack the domestic market. "Everything is really spread out and regional. I think the American people suffer from a lack of press. European press is very important. Here, television is what's important. Press makes more of an organised statement. The printed word is where it's at. Not some creep sitting on TV saying, 'Hi, there. Blah, blah, blah. Bye, there.' American culture [no] has definition because TV has no awareness. I think that the future hope of TV lies in video cassettes."

To address this lack of recognition, Blondie embarked on a three-week American tour with support from former New York Dolls frontman (and former lover of Debbie's) David Johansen. Irked by the legal hassles, Chris found it cathartic to be back on the road. "Being on stage is great," he declared. "What I don't like about touring is the rest of the day. You spend an hour having a good time, and you spend 22 hours sleeping or lazing about a bus. That's a real drag. I mean, you're never not tired on a tour. You're always tired because you always got to get up too early."

"Sometimes it's real tiring," agreed Debbie. "So we usually unwind after a show. A lot of times, the guys will go out, and they'll go to a discotheque or something like that. I don't really do that that much because I'm with

Chris. I think if I was on the road and single, I would definitely go out. You just can't go back to the room and sit there, especially in foreign countries. The TV goes off at an unreal hour, and it's boring. I read a lot when I'm on the road. That really saves me."

The tour, which finished in New Haven, Connecticut on November 16, banked around $2,000 per show for the band and saw them play to enthusiastic young crowds. "Our favourite audiences are those that applaud or dance. I like noisy crowds. I like them to yell. Whatever age. I don't care," remarked Deborah.

"I think the bulk of our audience is under 21," Clem added. "Jimmy got invitations to proms from teenage girls. We play to kids and they go crazy; they ask for autographs and everything. That's the way it should be. I think people intellectualise too much about rock'n'roll. It's fun to write about, but I don't think you should get too serious."

The New York Palladium concert on November 12 saw Blondie joined on stage by Robert Fripp who, in addition to adding his guitar flourishes to 'Fade Away And Radiate,' had become interested in contributing to Chris and Debbie's projected remake of Jean Luc Godard's cult 1965 science-fiction film, *Alphaville*. "It's contingent on three factors: the next Blondie album, and the tour to promote it; my solo album; and finding a producer," explained Fripp, who had screen-tested for the part of subverted secret agent Lemmy Caution. *Melody Maker* reported that the movie would be directed by Amos Poe, with Debbie taking the role of Caution's love interest, Natacha von Braun. Although both Chris and Debbie would continue to express interest in the project, *Alphaville* was never made.

"We blew it," Deborah admitted. "Chris and I started out with the idea to do a remake – we pursued it and got the rights from Godard, and we had characters lined up, and who was going to play what. But we didn't have any backing. Chris had done a whole lot of stills of how it was going to look … Fripp went to England and did an interview on it, and it just sort of blew it, in an odd way. I guess you shouldn't ever let anything out unless you're in production or something."

Fripp had also planned to feature Debbie as a guest vocalist on his debut solo album, *Exposure*, but this similarly came to nothing when Chrysalis refused her permission to contribute. "Our record company won't let us do anything with anybody, especially me," Debbie complained. "It's such a fucking drag."

161

More positively, 1979 rolled in with 'Heart Of Glass' released as a single on both sides of the Atlantic. With the aid of a video shot after the seven-inch had been issued, the song would surpass the popularity of 'Denis', hitting the top of the UK chart on February 3 and staying there for three weeks. This success took the band as a whole, and Clem in particular, by surprise, "'Heart Of Glass' was buried in *Parallel Lines* – we never thought of it as a single,' he explained. "We thought it was too weird with the sequencing and the drum machine at the beginning … We never really knew what was going to be a hit."

For British audiences, 'Heart Of Glass' was part of a post-punk *zeitgeist* that would see bands with their roots in the punk scene transcend their basic musical template and incorporate diverse elements into a palate of sonic experimentation. By the year's end, The Clash's *London Calling*, The Slits' *Cut*, The Gang Of Four's *Entertainment!* and *Y* by The Pop Group would all apply punk's unfettered energy to various forms of black music. At the populist end of the spectrum, The Police were already peddling an accessible line in sanitised cod-reggae, while a more valid chart phenomenon would emerge in the summer as The Specials kick-started the whole 2-Tone movement with 'Gangsters'.

"I am really excited about the 2-Tone band thing because that is really saying something," Chris later enthused. "It's great seeing black and white kids on stage together. In America blacks have contributed so much to our culture and they're still treated as second class citizens. I hate that racist shit. And [in the UK] the battle between mods and skins and punks is just stupid. It's missing the point that there is a common enemy, the greedy power-mad politicians and the fat bastard businessmen who sap our strength and steal our art."

In contrast, the US was polarised by disco. Whereas New York throbbed to a million sequenced beats while hip hop gestated in the streets, much of the American interior seemed less receptive. This extended as far as an anti-disco movement that culminated in 90,000 rock fundamentalists gathering at a Chicago baseball field to witness the detonation of a crate filled with disco records. Although the event was subsequently criticised as "a mass exercise in racism and homophobia, reminiscent of Nazi book-burnings", the truth is that it had more in common with *The Dukes Of Hazzard* than it did the *Säuberung* of 1933 – on being blown up the crate of records set fire to the field, which triggered a pitch invasion by hundreds of stoned yahoos, who wrecked the baseball equipment as the demonstration organisers fled in a jeep.

Irrespective of its comical aspect the disco backlash presented a genuine issue to Blondie, who were keen to score a US hit but unwilling to restrain their creativity. "We planned to release 'Heart Of Glass' as a single, but we wanted to hold it back, because we knew we were gonna get tagged with the disco thing," Chris revealed. "We didn't want to release it first from the album. The album was out six months before it came out."

"I thought it pretty funny," recounted Deborah. "People were furious. People were like, [hissing] 'Death to disco! How could you do that?'"

Perhaps surprisingly, given the resistance to disco and their poor commercial track record in the home market, Blondie's fears proved unfounded. 'Heart Of Glass' began to pick up airplay and sales, inching its way to number 84 on the *Billboard* Hot 100 by February 17, 1979, beginning a steady climb that would see the song top the chart by April 28. "We were in Italy when we found that it was number one in America and we felt so fucking vindicated and so cool, we were dancing around and popping champagne," beamed Jimmy.

With no national radio and little in the way of a countrywide music press, television was a key factor in the song's success, with the video and performances on NBC's *Merv Griffin Show* and the syndicated *Mike Douglas Show* bringing the band to nationwide attention for the first time. The importance of the visual media was not lost on the graphically inclined Chris, who would be instrumental in Blondie emerging as one of the pioneering groups of the video age.

As is often the case, reaching the mainstream required a degree of compromise – in this instance, the wholly uncontroversial lyrics were censored so as not to shock even the most easily offended. "They took 'pain in the ass' out of some versions of 'Heart Of Glass' for the radio," recalled Debbie. "But there was always a version available that said 'pain in the ass'. There was just a single version that didn't. That was good because we could put stickers on the album that said, 'Contains the uncensored lyric.'

"Our record company didn't see any hit singles on *Parallel Lines* at the time," added Clem. "Then 'Heart Of Glass' became a hit, and the album went back up the charts. It took around 35 weeks to get into the Top 10. Until The Go-Go's, we were the band to take the longest to get an album into the Top 10. *Parallel Lines* is a classic album. I think when people think of Blondie they think of *Parallel Lines*, 'Heart Of Glass.'"

Even before 'Heart Of Glass' went global, topping the charts in eight countries and making the Top 10 in several more, Debbie's profile had risen sufficiently for her to receive film scripts from directors and producers keen to capitalise on her evident cinematic potential. One of these was *Union City*, a psychological thriller set in the thirties, based on a story by mystery writer Cornell Woolrich and directed by New York filmmaker Marcus Reichert.

"Edward Lachman, who was the director of photography, met Debbie at a party and she said, 'I'd like to do a film sometime and I hear you're a good photographer,'" the film's producer, Graham Belin, explained. Debbie was offered the role of Lillian, the apparently timid wife of an obsessive accountant named Harlan played by TV character actor Dennis Lipscomb. "I play a very traditional kind of housewife who likes to keep the place looking nice," she stated. "Originally, she wanted her husband and she works at it. She always cooks his dinner and does his laundry and makes the house look nice and everything, but he goes down Tatty's bar all the time and gets loaded. And he gets crazy. He gets nuts. And in those days nobody went to psychiatrists, nobody knew anything, especially girls."

One of the main aspects that appealed to Debbie was how the character of Lillian represented a complete departure from her public persona. "I don't want to make a film based on music. I want a script that will establish me as an actress. Being a singer in a movie won't do it," she asserted. "That's why I did it. I wanted a part that wouldn't put me under the microscope."

It called for her to wear a brown wig quite close to her natural hair colour for most of the film, something that came as a shock to many who were expecting a character more consistent with her media image. "*Union City* was non-union, and it was a real low-budget production – nobody had a dressing room or anything like that," she recounted.

"She was unpretentious – she didn't lord it over us because 'Heart Of Glass' had just broken,' remembered Belin. "She was professional about everything, which is very unusual for major music stars. Working with her was a joy. Her abilities and potential as an actress are both great. She needs work, but for film she's fantastic because her face is so photogenic, and she's just herself in front of the camera. I think if she works with a more experienced director he'll bring her out even more."

Although her unexpected performance would garner critical praise, Debbie found that her creative courage was a double-edged sword. "They took it to distributors and everyone went 'Ah, Debbie Harry movie,' and they expected this big glamour thing, but it's very low-key and Debbie's role is just a role, plus it's this weird sort of underground movie," explained Chris, who supplied the film's jazz-inspired soundtrack.

"It's a strange little sleeper art film, not a picture that would get broad-ranging praise," added Deborah. "I think a lot of people were surprised that I made such a low-key film. I was criticised for not doing some big, splashy production, but, personally, I got very good reviews! I was shocked!"

Disappointed that *Union City* wasn't some kind of *Hard Day's Night* style vehicle for Deborah, distributors were reluctant to invest in the film. It was never given a general release in the UK and did not emerge in the USA and Canada until September 1980, several months after its premiere at Cannes. "Not that many people saw it," said Debbie. "The film business is a different world. The producers and directors don't want to take any chances. A film is a big project – there is a lot more money involved than on a record album. And a film takes three to five years to put together – to finance, to write, to produce, to publicise – so you can't just hire a 'name' on a whim. You've got to be absolutely sure the actor can handle it."

Some observers still conspired to miss the point. "Those two idiots who do film reviews, Fric and Frac [probably Siskel and Ebert], came on and said, 'Well, we didn't think Deborah Harry demonstrated the energy she's known for on stage.' I suppose she should have leaped into this thirties kitchen with a microphone," groaned Chris.

"I was being directed," continued Debbie. "That's the important thing. I was someone else's creation, not my own."

After Debbie and Chris completed work on *Union City*, it was planned for Blondie to return to the studio with Mike Chapman to begin work on their fourth album. However, the band's management situation remained uncertain and negotiations between themselves, Peter Leeds, Marty Silfen, Bert Padell, Chrysalis' Terry Ellis (as mediator) and Leeds' legal representative, Mike Mayer, continued with no apparent resolution in sight.

"That whole period was ridiculous because we started to make the album in February, but we didn't actually get anything done," recalled Nigel Harrison. "We booked some studio time, which we cancelled at the last minute. That cost us ... $18,000 or something. We tried to get it together for three or four days. There were so many hassles going down with the management thing."

Instead, the group travelled to the West Coast to film performance spots for a variety of mainstream chat shows, before flying to Europe for a promotional tour aimed to coincide with 'Heart Of Glass' rising across the continent. "We were now the biggest pop stars in Europe, zooming around in limousines to the best restaurants, but meanwhile, we were totally zonked out and unable to eat, feeling like we were a hundred years old," said Debbie. "Everything seems to balance out. You always pay for what you get. And as you get to know what the price is, you get a better idea of how far you want to go and how much you want to pay."

The promotional jaunt paid off. In addition to unprecedented sales for 'Heart Of Glass', when 'Sunday Girl' was released in April the single made the Top 20 in eight European countries, as well as topping the chart in Australia. Assisted by a French language version on the 12-inch, it provided the band with their second British number one but, despite the label's efforts, failed to chart in the US.

"The way they merchandised and marketed me had a very unthreatening tonality," Deborah observed. "Chrysalis wanted desperately to get Blondie records on the radio in the States and punk was completely *verboten*. Everybody viewed it as being threatening and dangerous, sick and bad. So they really made an effort to make me appear somewhat palatable."

"We've simply been too busy elsewhere to really start working the States," explained Chris. "And then our previous promotion company didn't help. First there was that 'Wouldn't you like to rip her to shreds?' ad campaign which was sexually exploitative to say the least and exploitation is our subject matter, not our trip. Then the 'Blondie Is A Group' number which was a defensive campaign. Anybody who knows our music knows we're a group and whoever cares about the rest will just pick up whatever they want anyway."

"We're sort of tottering on the edge of this pop thing, that's totally legitimate and commercial, and something that's totally suspicious," expounded Debbie. "That's the line we walk and that's the image we have.

The odd thing that happens is we have this number one hit all over the world. The really radical kids reject us because we're too smooth and then the people that are too smooth look at us in horror and think that we represent radicals."

"The hard part about success is that all these people that you like turn against you," added Chris. "Here's the band. They starve. You have no money. You sign bad deals, sign your life away. You spend all your time and unearned money getting out of the bad deals. Then all the people you respect turn around and say, 'You sold out. You suck. Well, fuck you.'"

With studio time booked for May and few gigs on the horizon, the band was becoming a little tired of all the promotion. "I suppose I'm just going to have to get used to this," grumbled Frank. "I really miss playing live, that's what it's all about for me. I can't remember when we last did a live show. And after this we do two weeks' TV promotion and then back to New York to start work on the new album."

While Jimmy occupied himself at Max's and producing a group called The Student Teachers, Clem kept busy by taking on session work with bassist Phil Chen. Meanwhile, Chris and Debbie blew off steam by appearing on *TV Party*, a cable access TV show hosted by writer and Warhol associate Glenn O'Brien. Broadcasting from a small studio on 23rd Street, the anarchic show ran for four years between 1978 and 1982. Covering music, art and fashion, the series featured a wide range of guests and a notoriously spicy phone-in feature. Debbie sang and helped out behind the scenes, occasionally manning a camera, Warhol assistant and violinist Walter Steding led The TV Party Orchestra and The Patti Smith Group's Richard Sohl manned phones, while regular guests included David Byrne, Robert Fripp, The Clash, Nile Rodgers, The B-52's and local groups like DNA. When Blondie were away, Chris and Debbie sent in video reports.

"I guess it was punk TV," stated O'Brien. "We were anti-technique, anti-format, anti-establishment and anti-anti-establishment. We thrived on disaster." Chat-show heavyweight David Letterman declared, "*TV Party* is the greatest TV show anywhere, ever."

"The *TV Party* situation was just really great," enthused Chris. "It was kind of like going to our own club once a week. There was maybe a hundred or so people and we'd gather in this studio. I don't know who we were actually reaching but it was a lot of fun and enjoyable. The show was a great experiment."

"All these projects act as a valve and give us a lot of satisfaction," Debbie explained. "There are so many strong personalities within the band that you have to find a channel to release the rest of the energy, otherwise you get a lot of bickering."

In addition to becoming involved in broadcasting, Chris took his first steps into production, manning the desk for violinist and *TV Party* regular Walter Steding's eponymous debut album. "Producing him is great because there are no preconceptions whatsoever, and there are no references to music or anything else that I can think of except to jazz and that isn't deliberate," declares Chris. "It's sorta like psychedelic jazz. It has a good sense of humour, too, which appeals to me. It satisfies my desire for abstraction. Blondie's music is much more regimented and mapped out carefully."

Released on Marty Thau's Red Star label, the album also featured guitar contributions from Robert Fripp on a radical overhaul of 'Hound Dog' and provided Stein with yet another outlet for his creativity. "It's easier for me to create things now, because I feel like there is really an audience and people will look or listen to whatever I do. We always wanted Blondie to be a multimedia commune. It's not supposed to be just a band. Actually, we're gonna go into religion pretty soon," he grinned.

In April 1979, work on the album that would emerge as *Eat To The Beat* began with a series of rehearsals. "Everyone was a little nervous and that was good," insisted Mike Chapman. "Songs came in bits and pieces, but the bits and pieces were good ... This album was going to be a little more pop and a little less dark than *Parallel Lines*."

However, the producer's optimism was gradually eroded by the ongoing negotiations concerning Peter Leeds. "The meetings started at rehearsals," recalled Chapman. "Meetings with managers, with record company people, with agents, with tour managers, with accountants, with photographers, with journalists, with fashion designers, with gurus and various artistic vagabonds. They started eating away at my body and my brain. Every door I opened, I was face to face with another strange and pushy individual. Who were these people and why were they at my sessions?"

For Mike, it seemed that the music business was obstructing the business of making music. "We were looking for new management," confirmed Debbie. "That was very distracting, I'm sure he hated that."

Beset by constant interruptions, Chapman found it difficult to get the band to focus. This situation was exacerbated by the increased expectations that accompanied commercial success. "The record company wanted more of the same, but Blondie was not about that," asserted Deborah. "It's a building process, and all of our albums have continued to add new layers of development."

"There was a lot less pressure before, and we really thought we could go on living an innocent sort of lifestyle. But that's not very realistic. You can't go back to that. It's ridiculous. I think that's how a lot of kids are misled," mused Chris.

"It's easier on your conscience and it's easier on your sense of fair play, when you're just a low man on the totem pole," Debbie observes. "It's more genuine in terms of what rock'n'roll stands for. When you get up to this part it's so full of hypocrisy. The hustle is on just totally one thing. I suppose the bigger you get the worse it gets. I can't imagine what it'd be like to be The Who, or The Beatles or Stones. Oh my God! I can't imagine what those people live through."

To further complicate matters, Chris was dividing his time between Blondie and producing French leftfield disco duo Gilles Riberalles and Eric Weber (aka Casino Music) for ZE Records, only working with his own group when absolutely necessary. At the time ZE was the hippest label in town, started by Mothercare heir Michael Zilkha and French punk pioneer Michel Esteban to capture New York's thriving downtown post-punk scene. The label released August Darnell's productions, Suicide, The Contortions and what became known as the 'Mutant Disco' movement. Chris worked at Bob Blank's Blank Tapes studio, then the epicentre of the 'No Wave'/post-punk scene. Taking on this enormous workload set the tone for his next three years, when he would juggle the increasingly successful Blondie with outside productions, collaborations, his involvement with *TV Party* and, later, running his own record label.

Unsurprisingly, the stress and uncertainty began to take its toll on the six human beings that made up Blondie. There were arguments and internal divisions started to emerge.

"As the weeks went by and the meetings went on, we were beginning to submit to the pressure," remembered Mike Chapman, who also had to cope with a marital break-up during this period. "The group's attention was less focused on the music, and I was trying to squeeze the sessions in between negotiations. There seemed to be three different camps in the group: Debbie and Chris were – as always – together; Jimmy and Clem had formed an alliance; and Nigel and Frankie were a team. This was beginning to get really unhealthy."

As the negotiations and disputes persisted, the album slipped behind schedule, forcing Chapman – who had wanted to record the album nearer his home in Los Angeles – to relocate the sessions from The Power Station on West 53rd Street to Electric Lady Studios in Greenwich Village. "This was really disruptive," he added. "Having to break down all our equipment and console set-ups ate away at our time and caused even more disagreements. I was fighting with everyone."

To escape the increasingly combustible atmosphere engulfing Blondie in the studio, both band and producer took to hanging out at Studio 54 – just a short walk from The Power Station on West 54th Street. In addition to being the epicentre of New York's burgeoning disco scene, Studio 54 was where celebrities mixed with the ultra-hip unknown to indulge in lines of white-powdered decadence.

"It had this sense of danger. It was private and exclusive in a weird way because nobody really knew or cared about it," Deborah explained. "And yet all these people were being as reckless as they could. People were exotic in their dress. People don't really even dress that way any more – having a sense of costume and personal style. I don't mean just going out and buying stuff off the rack that's glittery."

Throughout the seventies, New York had three main underground musical movements gestating within its city limits: punk rock downtown, disco and, later, hip hop in the South Bronx. While the scene attracted by the soiled glamour of The New York Dolls bustled at the Mercer, nearby clubs like the Gallery shaped modern DJ-ing, clubbing and 12-inch remix culture – a world apart from the crass commercialisation which swept the globe after *Saturday Night Fever*.

Discos initially appeared at midtown New York niteries such as Le Club (founded in 1961), Arthur, Ondine and many subsequent nightspots, including early super-club The Cheetah on Broadway and Third Street. While operating in midtown, discos were the domain of the elite, the rich and the celebrated. When Salvation opened in the former Café Society space on Sheridan Square, they invaded the downtown area as DJ Francis Grasso became the first to turn playing records into an art form, playing mainly black music. In 1969, Grasso moved to Sanctuary, the world's first openly gay disco. In a former German Baptist church on 43rd between Ninth and

10th Avenues, he used an early predecessor of the modern DJ set-up to play anything from James Brown and Motown to The Doors, Osibisa and, as the club's anthem, African drummer Olatunji's 'Jin-go-lo-ba'.

The roots of modern dance music can also be traced back to 1970, at David Mancuso's hedonistic but musically devotional all-night loft parties at his Broadway abode. These were intimate invite-only affairs which numbered Larry Levan and Frankie Knuckles among their acid-guzzling crowd, before both started playing records at the infamous Continental Baths on the Upper West Side. In 1973, Nicky Siano's Gallery appeared on 22nd Street; like a drug-fuelled younger brother to Mancuso's loft, it was closest to what would coalesce into the popular notion of 'the disco' later in the decade.

Until the mid-seventies, discos existed as a parallel New York underground movement to punk and the *avant garde*, but, as hit records were spawned from the enthusiasm of its flamboyant crowds, disco unleashed innovations such as Tom Moulton's remixing of existing tracks and 12-inch singles improving the sound quality of tunes, as with studio pioneer Walter Gibbons' sumptuous rework of Double Exposure's '10 Per Cent'. It started cross-pollinating with the city's other musical strains, slowly infiltrating the mainstream.

Disco originally attracted the black and gay demographics, but it became a worldwide phenomenon – largely thanks to *Saturday Night Fever*, which presented the world with a far different picture of how the movement started and operated by homing in on suburban Italian-American enclaves. Consequently, disco was much derided at the time but seems inestimably influential in hindsight – not least on Blondie.

By 1978, although New York's most exciting dance inferno was Larry Levan's Paradise Garage on King Street, its most famous celebrity magnet was Studio 54. It became notorious for co-owner Steve Rubell's ruthless door policy, which had even excluded Chic's Nile Rodgers – prompting him to write 'Le Freak' (or, as originally titled, 'Fuck You') in 1978. Blondie, however, were A-list enough to sail past the velvet rope – especially in the company of Andy Warhol. Inside, the former opera house was cavernously exotic, dominated by a huge hanging moon and coke spoon.

The venue had also provided the setting for a party thrown to celebrate the success of 'Heart Of Glass' by Warhol, who cited Debbie as his favourite pop star. Although she and Chris, in particular, had orbited the fringes of

Warhol's circle for more than a decade, it was only now that both parties got to know one another. Recalling his early impressions of Deborah, Warhol observed, "Blondie – Debbie – was sweet, her hair was fixed up and you'd never believe she's in her thirties – no wrinkles and so pretty. She spends all her money on make-up. She must not have been pretty all these years, though, or I would have noticed her. She must have tried to look bad or something. But I guess some people look better, actually, when they get a little older. I didn't know what to call her. I guess I call her 'Debbie'. But when I introduce her, I call her 'Blondie'. But Blondie is the name of the whole group."

"In the seventies he and I became friends, or I was always on his invitation list at least," explained Deborah. "The thing is, he was a terrific listener, that was his genius, really. He just sucked it all in, and made a point of never saying too much. That's a skill."

Given Chris and Debbie's artistic leanings, it's hardly surprising that there was a natural connection between the couple and the artist who had been among their key cultural influences. "That's what Blondie came out of – we all had that influence. Chris and I came from an art background, and it's part of the way we think. There was also our association with Warhol, and Chris was very friendly with William Burroughs. Chris went to art school, and would either have become a photographer or a painter – and then the music evolved," said Debbie.

"In the truest sense of the word, pop music is very influenced by cartoon art. That brevity, that abbreviation, the knowledge that everyone understands. I'd say Andy was the Svengali of the downtown scene. He was very in touch with what was going on, and excited by it. He was very kind to Chris and myself, he invited us to a lot of different things. He was a social butterfly, that was part of his ritual."

In addition to socialising with the band at Studio 54, Warhol also invited them over to The Factory, by now in its third incarnation at 860 Broadway. "We were in the library and he had these big stuffed dogs. And you'd be there eating a baloney sandwich with Andy Warhol. But it's ironic that in the *Diaries*, he's almost trying to convince himself how well off he is. He's always dropping names as if he weren't sure of his elevated status," Jimmy remembered.

"The thing about Andy was that he always made parties or events a special thing. And when he died [in 1987], you sensed that the events became much less," added Clem. "You miss that now in New York. He was like a barometer, a godfather to the whole scene."

Debbie, of whom Warhol created a Marilyn-style portrait in 1980, found the artist's unique personality and detached manner thoroughly magnetic. "Andy was a great guy. He was an amazing listener. Sometimes people want to talk too much but you get more if you listen. He was incredibly casual about everything. I think the best thing he taught me was always to be open to new things, new music, new style, new bands, new technology and just go with it. Never get mired in the past and always accept new things whatever age you are," she recounted. "Had he lived, we possibly would have become better friends. I looked up to him tremendously. I thought he could do no wrong – he was wonderful, outstanding, a genius. But if there was a relationship between us, I don't think I really understood it. I guess he could count on me for being straight with him because I was too fractured in my own mind to possibly be devious with him, and he liked that."

Back in the studio, it quickly became evident that, while the group were assimilating new influences from the pounding beats that resonated around Studio 54, they were also soaking up the abundant drugs. "They found their way into the studio and presented us with yet another obstacle," Chapman opined. "The more drugs, the more fights. It was becoming a real mess. The meetings were still going on and now it had turned into, 'Just call us when you need us, Mike.' Hard to make a record under those circumstances."

"Drugs were an escapist thing," Deborah observed. "It just created an alternative universe. I don't think it produces a new kind of sensitivity; I think it actually dulls your sensations. It doesn't help you in the long run because of all the complications you have to deal with and it can kill you but it does alleviate. It's a form of medication."

It seemed that the sessions were teetering on the edge of collapse. Compelled to take the expensive option of working up songs in the studio, the band felt the pressure being cranked up yet another notch. "Blondie started out with uniqueness but as soon as it became commercial then it was a routine in a way. We couldn't really escape it. The demand for the repetition of that same product was ungodly in a way. But I think that's the problem with art and commerce really," remarked Debbie.

"On *Eat To The Beat*, some of the songs came out really good and some of them were just an afterthought, some of them became just filler," Chris insisted. "There was a big rush to get it out and then it didn't matter anyway because it all got tied up with legal things, so it's ironic."

Adopting a looser approach than he utilised for *Parallel Lines*, Chapman was delighted as the album finally started to take shape. "While we were making *Eat To The Beat* in New York, I said to Blondie that I felt they were something like the new Beatles, because they came up with these extraordinary ideas, all of which were different, and which produced so many hits," he recalled.

"We got better at what we did," added Deborah. "There was an advancement of technology and the different sounds we could bring in. Chris had a synthesizer that could talk! We were pretty open to experimentation."

The band responded to Chapman's more spontaneous method by pulling together a series of impressive tracks just at the moment it was absolutely necessary to do so. "'Dreaming' was recorded live," explained Jimmy. "'Living In The Real World', the song 'Eat To The Beat', the basic track for 'Slow Motion' – we did all that stuff live, it was great. Only 'Atomic' and one other song were done with a click-track. By *Eat To The Beat* Chapman had really sharpened us up."

"'Atomic' was supposed to be the last disco song. We said we'd do one more disco song and then that was it. 'Atomic', though, sounds like Duran Duran to me," added Clem.

"There was lots of guitar, and I was free to do what I wanted," continued Frank. "For me, they're so good, because they're all so different – 'Victor' was a good song, because I wrote it. The musical idea came from Russia, somehow. The theme there was a Russian thing. 'The Hardest Part' was a good song, too. 'Die Young, Stay Pretty' – Debbie came up with the concept."

"Jimmy came up with the idea of reviving 'Die Young, Stay Pretty', which was an old song of ours," clarified Chris. "We wanted to do a reggae song and that number had always been arranged that way. We thought 'The Hardest Part' might do something in the States as a single but one thing I've learned is that one never knows. So much of it has to do with politics, craziness. If hit records only concerned people's taste and not all these weird prejudices about what type of music it is, they would be a lot easier to pick."

Like 'Heart Of Glass', 'Atomic' was the most radical song on the album and was ultimately plucked to provide the disc's biggest hit single. Similarly adventurous was the thunderous 'Dreaming', which showcased the band's developing ability to create an expansive sound and also found its way onto a seven-inch.

"The reason why 'Dreaming' came out the way it did is because [Chapman] really gave me free rein and it was really a surprise," remembered Clem. "That take of 'Dreaming' was just me kind of blowing through the song. It's not like I expected that to be the take. I was consciously overplaying just for the sake of it because it was a run-through. I always say 'Dreaming' would have been a bigger hit had I not played like that. It was Top 40, but it was never a huge hit."

'Sound-A-Sleep' was equally left-field, drawing inspiration from the kind of gently crooned lullaby hits that had been a staple of pre-war radio. "It's supposed to be like regular old style traditional music," explained Chris. "I think maybe the next album is going to be big band hits of the thirties and forties. At the end of the show we play the track without the vocal. That tape is a rough tape we made while recording in the studio."

Whereas 'Slow Motion' took its cue from Motown, the sonic sheen that Chapman imparted to 'Die Young, Stay Pretty' can be viewed as one of the few occasions where his production works against a Blondie song. While the album version is a light slice of ersatz reggae that veers perilously close to the kind of cultural imperialism found on 10cc's 'Dreadlock Holiday', live it was an altogether more dub-wise experience.

"There's no doubt in my mind that a record producer's job is to be in total control of a recording session," asserted Chapman, "he not only has to take the rap at the end of the day for choosing the right or wrong songs, but he has to make sure that the arrangements on those songs are correct, that the atmosphere that's created on the record is right for the song, that the song is right for the image of the band. With Debbie and the rest of the people in Blondie, they leave everything to me – all they do is come up with these genius ideas, and then they give me the responsibility of putting them together."

"Mike Chapman actually inherited a lot of the efforts of what we did way back then," observed Craig Leon. "But I don't want to slight him, because in my opinion he is probably the greatest producer of the seventies pop era. And he really made Blondie into something commercial and worldwide when he got a hold of it."

Despite the sense of urgent innovation that makes *Eat To The Beat* both diverse and vibrant, there were limits to the levels of experimentation.

"Vocally, I wanted to do something different, so I tried inhaling helium which no one liked," revealed Debbie. Although she later observed that the disc may have been "too accessible", there was a general feeling of satisfaction and relief when the album was sent for final mixing in June.

"I considered this to be my album in a lot of ways. I'm all over the place on it, but not in a negative sense," declared Clem. "The songs are very up, and there are a lot of punk rock elements. That's our most rock'n'roll album. With a title like *Eat To The Beat*, it has to be."

"Even though America chose to pretty much ignore our first two albums, before picking up on *Parallel Lines* and the 'Heart Of Glass' single, in a way we're already at the crossroads of our career," Chris remarked. "*Eat To The Beat* is … the first one that the American public has been waiting for. Now, there really isn't another 'Heart Of Glass' amongst the tracks, but I honestly believe it to be our best effort and I guess it will enjoy mass appeal on the strength of us now having so many fans."

Exhausted by the problems that had extended the album sessions, Mike Chapman was keen to return to LA. Reflecting on the completion of a difficult job, he admitted to uncertainty as to what had been achieved. "It was hard to have a positive attitude when the project was finished. I wasn't at all sure what we had made. I was tired and I wanted to go home. I seem to remember all of us feeling that perhaps this was the end. Was this record good enough? Was this the record that the public was waiting for, or was it just the waste of seven sick minds?"

Jimmy, however, was far less equivocal: "If there's no Mike Chapman, there's no Jimmy Destri on the next album."

At the end of June 1979, Blondie set out on their now customary round of post-recording gigs. This time they accompanied the Dave Edmunds/ Nick Lowe vehicle Rockpile on a six-week US tour, which ended in Los Angeles on August 15. Relations between the two bands quickly became competitive largely due to the penchant of Jake Riviera, boss of Rockpile's label Stiff Records, for stirring things up. In order to pour oil on increasingly choppy waters, the imposing Mike Vosburg was sent along to quell the bickering – partner of Alice Cooper/Teddy Pendergrass manager Shep Gordon.

Gordon's involvement spoke volumes. During the tour, it was officially announced that Peter Leeds was now no longer connected with the band and that Gordon would assume the role with effect from August 1. This came as a huge relief to the group. "Shep Gordon has a knowledge of show business which, no matter what anybody says, is really what the record business is. And, we hope to use his vast knowledge and I think he hopes to use ours to reach a mutually happy medium – not a compromise," declared Chris.

After months of wrangling, Debbie was delighted. "We constantly had to fight to maintain what we, as a group, honestly felt that we were, but with our old management there was absolutely no simpatico in the relationship whatsoever," she asserted. "I'm the first to realise that certain images of the group have been shaped but perhaps in the coming year we'll have the opportunity to put new and more valid ones across. OK, so it might not be easy. But I don't think it could have ever come across before under our previous managerial set-up and, again, I'll be the first to admit that it was a very serious and important failure. It was really destructive in terms of projecting a long-term career."

Shep Gordon's career was intrinsically linked with that of Alice Cooper, whom he'd managed since 1969 and guided to fame and fortune. A sharp-witted New Yorker, he'd got a toe hold by becoming the West Coast agent for The Left Banke, who had a Top 10 hit with a cover of The Four Tops' 'Don't Walk Away Renee'.

While in LA, Shep encountered Janis Joplin and, through her, Jimi Hendrix – who'd been introduced to Alice and knew he was looking for a manager. Gordon jumped in and signed Alice Cooper (then a five-piece band, just like Marilyn Manson later) to his new company Alive Enterprises, overseeing their deal with Frank Zappa's Straight label. Zappa's manager, Herb Cohen, wanted Alice's publishing, but Gordon intervened and retained 50 per cent for his new client. He later admitted that he hadn't a clue what publishing was, but his instincts told him that, if Zappa and Cohen wanted it, it was obviously worth something. Shep Gordon and Alice Cooper never looked back.

Although he was already known to Debbie and Chris, Gordon was recruited by means of a recruitment process Nigel Harrison found particularly tiresome. "Very few groups have had to sit in a room while 36 managers try to sell you on why they're so wonderful," asserted the bassist.

"I don't trust any of these people; it's just a business, and I hate the business side of music. The first few weeks the whole band would go, 12 to 2, at our accountant's office. As the days went on just Clem and I went there, then I'd go there alone to talk to managers, 'cos no one wanted to know about it. We were making *Eat To The Beat*, and it just doesn't go with the creative process. Some of these guys are more show business than the groups themselves."

The downside of jettisoning Peter Leeds was that the settlement guaranteed their former manager 20 per cent of the gross on any future Blondie or Debbie Harry product originated at Chrysalis. "Even though financially we all sacrificed a lot... and I do mean a lot, it really wasn't worth all the hassles. You've just got to put it down to experience," affirmed Stein – though he was later forced to admit that the prospect was galling: "When you see yourself producing these huge sums for other people, it's hard sometimes not to feel bitter. I just can't cut off my emotions and not be upset."

Still, the resolution of their management hassles served to lighten the mood. The following month saw the release of *Eat To The Beat* which, although it stalled at number 17 in the US, would still go on to achieve platinum status. In Britain it rose to the top of the chart by mid–October, consolidating the group's status – and providing them with a springboard for further innovation.

Chapter Ten

Walking On Glass

"We're definitely not an underground group any more ..."

Clem Burke

With *Eat To The Beat* sitting proudly on top of the UK album chart, 'Dreaming' made its debut on the Top 40 at number seven before rising five places the following week – kept from the top spot by The Police's 'Message In A Bottle'. As the record slowly slid down the Top 10 over the next fortnight, Clem tempered his disappointment. "English audiences are notoriously fickle. They go off people after a while. It's been done before. We're so spoiled by having all those number ones ..."

In the US the single stalled at number 27, despite an irrepressible performance on NBC's *Saturday Night Live* which saw the band blast through both 'Dreaming' and 'Union City Blue'. (Two months later, Jimmy Destri would be back on the show with David Bowie.)

In November 1979, the group travelled to Austin, Texas to take part in the shooting of *Roadie*, where they played one of the bands for which the movie's eponymous hero – played by Meat Loaf – worked. In addition to featuring in a fight scene with a café full of dwarves, the band got to perform several songs, including a cover of the Johnny Cash standard 'Ring Of Fire'.

While Debbie and Chris had already amassed a fair amount of on-set experience, the rest of the band found the process of filmmaking less than exciting. "I think it's just the hanging around and the boredom, man. It just gets you pissed off. You get *real* irritable when you gotta sit around all day doing nothing," griped Frank. "When we played those first three songs, that was the best time I've had since we've been here. Like *playing,* actually *playing* without having to think about whether we're gonna have to do it again 20 million times, or trying to think about cameras and all that shit."

"We told them to get us six Space Invaders games, which I really didn't think would be that hard to do," added an equally bored Clem. "A couple of dirt bikes and some Space Invaders games. I'm surprised they didn't – especially because we have to be here every day."

The United Artists movie – which also featured Alice Cooper (like Blondie, managed by Shep Gordon), Roy Orbison and Hank Williams Jr. – received its Stateside release in June 1980 and pretty much sank without a trace. Around the same time there was some discussion about Deborah being cast as the seductive Princess Aura in Universal's big-budget remake of *Flash Gordon,* initially set to be directed by acclaimed filmmaker Nicolas Roeg. "I was really excited at the idea of Nic directing me," enthused Debbie. "But Nic and the producer, Dino De Laurentiis, had a falling out and Nic backed out of the project altogether. The next director [Mike Hodges] didn't want me. It was as simple as that. I would have done it with or without Nic."

As 'Dreaming' slid out of the British chart, Chrysalis sought to maintain sales momentum by releasing 'Union City Blue' on November 23. The single would peak at number 13 in mid-December, coinciding with the group's return to the UK for a major headlining tour. The tour was heralded by a return promotional visit to Our Price Records in Kensington where crowds brought the busy shopping thoroughfare to a standstill for the second time in just over a year. "I stuck my head out the upstairs window of the shop and the crowd cheered," recalled Deborah. "Then Jimmy stuck his head out the window and yelled, 'Do you wanna see her again?' Everybody went, '*Yeeeaaahhhh*!' So I stuck my head out the window again and another cheer went up. I was plucked."

After recording 'Dreaming' for the Christmas edition of *Top Of The Pops,* the tour started on December 26 in Bournemouth. As if to underline that the group were returning as stars to the country that first embraced them, Blondie's Glasgow Apollo show on New Year's Eve was broadcast live on

BBC's *The Old Grey Whistle Test*, where they were joined on stage by The Strathclyde Pipers for 'Sunday Girl'.

Despite their exalted status, the group had fought to play eight nights at the more intimate Hammersmith Odeon instead of one or two gigs at Wembley Arena, resulting in some of their best ever shows, as a relaxed Debbie interacted with the crowd in a party-like atmosphere, even handing beer to waiting fans before the Saturday matinee. Choreographed by their old associate Tony Ingrassia, now resident in Berlin, she described performing as "surreally effortless ... I would try to take the audience on Blondie escapades and emotional voyages, and this worked very well for me."

During the encores, Iggy made a surprise appearance for 'Funtime' while every show saw Robert Fripp reprising his role on Bowie's 'Heroes'. ("'Heroes' is one of those songs; Bowie's 'My Way', God, operatic," gasped Debbie.)

Going by what happened on the coach trip during Blondie's previous visit, co-author Kris wasn't even down on the timetable for an interview this time; there was just the Sunday afternoon of January 13 set aside for 'hanging out with Needs' – the afternoon of the final night of their Hammersmith Odeon stint.

This time, they were staying at the plush Carlton Towers in Knightsbridge, a far cry from the glorified bed-and-breakfast of that first trip. Although I'd spoken to Chris on the phone, I admit I had the odd qualm about seeing them for the first time in over a year after reading several tabloid reports which portrayed Debbie as a recluse, holed up in her hotel room eating nuts and melons. Maybe they'd changed? Maybe Debbie had become the peroxide recluse basking in fame, ensconced in her fortress, taking Concorde to the corner shop and bereft of spirit and enthusiasm as some reports would have you believe.

I had nothing to worry about – the day the papers said she was imprisoned by her fame, Debbie was out shopping in a wig and giggling at the story on the news-stands. It was three o'clock in the afternoon when I was summoned to Chris and Debbie's room from the foyer. They'd just got up, and the breakfast was being wheeled in as I arrived, finding Debbie hanging out of bed sporting the Day-Glo-striped mini-dress she wore on Blondie's recent Whistle Test appearance.

Her recently trimmed hair is tousled, face devoid of make-up and she looks in fine fettle. Chris sprawls on the bed next to her, barefoot and relaxed.

Of all the times I'd met Debbie, I'd never encountered her in such ebullient spirits, even bouncing up and down on the bed with a big grin across her face, dispensing a contagious flow of buffoonery and easy chatter, interspersed with discussing details like stage volume and the madness of the year they've had since we last met in late 1978. In short, she radiates, especially when she laughs, which is often.

While Debbie bounces on the bed, pours coffee and hops around the room, rarely in the same place for five minutes, Chris stays in the same position, a half-smile on his face as he expounds on the current tour and other issues of the moment. The couple seem very content despite their intensive daily work schedule, still demonstrating an intimacy and warmth which dispels any notions of arrogance or conceit. Their close bond was always what protected them from becoming victims to the madness and chaos that enveloped Blondie from the start.

We started talking, I turned on the cassette recorder and ended up with the longest interview I'd done with them, or anyone else at that point. The resultant feature ran to seven pages and was framed by Blondie's third Zigzag cover. It was no secret that Debbie hated interviews because she always got asked the same things. We just chatted and it flowed to the extent that I was compelled to excise some of our conversation from the finished piece for fear of litigation.

The mood was noticeably lighter because it was the first time they'd played the UK under new management. Previously, Debbie and Chris had often been seething about Peter Leeds. This time, they were able to enjoy the experience and appreciate the adulation and affection that greeted them throughout the trip.

"That's the reason we came," asserts Debbie. "We came here for our audience. It's inevitable that part of the game is to get the press but it's really silly, I wish that these people really had to do something off their own initiative, something creative so they could see what it's really like, because they're full of shit. Plain English, they're full of shit."

"I feel the same way," adds Chris. "We're not doing a show for the critics, especially this time around. We're doing it for the fans."

As usual, the quaint British custom of finding fault with Blondie was initiated by a couple of live reviews that criticised Deborah for moving around too little. "I move all over the place," she contests. "They must be fucking crazy! I sometimes think they don't even watch the show. I got one review from some girl up north, in one of the local papers and she said I had on a gold sequinned outfit and that we did less than an hour. I think she was home watching TV. She didn't see our show because we played for almost an hour and 45 minutes and I had on a green jumpsuit. They say I don't move around enough – they come in for one song, like I stand still in a couple of songs because it becomes redundant to keep doing the same thing. There's a limited number of moves that you can make that carry it off. I was standing stock still for 'Shayla'. What am I supposed to do? Run around during a ballad? Yeah, sure! I'll trot back and forth, run up and down those ramps and make it look realistic.

"I'm really surprised at a lot of things. I don't know, I don't think anybody really knows what the fuck is going on any more. I think everybody is so ditzed out and struggling so much just to survive that they can't be rational. I don't think anybody's very rational any more. Criticism means less and less and less to me, whereas now it should be meaning more and more. When I see something in a newspaper that tells me something about the music or lighting or things that are really important to me, I read 'em. But when it comes to slagging me off as some kind of she-bitch ... those aren't the reasons that I do what I do."

"I'm still happy with 75 per cent of the coverage," states Chris. "We expected a backlash for the album, so I guess it came later for the tour. I think the idea of a review is sexist crap because they can't tolerate the idea of a woman having any power. [To] put down Debbie based on her sexual stance is a bunch of bullshit, but if they want to put us down on a musical level, that's great. That's what I consider criticism."

"That's why I go on [BBC Radio 1 singles review show] Round Table," Debbie interjects. "Here I am, sort of on top of the heap in terms of a lot of new groups coming up and I've the opportunity to go on national radio and slag off the competition. I can destroy the competition verbally. God knows how much I could really do to somebody's career. But when I go on there I'm really cautious about listening to what things are and I evaluate different sections of the song and I give my review on that, because that's what I am, I'm a musician and I'm an artist and when I listen to something there's content to be evaluated rather than a social attitude. I really liked listening to The Pretenders' record and I heard some reggae I really liked. I don't remember all the songs that I had to listen to because there's quite a few, but I certainly try and treat people as I wanna be treated, and I certainly don't want everybody to like everything that I do, that Blondie does, because I think that's an impossibility."

Heedless of any sniping from the press pit, the four-week-long tour showcases the group at their best yet, as Ingrassia's choreography combines with Blondie's most assured performances to create an audiovisual feast. "We're a lot more confident now. I haven't been smoking or drinking before any of the shows," admits Stein.

"Me and Chris go on stage totally straight," Deborah confirms. "I don't do anything any more, I just go on totally fucking straight, and it's really cool. I really had a good time on stage on Friday. I took it for granted Friday was gonna be press night and I figured I'm not gonna get uptight about anything, because I wanna have a good time and I did, and I know that it showed. I think we got the audience up in a real way, God bless 'em – we weren't demanding of a reaction, they just did it, they responded. That was really cool ... I get more inspired because I've more control over what I'm doing now than ever before. I'm singing much better now."

Freed from management and legal hassles, the sextet found touring far less exacting than on previous trips to Europe. This is despite a schedule that sent them ping-ponging up and down Britain, returning to play their final Hammersmith shows after a two-night excursion to Paris. "This time is really one day after another. There's no pauses. We've days off but there's days of travelling and press when we're not doing shows. We're here only for two or three weeks total so everything's jam-packed in," explains Debbie.

"We're not making money on this trip. If we're lucky we'll break even," adds Chris.

"Even the last major tour here lost money, several thousand pounds," Deborah reveals. "So touring is definitely an outmoded way of making a living."

Even so, rather than taking the low-maintenance option and packing out Wembley Arena for a couple of nights, the band afford their fans a greater level of intimacy by sticking with smaller venues. "The promoter was begging us to do bigger gigs," says Deborah. "We had to go to war for that too, to do the gigs that we wanted to do ... I wouldn't mind playing Hammersmith Odeon for a week."

The only downside came in Edinburgh, when a member of the lighting crew named Eddie was badly burned when a flash pot prematurely detonated in his face. "It was awful," shudders Debbie.

"We got another man but the lights are about 50 per cent of what they were," explains Chris. "One of the worst things about this is disappointing people. The more successful you are there are a lot of people who have good

reason to wanna talk to you and get to know you, and you can't do it. I used to be able to hang around in the front and talk to the kids. Now you can't. Debbie used to hang out in the street if the weather was good.

"Doing the shows is great, and the money we do have is great. I can buy things like video cameras. We're able to equip ourselves now. I don't really think I'll go in for buying Rolls-Royces and that shit ... I'm a little disturbed by the commercialism of the whole thing. Just the way that Blondie is. I think now we're so successful we can reach people. We can still reach those kids maybe with a different message, something else.

"I've a feeling the next album may not come out for quite a while, because we can't do another album in the series of 'Blondie's Smash Hits'. It has to be something different. I don't know how it's going to be yet. The gap will be much longer than before though," he continues. "Next time we come back we'll do fucking stand-up gigs. We can come back and play four or five nights in every town in a small place, if we can get it together."

By now it was time for Debbie and Chris to get ready for the gig so I wandered off. As I said, the show was dynamite. Afterwards there was a party. Last thing I remember is Debbie and a visiting Joan Jett in the bathroom plastering my eyes with black stuff for Chris' video camera. He still mentions this footage today.

Or, in Chris Stein's own words:

My main memory of Needs and our association is reinforced by a little bit of video I shot of him many years ago. During a period in the late seventies-early Eighties, I dragged around the world a very primitive and bulky VHS video recorder; the battery was larger than many of today's high-end professional cameras, the camera was the size of a small suitcase. This segment of video is of Kris, Joan Jett and Debbie in a bathroom during a star-studded party that had been thrown for Blondie at a London hotel. It was attended by Mark Hamill, aka Luke Skywalker. In the clip Debbie is applying eye make-up to Joan and Kris. The three of them look fantastic in spite of my sarcastic complaining that his presence is 'lousing up the best shot in the movie'.

The final Hammersmith concert on January 22 provided a suitably triumphant climax to the tour. After support from Holly And The Italians and The Selecter, Blondie steamrollered through a powerhouse set filled with hits, fan favourites and well-chosen cover versions. As the sweat-soaked throng clambered over seats demanding more, the group returned to the stage without Clem, so Debbie took over on drums. "I just jumped on, but I wasn't very good," she laughed. "In Iran, they'd cut off your hands for playing like that."

As befitted a band who'd achieved a string of hit singles and developed a huge following capable of bringing city-centre traffic to a halt, the group flew home to New York via Concorde.

"It's a thrill," reported Debbie. "I think now it's become easier. Since we've had our new management everything's become a lot easier and a lot clearer. Everybody's becoming a lot more aware of what their responsibilities are. And everybody's much happier, I think. Much more relaxed."

While Blondie had been conquering the UK, Chrysalis tried to build on the American chart success of 'Heart Of Glass' by releasing 'The Hardest Part' as the second US single from *Eat To The Beat*. Not the most obvious choice, it made little impression on the *Billboard* Hot 100, only managing to reach number 84.

The label's legal department had also swung into action on behalf of its investment, preventing the release of a cover version of Ronnie And The Daytonas' 1964 hit 'Little GTO', recorded by Blondie under the pseudonym New York Blondes as a favour to KROQ DJ Rodney Bingenheimer.

"Rodney convinced Clem that we do backing on 'Little GTO', so we said, 'OK,' and went and did it. I did a guide vocal in one take to show Rodney the song … some of The Beach Boys and their wives were on that single too – the backing vocals are flawless," explains Debbie.

"We did it for Rodney so he could make a couple of bucks," adds Chris. "Needless to say it didn't come out. They pressed up about 300 with Rodney singing. Between him and Greg Shaw of Bomp! they got the damn thing released on Decca Records, with Debbie's vocal. When they did Chrysalis proceeded to sue them."

A more legitimate release emerged in January in the form of an *Eat To The Beat* 'video album' on Warner. Featuring staged performances of all 12 tracks from the original disc, the project broke new commercial ground. "The importance of the visual side of what we do is an automatic assumption on my part," asserted Deborah. "I've always noticed that the best groups were always very visual groups. That's a special thing: there's no place else except in rock'n'roll where that is represented – a 50/50 representation of visuals and sound."

Shot over a long weekend, the clips presented what Debbie described as "a very simple representation of a band's performance", with only the expansive promo video for 'Union City Blue' being in any way cinematic.

"We eventually went down to Union City and we have an aerial view with a helicopter and the whole bit way down there on the dock. It comes from across the river," recalled Nigel.

As an exercise in merchandising, the project was undermined by the prohibitive cost of pre-recorded videotapes at the time, but for Chrysalis – keenly aware of the impact the promotional video to 'Heart Of Glass' had made in breaking the band in the USA – it meant that there was a film available for any track on *Eat To The Beat* they might later choose to release as a single.

The next of these turned out to be 'Atomic' which, backed by 'Die Young, Stay Pretty', was issued in both the UK and US on February 7, 1980. The song thundered into the UK chart at number three; back home, its fusion of new wave and disco failed to emulate the success of 'Heart Of Glass', barely bruising the Top 40, despite a promo video where Debbie turned a black plastic bin liner into an iconic outfit while the group performed in a hastily constructed post-nuclear dancehall.

Undaunted, Chris remained committed to transcending musical boundaries. "One of my goals is to try to synthesize different kinds of music that'll bring people together," he declared. "I definitely see a return toward R'n'B and soul music. I think the fucking anti-disco movement is a bunch of bullshit with *very* heavy racist overtones. And if you'll remember correctly, back in the late sixties, all the great black music that people now accept as the best – The Supremes and The Four Tops and all that stuff – was considered sort of the same way that disco music is considered now."

As if to validate Chris' ethos, Blondie's next American single would combine elements of rock, disco and the nascent electronica subgenre, breaking new creative ground while providing the group with their biggest hit yet. Recorded at The Power Station back in August 1979, 'Call Me' was a collaboration between the group and Italian producer Giorgio Moroder who, along with lyricist Pete Bellotte, had shaped Donna Summer's sexy synthesized disco hits. "It's the theme song of a movie called *American Gigolo*," explained Chris. "It's a real hard rock song, not like disco. Giorgio was great. He wrote the song and Debbie wrote the lyrics. He listened to all our albums and put together the ultimate Blondie song."

"We went over to the hotel and he played us the movie on video and I just got my impressions of it and I tried to think of what it would be," Deborah recalled. "Giorgio's original idea was to call it 'Man Machine' because the man was just like the sex machine, and he had these lyrics he had written but he definitely wanted me to write something better."

"Debbie's lyrics are much more subtle than the ones he wrote," added Chris. "His thing was very direct like saying, 'I am a man and I go out and I fuck all the girls.' Debbie's lyrics are a lot more subtle and the movie in a way is not that blatant, it is sort of subtle."

"*American Gigolo* has some things that are really nice about it, it has a very great look," remarked Debbie. "The thing that I was really fascinated by when I saw it was the muted tones and hi-tech look of it, so that was the first verse about colours: 'Colour me your colour baby/ colour me your car.' It was like teasing too because the thing about the movie was that he was always, 'Call me! Call me if you want me to come to you.' You know, 'Cover me.' And it was like these little commands had this macho quality through his being a male hooker, you know that kind of demanding business. So it really fell in easy for me. I got real enthusiastic. The first verse came real fast and then the others were just there."

"[Moroder] had this basic synth track, Debbie had the vocal thing," said Frank. "I did the guitar part that goes 'duddle-a-dah, duddle-a-dah'. All of a sudden, the song took on a whole new thing."

"Frankie played some great stuff on it," added Clem. "'Call Me' was something that we really needed; it got us to the next level, and another number one."

In late February, 'Call Me' was released in different versions by three different US record companies – Polydor's movie soundtrack version, Chrysalis' seven- and 12-inch singles and also a Spanish version called 'Llamame', aimed at Latin territories but also released on 12-inch by top New York disco label Salsoul. This version exemplifies the way in which Blondie assimilated musical developments from the New York streets, adding them to their ever-changing sound palette. This was a two-way cultural exchange – no other white rock band was feted to the extent of appearing on the city's coolest disco imprint. "I've always equated our work with Bowie who's always changed his style," observed Chris. "All the great groups – The Beatles and the Stones – have changed their style. There's so much brain stuff going on in the band that it's very difficult to put it all into one outlet."

'Call Me' spent six weeks at number one in the States, topped the US dance charts and became Blondie's fourth British number one in little over a year when released in April. With no firm plans yet in place for a fifth studio album, the success of 'Call Me' opened up the possibility of Moroder coming on board as producer. "We wouldn't mind working with Giorgio," said Chris. "I don't know if we'll do the next one with Chapman anyway. I don't think we can do a third album in this series, not another album that's like a string of singles. We'll do something else, some longer songs."

Despite his growing interest in production, Chris insisted he had no intention of taking on the dual role. "I never want to produce a Blondie album because it's too much responsibility. A guy like Chapman or Giorgio Moroder can teach you a lot of things. I don't yet have the experience."

As 1980 progressed it seemed as if Blondie – Debbie in particular – were appearing across all facets of the media. In addition to hit singles, video albums and film soundtracks, Deborah started showing up on television as part of a high-profile advertising campaign for Gloria Vanderbilt branded jeans. "It's like a non-commercial," observed Chris. "There's no mention of jeans in it. It's just like Debbie walking down the street and her outfits change but that's about it. There's another jeans commercial here with a voice just like Ian Dury, heavy rhythm disco new wave bullshit. It's very funny."

"It was something that Shep Gordon did," Deborah later explained. "At the time, personalities and jeans were a big thing, and all of a sudden I had this ad campaign all over TV and it was for a lot of money, I'm sure it was around $200,000. At that time it was a lot, probably not compared to what people get nowadays. I guess I must've owned a pair, but I can't remember. I wasn't really into personal names or signature jeans."

"Debbie got more money from the jeans deal than both of us have for our record sales," added Chris. "Now we have good credit. We were so happy to do the commercial, though, we would have done it for nothing."

In June, Debbie travelled to England to film a guest-star spot on wildly popular family television programme *The Muppet Show*. Sandwiched between the Cannes premiere of *Union City* and the US opening of *Roadie*, the shoot gave Deborah the opportunity to branch out into mainstream light entertainment. She performed 'One Way Or Another' ("I'm gonna get ya, get ya, get ya, get ya") backed by a Muppet version of Blondie, as the show's cloth curmudgeons Statler and Waldorf cracked, "Who was she looking for anyway? The guy that booked her on this crummy show?" She also got to help the Frog Scout troop with their punk merit badges, duet with Kermit on 'Rainbow Connection', join some Technicolor-haired punk Muppets for a version of 'Call Me', and appear in full Frog Scout regalia for the finale.

"That was a real good experience, working with those people. You can't make a fool of yourself. They're very clever, the way they write things. [Jim] Henson is a genius," insisted Debbie. "I didn't suggest anything in particular that I wanted to do on the show – I left the choice of sketches and songs to the experts. After all, they know the show better than I ever could, even though I am a devoted fan. My only regret is that I don't have a scene with Miss Piggy. I thought it would be nice if we could fight over a feather boa or something but I'm told that she doesn't really like working with the lady guests. She saves herself for guests like Roger Moore – not that I blame her. She's a very astute lady!"

Shortly after the *Muppet Show* shoot, the first biography of the band was published. Written by gonzo music journalist Lester Bangs, *Blondie* combined an idiosyncratic account of the group's history to date with the author's own critical observations – much of which centred around a kind of *faux*-distaste for the way in which he perceived the band were using sex to sell records. "I was surprised by that book," stated Debbie. "We had known Lester for a long time; I was shocked that he was so hostile. What I do is, in a sense, nothing new. Yet I combine two, more or less, opposites. On the one hand I entertain in a very traditional way with the image of the beautiful female singer, though that can be very bland. But then I put a lot of feeling and information into the lyrics. Maybe that is scary. A lot of people don't want to look at, or confront that."

"Lester's point was to make money. But he didn't because the book didn't sell. Because our fans were, all in all, pretty disgusted with it," added Chris. "I just don't believe that in order to be true men and women, we have to become sexless creatures that gradually grow together. Yet a lot of people feel that's the true sexuality; this sort of Big Brotherland where everybody wears coveralls and has shaved heads … maybe that's the kind of world Lester Bangs gets excited by. In his book one of his main theses was that every little boy really wants to beat up his favourite poster girl to prove that she's a piece of meat like everyone else. So maybe he would be happier in a world where everybody was the same."

Bangs subsequently insisted, "I would like to see a world where men and women begin to see each other as they truly are and not as icons of frustration and contempt. But I can see Debbie being bugged because I also said in the book that she wasn't my type." (Hardly likely, given Bangs' slobbish, unappealing appearance and penchant for overbearing sexism.)

Despite Blondie being highly visible in the media, 1980 was the group's least active year. Since returning from Europe they had taken a break from touring and the continuing uncertainty about the next album only served to extend this hiatus. Giorgio Moroder was eliminated from the list of possible producers when it became apparent that his Eurodisco orientation didn't mesh with any direction the group wished to take.

"I don't think we could have done a whole album with Giorgio – he just didn't have any rock'n'roll roots," explained Clem, who expressed a preference for recording at Abba's studios in Sweden, before suggesting sessions at Abbey Road with Paul McCartney. Phil Spector presented another option, but reports of his obsessive, gun-toting behaviour during the making of The Ramones' *End Of The Century* scared Blondie off. Chris was becoming increasingly besotted with the idea of hiring Chic to handle production, but that would keep. As the summer reached its end, it was decided the group would stick with what they knew best, travelling to Los Angeles to record the album that would become *Autoamerican* with Mike Chapman.

"With *Autoamerican*, there was no rehearsal done at all, we just walked into the studio blind with a sketch of a few songs, and how that album came out, I really don't know," Chapman recalled.

It was to be recorded at United/Western Studios on Sunset Strip, established in the late fifties with financial backing from Bing Crosby and Frank Sinatra. "It was our turn to go out there for Mike," explained Debbie.

"I knew this was the right thing to do and felt sure that a dose of LA would bend the music," Chapman asserted. "They all loved LA anyway. They just didn't like to admit it. It's a New York thing."

Chris was not so sure. "I'm not used to it out there – it's difficult for me. It's a pretty strange place – probably one of the weirdest places in the world.

It's like a big *Ripley's Believe It Or Not* ... The whole state is like a giant Disneyland. No, I shouldn't say that; Frisco seems like a normal European sort of town ... except for the fact that half the population is homosexual, there's nothing unusual about it. In LA though, everything seems big and plastic."

With only the bare outlines of their new material prepared, Chris saw the opportunity to take Blondie's sound into uncharted realms. "I'm determined not to stagnate in the music we produce. It's always easy to accept the unsuccessful artist and say, 'Well, he's more pure because he's not successful and has nothing to lose.' But we're still trying to turn things over and make a change."

"We wanted to get away from a mould," he would retrospectively explain. "I was really angry at the time; a lot of that stuff was a slap in the face to critics and people with preconceptions about what we were and what new wave music was supposed to be. I was appalled by the way new wave was being absorbed into the mainstream. By the time we did *Autoamerican*, new wave had been totally absorbed, the same way hippies were absorbed."

Although he admitted to surprise when Blondie arrived in LA without Frank, who would "come when he was needed", Mike Chapman was immediately impressed. "They all came with ideas. Great ideas," he recalled. "We would have an orchestra, a jazz great or two, some horn sections, a cover of a great reggae song, and – as Chris put it – 'a rap'. I wasn't too sure what he meant, but it sounded good and it was his idea, so it must be good."

"*Autoamerican* solidified our relationship with Chapman. After that we felt a lot more committed to each other," said Chris. "He agreed that we should get away from standard rock. We didn't want to do what everybody expected us to do, which would have been 'Call Me'-type stuff."

The album's basic tracks took over a month to work out and lay down. "The feel of the songs was closely examined," recalled Debbie. "There were plenty of differences of opinion. Lots of time was spent discussing, hacking it out, trying to satisfy everyone."

Studio A was situated on a particularly sleazy stretch of the Strip, where darkness brought out all manner of winos, hookers and ne'er-do-wells. At one point Chapman was called home to Australia, due to his father's death, leaving Blondie to get up to no good in LA. Debbie would later confess to having no recollection at all of what transpired. On Chapman's return, they relocated a block down the Strip to Studio B for vocals, overdubs, orchestra and horns. This was the facility that had hosted the likes of Elvis, The Beach Boys, The Rolling Stones and The Righteous Brothers.

Chris and Debbie's determination to transcend musical boundaries defined *Autoamerican*, as the couple seized the creative reins. Only Jimmy Destri's 'Angels On The Balcony' and 'Walk Like Me', along with the Harry/Harrison composition 'T-Birds', conformed to the sonic lineage of the group's previous releases.

"Chris took the most interest in the whole album," remarked Jimmy.

"It's being in the right frame of mind," Chris explained. "Sometimes you have spurts like at the moment – six or seven songs, but another time there's nothing at all. I always write music, I'm not too good at lyrics. I never wrote prose or poetry, but Debbie always has and I think she's getting better and better at lyrics. She's responsible for all the stuff that really gives it its character. All our stuff is taken for granted now, and that's why it's our duty now to find some new avenues."

"I like to sing freestyle into a tape recorder," added Deborah. "I improvise and listen to it back. Sometimes I get an idea, I just try to make up embellishments and it's easier with a cassette machine. Nowadays I seem to come up with attitudes and feelings first and just go with that. I just try to ad lib it."

To fully realise their vision, Debbie, Chris and Mike Chapman – who found himself standing in for the absent Frank on second guitar – enlisted a wide range of additional singers and players. Experienced arranger Jimmie Haskell worked tirelessly with a 30-piece orchestra brought in to enhance the two tracks bookending *Autoamerican* – Stein's cinematic instrumental opener, 'Europa', and a cover version of Alan Jay Lerner and Frederick Loewe's 'Follow Me', from the 1960 musical *Camelot*.

In many ways the most controversial song on the album, 'Follow Me' was viewed by Chris as a perverse form of radicalism. "I went to see *Camelot* and 'Follow Me' stuck in my head. By doing something corny like that I was trying to wake people up to the validity of that type of music. I felt new wave fans were getting as stuffy as opera lovers: 'I can't listen to that – it's about teenage suicide and doesn't have raging guitars in it.' The band thought I was insane," he explained. "People have these preconceived ideas about what it's cool to listen to and we wanted to expose our fans to different types of music, to open up their brains a little. I believe punks are just as stuffy as opera lovers. If you force a punk to listen to Wagner or

Camelot by Lerner and Loewe, he will reject the image of the music rather than listen and hear the melody."

Saxophonist Tom Scott − best known for composing theme tunes to such TV cop shows as *Starsky And Hutch* and *The Streets Of San Francisco* − was hired, along with pianist Steve Goldstein and bassist Ray Brown, to provide Debbie with a suitably jazzy backing for her slow-burning 'Faces'. Written entirely by the singer, the haunting ballad has her trading vocal lines with Scott's sax as the realisation of an idea she had developed over an extended period. "I was working on it for five years. I'm lying. Six years," she revealed.

Jimmy, who admitted that the track's keyboards were beyond his technical capabilities, observed, "'Faces' is totally Debbie. I can tell she's been holding it in for a while, with all those Bowery references."

"We tried to consciously make it a depression era song, for the eighties depression," stated Stein. "It's about bums on the Bowery. I think that's really the key song on the album."

Elsewhere, vocal duo Howard Kayman and Mark Volman (aka former Turtles members Flo and Eddie) provided backing vocals for 'T-Birds', while percussion trio Ollie Brown, Emil Richards and Alex Acuña were brought aboard for *Autoamerican*'s other cover, a reworking of The Paragons' 1967 Jamaican rocksteady single, 'The Tide Is High'. "The song gave me the chills," recounted Chapman. "That's the number one record," he told Deborah. "The track felt perfect. The percussion players added the next dimension. Debbie's vocal was magic, and the strings and horns put it over the top. I asked them to play it without reading or running through their parts. They thought I had lost it, but they did it. The result was loose and added a wonderful atmosphere to the overall picture."

Blondie had actually debuted a gloriously ramshackle version of 'The Tide Is High' on *TV Party* some weeks earlier, with Walter Steding adding some uniquely discordant violin. "I wish I could have strangled Walter and dragged him off the stage because he was so unbearably out of tune in that," asserted Glenn O' Brien.

In terms of innovation, 'Rapture' was the album's standout track. Like 'Heart Of Glass' and 'Atomic', it demonstrated how Blondie's penchant for experimentation was most effective when the group incorporated elements of dance music. Once again Debbie and Chris returned to the New York streets for inspiration, referencing the emergent rap scene that had ripened throughout the previous decade.

The initial development of rapping, turntabling and break-dancing had run parallel with the downtown punk scene, gestating in the housing projects of the South Bronx since 1974. This slow street-level evolution continued unrecorded for another five years, before The Sugarhill Gang's 'Rapper's Delight' propelled the medium to mainstream attention. Just as Television and The Ramones represented what had been going on at CBGB's before Blondie became its first hit-makers, 'Rapper's Delight' echoed the scene amid the urban ruins, presenting hip hop as a major new cultural force. On the streets it represented primal expression for kids with nothing to lose, many initially just looking for escape and a few minutes of self-earned glory, rather than the big dollars that came later. By the 21st century, the music would become the biggest-selling musical genre in the world (albeit often in watered-down or horribly mutated forms).

The genesis of hip hop can be attributed to three prime movers: DJ Kool Herc, Grandmaster Flash and Afrika Bambaataa. Although all were ostensibly DJs, each brought a different crucial element to the movement, with Herc widely credited for originating the form in its rawest state. Born Clive Campbell in Kingston, Jamaica, Herc had arrived in New York in 1967 and set about applying elements drawn from his native sound-system culture (such as the verbally dextrous practice of 'toasting' over records) to the funkier offerings of artists such as James Brown and Jimmy Castor. The foundations of hip hop were laid in 1973 at a Sedgwick Avenue housing-project recreation room, where Herc started extending the percussion breaks in records, whipping up the dancers who unleashed their break moves with party cries like, "This is the joint!"

Herc's reputation rapidly became as immense as the scale of his parties, sometimes held in parks with equipment powered by hotwired street lights, inspiring others to take to the decks. Teenage electronics boffin Joseph Sadler, of blitzed-out Fox Street, witnessed Herc around this time but, rather than copying his sometimes clumsy method of switching from break to break, became convinced that the seamless beat-mixing techniques being pioneered by Manhattan DJs such as Pete DJ Jones and Grandmaster Flowers could be applied to Herc's break-isolating methods. The young boffin went off and constructed his own primitive double-deck set-up, while developing the 'quick mix' technique which would ultimately lead to the turntablist's arsenal of cutting, back-spins and scratching. By the following September of 1978 he had renamed himself Grandmaster Flash and could fill Harlem's Audubon Ballroom with break-dancing party fiends, many hatching their own takes on the emerging new style.

Former Black Spades warlord Afrika Bambaataa came from a broader social angle, having rejected and then confronted the violent gang life dominating the South Bronx to establish his Zulu Nation, which brought together previously warring factions under one banner. Bam was also known as the 'Master Of Records', on account of the wildly eclectic musical menus at his parties in the South East Bronx. By 1977, hip hop had replaced (although it still sometimes accompanied) the thug life as the main obsession of disaffected Bronx youth, as Disco Fever – a rampant hothouse which showcased new names – provided the movement's sometimes highly dangerous epicentre.

Until the release of 'Rapper's Delight' in late 1979, the South Bronx and parts of Harlem had kept this new movement to themselves, many DJs and MCs even turning down offers to appear on vinyl (although there had already been low-key rap outings such as 'Vicious Rap' on Winley Records). It was finally down to New Jersey-based music business veterans Sylvia and Joe Robinson (the former once a successful solo artist in her own right) to corral some musicians into replicating Chic's 'Good Times' groove for nearly 15 minutes, driven by ubiquitous session drummer Pumpkin. After being turned down by several MCs, Sylvia roped in a motley crew including Big Bank Hank (a bouncer who also worked in a pizza joint), Master Gee and Wonder Mike, using rhymes built on quotes from Bronx MC Grandmaster Caz's notebook.

Chic's Nile Rodgers first heard 'Rapper's Delight' at a club and – although he initially claimed publishing rights for himself and partner Bernard Edwards, on account of how the whole track was based on the 'Good Times' groove – later cited the track among his all-time favourites, as important and innovative as his original 'Good Times' had been to the disco genre. 'Rapper's Delight' made number 35 on the US charts and went Top Five in the UK, resulting in an eye-opening *Top Of The Pops* appearance. However, The Sugarhill Gang were roundly decried by the close-knit Bronx community, who felt they'd been beaten to the big prize (while forced to admit it was their own obstinate fault in most cases). But the floodgates were now open. Flash was soon appearing on record with the Furious Five, accompanied by a welter of MCs and crews, initially on

Bobby Robinson's Enjoy and Sugarhill before the major labels started their inevitable bandwagon rolling.

Hip hop was still an underground uptown movement when it came to the attention of Debbie and Chris, largely through the uptown/downtown character Fred Braithwaite, who actually hailed from Bedford-Stuyvesant in central Brooklyn. Better known as Fab Five Freddy, whose name would soon be immortalised in 'Rapture', Braithwaite initially showed up on *TV Party* as a graffiti artist, making a carriage-long replication of Warhol's Campbell's soup cans painting on the city's subway system – an early example of uptown hip hop culture in graphic form. Freddy's grandfather had been an associate of civil rights activist Marcus Garvey, while his father was in the audience at the Audubon Ballroom when Malcolm X was shot. This instilled a sense of self-awareness in Freddy who, along with being a regular at Brooklyn appearances by Grandmaster Flowers and Pete DJ Jones, also drew upon a wide range of influences that encompassed Caravaggio, impressionism and Warhol, assimilating them all into his own nascent graffiti style. He became part of Brooklyn's Fabulous Five graffiti crew after befriending legendary artist Lee Quinones – hence the 'Fab Five' tag.

Freddy's godfather was master drummer Max Roach, the family home often playing host to leading musicians of the day such as Bud Powell and Thelonious Monk. He later claimed to have introduced uptown culture, art, hip hop, breaking and rapping to the downtown post-punk and art scenes, his co-conspirators including artists Keith Haring and Jean-Michel Basquiat.

"Freddy brought Debbie and myself to a big festival at a Police Athletic League place in the Bronx; that's a bit like a community or leisure centre," recalls Chris. "We were the only Caucasians in attendance; even Freddy was razzed by the crowd for wearing a then-unfashionable porkpie hat and white shirt and tie – a sort of dread style that at the time hadn't been seen outside of the UK. At the time, the hip hop uniform had to be topped off by a massive wool stocking cap that often had cardboard in it to make it stand up higher. But everyone there was quite polite to us. I overheard some kids talking who thought we were part of Kool And The Gang."

Suitably bitten, Chris started writing what would become 'Rapture'. "'Rapture' is not truly rap," explained Debbie. "It was an homage, dedicated to the form. We were hanging out with Fab Five Freddy. He would come down to CBGB. Some of the taggers would too. We met Grandmaster Flash and some of The Sugarhill Gang. They were all so cute. I remember Chris and I were lying in bed one day. He was smoking a joint, going, 'We should do a song called "Rapture".'"

"The whole rapping thing is totally fresh," observed Chris. "It's the closest thing I've seen to new wave/punk in a long time. There are millions of one-off singles being produced, the same as rock kids were producing their punk singles. The real stuff is not even available to the general American public."

'Rapture' was worked up in the studio. "Debbie and Chris had the verses and choruses written," remembered Mike. "I was told that a large hole in the second verse would contain the rap and a guitar solo – a guitar solo that Frankie would be flown in to record … Tom Scott came in and wrote the horn parts with us and then played them all."

Debbie and Chris lashed the rap together in a few minutes and the song was recorded in two takes. "I'm really proud of my playing on 'Rapture'," enthused Clem. "*Autoamerican* is the album where I gave up wanting to play like Keith Moon and decided I want to play like [jazz and blues drummer] Steve Gadd. *Autoamerican* was fun; we got to spend two months in California. I'm always up for a free ride."

However, in retrospect Nigel was less certain of Clem's positive attitude. "I think Clem felt a little odd about *Autoamerican*. After doing *Eat To The Beat* he couldn't really lay into it; there's only a certain way you can play 'Rapture'."

"There was a running joke about *Autoamerican* in the studio," Jimmy recalled. "It was going to sell 14 copies and get all these awards from critics, or critics were going to hate it and it would sell millions. There were a couple of hits on the record and the rest was just esoteric and fun. I loved it. That's one of the few Blondie records I walked away from proud. I thought, finally we took a chance; we did something different. We let go."

"I really like *Autoamerican*," enthused Chris. "I was heavily involved with that one myself. I had that crazy instrumental at the beginning. *Autoamerican* was the closest we ever came to a concept album, which is something we had always talked about before."

Mike Chapman subsequently compared the album to The Beatles' *Sgt Pepper*. "I'm proud of it, I think it's a wonderful album, and most of those songs were constructed and written in the studio. It didn't take that long really, and it was only because I had total control over the situation that the record was able to be made as efficiently as it was."

Autoamerican achieved Debbie and Chris's avowed intent of creating a hugely diverse album. It provided Debbie with a variety of backdrops on which to project the full range of her vocal talent. "We tried for that versatility on earlier records, but I don't think we pulled it off until now. My voice hasn't changed, but I know I've improved as a singer and recording artist. I also believe my attitude and my ability to express moods has really gotten better," she declared. "It's like a fuzz box or a wah-wah pedal. You can get all these different qualities and attitudes in your voice by just changing the tone. It's like the same notes with a different style."

However, experimentation and diversity tend to be unpopular with mainstream record companies marketing a new album by a successful act. Ideally, they prefer minimal variations on an established theme. True to this maxim, Chrysalis recoiled from what Blondie and Chapman set before them. "The pressure with *Autoamerican* came after it was released," Clem explained. "The record company went through the roof because the album was so weird to them. They didn't hear any hits. They just heard strings and mariachi horns."

When it was released, on November 14, 1980, the press largely sided with the band's record label. In *New Musical Express*, Cynthia Rose posted a particularly uncomplimentary review: "The band have drifted steadily further and further into 'eclectic' experiments which found them waxing patriotic in the express lane, and treating the world – musical and material – as one vast quarry from which it was OK to take more and more and cool to give less and less. *Autoamerican* is the *reductio ad absurdum* of this O Sweet Land of Circuitry-style of New York minimalism and pretension." She concluded by insisting, "*Autoamerican* is just a half-baked (cable) TV dinner, and it's full of unhealthy preservatives and artificial sweeteners. So leave it in the fridge where it belongs and don't take it out to thaw – no way should this band be taking the temperature of your present."

Elsewhere, the album was lambasted for a "fake aesthetic" in the *New York Times*, *Rolling Stone* accused Chris of "trying to destroy pop music" and *Sounds* gave the disc a one-star review, asking, "Can't someone stop these people?"

In *Trouser Press*, Ira Robbins was more balanced. After noting how "*Autoamerican* displays the band's basic flaw: lack of direction and a musical confusion that is almost unbelievable," he recognised it as "the most interesting and (dare I say it?) cohesive album Blondie has made. There's no logic to it, very little resemblance to previous work, and the only emotional content lies in wry New York lyrics – yet Blondie has reached a new stage in their career: they finally sound at ease on record, and can be counted among the major American rock bands."

"This LP's aimed at the real street people. The hip hoppers and the rappers," countered Chris. "The new wave is plastic. They're just our next generation of computer programmers." Regardless of how something like 'Follow Me' might go down in the South Bronx, his belief in *Autoamerican* was validated by its commercial success. In addition to spawning two US number one singles in 'Rapture' and 'The Tide Is High' (the latter matching that achievement in Britain), *Autoamerican* made number seven on the *Billboard* chart and number three in the UK.

"We put out a whacko album with all kinds of crazy shit to open everyone's head up a little bit, and half the critics freaked out," concluded Chris. "Whatever you do, reviewers are always divided in thirds. They either like it, hate it or have mixed feelings about it. It doesn't have anything to do with quality. It has more to do with selling advertising."

"Chris took some chances with his ideas and his writing. I think a lot of those songs' popularity is really due to a lot of his ideas. He's really responsible for 'Rapture' and for the sound of 'The Tide Is High'," Deborah declared.

Asked about the impact of 'Rapture,' Fab Five Freddie observed, "It was the first time that a mainstream audience had a peek at what was about to become this huge movement called hip hop."

'Rapture' subsequently became the first ever rap tune broadcast by MTV in 1981. The video was set in the East Village, with dancer William Barnes (who also choreographed the piece) as 'The Man From Mars', while Andy Warhol lends support via his presence and Fab Five Freddy, Lee Quinones and artist Jean-Michel Basquiat all make cameo appearances – the latter covering behind the decks for a no-show Flash. The US 12-inch was longer, with a verse in French, while Mike Chapman remixed the extended UK version.

After the advent of sampling technology later in the decade, 'Rapture' would become a target for plundering: including Foxy Brown's 1996 hit, 'I'll Be', KRS-One's 'Step Into A World (Rapture's Delight)' the following year and Destiny Child's 'Independent Woman' (2000), while Erasure covered the song on the US version of their *Cowboy* album, with Vince Clarke rapping. 2005 saw Go Home Productions' acclaimed mash-up of the song, splicing it with The Doors' 'Riders On The Storm' to make 'Rapture Riders' on *Greatest Hits: Sight And Sound*, after approval by the band. Alicia Keys also covered 'Rapture' for the *Sex And The City 2* soundtrack.

"It remains to be seen what effect the record will have," mused Stein at the time. "We wanted to make music that would cross over. I would like to see the record help resolve racial tensions by bringing different audiences together. When the new wave kids and the rappers get together, that'll be something. Eventually, they'll all meet in the middle, where you'll have a strong race of young people that won't be divided by stupid racial issues."

Chapter Eleven

Six Like Dice

"For a lot of bands, the one concept becomes their world. Blondie was all about change."

Debbie Harry

As 1980 gave way to '81, it sometimes seemed as if Blondie was everywhere. The US and European chart successes of 'The Tide Is High' and 'Rapture' ensured the band were constantly on the radio and TV. Debbie and the group looked out from dozens of magazine covers, while their name and image adorned thousands of T-shirts worldwide. In fact, just about the only place one was unlikely to encounter Blondie was in a concert hall. By the third week in January, a year had passed since the band left the Hammersmith stage at the end of their triumphant British tour. Now that they had finished dissecting *Autoamerican*, the music press noticed that it had been over a year since Blondie last played live and began to speculate. Rumours that the group was divided by internal bickering began to circulate; it was suggested they had already played their final gig and were about to split.

Blondie were quick to counter. "Any band that's successful automatically gets break-up rumours," observed Chris, who also denied that there were any tensions among the sextet.

"We're definitely not breaking up," affirmed Clem. "There's no reason to break up. The band isn't divided; there's a lot of common ground."

Jimmy was equally relaxed. "I don't care about rumours. It's funny; I was over at Debbie and Chris's place, sitting around, playing guitar and going through the papers seeing how many times we were breaking up. If only these writers could see us hanging out together. We like each other a lot more since we don't have to work together as often because of *Autoamerican's* success."

"I don't feel any responsibility to go out and give a bad show right now. We'll work again, but we'll only tour where we want to," Deborah declared. "You get nuts. You do these gigs in the most awful circumstances. You go do a soundcheck and it's like, 'Heyyy, maaan, you got an extension cord?' Somebody's vomiting; you step in dog shit; you sit in a dressing room with three inches of water on the floor. That's what makes it so exciting, but that's why people flip out."

However, she did reveal that there *had* been some personality clashes. "I will admit to certain divisions within the band existing up to and through the last tour and I think cooling it is the answer."

"I don't think we've found a communication on stage yet," observed Destri. "There was too much ego in the group; we were six musicians thrown on stage and blasting each other out ... We'll work again, but we'll only tour when we want to. We've suffered enough."

Whether this was a rationalisation or a declaration of unity, it was apparent that the personnel dynamic within Blondie had altered since the release of *Parallel Lines* in 1979. Successive albums had seen Frank Infante's role in the studio significantly diminished. Although he had co-written 'Victor' for *Eat To The Beat*, his guitar contributions to the album were reduced and he was only brought in to provide overdubs for *Autoamerican*, a disc for which he received no writing credits.

Despite this, Infante remained an important part of the band's live show. But now there were no live shows. "Debbie and Chris were pulling away from the whole band situation," Frank later asserted. "I guess Chris wanted to be the only guitar player, I don't know. There was a lot of friction at the time."

"They went through the same thing a lot of groups go through, where there's success and then everybody's ego gets inflated," remarked *TV Party* host Glenn O'Brien. "In the old days of jazz you'd have a group and there would be a leader and there would be sidemen. But then the whole notion of the pop group came along, and even though Chris and Jimmy were the principal songwriters, and Chris in a way was the musical director, and Debbie the star, all of a sudden Frankie Infante thinks it's a democracy. And I think that democracy and successful bands is just something that's never been resolved."

"You know how difficult it is to keep a cast of people together without fighting and little bits of ego getting in the way," said Debbie. "It's difficult, understandably difficult. And you have this situation with the added influence and destructive element that money can put on your head. Imagine what happens when you're out there and there are lots of people that are making money off of you. All kinds of things happen. People get weird ideas and paranoia. This is what I mean by this thing that happens in the industry. It happens to bands all the time – it's very hard to keep groups of young people together and motivated."

As is the case with most groups, there was an unspoken hierarchy within Blondie. Frank, like Nigel Harrison, had not been an original member and was therefore at the foot of the totem pole. Unfortunately, he clashed with Debbie and Chris far more often than Nigel, which in turn ensured the group's principal duo saw him as dispensable when it came to weeks holed up in a studio. Unsurprisingly, it led to Frank feeling marginalised, exacerbated by the lack of gigs and reports of Chris telling *Rolling Stone* that touring was "for morons".

"That was misconstrued," Stein clarified. "What I meant is that if a band has to tour incessantly, it's not really for morons but it's just for people who don't have the right kind of hook that can be grabbed by the media. Bands like Kiss and Rush have to tour constantly, because they can't get the right type of media coverage. That doesn't necessarily mean it's moronic, but it's a lifestyle that we don't adhere to. We want to use the media – which is there to be used, after all."

But in terms of interacting with the media, the way in which Deborah's image enveloped the whole band became a bugbear. "There came to be a problem in the sense of 'Blondie' – who is Blondie, Blondie, Blondie," she explained.

"That's all the tension ever arose from," added Chris. "If Debbie was a guy we would never have had the same situation – or if we were all girls."

"It's very selfish for me and the other guys to be part of this group when we're all equal partners in someone else's image," agreed Jimmy. "Debbie's gotta be the face but we're all collecting off it anyway. Sometimes I think it's a little unfair: Why am I sitting at home building plastic models when she's in LA doing nine interviews in a row? But I never thought she'd be anything less of a star than she is, so I don't feel confused, upset or pushed aside. Debbie wanted to be the face, the focal point. She's got it."

"Everybody wants to think that they're what everybody's coming to see," said Chris. "Me being together with Debbie and shit, I always had a different perspective on it. I don't know, maybe if she hadn't been my girlfriend maybe I would have had the same kind of feelings, I really don't know. I like to think I'm smart enough to not get absorbed in that shit, it's hard to say."

"The thing that gets me about it was that I was Blondie. But the group was called Blondie," Deborah observed. "Now for all the mistakes and all the things that happened within the band, I'm where the buck stops, that's it. Whether it was my fault or not. Whether it was my decision or not."

As Debbie was feeling the pressure of being the focal point while others believed they were being edged to the sidelines, extracurricular activities provided a release. "One night I sat up thinking I was in pretty interesting circumstances," recalled Clem, who later admitted he saw hardly anything of the group as a whole for long periods during 1980-81. "With the Blondie lay-off, I wound up doing [the Devo song] 'Come Back Jonee' on *Saturday Night Live* with Debbie and Chris, a Michael Des Barres English tour with Nigel, some tracks on Joan Jett's *Bad Reputation* album with Frankie, Jimmy's solo album, and I played on Iggy Pop's tour last year [1981] with Gary Valentine. I guess that's the luxury of being a drummer, especially if you're a very damned good drummer."

Aside from working on his solo debut, *Heart On A Wall*, Jimmy also took time out to produce the *Marty Thau Presents 2x5* compilation for Red Star Records, while Clem produced two power-pop singles, The Colors' 'Rave It Up' and 'Something On My Mind' by The Speedies, both issued in 1980.

Ever the polymath, the early eighties found Chris busiest of all. "Everything sort of came at once. I just finished working on *Polyester*, the new John Waters movie with Stiv Bators, Divine and Tab Hunter. I got into that through the guy who's sound man on *New York Beat*, which is Glenn O'Brien's and [writer/director] Edo [Bertoglio]'s movie. That movie could be really exciting, it's what should've been done in 1975 ... I've worked on that soundtrack. The idea is to get a lot of people who are in the movie involved in the soundtrack, like John [Lurie], James [Chance]."

He also produced a single for Walter Steding, helped saxophonist John Lurie's Lounge Lizards get an album deal and teamed up with Debbie to write some songs for a Canadian cartoon called *Rock & Rule*, which also featured contributions from Iggy Pop, Lou Reed and Cheap Trick. Chris also moved to the other side of the critical fence by writing an account of the recording of *Autoamerican* for *Creem* magazine.

In April 1981, Chris and Debbie undertook the most significant side project when they teamed up with Chic's Bernard Edwards and Nile Rodgers to record *Koo Koo*. Although the album was very much a collaborative effort, it would be marketed as Deborah's solo debut. More importantly, outside the confines of a group format, it allowed the couple free reign to experiment with the elements of black music they were increasingly fascinated by."By the time we'd finished *Autoamerican* ... Blondie was not changing enough for my tastes," declared Debbie. "We were worried that it was becoming a static safety thing that was there. Everyone could just step into it and there would be an audience and money. This has never been my goal."

Glenn O'Brien's weekly *TV Party* free-for-all was becoming more chaotic by the week, the range of guests widening to encompass Bernard and Nile, who duly established a rapport with Debbie and Chris. Rodgers spent one show manning the live phone line, handling stunningly ignorant racist calls with grace and cool. As their relationship developed, some form of collaboration seemed logical. To those who knew Blondie and appreciated their downtown New York ethos, it made perfect sense. To disco-hating bigots, however, it was as if they were prostituting their pop purity to Studio 54.

Nile Rodgers and Bernard Edwards first met in 1970 as session musicians working in the New York area, forming ill-fated rock groups before being joined by former Labelle drummer Tony Thompson and forming a covers band. After gaining singer Norma Jean Wright, soon replaced by the unspeakably sensuous voices of Luci Martin and Alfa Anderson, they started exploring disco. The subsequent demos led to a deal with Atlantic Records, who unleashed a string of epoch-making singles: 'Dance, Dance, Dance (Yowsah, Yowsah, Yowsah)', 'Everybody Dance', 'Le Freak', 'I Want Your Love', 'Good Times', 'My Forbidden Lover' and 'My Feet Keep Dancing'. By 1979, Nile and Bernard were working further wonders with Sister Sledge, including the anthemic 'We Are Family', 'Thinking Of You' and 'He's The Greatest Dancer'. It was like having a new Motown.

The coolest studio band of the moment and the last word in elegance, Chic broke the disco mould that had solidified after the original Philly soul templates mutated into conveyor-belt corn. Their blend of liquid funk grooves, wittily sensual lyrical flights, monstrous choruses, Robert Sabino's grand keyboard embellishments and what Primal Scream's Bobby Gillespie calls "icy cocaine strings" transformed dance music into heavenly soundtracks of syncopated funk and emotional resonance. To dismiss Chic as emblematic of some anti-rock phenomenon was so thoroughly misguided that it became a crusade in some quarters to spread word of their excellence.

It took Danny Baker, co-founder of punk fanzine *Sniffin' Glue*, *Zigzag* contributor and *NME*'s sharpest young gun, to put everything in perspective: "Chic are that James Brown riff in modern times. They repeat it, always altering and building, and hang the extremely desirable Alfa Anderson/Luci Martin vocals right up front where they can do the most harm … The group is the vehicle for two incredibly gifted musicians in Nile Rodgers, the ace pace flicking rhythm-guitar, and Bernard Edwards, who is the world's greatest bass player bar none and that's fact. Between them and the explosive outfit they've gathered together and who enrich their ideas – even their string section is a permanent Chic crew – Chic are currently making some of the most exciting and strongest music available in any field or civilisation."

Inevitably, the rapidly evolving dance scene emulated Chic, in a similar way to how others followed Blondie's punk-propelled approach to pop. Although appearing to represent polar opposites of the musical spectrum, there were further striking parallels between Blondie and Chic who, along with the ubiquitous Abba, had been probably the biggest chart bands in the world in 1979–80. Apart from both being blessed with a sense of often mischievous humour, both outfits' twin dynamos felt stifled by the formulas on which their success was predicated. While Debbie and Chris were creating *Autoamerican*, Nile and Bernard went against their own established grain to produce *Real People*, their priapic dance-floor glow replaced by personal statements such as 'Rebels Are We,' or the title track's bitter comments on the negative aspects of success: "I'm so tired of hypocrisy … I want to live my life with some real people."

In hindsight, *Real People* can be viewed as clearing the air for *Koo Koo* and the producers' subsequent career triumphs with Bowie and Madonna. "It was a combination of factors working against us," Bernard later explained.

"The attitude people have to you. Previous to our success everyone was rooting for us. Then all of a sudden, when we made it, they turn against you. Nile and I were hurt and angry. It's hypocritical, but there's very little you can do about it. You can decide if you're going to write about it or not. We decided to write about it."

Both parties were ready for a new challenge. When it was announced that Debbie and Chris would be working with Chic on an album, many expected a sublime combination of Blondie art-pop and sophisticated disco, a delirious 'Rapture'/'Good Times' hybrid that could well have been the biggest record of 1981. Instead, all concerned had a blast by experimenting with many different styles – as long as they weren't their own. The result was a bold, playful statement that declared how neither party would be defined by commercial expectations.

Shortly before starting the project, The Chic Organisation had turned down a personal request from Aretha Franklin for a disco makeover. "We knew those guys from Chic and went round to see them right after they finished Diana Ross," explains Chris of the Motown star's 1980 album *Diana*, which would yield the hit single 'Upside Down'. "They played us their production of the Diana Ross record and I thought it was really fantastic. I said, 'This'll put Diana Ross back in the charts!' Then, after that they had all this hassle with Motown wanting to remix it all, which is really stupid, but it was really successful anyway. We had all this in common. Then, when 'Rapture', which is really an homage to Chic, crossed over we started getting more of a black audience in the States. We admire them a lot, so [*Koo Koo*] seemed like the right thing to do. If it wasn't for linking up with those guys, I don't think we would have done the solo album so soon."

'I don't think we would have done it if they hadn't said, 'Yeah, we got the time,'" agrees Debbie. "It really was fun to do, so much. We had a lot of laughs, I'm telling you. Sometimes my face would hurt from laughing. God, they're so crazy!"

The sessions, which would last five weeks, commenced with Nile treating Debbie, Chris and the other Chic musicians to an early morning ride along the East River in his speedboat. "We had to hold on for dear life," recalled Debbie. "I liked it, but I was screaming and Tony Thompson was up front screaming too. Nile was driving us all crazy, because he likes to go so fast, and we were in terror throughout the ride. Suddenly we were at the beginning of the bay heading out toward Long Island. The swells were huge, there was a big wind, and we went right over a huge log … That's when we realised the water was too high and everybody went berserk, cursing at Nile, who was having a great time, to slow down."

"It was fun," says Chris of the sessions. "They started off telling a lot of race jokes and making us feel inferior for being white. The engineer, Chuck Martin, was telling jokes about doing dog barks [as heard on 'Jump Jump']. It was worse than Chapman. That's great. I think a lot of it comes across on the record."

"To me, each producer produces you differently every time. Michael Chapman always made me very compatible with the Blondie sound. He used to equalise my voice electronically, and do certain things to it to make it have that sound," Deborah explains. "In some ways I insisted on it too because I always used to say, 'I don't want to hear a lot of bottom on my voice.' I went for a more trebly sound so I could cut through a lot of the instruments, because it was like that wall [of sound] business. I think there was a lot more space in the *Koo Koo* kind of music. Chic just have a different way of doing it. It was pretty much a straighter production, a lot rawer and a lot funkier. I don't think there's *any* equalising on my voice.

"They're like the cream, those guys. They're really fucking great. I can't say it enough; I'm amazed. A lot of people in the States don't even think they know how to play, think they're just producers. Yeah well, that's certainly not the Chic fans. I think people that are not really disco fans think those guys are slick disco producers, but really it's amazing; their rock history really is funny."

"We used to get a lot of flack because people didn't know whether we were white or black," remembered Bernard of their funk-rock group The Boys. "We've always thought that's why we've been successful. We must go against the grain. If we didn't, we'd turn into just another R&B band, or black guys trying to be a rock'n'roll group."

"They felt very confident about it," recalls Debbie of how all concerned sought to broaden their creative horizons. "They were looking for a chance to break out of their format as Chic as much as Chris and I were looking for a chance to break out of our format with Blondie. Really, we were both equally in the same position. They had been totally identified with that sound they had and Blondie had been identified with that sound they had, and then we got the chance to do something together. There are pieces of both those things, and you can hear them. It's nice, I really like it. I'm nuts about this record. I always do this now, it's getting to be boring, even to myself: each time we come out with a record I like that record better, but this is the one I like best."

"The reason why we get along so well with Debbie and Chris is because what we do is something that they've been doing and something they like to do," enthused Nile of the fusion of post-punk rock and funk. Each songwriting partnership wrote four songs and collaborated on two, with a band based around the core Chic trio of Nile, Bernard and Tony Thompson with Chris also contributing guitar. Opener 'Jump Jump' features Debbie with a frisky jazz element in her voice as the Chic contingent drop the kind of taut funky backdrop they could do with their eyes closed, Bernard's ever-probing bass blasting to the fore as Devo's Mark Mothersbaugh and Jerry Casale add backing vocals to the cross-cultural stew.

Issued as the second single from *Koo Koo*, Bernard and Nile's 'The Jam Was Moving' is a kind of precursor to Cameo's 1986 hit 'Word Up', with additional spiky shuffle and an 'Eight Miles High' guitar quote. 'Chrome' is the kind of exotic mid-tempo outing which Blondie had become adept at, in which Debbie sings about "changing colours like a chameleon". "I wanna become like the chameleon in 'Chrome', I wanna do it all, I don't want to do one thing," she asserted. "It's just a fantasy based on Truman Capote's book [*Music For Chameleons* – his semi-fictionalised anthology of articles originally commissioned for Warhol's *InterView* magazine, while Debbie's lyric was a more literal fantasy of physical transformation]."

"It's old, I've had that for quite a while," revealed Chris. "It was written for *Alphaville*. It's supposed to be like flying at night, that kind of imagery."

'Surrender' could be the quintessential Chic outing, a scrub guitar-infused funk-up that sees Nile on blazing form, spliced to a tightrope bass-drum interplay. Harry/Stein's 'Inner City Spillover' flows over Chic's first and only stab at reggae, its lyrics referencing 'red card' – a three-card monte street hustle. "The black kids set up little cardboard boxes and try to get tourists. One kid's a lookout for police."

"There's a big difference in reference points too," explained Chris at the time. "Because there's not really such a thing as reggae music with black kids in the States. In the States they listen to Chic and that's really street music. And there's the whole rapping movement. [In the UK] kids heavily identify with reggae. In America, it comes out of disco, out of funk. The rapping thing's the first real black movement that's come out. It's thriving. Racially, it's totally mixed. There's no segregation in the New York rock scene."

The album's debut single, 'Backfired', is adorned by Rodgers' steely guitar sound, which the Edwards/Thompson rhythm section locks into the set's toughest groove, elaborating on themes found on *Real People*, as Nile's lyrics lambast music-industry parasites. "There's so much bullshit that goes down," he explained. "People give all this stuff to bands, all these promises. They're just charlatan-type fast-talkers who try to pull the wool over your eyes."

Anyone hoping Debbie would drape her velvet tones over one of Chic's exquisite ballads was rewarded by sepulchral jazz croon 'Now I Know You Know'; time stands still as the band work their understated, languid majesty. Midway, its curious wind-tunnel resonance blows in a jazz zephyr for a few bars. "That's one of Nile's favourites too – maybe 'cos he wrote it," smiles Debbie. 'I'm really perplexed that people haven't jumped on that more. I thought that was really the most outstandingly, strikingly different thing."

"Vocally, we really brought her out front," observed Bernard. "We thought to ourselves, 'Debbie, sing a ballad?' But, most of the people we told about it thought it was a really great idea. For Nile and I, it was the exposure. For Debbie, it was something new, something different. She told us she loved our work and wanted to sing on some of our music. And she sounded real sincere. She just didn't want to keep doing what was expected of her. She's real aware of what's going on."

Interestingly, one of *Koo Koo*'s two four-way collaborative efforts, 'Under Arrest', is the song that veers closest to Blondie's early signature sound, while Chris and Debbie's 'Military Rap' adds bugle calls to a new-wave gallop that the Chic contingent found challenging. "They'd never recorded anything that fast, not since the days they were a rock band; that blew their minds," Chris recalls. "They'd never had people telling them what to play before. I did a lot of the basslines."

Eastern-infused disco closer 'Oasis' was the second collective collaboration. "It's the old Islamic disco song that people have been talking about in New York for years – 'Let's have a hit in Tehran,'" offered Chris. "On *TV Party* we have Islamic disco and stuff like that. *TV Party* is real crazy ... that's where the Islamic disco thing came from. We did the track and were listening to it and we decided to take the snare drum out, and that was it! Now it sounded authentic."

"Nile's working [album] title was *The Niggers And The Bitch*, which we decided not to give to Chrysalis," deadpanned Chris. "Doing that album really brought home to us how much fucking racism there is. We were getting – 'You can't do that, it's too R&B.' The inverse of that is when Chic started out, they were a rock band and they'd send their tapes to the record companies and be invited up. And they'd walk in and when the companies saw what colour they were – forget it. 'Why don't you play soul music?'"

"Personally, I don't think it has anything to do with music. It's racial," Deborah asserted.

"I think there's racism in the rock community that says white people can't make black music because they're trying to sound black," Chris observed. "That was never our point – we're not trying to be anything, just trying to make music. And there's another sort of racism that says contemporary black music is not acceptable – that after it's sat around for 10 years, it's safe and it's cool. I mean, at the time of Motown, in the mid-sixties, the blues were accepted, but Motown itself was considered, like, background music. I remember how kids felt about The Four Tops back then."

Chrysalis threw a lavish party to launch *Koo Koo* at Covent Garden's Sanctuary spa in central London on July 27, 1982, laying out an extravagant spread. "It was something for the journalists," explains Chris. "We okayed a guest list of 100, then about 500 showed up. What the hell … I don't know if we would do that again. I guess everybody goes nuts about the expense and Debbie with a bodyguard and all that crap. And it was just too hot. I had a good time. I don't know if Debbie had a good time. I was prepared to be uncomfortable."

The *Sun* tabloid focused on Deborah's discomfort, rolling out clichés under the headline, 'It's too hot for the Blondie Cinderella!', traducing 'delicious Debbie' with the title 'The Cinderella of Pop' and describing how she left at midnight, "looking tired and distressed", having only stayed for a bottle of Perrier water. The tabloid concludes that 'the wild, wild Debbie Harry party" had to be the last of its kind in terms of expense, describing the buffet and observing how people were making off with whole crabs under their arms. (They also mentioned Chris' new beard, quoting him as saying, "I just got fed up with shaving. Debbie doesn't mind the beard. She calls me her bit of rough.")

Kris Needs was present at the launch:

Meeting my plus-one Jah Wobble in the pub beforehand was always likely to make for an action-packed evening and I later awoke in an industrial dustbin. This was after the back of my head appeared in The Sun next to a green-wigged Debbie and I got to meet Nile Rodgers: charming, larger-than-life and having a blast. It turned out he was an avid Zigzag reader, which clinched a Chic interview later in the year. I asked Bernard Edwards what it was like working with Debbie and Chris.

"The recording wasn't difficult," he replies. "Me and Nile used to work with three or four people in a band all the time. This record was going back to that kind of thing. We had a ball. We got real close to each other. There was great communication once we got in there."

"We learned a lot from that," adds Nile. "It was a very good experience. When we did that album everyone was expecting a combination of Blondie and Chic. They thought it would be the ultimate commercial venture, with the best elements of both. But we didn't do that. I know it's not gonna sell, but I had to play it like that.

"There's a lot of good stuff on that record. 'Surrender' – that's one of the hippest guitar solos I ever played! The trouble is there's nothing traditional you could put your finger on. Everyone expected it to be the ultimate commercial seller, but instead of that we tried to make it more of an artistic endeavour communication thing. Once you get to a certain point in your career it's important to make that kind of album, where you want to say something else."

Although it reached number six in the UK and bruised the US Top 30, the album's blend of inner city funk, angular post-punk and Islamic disco confused both groups' fans. "I really like that record." Debbie declared in 1987. "I still think it stands up today. Except for probably a little bit of remixing, it's really good material. I was really surprised that it never did anything … it was mostly the record company. They didn't want me to go solo. They didn't want to lose Blondie. Just my opinion, of course, but I have pretty good grounds for my opinion."

In keeping with the spirit of confounding expectations, Debbie subverted her public image by returning her hair to something close to its natural brown colour. "I just had to do something different. That's all. I got tired of it; I'd had blonde hair from – what – 1973, all the way up to 1980. That's a long time to keep bleaching your hair one colour. And how can you stay one way for such a long time? It got so that people were telling me what I should look like," she explained. "I couldn't fairly to the rest of the guys in the band take Blondie's identity and then go and do a solo project. I thought that would have been really rude."

For the album sleeve, Debbie and Chris brought in acclaimed Swiss artist H. R. Giger to impart his uniquely visceral style to the visuals. "We knew his stuff before *Alien* [the classic 1979 movie for which Giger acted as production designer]," says Chris. "We knew he could do something which had a lot of impact and was memorable … It's always so difficult with Blondie because everybody has to look good!"

"Ever since we met Giger at the Hansen Gallery in New York nearly two years ago, we've thought of working together," recalled Stein in 1981. "Similar loves for science fiction, skulls, and pagan archetypes forged an automatic union. We remembered his posters in the late sixties when he was the first European psychedelic-poster artist. Then we knew of him as the artist of *Alien*. And we found out that Giger began listening to us while working on *Alien* in England. Our ascendance paralleled his as we simultaneously became aware of each other."

"I asked [Deborah] to make a portrait of herself to give to me," Giger explained. "At the time, a friend of mine was a doctor who made acupuncture where they went into your ears with little needles. I was very impressed by this, so I took very big needles and I used them for her portrait – I stuck them through her picture. Then I airbrushed it so that it looked like the needles went through her head to suggest stimulation, to turn on the four elements – Earth, Air, Fire, Water … She was very pleased but I think some people thought it was like voodoo, when you stick needles into a doll and make magic, but that's not what I meant by it."

The multiple facial piercings of Debbie represented a shedding of her Blondie persona, a progression away from the band's established image and the way she had been marketed. "We did want to cut down a little on the exploitation end of it," stated Chris. "Maybe it means Debbie's just sick of her face. It's hard to say, but I've never liked the merchandising of Blondie and all that crap. We're just trying to cut it down a bit."

"There were some problems with the fans," conceded Debbie – although their concerns were more mundane. "A lot of them felt I was killing off or deserting Blondie by going brown-haired."

Any concern felt by Chrysalis about Debbie's makeover was undoubtedly heightened when promotional materials featuring Giger's *Koo Koo* cover image were banned by London Transport, the BBC and a number of record shops. "It didn't bother me that it was banned, but I was surprised," recalled Deborah. "I guess it was ahead of its time, as were a lot of things we did. H. R. Giger had just won the Academy Award for his work on *Alien*, he was a huge name and his images were known the world over – and more importantly, it was such an incredible image. It was his idea, his design, and he had a whole philosophy around it. There was a Frankenstein element to it, with him being such a sci-fi freak. I guess the piercings were just a little bit too realistic."

"We knew the cover would cause a reaction, but maybe were overconfident, even naive, to believe it would simply be taken as art," mused Chris. "It was a risk we were willing to take."

Debbie also worked with Giger and his team of assistants for videos of 'Backfired' and 'Now You Know I Know". "Working with Debbie was very good, she was very professional," Giger recounted. "I had worked with the human form before and made costumes for the theatre, but I thought Debbie looked really beautiful, really strong."

The media's focus on Debbie's change of hair colour served to highlight just how recognisable she had become over the last two years. Aside from the pressures of fame that accompany fronting a globally successful band, the strength of her image had also encouraged labels such as 'The Face of the Seventies' or 'The Face of 1980'. The history of 20th-century popular culture is littered with salutary tales of those unable to cope with the very specific pressures of celebrity. From Marilyn Monroe to Amy Winehouse, there are dozens of public figures who have imploded beneath the gravitational force of stardom. "I fully intended to be famous, ever since I was a little girl," Deborah explained. "I focused on it mentally and spiritually – on the idea of fame and the fantasy idea of Marilyn. I loved it. Then I hated it. I am truly not the person who wants to have all that exposure. In the eighties, I found that there was no place I could go, and I found that very uncomfortable. I lost all my access to street life. So then I didn't want to have a public life any more. It took away from the love that I had of the artistic thing I was doing."

Although Debbie and Blondie became well-known after the release of *Plastic Letters*, it had not been until *Parallel Lines* broke the group as a major international act that a sense of separation from the intimate scene that spawned them truly set in. In the two years that followed, Deborah was catapulted across the media at an accelerated rate, making the whole experience far more intense than if Blondie had risen to prominence more gradually.

"It really was just a lot of work always being propelled at a faster rate – an unnatural rate – trying to keep up. It was like being marched straight into the sea, always facing deadlines and so on," she admitted in 2003. "It wasn't how I imagined it to be. I think now I'd deal with it in a different way, as a game. I took it all very personally. I didn't consider myself to be 'in showbiz' – I wanted to be an artist – but I started to like it and got to being good at it. I'm good at it now and I wish I'd handled it better, that I'd been more astute as a business person. If I have a regret, it's that I didn't have that information."

Unlike many of those who found celebrity impossible to cope with, Debbie had a stable relationship that provided a bubble of comfort into which she could retreat. Hers and Chris' relationship had lasted for eight years and seen them share things that most couples never experience. Although it served to strengthen the bond between them that would endure even after they ceased to be an item, it was hardly conducive to domestic harmony.

"It was difficult for Chris and me when I became so famous," Debbie later recalled. "Because Chris is very protective, and it was beyond his ability to be the man in that situation. Witness Sean Penn and Madonna – it's not possible for any couple. And we'd worked for seven years non-stop, and it was just chaos. There was a lot of pressure."

"We have a normal relationship," Chris asserted to the contrary, at the time. "Our roles are hard to nail down because we flip-flop and take opposite sides as well. We have a very fluid relationship that can adapt to just about anything."

"I think I have a better understanding of the business world than he does," Deborah added. "Chris has a better sense of time and logic. How things will actually happen. Sometimes I can't bear to answer the phone, so Chris will do all the business that day. And then, the next day, I will do it. We support each other."

Only six years before, Chris and Debbie had lived in a rundown Bowery loft where it was possible to find a dead bum on their doorstep and not be profoundly freaked out by it. Now the couple's experiences of invasive journalism and obsessive fan interest fostered feelings of isolation and suspicion.

"One night my garbage disappeared from in front of my house and I thought, 'Oh God, what if it's that guy who goes around picking people's secrets out of their trash?' So there I was – tearing up and down the road, looking for my garbage, and … I found this bum, just rooting through it for something to eat," recounted Debbie. "It was like, 'Oh shit!' And I had to say to him, 'Listen, you picked a good night here 'cos I just happen to have thrown out some food today.'"

Not all of her concerns were unfounded, as her fame had served to mark her parents out for unwanted attention. "There was one particularly horrifying letter all about money – he was in prison, waiting to get out," she recalled. "I thought, 'Oh my God, it's like *In Cold Blood*.' I told them never to talk to anyone."

Although Debbie had always wanted to be a star, the bohemian outlook she shared with Chris ensured she would never become the kind of celebrity motivated only by fame. As much as Blondie's management, their record label and the media had sought to shape her into a consumable product, Debbie's artistic sensibility led her away from becoming a commodity.

"What I really wanted to be was a beatnik, I really wanted to be an underground artist," she asserts. "That was really where my thrust was, being a pop star – I thought it was such bullshit, you know? I knew it was bullshit, I didn't really give a rat's ass about any of it, I wanted to be famous, but I didn't really care about carrying it on."

Both *Autoamerican* and *Koo Koo* are indicative of how Debbie and Chris prioritised creativity above commerce and celebrity. "You do have a choice," Deborah declared. "You can get away. You can say, 'Either I'll stay here in a predictable world with everything controlled for me or I can close myself off from it.'"

In June 1981, the week before Debbie and Chris flew to Zurich to hook up with H. R. Giger, another link with their New York roots was severed when Anya Phillips succumbed to cancer. Anya had been one of Deborah's closest friends since they had both worked as waitresses at White's Bar during the earliest days of Blondie. While Debbie had concentrated on her group, the notoriously strong-minded Anya worked as anything from stripper or dominatrix to clothes designer to make ends meet. When conservatory-trained saxophonist James Siegfried (aka James Chance) arrived from Wisconsin, first appearing with Lydia Lunch in Teenage Jesus And The Jerks, Anya had become the manager of his group, The Contortions, and the couple later became an item. After Teenage Jesus, their wired maelstrom of clipped funk, barbed-wire vocals and manic sax caterwauling made them the most infamous group to emerge from the 'No Wave' movement.

Along with Steve Mass and Diego Cortez, Anya was co-founder of No Wave epicentre The Mudd Club on White Street, which opened in October 1978. Blondie were regulars at the venue, along with Johnny Thunders, Lou Reed, David Byrne (who name-checked it in Talking Heads' 'Life During Wartime'), The B-52's, Walter Steding and most of the *TV Party* regulars. This drug-charged den of unfettered hedonism, which featured gender-neutral bathrooms and pop artist Keith Haring's rotating gallery on the fourth floor, presented underground bands of the day along with literary titans such as Allen Ginsberg and William Burroughs. Initially intended as a downtown riposte to Studio 54, it later developed a similarly exclusive door policy, gradually losing its initial sense of danger and excitement, before closing in 1983. For a maniacal few years, New York's underground, its veterans and new bloods had been able to boast their own clubs, a regular TV show and a healthy representation on vinyl.

Anya had been at the centre of a scene that originated at CBGB's and took off into wildly experimental, often confrontational new directions. Fiercely independent, she initially refused to even recognise the disease that would cut short her life. "Anya never really came out and said, 'I have cancer,'" explained designer Sylvia Morales, a friend of hers who had recently embarked on a decade-long marriage to Lou Reed. "She said that they had found this lump behind her ear, and that they were looking for other lumps ... I don't think she accepted it for a long, long time."

When it became impossible, even for someone as self-possessed as Anya, to ignore the effects of the disease, Debbie helped her receive care at the Westchester County hospital, where she died on June 19. "Anya's death seemed to mark something, perhaps the coming of the real world," reflected Debbie. "The period 1975-1980 was a time in which people insisted on being allowed to do what they weren't supposed to do. Anya symbolised that period. She was a powerful energy source that's now missing from the scene, an example of how intense willpower is charisma. As a Chinese woman she was a symbol of intensity, but she was also very romantic even though she would say hard things and act cold sometimes. I think Anya meant many things to everybody, because she was so ferociously strong. Most of the people who started at the same level as she did never got anywhere. Apart from being a photographer and actress, Anya succeeded in the things she tried. She helped shape the concept of The Contortions. I guess certain sections of a scene always get marked off by death. Anya's was a particularly personal loss for us. I wish she hadn't died."

"She was unique," observed Chris in 1999. "I have Anya's ashes downstairs. James [Chance] was always afraid he'd leave them somewhere. He keeps saying he wants them, but he never comes to get them, maybe because they'd make him sad. Anya was a really strong girl who did really powerful things. I'm honoured to have them here."

Issued at the end of July 1981, *Koo Koo* was trailed by the single release of 'Backfired', which suffered from a lack of airplay and failed to make the Top 30 in America or Britain. Three months later it was followed by a seven-inch of 'The Jam Was Moving' that came with little publicity, stalling at number 82 in the *Billboard* chart.

Chris admitted to being disappointed with the way the album had been received. "More so in the States where we had this blatant racist reaction. Some of the stations were saying we can't play it because it's too R&B. But in the States you have a white chart and a black chart, so that's appalling."

Equally disappointing but perhaps understandably so, Debbie's nascent solo career drew little support from within Blondie. Nigel Harrison admitted her and Chris' link-up with Edwards and Rodgers had generated "a little paranoia", while Clem observed, "I don't think that album was very good. I don't think that Nile Rodgers and Bernard Edwards were the best producers for her."

Perhaps these reactions stemmed from a sense of disappointment at Blondie's recent inactivity. A year after the band had travelled to Los Angeles to record *Autoamerican*, there was still no concrete date to commence on a sixth studio album. "I don't feel under pressure to do it," Deborah asserted. "I think it's much better to do something that's good and right and that everybody wants to do than to do it because the record company thinks it's time. I will definitely not do that."

Instead, Chrysalis released *The Best Of Blondie* in October 1981. The 12-track retrospective was freshened up by four 'Special Mix' tracks that saw Mike Chapman remix 'Heart Of Glass', 'Sunday Girl', 'In The Flesh' and 'Rapture', largely by incorporating elements of alternate takes into the single version. Although the compilation reached number four in the UK, it would merely brush the *Billboard* Top 30. As the autumn drew to a close, the news that Blondie would reconvene to record before the end of the year drew sighs of relief from a record label desperate for new product.

Chapter 12

No One Can Say We Didn't
Hold Out For 15 Minutes

"We definitely didn't come from showbiz families where we were counselled or tutored for our entire adolescent lives. We weren't groomed for success, that's for sure."

Debbie Harry

W hen Blondie went into The Hit Factory to record their sixth studio album in late 1981, there was little in the way of unity or enthusiasm. Although Clem was happy enough to be back in action and Nigel returned to the studio in businesslike fashion, Jimmy was disappointed by the poor critical reception and minimal sales that greeted *Heart On A Wall*, his recent new-wave/power-pop long-player. "It was a real horrible record, for a lot of reasons – because Jimmy can't sing for starters," Burke observed. "I don't think the timing was right for any of that stuff."

Having spent much of the last two years seeking to expand their boundaries, both Debbie and Chris had reached a point where the band's next album seemed little more than a contractual obligation. Chris' focus was on getting his new record label, Animal, up and running, while Debbie remained engaged by the possibility of a career as an actress. Neither was bursting with fervour at the prospect of climbing back on the album/tour merry-go-round.

"I never have any difficulty making my own decisions about what thing to do next, but in the group it's hard," stated Deborah. "I think I really have a strong sense of what's right. But it just seems like your mind is travelling at one rate and the physical world is travelling at another rate. The record business, God knows what rate that's travelling at. So by the time a record comes out it's like you're not even there any more. The record comes out and it's like, 'God, I have to promote this for the next six months?' I feel like hiring a bunch of clones to go out and do it."

Aware that they were obliged to produce several more albums for Chrysalis, Chris quipped, "We could just improvise it … Play for 10 hours and then put it together. I'm not sure at all what it's going to be like."

Frankie, who'd been a peripheral figure during the making of *Autoamerican*, was now so far out of the loop that the sessions got under way before he realised Blondie were back in the studio. "All I know is, the record was going down without me being involved in the basic tracks, and I got the lawyer involved," he explained afterwards. A settlement was reached before the matter got to court and Infante permitted to overdub his guitar alone, after the rest of the group had laid down their parts. While this latest development in what he saw as a campaign to marginalise him may have lodged in the guitarist's mind, his contributions certainly didn't. "You could play me stuff, and I could say, 'What is that?' I don't even remember where I did it!"

In addition to internal rancour and lack of interest, cocaine consumption by certain members was approaching heroic levels. And, while Blondie operated within a culture where record labels were happy to lay on generous amounts of blow to aid creativity, there was plenty of self-indulgent evidence on vinyl to prove it did precisely the opposite. In any event, it was hardly likely to calm already stormy waters.

Returning for his fourth time, Mike Chapman sensed an air of finality. "I knew that we were in a different and far less accessible artistic space. And that worried me. I could tell that things were different now, and I knew that this would be the last Blondie album."

So far as Stein was concerned, his recent experience behind the mixing desk had enhanced his appreciation of Mike's talents. "I've never walked away from a record thinking it was finished, but one thing I've learned from producing all these other people is to let Chapman do it."

Chrysalis was also worried about its investment's ability to extend its run of hits. "They said, 'Well, we hope this isn't another album like *Autoamerican*,'" recalled Clem, who shot back with, "What do you mean, you hope there's not gonna be two number one singles on the album?"

"Both Debbie and Chris came to this latest project full of doubts and fears," said Chapman. "They seemed almost disinterested, although they put on a brave face."

Irrespective of any misgivings, the one thing that Blondie – Chris in particular – was never short of was ideas. "This was the first album done pretty much in the studio, with very little pre-production," he remembered. "We wanted to experiment, to stretch the limits a little. The record evolved during the session. Nigel had lots of idea tapes. 'Orchid Club' was a simple riff that we structured; 'War Child' was the same thing. I had the theme and title of 'English Boys'."

"I brought in a tape of 'War Child', and the band really jumped for that one. Chris thought it was like The Jackson Five. My other song on the album, 'Orchid Club', was kind of a Marvin Gaye cop," added Nigel.

"'Danceway' is my little story about my band," continued Jimmy. "Debbie said, 'Write a song about us.'"

With sufficient ideas germinating in the studio, it was decided that only one track would be a cover version – a radical reworking of girl group The Marvelettes' 1967 hit, 'The Hunter Gets Captured By The Game'. The Smokey Robinson-penned song also provided the album with its name: *The Hunter*.

"I thought we were gonna do 'The Hunter Gets Captured By The Game' like The Marvelettes' original," Harrison observed, "but I think Chris and Mike decided they wanted it real primitive-sounding. When I hear it I keep waiting for the whole drum kit to come in."

"I don't think that song's ever been covered the way we did it. We tried to get a *King Kong* feeling," said Debbie. "We identified with both hunter and hunted, but obviously we were more of the hunted at that point. We were really marked for slaughter and decimated by a bunch of different people right around then."

The Hunter continues the musical diversity of Blondie's previous two albums, presenting an extensive range of styles. The opening track, 'Orchid Club', has a distinct Latin vibe that rolls into the horn-driven mariachi/calypso whimsy of 'Island Of Lost Souls'. "The horn section that they brought in to play on 'Island Of Lost Souls', and whatever other tracks we used them on, they were all a bunch of junkies – Puerto Ricans that they'd come across," Chapman recounted. "Great players – and they were all junked out of their minds. The whole session they were sweating profusely and disappearing to the bathroom and coming back. I was like, 'Even my horn section are junkies.'"

"The difference with this album is that before we used session players for the horns, while here it's guys off the street," confirmed Chris.

Reflecting the eclecticism, 'Dragonfly' splices Debbie's sci-fi infused lyrics to Chris' diaphanous funk, while another Harry/Stein composition, 'The Beast', is a kind of 'Rapture' sequel that features another Debbie rap underpinned by a melange of wailing guitars and pounding drums. "That's just a rap song about the devil," she explains. "Going out for the night like he was just a regular guy."

Originally recorded for that year's James Bond movie of the same name, but passed over in favour of Sheena Easton's theme, 'For Your Eyes Only' strikes a suitably expansive tone, with Deborah's lyrics imparting an appropriate air of mystery and adventure.

Chris' 'English Boys' is a gentle, synth-infused ballad topped by Debbie's lyrics which vaguely hint at an antiwar message. 'War Child' likewise sees Blondie exploring the field of human conflict, its lyrics citing both the PLO and Khmer Rouge as the track lurches in a direction that Giorgio Moroder might have propelled Blondie in. 'Little Caesar' brings back the horns for a sultry shuffle, while 'Danceaway' – one of only two Jimmy Destri-credited tracks on the disc – showcases the keyboardist's sixties chops across an upbeat slice of Motown-infused pop. His other song, on an album dominated by Chris and Debbie's material, '(Can I) Find The Right Words (To Say)', is less engaging as its slightly disjointed arrangement is made jarring by Deborah's strident delivery of her lyric.

While *The Hunter* fulfilled its brief of encompassing a wide range of musical styles, it lacked the sense of new ground being broken that energised Blondie's previous albums. Despite this, Nigel remained upbeat. "The challenge now is just to keep growing," he observed. "This last album we definitely grew, and I know we're capable of more. There's no way we can ever backtrack."

"*The Hunter* is the composite album. Every phase that Blondie's been through manifests itself on this disc," insisted Clem. "It was the first time

I'd ever felt confident, I really thought I was at the top of my game, playing well. We made a good record, in a lot of ways."

"The entire project was a struggle," countered Chapman. "Nothing went well. Chris was not well. Debbie was not happy. Jimmy had some really bad problems. Clem was complaining about everything. Nigel seemed worried about everything. Frankie, of course, was gone ... The wonderful world of clever and intensely catchy pop songs had turned to hell."

With *The Hunter* recorded but without a firm release date, Chris refocused his energies on Animal Records, the label he initiated at the urging of Walter Steding which had secured distribution through Chrysalis. Initially, Animal had been devised as a means of representing the post-punk scene on vinyl, providing an outlet for downtown friends and artists and Chris' own productions, pledging to restore "loudness and craziness" to the "staid and conservative" music scene.

Another key factor in convincing Stein to helm his own label dated back to the winter of 1980, when he produced a demo for The Lounge Lizards and had to deal with the ignorance of record company A&R departments before the group were finally signed by EG Records. It took two years for Chris, helped by Jeff Aldrich, Chrysalis' Vice President of A&R in LA, to get the right deal for Animal, demanding that its artists sign one-off deals and keep their own publishing.

Originally, Chris was going to call his label 'Skull', but Chrysalis was less than keen. "The Chrysalis people thought 'Skull Records' was kinda down, and I could see it was a little limited," he conceded. 'Animal' came from the notion that all record companies are corporate beasts. Although approved by Chrysalis as a kind of vanity project to keep one of its stars happy, the label's subsequent success would prove its merit – although Chris financed many activities himself and deals were often done on the basis of a handshake.

"Chrysalis were really resistant to the concept at first," said Stein. "They really wanted to have options on the artists and I wanted to do something more modern. But at least they were open to an alternative label approach, because they'd had the 2-Tone thing and also Takoma, the obscure little folk label they picked up."

Operating out of Shep Gordon's Alive Enterprises suite, Animal's office was run by former head of EG management Ed Strait (as suggested by Robert Fripp). "There are still all the same problems in any big sort of corporate monstrosity," stated Chris. "But for an outfit like them to cater to The Gun Club when they aren't signed to them and could go to another label in a second, that's a plus. They really have been open."

Animal's first high-profile release was Iggy Pop's *Zombie Birdhouse* album. Iggy's recording contract with Arista had come to an end after his main champion at the label, Charles Levison, took a new post at WEA. Chris agreed to release the next album, advancing $50,000 to Iggy, who spent six weeks writing material with guitarist Rob Duprey at the latter's home studio on Sixth Avenue. At this time, the former Stooge was living in an approximation of domesticity in Bensonhurst, Brooklyn with his girlfriend, Esther. With Chris producing and playing bass and Clem providing drums for the sessions at Blank Tapes – Bob Blank's studio lifeline for the downtown scene, particularly ZE artists – the album came in under budget before May 1982 was out.

After having to bow to commercial demands on his Arista albums, Iggy seemed to view the sessions as a creative catharsis, eschewing any energised rock'n'roll in favour of the dark experimentation that suffused *The Idiot*. Taking further cues from his Bowie period, Iggy's lyrics are evidently influenced by the Burroughs/Bowie cut-up technique and often slip into a form of free association. It's an album of bold gambles, some of which work and others don't, but Chris could have done a lot worse than to launch his new record label with 'the Mighty Pop', who described the album as "a solid piece of work".

"I think Ig really got pushed into this American mainstream rock'n'roll thing the last couple of albums; I just wanted to see him be really free to go crazy," Stein explained. "When we did his vocal sessions, he really was just totally crazy … the line about 'zombie birdhouse' was just completely improvised … when you listen to the record you can hear some hesitation after 'zombie' and suddenly it's 'birdhouse!' – like, 'There it is, figure it out! … I didn't even know what Zombie Birdhouse was until he came back from Haiti with a photo of the club … When Debbie and I saw that we thought maybe Zombie Birdhouse was this little club of Iggy's brain where he goes to!"

Summing up his Iggy experience now, Chris says, "It was really ironic that, at the time, Iggy couldn't get a decent deal, so he did a record for my very casual company; there were no contracts. Then the very next record that he did was the one with 'Real Wild Child' on it, and that one really elevated him."

Former *Punk* artist/editor John Holmstrom, who designed the Animal logo, commented, "Chris isn't stupid! I think he's the only guy from Blondie that will land on his feet. If some bigger company picks up, say, Iggy, he'd love it … Chris is open to that. I just hope he can afford to continue like this. I mean, it's brave of Chrysalis with Blondie going out the window [in terms of declining sales] and Pat Benatar on the way out the window – what else do they have? Jethro Tull?"

Zombie Birdhouse was followed by a stream of idiosyncratic releases on Animal from friends such as Walter Steding, Snuky Tate, Tav Falco's Panther Burns and James Chance, representing the original No Wave. The next landmark Animal release saw Chris producing Jeffrey Lee Pierce and his Gun Club, emerging with the hauntingly atmospheric *Miami*. It was both fitting and touchingly loyal that Pierce should get his big break courtesy of Chris. He had been a fervent Blondie devotee since witnessing the first West Coast gigs in early 1977, concealing himself in a shopping trolley to sneak into their hotel and earning an appointment as their fan club president. For years he dyed his hair blond in a dishevelled imitation of Debbie's, even down to the hard-to-reach dark part at the back.

The Gun Club were a band out of their time and out of their minds. They never got full credit for fearlessly creating a template which others later capitalised upon, diluting the original concept. Jeffrey plugged into the dark main artery of the blues itself, a demonic mess of paradoxes belching out disarming beauty or apocalyptic rage. While much of LA's punk scene took inspiration from the usual three-chord sources, Pierce gouged much deeper into America's roots music: blues, folk, jazz and country, tossed in a blender full of drugs and liquor then taken to hell and back.

Jeffrey was born in El Monte, near downtown LA – one of the few parts of the city to bear a resemblance to New York's funkier neighbourhoods. He was a natural born rebel, dressing glam-punk-pimp-cowboy style. His creative passions were ignited by Blondie, who became a fixation for the rest of his life, Pierce often going dewy-eyed at the mention of Debbie's name. He combined and conflated the bad side of Jim Morrison without the sex, the unpredictability of Iggy Pop without the self-mutilating gymnastics and, sometimes, the drugged ruin of Elvis without the rhinestones. Despite (or maybe because of) his personal dissolution, Jeff's voice could send shivers down the spine.

Also featuring drummer Terry Graham, guitarist Ward Dobson and bassist Rob Ritter, The Gun Club thrashed around LA's club circuit until they made an album for Bob Biggs' Slash Records in 1981. They speed-recorded *The Fire Of Love* in two days, emerging with an awesome distillation of raw blues, rockabilly and punk, topped by Jeffrey's evangelical screams and harangues. Its impact and Jeffrey's established Blondie connection secured a deal with Animal Records, an association that would lead to The Gun Club releasing more records than anyone else on Chris' roster.

"In LA, there's like this real hierarchy of coolness that's supposed to be real important and they were always in and out of it," Stein observed. "Jeff sort of went through all this stuff fast that we also went through in Blondie. I was just intrigued that there was this bunch of young kids in LA who were into this stuff I was into in the sixties – fuckin' old blues."

Miami was recorded at Blank Tapes during June 1982, with Chris turning in a powerfully atmosphere-drenched production. Determined not to allow contractual restraints to prevent her involvement, Debbie provided backing vocals credited to 'D. H. Laurence Jr.' on the contagious 'Watermelon Man', which also featured Chris on bongos and a Walter Steding violin contribution.

"I've known Jeffrey a long time, since Blondie first went to LA," Chris explained. "When we met he was a very sad person; he's a little happier now that he's found what he wants to do. He was like this lost kid hanging around us seeking this thing, but he didn't know what it was. He used to send me tapes; the only reason we did 'Hanging On The Telephone' was because Jeff sent me a tape of it."

Chris' production drew criticism from those who were hoping for a re-creation of the abrasive punk attack of the band's live shows. Today he remains justifiably proud of the album, saying, "The Jeffrey saga is seemingly a long one. I have gotten flak from Gun Club members who played on *Miami* for not having a 'hard rock' enough approach to the production. I don't recall any of them voicing concerns at the time. Jeffrey and I spent a lot of time thinking about what the record should ultimately sound like. He really wanted to get away from a standard punk rock approach and reach into the world of so-called 'normal' music by making more references to country, et cetera. Jeff was the one who brought in a pedal steel guitar player. I know for sure he liked the record."

With ZE records starting to flounder, James Chance made the logical move of recording an album for Animal, revisiting the James White And The Blacks persona devised by his late girlfriend Anya Phillips, in which he had recorded *Off White* with members of apocalyptic jazz band Defunkt. Live, Chance's crowd-baiting onslaughts had achieved an Iggy-like notoriety, giving him a reputation that hardly helped his career. His music remained a sabre-toothed mixture of hellish caterwauls and taut funk backdrops, East Village aural anarchy playing havoc with 'That Old Black Magic'. Over 30 years later, it's apparent that Chance was sparking a rebirth of the cool in New York's post-punk hotbed.

"James is a real controversial figure," claimed Chris. "People either hate him or love him; there's no middle ground. Ever since he was jumping into the audience and getting into fights, that's how it's been. James did his own thing and his own cover and everything; that LP was recorded last spring. James has been through lots of weird trips but he is what he is; a real original … He's always tried to maintain what he thinks is right. He's an honourable person and he is sensitive. We've been friends a long time … People are not gonna readily accept his record, but James is aware of that …The record's really *thick;* it's the most heavy produced record he's ever made."

Other records released by Animal in 1982 now seem like curios from an era of unfettered adventurism. Previously, Walter Steding's sole recorded output outside the *TV Party* studio had been 1980's 'The Poke', produced with Chris as the lone release on Andy Warhol's Earhole label (now a three-figure collectable for Warholites and Blondie completists). The track is revisited on *Dancing In Heaven*, a Steding-produced melange of post-punk quirkiness, multi-tracked vocal convolutions and occasional funk undertows, recorded at Blank Tapes. The back cover shows Steding and a worried-looking Warhol − billed as the album's 'executive producer' − clamping his hands over his ears.

Snuky Tate made his long-playing debut with the multihued hallucinogenic sonic collisions of *Babylon Under Pressure*, which he described as, "Like Ray Charles and reggae, but space stuff and salsa music at the same time. Actually it's completely insane. It's like Ray Charles on acid."

Tav Falco and the Panther Burns released the rambunctious four-track *Blow Your Top* EP. Named after the legend of a demonic panther that stalked and terrorised a 19th-century plantation, The Unapproachable Panther Burns' 'art damage' project was the 1979 brainchild of confrontational performance artist Tav Falco and the late Alex Chilton. After impressing

Rough Trade's Geoff Travis at a New York show, an album was recorded at Sam Phillips' Memphis studio but rejected. The group, now including future Gun Club guitarist Jim Duckworth, tried again at Ardent studios, recording everything in one take to emerge with the sizzlingly shambolic rockabilly hellfire of *Beyond The Magnolia Curtain*. When Panther Burns took to the road, Chilton departed and former Lydia Lunch drummer Jim Sclavunos (now an integral part of Nick Cave's Bad Seeds and Grinderman) joined on drums. Soon, Falco was being embraced by the Mudd Club scene, sufficiently captivating Chris to place them in the same Plaza studios where Blondie had recorded their early albums, resulting in the tightly energised *Blow Your Top*.

Speaking now, Chris remembers this time with much affection, while acknowledging that trying to balance a record label with Blondie ran him into the ground. In New York at that time the energy seemed to be buzzing out of the subway vents and, if one's energy flagged, cocaine was omnipresent. "The Animal Records thing was satisfying because, in retrospect, we – and there were only two people who made up the 'company'; me and Ed Strait – got some memorable recordings out. I think about 12 albums and maybe twice that many singles. The best known is probably the *Wild Style* soundtrack."

Animal briefly embodied the rampantly creative downtown spirit. The *Wild Style* project now stands as a remarkably prescient landmark, one of hip hop's most crucially vibrant early documents, setting footage of rapping, turntabling, graffiti and break-dancing against the cavernous ruins of the South Bronx. Producer Charlie Ahearn's movie was the first to depict the neighbourhood's hip hop culture, aided by a cast including Freddy Braithwaite, Lee Quinones, Lady Pink, Rock Steady Crew, Grandmaster Flash and the Cold Crush Brothers.

Whereas Malcolm McLaren diluted what he witnessed on one personally terrifying night at a South Bronx jam to create the globally successful *Duck Rock*, Chris and Fab Five Freddy went straight to the source, secured the originators and (crucially) documented its outlaw excitement in the movie and on the soundtrack. The latter's mix of infectious old-school rapping and smoking funk-based grooves (whipped up by Chris, Steding drummer Lenny Ferrari and bassist David Harper), laced with dub-fired mixing-desk trickery, was truly ahead of the coming hip hop wave. The album's credits boast several nascent talents who would go down in folklore: Grandmaster

Caz, Double Trouble, Grand Wizzard Theodore, Cold Crush Brothers, Kevie Kev and Chrois, plus Debbie's favourite, Rammellzee (soon to cause a stir with 'Beat Bop'). Unfortunately, most would be lost in the gold rush which strangled much of the movement's raw street spirit.

"We never even met!" laughs Chris. "It was done like how people work today on the internet. We just traded tapes back and forth. They had bass and drum parts, then I came in and did weird electric guitar stuff, while Freddy added sound effects like electric shavers and police sirens. Then the finished thing was pressed up and made into a hundred white label copies. Guys would beg me for copies.

"They were initially just given out to people who were working on the film to use to scratch with, but everyone gravitated to this one track called 'Down By Law'. Caz cut it on turntables and sent me a tape of his cut version, then I synchronised a bunch of synthesizers to the cutting, which I'm sure hadn't been done prior to that."

While the movie soundtrack was released on Animal in 1983, the Caz-Stein collaboration came out as a 12-inch singe entitled 'The Wild Style Theme', which now sounds uncannily like an instrumental blueprint for The Stone Roses' 'Fools Gold'.

Amid this maelstrom of activity, it was apparent that Chris' focus was now primarily upon Animal Records, with Blondie a third consideration after Debbie's solo career. "We're gonna do another solo album with Debbie, which Mike Chapman will probably produce; I don't know how long we'll keep it together with Blondie. Animal seems to have evolved when the timing was really right ... It's like Zen, y'know? When you don't have the desire for something, that's when something happens. It's when you define something and say, that has to happen – that's when you'll find that you can't make it happen."

With *The Hunter's* release finally set for late May, Chrysalis trailed the album by issuing 'Island Of Lost Souls' on seven-inch, supported by a rather unreal video that set Debbie and the group down in a Scilly Isles approximation of a *Fantasy Island* tropical paradise. Chris, Jimmy, Nigel and Frank were asked to caper around pretending to play a variety of wind instruments. Infante was still 'travelling separately' from the rest of Blondie and found the shoot a fraught experience: "When we did the video — talk about island of lost souls, man, lemme tell you! When I was there, nobody would talk to anybody else; my lawyer said, 'Don't talk to anybody, don't hit anybody.'"

Although sections of the music press dismissed the single as an attempt to replicate the commercial success of 'The Tide Is High', 'Island Of Lost Souls' cracked the *Billboard* Top 40 and narrowly missed out on the UK Top 10.

Just ahead of the album's release, Blondie made a high-profile trip to the UK to announce a September 1982 tour, mark the release of *The Hunter* and participate in the launch of Victor Bockris' *Making Tracks: The Rise Of Blondie*. The book launch took place at the B2 Art Gallery in Wapping High Street — at that time basically a near-derelict Thameside landscape of abandoned warehouses and trailer cafés. It resembled some pre-gentrification areas of New York, with this little gallery pointing toward a similar redeveloped future to Manhattan.

Despite the less than salubrious locale, nothing could stop the media converging on another label-funded Blondie blowout. Despite adverse reactions to recent records there was still feverish interest in Debbie, while the band had bowed to pressure and booked four nights at Wembley Arena as a climax to their forthcoming UK tour.

Kris was present at the Blondie/Bockris book launch:

At the time, the group stated that they were happy with how The Hunter had turned out, a beaming Nigel Harrison declaring, "We did it really fast, just went in there." Of course, the bad reviews had riled Chris, who reacted with a contemptuous shrug: "Yes it got slagged. What a surprise! Where's the spirit, chaps? What did they say? I wouldn't know, I never read them."

Debbie, resplendent in a blonde wig, seemed quite relaxed at first, finding time to tackle a trifle amidst the meeting, greeting and posing for photographs. For much of the bash, I stood at a far window with Chris, sundry band members and Victor Bockris. Chris looked thinner but was his usual dry, acerbic self, unable to stop enthusing on upcoming Animal projects such as Debbie's second solo album, which he was thinking of asking Chapman to produce. He gave me a guided tour of the photos adorning the gallery walls; "There's the box where I kept my comic collection before it got lost in the fire ... That's Debbie in Marilyn Monroe's dress ... The Ramones before they got leather jackets."

After the party, the group embarked upon a punishing schedule of early-starting interviews and TV appearances, before popping off to the Scilly Isles for the 'Island Of Lost Souls' shoot. Following a brief overstay caused by fog descending on the Isles, the behind-schedule group jetted over to the continent to fulfil further promotional obligations. They then returned to London, where Debbie was scheduled to host Top Of The Pops alongside John Peel. Arriving at the BBC's Shepherds Bush studio in the afternoon, Blondie set about rehearsing in that little studio which always seemed so much bigger on the TV. Debbie and Peel were already making a great double act, trading banter, John the epitome of warm charm, maybe thinking he was a very lucky man, as more often he was paired with Jimmy Savile.

With Debbie changed into blonde wig and green dress, the red light was about to go on so Chris and I made for the studio and were summarily refused entry. A combination of new fire regulations enforced by the consummate jobsworth meant we had to watch from an observation room miles above the studio. Debbie didn't realise that her partner hadn't been allowed in until near the end of recording, which had included the 'Island Of Lost Souls' video and gone very well, thanks to the good-natured chemistry between Debbie and Peel. Understandably, she threw a minor shitfit. Although Denny Vosburgh [Shep Gordon's assistant] blasts a producer who apologises, it was evident that behind her favourite wraparound mirror shades Debbie was pissed off. So the last time that I would see Debbie and Chris together as part of Blondie finished under something of a black cloud. They were about to return to New York and start rehearsing for the tour next day. "See you in September" were their final words.

Any criticisms levelled at 'Island Of Lost Souls' paled into insignificance compared to the opprobrium that greeted the May 27, 1982 release of *The Hunter*. While *Musician's* Mark Roland described the album as comprising "all hot sauce and no enchilada", in *New Musical Express* Adrian Thrills heaped on the disapproval: "This is the sixth Blondie album, their worst to date. At a time when the best new British pop is pushing forward at an invigorating post-punk pace, Blondie could hardly sound any safer, saner, stodgier or more senile," he blasted, dismissing the group as "just a bunch of loveless old lags; pale, middle-aged hipsters politely fading into the wallpaper at a house-party for bright young things." Thrills eviscerated the original material: "Had they been sent as demos to a record label, they would have been rejected outright by any quality-conscious A&R man, yet here they are on hard, black vinyl, obscene and embarrassing to the point of grotesque self-parody." Finally, he critically consigned *The Hunter* to the sump pit usually reserved for money-spinning pap: "This album will doubtlessly sell and sell. Sadly, there are still a lot of people around who will buy a Blondie record on face value. On musical merit, however, *The Hunter* deserves to be the final nail in their coffers."

Whatever the merits of Thrills' musical criticism, he was inarguably wrong about one thing – *The Hunter* only sold in similar numbers to its preceding single, making number nine in Britain and hovering just outside the US Top 30 for a week. Debbie believed the album was poorly promoted and it was certainly true that Chrysalis – which had just undergone a management shake-up – did not put the push behind *The Hunter* that *Eat To The Beat* and *Autoamerican* had enjoyed. "There were changes going on at the record company as well. There are usually personnel changes at a record company every five years and those are deadly to an artist because very often the people who sign you aren't there any more and the new honcho who comes in isn't really interested in old artists," she asserted. This was further evidenced by the lack of any funds being made available for the filming of a video to promote the single release of 'War Child', which slipped out with minimal fanfare across Europe and Australia in July. Unsurprisingly, the single flopped – only making number 39 in the UK.

Although Blondie's British fans had been divided by *The Hunter*, expectations generated an optimism among those who waited patiently to catch the band live. However, this was undermined when the tour was cancelled due to slow ticket sales. Instead, the group returned to the stage (for the first time since January 1980) with the Tracks Across America tour, opening at Baton Rouge, Louisiana on July 23, 1982. As the band took the State University Assembly Centre stage, two things were immediately apparent. Most obviously, Frank was absent, having been replaced by session man Eddie Martinez.

"It was, 'Frank, there's a problem,'" recalled Infante. "And I said, 'Get somebody else, and pay me as if I was there.' The vibe wasn't the same. I didn't go to any shows, but that's what I heard from people who did."

Those who looked a little closer might have noticed Chris had lost a considerable amount of weight and was looking more than fashionably gaunt. "Nobody knew what was wrong," Glenn O'Brien recalled. "We thought maybe he had AIDS, but how did he get AIDS? He didn't do any of the things you're supposed to do to get AIDS? You could see he was like a skeleton."

Although, thankfully, Chris was not infected with HIV, he was obviously unwell. He'd experienced some chest problems the previous year, which he and Deborah had ascribed to asthma. However, as Blondie tracked across America, it was clear that the guitarist was struggling to cope with the rigours of being back on the road. His reaction to a pre-tour pep talk from Shep Gordon clearly showed where Chris was at. "He said, 'You can go out and be millionaires, or sit at home on your ass, and sell a lot of records,'" recounted Clem. "And Chris said, 'Well, I'll just stay home, then.'"

"The tour was a disaster, it was just horrible," Nigel insisted. "We were booked into gigs that were 20,000-seater places and there was only 9,000 people there. And at that point that's when Chris really started to look pale and skinny."

By the time Blondie reached New Jersey on August 14, both Chris and the band he played such a key part in were visibly fraying at the edges, putting in a lifeless set before a disappointed crowd. "Chris was sick by then. He weighed about 120 pounds," recalled Deborah. "It was difficult for him physically and total stress time for all of us. We didn't know what was wrong with him yet. It was horrifying. And there were so many fractures within the band. They kept getting bigger. Management wasn't interested and eventually just walked away."

"It was like a changing of the guard," Clem observed. "Nigel and I got Duran Duran to open for us; by the end of the tour, they were the success, we were the failure."

Chris did his best to remain upbeat. "Every big group has gone up and down. The question which makes existing relevant is whether or not you are making any statement." But it was difficult to understand what kind of statement a poorly attended tour by a conflict-ridden group, led by an evidently unwell guitarist, could make.

In common with the rest of the band, Debbie was finding the going tough. "In a lot of ways as a performer it's easier to be the underdog," she asserted. "When you come out on stage I think it's more of a challenge to have people like you. Also, sometimes you come out on stage and everybody's ready for you, and you just don't come up to their expectations, because everybody's fantasy is always more than reality – then it makes it very hard."

A week later, after a gig alongside Genesis and Elvis Costello in Philadelphia, Chris could no longer continue. He'd been unable to swallow and had found it difficult to eat. Weakened by the as-yet undiagnosed illness, the rigours of touring and running a record label, and overenthusiastic drug consumption, he finally collapsed.

Chris Stein was rushed into hospital and, after 10 days of tests, was diagnosed as suffering from *pemphigus vulgaris* – a rare autoimmune disorder that causes blistering of the skin, sores, and damage to the mucus membranes. If left untreated, the disease – which most commonly affects middle-aged or older people – can be fatal.

"It's a genetic disorder, even though nobody in your family necessarily has to have had it," explained Chris. "It's pretty rare. I got one letter from a guy who had it. But I also got tons of weird letters. Everything you could think of."

Chris had been unaware that his life was in danger and was reluctant to stay in hospital. "If I hadn't been doing what I was doing it wouldn't have happened. When they first put me on the steroids, I had some really great hallucinations. I had no conception of where I was. I felt like I was everywhere in the world. It was like an astral tour. I'd wake up and think I was in Cuba or Hong Kong."

"He was still on the road," added Debbie. "He didn't know who people were."

Initially he downplayed his condition, preferring to talk up the band's future: "Ironically the shows were the best received of any we've ever done and the reviews were also the best – although the *previews* were universally moaning and groaning on about 'art'. Being associated with art is really a negative thing. But ticket sales abroad were down and everybody was tired so we figured we'll end it now and see what happens. Go on to the next thing, which is Debbie's solo project."

It became apparent that Chris' condition precluded any quick return to performing or recording. "Chris and I had talked about taking a year off," Debbie revealed. "He was working very hard with his label Animal Records, and he'd produced *Zombie Birdhouse* and the first record of The Gun Club, plus with the Blondie pile-up and responsibilities, it all got to be too much."

In the late summer of 1982, without any fanfare, public acrimony or even a press release, Blondie simply dissolved.

Looking back from a perspective widened by nearly 30 years, Chris reflects on the way in which Blondie broke up. "As far as why the band split, there were so many causes and a lot of negativity … getting older gives one a different view of just about everything … I'm sure I said some really stupid shit — it was a period of stupid statements. Looking back from the 21st century, I often wonder about some of the things people said back then about Blondie, about how some of the crazy criticism and mud slung at us would hold up in today's context, in light of all that has come after … For example, how would Lester Bangs' severe comments about Debbie and my selling out and exploiting her sexuality — for one, 'selling out' implies that you get paid but that's a whole other story — hold up in the cold light of Britney and all of her ilk? Deb got so whacked for doing what in retrospect was absurdly innocent compared to what's become the norm now, not only the norm but embraced by the masses and the media."

"It was a gradual thing to end Blondie. It wasn't totally my decision," Deborah explained. "We had all outgrown it and wanted to do different things. So we stopped. I wanted people to know there was more to me, as a person, than the sort of cartoon character we had created. It wasn't enough for me to be treated any more like I was Blondie. I had to let people know there was something else happening there. I wanted to be an actress, and that's what I want more than anything now — to be recognised as an actress. It's important to let people know I'm not Blondie, I'm Debbie Harry."

"The drugs were a tremendous downfall for us, because we were with management that was really OK with cocaine use — that was fine, but once you graduated to heroin use, you were fucked," stated Chris.

"I think that probably the main contributor to the band disbanding is our drug problems," agreed Jimmy.

"Everything fell apart and I don't think that anyone could hold Blondie, as individuals or the band, responsible for all of that," Debbie summarised. "It just was this kind of eruption or disintegration of the whole fucking machine simultaneously. It's just a very rare kind of occurrence and very sad. It was mind numbing, actually. We had worked practically non-stop for seven years, so we were probably over-worked and over-tired and the whole thing was just badly handled. I think we were mismanaged from the get-go. If it hadn't been for the fact that Chris and I were a sort of grounding force in the band, almost parental in a sense, that we represented some kind of solidity to the other guys, we probably wouldn't have lasted as long as we did."

Disappointed by the end of a key phase of his rock'n'roll dream, Clem noted, "It's frightening to see how successful the band could have been. It was a great success, and a great experience, but a lot of things could have been done a lot better."

Chapter 13

The Ice Cream Years

"Stories of my sainthood have been much exaggerated."

Debbie Harry

In the aftermath of Blondie's dissolution, the band's constituent parts scattered in search of new outlets for their talents. Disappointed by the way in which *Heart On A Wall* had been received, Jimmy set his sights on production, travelling to Europe with a view to working on the other side of the mixing desk. Although he met with U2 manager Paul McGuinness, nothing transpired and Destri returned to Brooklyn, where he went into the building industry. "I bought a company that bought and sold old buildings and renovated them," he explained. "It's a little more complicated than construction and I made a lot of money, which was good because when we left Blondie I had no money."

Nigel hooked up with his old Silverhead frontman Michael des Barres' latest project, Chequered Past, a dissolute supergroup that also included former Sex Pistol Steve Jones. Harrison was joined by Clem and Frankie, the latter not sticking around long before he was lured away to tour Australia and Japan with Iggy Pop. "I didn't call him, he called me," Infante declared. "He just let you do what you wanted, everything was real cool. He'd encourage you to get wild."

Frankie's guitar berth in Chequered Past was taken by another Iggy sideman, Tony Sales, and the group toured in support of Duran Duran, INXS and Little Steven before recording an eponymous album for EMI. After they split in 1985, Harrison became involved with soundtrack production and band management, while Burke travelled to Britain, appearing on Pete Townshend's *White City* album before joining The Eurythmics.

Chris had been forced to curtail his work with Animal Records when he fell ill, which meant the cancellation of projected albums by Fab Five Freddy, rapper J Walter Negro and several soundtracks. Any thoughts of a second solo album by Debbie were also abandoned. "I've put my life on hold till he's well again," she said. "I just can't think about anything until Chris has recovered. My life, my career, my home – they mean nothing to me while he's like this."

Although Chris' illness had been diagnosed, he remained in a serious condition. "He's so weak he can't stand on his feet," Deborah explained. "He lies in bed all the time."

Debbie was a constant presence at his bedside during his confinement at Lenox Hill Hospital, an acute care facility on the Upper East Side. What she subsequently described as "the worst time of my life" was made more trying when sections of the press – who had been at the hospital, covering the birth of Jerry Hall and Mick Jagger's daughter Elizabeth – caught wind of Chris' alarming physical state and Debbie's regular visits. Seemingly scandalised that she had not even bothered to visit a stylist before arriving to watch over her partner, New York's tabloids ran photographs of Debbie looking far from her best – alongside sensationalist copy that insisted Chris was dying and she was falling apart.

In some respects, being cast into the role of carer can present more difficulties than for those requiring care. While Chris was under heavy medication, drifting in and out of consciousness, Debbie was left to cope with the complete abandonment of her previous lifestyle. "When Chris got ill everything changed," she observed. "I was suddenly holding everything together. It was the hardest time, it got unequal. He was never mentally incapable, always astute, but it forced me into different areas. I didn't fit that role of keeper very easily. He had always been the mentor. He had always been the funny one and suddenly it was not light-hearted. Before then I'd always felt perhaps too serious."

As Chris' health slowly stabilised, Deborah found that her summary removal from the music business and all its concomitant pressures afforded the opportunity to reflect and reconsider. "I think that, up until that time, I had a lot of what you would call 'childish ways' and then the idea of taking complete responsibility for my life and not seeing it as just sheer fate or luck really hit home," she recalled. "Everything had been so intense. Just thinking about it I'm getting dizzy. There was no escape, no respite. What really brought me down to earth was Chris being sick. When that happened, I just said, 'I don't have time for this bullshit.' And I just washed it out of my character."

The regime of steroids employed to counteract *pemphigus vulgaris* began to reap benefits, as the disease eventually went into remission. Despite being allowed home under observation by a doctor from New York Hospital, who regularly monitored his blood, Chris still suffered from the effects of both the disease and its treatment. "Steroids change your whole metabolism. They're weird," he observed. "The proteins that bind your skin together break down, and you just sort of dissolve. You get a lot of sores – I still have the scars."

"This disease was incurable before steroids," added Deborah. "Before that you would die from associated infection because your skin would be all open and your immune system goes completely *ferkakte*, right? So then you catch everything. If he hadn't been fairly young when he got it, it could still have killed him."

With the critical phase of Chris' illness behind them, the couple immediately found that they were facing another crisis – they were broke. "Overall we just got completely fucked over," explained Stein. "It was a period when musicians still lived in a state of serfdom. We trusted people who weren't trustworthy ... and they cleaned us out."

"Things were really bad in 1982 and 1983 – when Blondie first broke up," Deborah recounted. "I didn't know what direction to go in; it was a very scary period all round. The IRS had closed in on me and Chris for various reasons, and at the same time Chris was sick. It was pretty damn heavy and it all started in 1982. It was awful – they took our house, everything."

As unpaid tax bills were brought alarmingly to light, this was an issue that affected the band collectively. "We had a letter from our accountant basically saying, 'Don't expect any more money, it's all over – basically there's $25,000 left in the Blondie account. Make arrangements to pay your bills, don't count on another penny from Blondie,'" said Nigel.

"We were all in a tax hole," added Jimmy. "I think Chris owed nearly a million dollars, I owed half a million dollars. After all of that work we wound up in the red."

It seemed unbelievable that a group who had sold well over 20 million records worldwide could find themselves so far in debt, within months of disbanding. Although the band had enjoyed the material and chemical trappings of success, running up the usual expenses which are then deducted from royalties, the extent of their debt was staggering.

"It's just that we were being fleeced so badly," stated Chris. "The first two years we made a lot of money, and this accountant that we had just didn't pay our tax bills. Everyone went on these horrendous back taxes for years and years ..."

"We were very bad at the business side and we lost a lot of money," Deborah later admitted. "At the height of our fame the thing that caused us the most stress was the business – we knew we didn't have a handle on it and we knew a lot of cash was flying away. When you get into a band you think it's all about music. It's all you know about and it's all you want to know about. The reality is that most young musicians could do with a crash course in accounting. It's a weird situation to be really famous, really busy and yet to have this feeling all the time that you're not being properly looked after. If I could give my younger self any advice it would be to keep an eye on the business side of things."

"I had a horrendous tax debt for about 20 years," revealed Chris. "I try not to feel bitter. Debbie keeps reminding me that it's our own fault and we should have paid better attention, which is the case. But I have no head for figures."

In February 1983, Debbie returned to the public eye when David Cronenberg's *Videodrome* was released in the US. Filmed in the previous summer, the movie tells the tale of Max Renn (played by James Woods, shortly before his co-starring role with Robert De Niro in *Once Upon A Time In America*), a small-time cable TV channel owner who stumbles across a coded broadcast containing extreme violence and using high-frequency signals to reconfigure viewers' perceptions of reality. Cast in the role of Renn's girlfriend, Nicki Brand, Debbie is drawn into a sleazy web of deception and body horror. "I played the seductress, the temptress. I was sort of like the embodiment of the video creature," she explained. "Don't ask me whether she was really a real person or an electronic being, because I didn't write the fucker! Ask Cronenberg. He said, 'I wrote this part for Blondie,' and then I showed up with red hair and he said, 'Oh, I guess that will be OK.'"

"There was something in my music that David used as a reference for writing the part of Nicki Brand," elaborated Deborah. "He told the producer this, who then asked him why he didn't cast me? And David said, 'No, I'm sure she can't act. I want to get somebody I know can handle the role.' Finally the producer convinced him to try me out. So I got a screen test and got the part."

Following cult success with such visceral fare as *Shivers* (1974) and *Rabid* (1976), Cronenberg's directorial career was shifting into high gear in the wake of 1981's psychic thriller, *Scanners*. With a budget in the region of $6 million, *Videodrome* represented a step up from *Union City*. "I need a lot of explicit direction," explained Debbie. "I need to be told more than an experienced actress would need to be told. Cronenberg said to me that he would tell me exactly what he wanted me to do, and that he wanted me to try and do that, more than someone else who had done a lot of film work and would be given more freedom. But that was all right with me."

Although Cronenberg's script demanded that Debbie shoot scenes involving partial nudity and physical mutilation, she had little problem once it was demonstrated that these aspects were in no way exploitative or gratuitous. "From the first I just wanted to be reassured that she would end up on some kind of positive note. Because I find that I'm paranoid now about getting into acting categorised as the 'Bad Girl', or the evil sex caricature, or whatever."

Although the narrative fails to arrive at any such unequivocal conclusion, Debbie believed that its exploration of issues such as passivity, exploitation and media manipulation validated *Videodrome*'s more extreme aspects. "It is a fascinating idea that something essentially passive – whether it's a media image or the media itself – can be more destructive than active weaponry."

"One of the scenes I found extremely difficult. In a shower – it felt awkward and didn't seem right," Deborah recounted. "But that was cut. The other two scenes were a lot easier. Partly because Jimmy was so great to work with, and partly because everybody was so careful to create the right atmosphere for me. Of course, there were the minimum amount of people on set. I think Jimmy was more self-conscious than I was, or afraid that I was self-conscious and consequently self-conscious on my behalf. It was very funny actually. I was standing there with a towel wrapped around me wondering how on earth I could go through with the scene. 'I can't do this,' I thought. 'What am I doing?' Then I thought, 'You stupid fool, what are you doing here if you can't do this? Just do it.' So I did it then the fear was over. Once that happened it was fun. Once I get past a certain point I'm not shy any more."

As with the role of Lillian in *Union City*, Deborah's portrayal of the cipher-like Nicki was well removed from the image she established with Blondie. Although she had been offered a number of lucrative parts in rock-themed movies, she was determined to develop a separate identity as an actress. "The scripts are usually not written very well, really unimaginative and incorrect as far as rock'n'roll goes. Most of them have been really horrible. I think I got two scripts out of about 150 that were worth doing ... I guess people always see you by what you've done, and there are very few people who have enough imagination to see you as something different. You either revolt everyone or turn everybody on by doing something new."

On release *Videodrome* drew generally positive notices, with many reviewers describing it as sufficiently audacious and fascinating to outweigh any sense of pretentiousness and self-indulgence. For Debbie it made a refreshing change from her experiences with the music press. "Film criticism is a whole new world," she insisted. "It's very remote — I've never met these people. I was totally amazed at the reviews I got for *Videodrome*. They were great — I expected it to be much worse. I was prepared! I think the film suffered more than I did, because of the gore at the end — but Cronenberg always gets slammed for that."

The movie fared less well at the US box office, where it failed to recoup the money invested in its production, although its subsequent release in foreign territories and steady sales on the developing video market went a long way to addressing this shortfall. "It was taken off for one reason or another, but during the time it was being shown it was in the Top 10," said Debbie. "I don't think it was a failure for me by any means. I think it's kind of confusing, but I thought it was a good part for me to do. Working with David Cronenberg was fun, but hard work towards the end of filming. It gave me the acting challenge I was looking for."

enduring item – Chris and Debbie in 1982. JANETTE BECKMAN/GETTY IMAGES

Chic's Nile Rodgers hangs with jade goddess Debbie in New York, 1982. MICHAEL PUTLAND/GETTY IMAGES

Designer Stephen Sprouse and Debbie give it the mean eye, ou on the town in 1982. RON GALELLA, LTD/WIREIMAGE

Blondie approach the end of the road in Toronto 1982 as Chris' gaunt appearance indicates just how unwell the guitarist had become.
MICHAEL PUTLAND/GETTY IMAGES

ebbie enters the squared circle for *Teaneck Tanzi* with actors Caitlin Clarke and Andy Kaufman. TIME & LIFE PICTURES/GETTY IMAGES

mes Woods gets physical with Debbie in David Lynch's groundbreaking 1983 film *Videodrome.* REX FEATURES

Deborah in solo action. IAN DICKSON/REX FEATURES

eborah with the Jazz Passengers – ensemble mainstay Roy Nathanson is pictured far left. ACTION PRESS/REX FEATURES

st reformation – Jimmy, Debbie, Chris and Clem line up for the second act. MICK HUTSON/REDFERNS

Tagged – Debbie is reunited with Fab 5 Freddie at the 2004 VH1 Hip Hop Honours event. STEPHEN LOVEKIN/FILMMAGIC

Delight and disharmony at the 2006 Rock 'n' Roll Hall of Fame induction ceremony. MIKE SEGAR/REUTERS/CORBIS

em and Frank renew their acquaintance at photographer Allan Tannenbaum's *New York In The 70's* book signing on April 2, 2009
Los Angeles. MIKE GUASTELLA/WIREIMAGE

venty-first century Blondie (L-R): Kevin Patrick, Debbie, Chris, Clem, Leigh Foxx and Matt Katz-Bohen in Culver City,
lifornia 2010. ALBERTO E. RODRIGUEZ/GETTY IMAGES

Still rocking – Chris and Debbie at London's Lovebox Festival, July 2011. SAMIR HUSSEIN/GETTY IMAGES

Despite little adverse reaction to *Videodrome's* scenes of torture and mutilation when it was released across 600 US cinemas, when Debbie arrived in London to promote the film's UK release, in November 1983, she unwittingly walked into a very British moral panic. Led by serial complainer Mary Whitehouse and her allies in right-wing newspapers such as the *Daily Mail* and *Sunday Times*, a campaign to enforce a ratings system on the then-unregulated video market had reached a hysterical pitch. At the urging of Whitehouse's minority lobby group, the misleadingly named National Viewers and Listeners Association, Conservative MP Graham Bright introduced a Private Member's Bill demanding that all commercial video recordings be subject to a strict system of classification. While the introduction of age restrictions that had applied to cinema releases for many years seemed logically consistent, some extremists saw the bill – which passed into statute the following year – as a golden opportunity to clamp down on any material they identified as offensive.

Unfortunately for Debbie, her promotional visit corresponded with a reading of Bright's proposed bill in the House of Commons. With any movie featuring adult themes now a political hot potato, a scheduled interview on BBC's *Breakfast Time* was cancelled, as were radio interviews and other promotional opportunities. "I think the controversy surrounding *Videodrome* in Britain has been stirred up by the Conservatives," asserted Deborah. "It has nothing to do with the film, it just has to do with their desire to control and to censor. But the guys from Palace [who distributed the movie in Britain] are thrilled because of the attention it has attracted."

"I got here and my PR said, 'There's a bit of a thing on, a bit of a controversy about this video nasty business,'" she explained. "We've had calls from ministers, town councillors and religious groups saying, 'We're not going to let this film in our town.' How do they know if they've never seen it? 'We don't want to see it, we don't want to know about it, we read about it – that's enough,' they said. That's funny, isn't it? It's a comedy almost."

Alarmingly, those who refused to allow logic to obstruct their opinions actually sought to blame Debbie for *Videodrome's* content – particularly the scene where a lit cigarette is tracked across her breast. "It's been, 'Why did you let Cronenberg write this thing?'" she marvelled. "I've not been held totally responsible, I've been held totally irresponsible with regard to the number of people who are going to go out and commit violent acts and perverted sexual things now, and 'My God, how did you do that to your chest!' They don't even say 'breast', it's 'chest'. It wasn't my 'chest', it was my tit!

"The most important thing to realise about it is that it has a very crucial message," Debbie concluded. "I really believe that. In fact, it's got a lot of messages. I mean, what place is video and television taking in our lives? There is a terrible danger that we are becoming what we watch. And I think *Videodrome* has driven that message home." (As director Cronenberg later conceded, the grand irony is that the 'message' is vaguely simpatico with the National Viewers and Listeners Association's own simplistic view.)

Having unsuccessfully read for a part in British director Alan Parker's post-Vietnam War drama, *Birdy*, Debbie – who had also previously been passed over for the roles of Linda Marolla in the Dudley Moore romantic comedy, *Arthur*, and Vikki LaMotta in Martin Scorsese's *Raging Bull* – directed her acting aspirations toward the stage. It resulted in her being cast for the shared title role in the American adaptation of Claire Luckham's wrestling-themed battle-of-the sexes drama, *Trafford Tanzi*. Transplanting the lead character's background from Manchester to New Jersey, the play was renamed *Teaneck Tanzi: The Venus Flytrap* for its US run.

Directed by debutant Chris Bond, the physical demands of the wrestling scenes were reduced by Debbie and actress Caitlin Clarke alternating in the lead role. Despite this, it still presented a considerable challenge for Debbie – who was also wrestling with heroin-related issues and closing in on 40 years of age, and whose only prior sporting experience had come as a high-school baton twirler.

"I was heavier for *Tanzi*. I thought that a lady wrestler couldn't be so thin. It really worked – I put on 10 or 15 pounds. I had my hair brown and very long when I started, and they made me cut it. It was very sporty – all-American – which turned me off," she recounted. "I went into training for eight weeks. We had the welterweight champion of Britain as our trainer ... it's real. You get hurt. I got beat to shit."

Although the play had been successful in England and its American adaptation featured *Saturday Night Live / Taxi* star Andy Kaufman (who would die of cancer the following year) as The Ref, *Teaneck Tanzi* suffered the ignominy of closing on its opening day at Broadway's Nederlander Theater.

"I was really disappointed it closed after just one night," said Debbie. "We had been doing the show for audiences downtown in a showcase kind of venue, and it was really popular. We did that for weeks, and it was doing great, but then the producers decided to take it to Broadway. However, I think if they left the show downtown, we would still be doing it. It was just too rough and tumble for Broadway, if that makes any sense, but it was great for downtown. It really worked. We had everyone in the audience cheering on different members of the cast. There was a lot of shouting and stuff going on. It was a little too funky for Broadway."

The critics panned the play. Writing in the *New York Times*, Frank Rich declared, "*Teaneck Tanzi* is an Americanised, retitled version of London's biggest comedy hit since *Steaming*, and its charm must have bailed out somewhere over the Atlantic. What we find at the Nederlander is a theatrical gimmick whose execution produces a pounding sensation in every part of one's head except the brain." While offering Debbie sarcastic praise for slurring some of her lines, Rich gave free reign to his disdain for the drama: "Because Tanzi and her antagonists are symbols devoid of flesh or blood, we don't care who vanquishes whom in the ring: they're all pop-up dolls. The wrestling, though noisy, is less convincing than an average Three Stooges melee. There are also songs, seemingly composed on a washboard. The instrumental accompaniment, led by an electric organ, isn't worthy of a seventh-inning stretch at Shea Stadium."

"The reason we closed," Debbie asserted, "was because of the critics. They really didn't like the show. They didn't understand it. They didn't appreciate the popularity of wrestling. [The critics] weren't into the audience participation, which was a very important part of that show. So, the show closed on Broadway despite advance sales and a certain amount of popularity through word of mouth."

Frank Rich also took issue with what he saw as the "anachronistic" nature of the play's feminist subtext, a criticism Debbie agreed with. "The so-called feminist content in that play is really old-hat, right? But when I talked to the people about doing it, we were talking about a lot of rewrites. I had a lot of ideas about it but ... *pfffft!* When the time came, they really just didn't intend to change more than a few words. That wasn't gonna make it work – America and Britain have totally different realities where that subject matter is concerned. And oh [groans], I was really sorry, because wrestling is so popular and it could have been so great ... The problem was I really tricked myself. I had it so rewritten in my mind, I was so into transforming it that — it rather sneaked up on me that they could be totally intransigent about changing it. About the basic orientation. But — it was still very good experience. Theatre is so rigid; it has its own hierarchies and discipline. And I had to go through it to find out."

Debbie's return to the world of cinema was in order to record vocals for Giogio Moroder's 'Rush Rush', on the soundtrack of Brian De Palma's high-octane update of *Scarface*. As a dancefloor filler the track was in a similar vein to 'Call Me', with Debbie's *yeyo*-referencing lyrics celebrating the septum-eroding lifestyle of the principal character, Tony Montana (Al Pacino). Released in February 1984 as Debbie's first post-Blondie single, the track made disappointingly little impact on the charts despite being a minor club hit.

It had been 18 months since Blondie broke up, but their influence was still evident at the forefront of popular music, particularly how elements of Debbie's style were appropriated by a new generation of vocalists. Although by no means a new phenomenon (in Britain, Kim Wilde and Hazel O'Connor had scored hits while taking cues from a still rolling Blondie bandwagon), by 1984 Madonna had assimilated elements of Deborah's image into a post-modern blonde persona that also referenced Marilyn Monroe, Marlene Dietrich, Jean Harlow and others. This combination proved to be a commercial gold mine, generating a string of hugely successful (if bland) hits supported by an assertive sexuality that largely owed its provenance to Debbie's Blondie persona. "There are two different ways to look at that," mused Deborah. "Homage or rip-off? There were a few incidences of direct … you know … lifts and others are just flattering references."

When Andy Warhol asserted that "Debbie actually was the first Madonna" in October 1984, it seemed unfair that her enforced recording hiatus had enabled others to cash in on her image — particularly at a time when she was facing financial hardship. "Sort of the same thing happened to Iggy Pop," she would observe in 2005. "His legacy and his reputation and his style have been copied, and he was a groundbreaker. He was so far ahead of his time that he was shocking everyone. He never really made a bundle of money, yet the people who followed after him did really well, and I just think sometimes that happens. Sometimes the people who were first don't really make the bucks."

Signed to Sire by Seymour Stein, who had started the label with Richard

Gottehrer in 1966 and later released The Ramones' and Talking Heads' early albums, Madonna Ciccone's emergence as a globally successful entertainer – between her debut single in 1981 and her first US number one with 'Like A Virgin' in November 1984 – initiated a lineage of marketable female vocalists who owed much to Debbie, including Wendy James, Courtney Love, Gwen Stefani and Lady Gaga. "I knew she was happening back in the early eighties, a friend of mine had some romance with her, but it all happened when Chris was really sick so I was paying most of my attention to him," Debbie recalled. "So I guess I didn't really catch onto Madonna until she was marching on up."

Aside from recording 'Feel The Spin' for the soundtrack of hip hop movie *Krush Groove* in 1985, in the mid-eighties Debbie disappeared almost completely from the public radar as she helped nurse Chris back to health. "I can remember Chris coming over to my apartment to meet William Burroughs," said Victor Bockris. "It was amazing to see him because he was a completely different person – so turned on, and so funny, just talking and talking. That was in 1986, and it was definitely the moment at which I recognised he was back completely. It did take a few years, because it wasn't just a physical illness. The fallout at the end of Blondie also created enormous stress. To get out of the tangled web they were when he fell ill was very complicated and took a long time and was very boring and stressful."

Chris emerged from his confinement weighing noticeably more than he had before he fell ill. "I have a sort of biker image now. I'm going to get a big tattoo on my stomach of an eagle holding a beer can in his claws," he laughed.

For Debbie, his recovery was a huge relief and, so far as she was concerned, reward enough for the devoted care she had provided. "It didn't seem like a sacrifice at all. Because our careers were so entwined, so enmeshed. We had always worked as a team. And being sick on your own is no fun," she reflects. "I would have expected the same from him. And I did do other things – different projects that just weren't so visible. But what many people don't realise is that, at the time Chris was sick, our record label had dropped us as well, our business had turned to shit, the tax people were attacking us. Everything sort of went down the tube at the same time, so it appeared that I was devoting myself to him – but, in reality, things had just collapsed. I was holding everything closer because we had everything to lose and we were losing most of it, after all that success."

"When I was loaded up with steroids, and who knows what other kinds of strange chemicals, my mood swings could be intense. Debbie was constant, though," Chris remembered. "Other people would have found me impossible to handle, but not her. She was amazing at coping with me, and did so in a way that was above and beyond any possible call of friendship or duty."

"It's taken a while, the recuperation, but he's really back to his former self," said Deborah. "He's got terrific ideas, as usual. He's a very creative person. He's never really stopped. One of the worst things about being sick is your mind keeps going and you're so limited. He never stopped thinking about things, so he's about to carry them out … It was frustrating for me too. I've felt really terrific since we've been working on the music again."

With Chris back in circulation, plans for Debbie's second solo album returned to the top of the agenda. Now managed by lawyer Stanley Arkin, who assisted Deborah in renegotiating her deal with Chrysalis, arrangements were made to record the disc at the Power Station and Electric Lady studios with J. Geils Band keyboard player Seth Justman producing. Although Chrysalis would release the album worldwide, in North America Debbie would be on the Geffen label. "Geffen is very artistically oriented," appraised Chris. "I'm not naming names, but a lot of these companies get so hung up on the business side of things that they totally lose sight of what's going on."

It had been more than four years since the couple last entered the studio to record an album. For Debbie, it was a challenge she approached with a degree of trepidation. "I was kind of lost after Blondie," she recalled, "but I kept on trying to figure it out. And then I wanted to make more records. I guess the best thing that I know now is what it really takes to be creative and to hold on to my artistic soul. And I guess I really didn't know that, I didn't know how to activate it. I think one of the reasons that I was so attracted to Chris is that he is so naturally adept at expressing that constantly. And it's taken a while just to become habitually in touch with that, and just to live my life like that."

Although the disc that emerged as *Rockbird* featured over 20 additional musicians and vocalists, the label was keen to relaunch Debbie as a commercially viable solo performer. To facilitate this, there would be none of the radical experimentation evident on *Koo Koo* or the last two Blondie albums. As Debbie stated, "They gave me money to make the record and now they have to sell the record to make it back."

Indeed, *Rockbird* is an entirely safe album, with many of Justman's arrangements typical of the sequenced and programmed fare providing hits for artists such as Madonna. 'I Want You', 'Buckle Up' and 'You Got Me In Trouble' are emblematic of the vaguely sassy, upbeat pop of the era, while only Chris and Debbie's title track and 'Beyond The Limit' (which she co-wrote with Nile Rodgers) possess the kind of urgent attitude that was always a key element of Deborah's material.

"I sort of feel like this record is maybe too mellow, or too nice, and not bitchin' or spunky or whatever as it could be," she mused. "But I'm coming out of a really quiet part of my life, been very involved with inner feelings, and the thing is very personal for me, it's just me. I'm not singing for five men, I'm singing for myself and I'm writing for myself. And that's what this record is. After I do some live shows, and after I get my ass kicked around by being in the business for a while and out in the real world, maybe I'll write something that's tougher, maybe I'll be tougher again. You know, I'm just a product of what everybody else is."

Released in a Stephen Sprouse/Andy Warhol-designed sleeve on November 29, 1986, *Rockbird* can be retrospectively viewed as a moderately successful attempt by an artist to find her feet after an extended break from recording. Commercially, it did little in the US but in Britain it sold relatively well, achieving gold disc status in the lower reaches of the Top 40. It spawned a global hit in the shape of 'French Kissin' In The USA', written by Chuck Lorre who would later go on to create the *Two And A Half Men* TV sitcom.

"To get an A&R department of a record company to back me, I had to do a song like 'French Kissin'," explained Debbie. "Which happens to be a good song, it's somehow a little more gutsy, but yet it can be commercial. They've made everything so cutesy from a girl point of view. There is no edge. And how many girl singers are around that are rock stars, or performers that are selling records, who can do that?"

The single made the Top 10 in Britain, Ireland and Australia, and its video secured Deborah airtime on the increasingly important MTV cable channel. Two other singles were also drawn from *Rockbird*: 'Free To Fall', a plaintive if pedestrian ballad, and the gently seductive 'In

Love With Love' – neither of which made any significant impact on the charts, although the latter did top the *Billboard* dance list. The album was only lightly promoted by Geffen, which at the time was concentrating on more easily marketable releases by Elton John, Kylie Minogue, Peter Gabriel and Irene Cara.

"I was really on their B-list and that hurt me a lot. It hurt me in business and it hurt me in other ways. I felt sort of worthless," Debbie recalled. "Had I stayed with the identity of Blondie, the industry would have considered me more of a sure thing. But because I veered off, it was hard for anyone to grasp – or to be bothered grasping – where I was headed. I wasn't a big enough world seller by that point to merit anyone giving me that kind of attention."

Sadly, Andy Warhol's contribution to the *Rockbird* sleeve proved to be among his last pieces of work. He died from a heart attack on February 22, 1987, while recovering from routine gall bladder surgery. Paying tribute to his friend, Chris observed, "I have a lot of admiration for him, as an artist. And whatever anybody says, he's been the fucking kingpin of the New York art scene for years. Also, I think he's been very radical."

"Here we are," Debbie said, "left here without him, and it's really been boring, I must say. It hasn't been as much fun. Andy was really great fun."

Rather than tour in support of an album put together in the studio and necessitating the recruitment of a new band, Debbie's focus returned to acting. She had already shot an episode of the *Tales From The Darkside* portmanteau horror TV series, which aired in October 1987. "It's a thriller kind of show, like *The Outer Limits*," she explained. "I play a witch who comes back in another body. It's called 'The Moth'." This was followed by an appearance in another television series, *Crime Story*. "I play a bimbette. You know, like a fancy hooker. I'm the comedy relief, so I got to do a bit of comedy, which was nice." She also got to do a little more comedy in the movie *Forever, Lulu*, a mildly amusing mystery directed by Amos Kollek (previously responsible for 1985 romantic drama *Goodbye, New York*) and starring iconic Polish actress Hanna Schygulla.

After a cameo return to gigging when she provided backing vocals for Lou Reed at a Madison Square Garden AIDS benefit show in December

1987, and an equally peripheral appearance in the teen comedy *Satisfaction* (1988), Debbie bagged the plum role of Velma Von Tussle in cult director John Waters' camp comedy *Hairspray*. Her association with the Baltimore director dated back to 1981, when she and Chris had written the title song to his earlier comedy *Polyester*.

Cast in the role of pushy matron, Debbie had once again selected a part that defied her established image. "She really wanted to do *Hairspray*, regardless of the fact that it may not have been the perfect next step or the exact order that she would have done things to benefit her music career," recalled Waters. "Anytime you confuse people by doing more than one thing, it sometimes works against you."

This time around, however, Deborah's adventurous approach paid dividends. Aside from demonstrating her talent for comedy, her portrayal served to cement her status as a gay icon among that portion of the demographic who routinely lapped up Waters' highly camp (and often scatological) comedies.

"I think gay men have always liked her maybe because it was easy to get dressed like her, even though no one could ever really look like her," remarked the director. "Hundreds of people stole her look anyway – every rock star did. But I still don't think about her as a gay icon, she's just an icon."

Debbie was equally complimentary about working with Waters. "John had a fevered approach to directing. He's very dedicated. He knows exactly what he wants. I'm not saying that it's mania, but he really does want a sort of madness, an almost clichéd kind of performance. He wants a very studied, cartoonish character portrayal. That really works with his scenarios. It just really works!"

The role of Velma Von Tussle also pitched Deborah alongside Sonny Bono, who had long retired from the music business to carve out a political career. "The best thing about Sonny was that he had a short fuse," she recounted. "He was a pretty nice guy but everywhere we went, people would come up and go, 'Hey, Sonny, where's Cher?' [The couple had divorced in 1975.] And he'd go so frosty all his limbs would seize up in anger and he'd go, 'If I hear that one more time …' It was like being haunted, poor guy … If that happened to me, I'd just tear my ears off."

Released in February 1988, *Hairspray* has proven enduringly popular – grossing around $8million on its initial release, it was subsequently adapted for a 2002 Broadway musical, with a big-budget remake hitting cinema screens five years later.

Despite Deborah's return to recording and the success of her performance in *Hairspray*, she and Chris had begun to drift apart. "Everything was sliding downhill, we were running out of money and stuff like that," he'd recall. "We had a really nice place uptown and we had to get a crummier place further downtown. We were both on methadone, which she went off pretty quickly and I stayed on because my condition was stress-related. Sexuality went down and we just went out of synch, I think."

"It was just a split, and it happened over a long period," explained Debbie. "I couldn't say how it started, or how it ended. It was a very intense relationship, a collaboration, a love affair, a business affair. I don't know if a relationship like that can go on for very long, really, because it was so very intense."

Given everything that they had been through as a couple, there was a definite poignancy to Chris and Debbie's separation. They had endured the poverty of their early years on the Bowery; the rollercoaster ride that was Blondie; the drug problems and the battle against Chris' illness. Given that many marriages fail to last the 15 years that Chris and Debbie spent together, it is hardly surprising that their bond endures to this day.

Although a comfort-eating Debbie, only recently over her junk addiction, would confess that she "was so messed up, full of ice cream … having a nervous breakdown of some sort", and Chris observed how her fast withdrawal from methadone "made her really nuts", there was no single quantifiable reason as to why they separated.

When it came, the decision to part was Debbie's, who moved out of their shared home to a nearby apartment. Despite this, the break-up was amicable and both parties continued to care for one another deeply. As for those seeking an explanation as to why two such evidently compatible individuals would choose to separate, Chris simply says, "The relationship just sort of ran its course."

Chapter Fourteen

Unfinished Business

"I think that you can adapt to anything, and if you aren't successful and you don't get big popularity, you can find happiness doing other things."

Debbie Harry

Although Chris and Debbie were no longer an item, it had little impact upon their ability to collaborate creatively. Within a year of their gradual late 1987/early 1988 separation, the duo began work on Deborah's third solo album, *Def, Dumb And Blonde* – co-writing more than half of the disc's 11 tracks. In many ways emblematic of its era, the LP bears many typically late-eighties production elements: processed drums, guitar and keyboards, clipped rhythms and multi-tracked backing vocals are layered to create a high-sheen sound. It was the work of many hands, with Debbie and Chris joined behind the desk by a whole committee of producers including Mike Chapman, electro pioneer Arthur Baker, Thompson Twin Tom Bailey, and Toni Colandreo – who'd previously contributed to 'Feel The Spin' and *Rockbird*.

In common with Debbie's last album, while *Def, Dumb And Blonde* encompasses a fairly wide range of styles there is nothing that could be described as radical. As with *Rockbird*, the disc represented another attempt to relaunch her career as a solo artist by applying her vocals to material that, in the main, had elements in common with the kind of songs making an

257

impact on the charts. "We felt this record has to be a reintroduction for us to our fans and to our record buyers," she explained. "We wanted to approach it like this. We did this for a very specific reason."

Unsurprisingly, any diversity of style evident on the album tended to be Chris' work. "His style of songs is very much his own," said Deborah. "We cover a lot of ground. We have a couple of really hardcore rock songs. And we have a samba. Then there's this rap/dance song that's really cool called 'Get Your Way'. Then another sort of really pretty, elegant song called 'He Is So'. Then there is this smoky kind of Dr John song called 'Lovelight', and Ian [Astbury] from The Cult singing on that. Then 'Liar Liar', which Jonathan Demme got for his picture, *Married To The Mob*, which has Gary Valentine on it."

Two of the songs written by Chris and Debbie reference Blondie's heritage in different ways: 'Maybe For Sure' combines the duo's girl-group influences with the kind of expansive sound that infused 'Union City Blue', while the retrospective sidewalk poetry of episodic closer 'End Of The Run' can be read as Debbie's elegy for the New York that spawned Blondie. "I think that is really a very beautiful piece of music," she declared. "This is a song about nostalgia and also about how some things become more important the further away they get, how it feels to be part of something unique and special. It's sad when those great personal moments pass away, but it's also great to be part of them while they're happening."

Aside from a sweetly seductive cover of Brazilian jazz vocalist and percussionist Naná Vasconcelos' 'Calmarie', the only track on *Def, Dumb And Blonde* not bearing a Harry or Stein writing credit is 'I Want That Man', written for Debbie by Tom Bailey and his Thompson Twins partner Alannah Currie. "The interesting thing lyrically, for Alannah, was that she was writing for a woman," observed Deborah. "She's usually writing lyrics that Tom can sing. This time out she was able to make a very direct statement from a female point of view. It was one of three songs they submitted for the album, and it ended up as the first single."

Catchy and appropriately assertive, 'I Want That Man' provided Debbie with a moderate hit, making number 13 in the UK and narrowly missing the top of *Billboard*'s modern rock chart. The single was promoted by a video directed by Mary Lambert, previously responsible for propelling Madonna hits such as 'Like A Prayer' onto the small screen. "It's a little story about me as a vampire waking up from the crypt by the sound of the music," explained Debbie. "Like the Anne Rice books. The music sort of wakes me up. And then I want all these things. I want that man and I want the pink shoes and I want to be alive … I wanna be turned on. And that's what happens. So I dance around and bite people and stuff. It looks quite beautiful, really incredibly beautiful. I've never looked so pretty on film before. I mean, I've always looked nice, but this one is really sensational."

Having fronted one of the first bands to truly embrace video, Debbie remained very visually orientated and was keenly aware of how, over the decade since *Eat To The Beat* had been issued on video cassette, television had become the preeminent medium for promoting music. This situation owed much to international cable and satellite channel MTV. "They're so powerful it's incredible," observed Deborah. "They can make a record happen. If I'm part of this industry and I'm competing in the business, then I have to find it equally as important for myself."

The Thompson Twins also contributed the sultry 'Kiss It Better', which included lyrics by Debbie and was selected as the disc's second seven-inch release, though it failed to repeat the sales and airplay of its predecessor. Deborah's new US label Sire, and Chrysalis – which had retained the rights to her releases elsewhere – plucked a further three singles from *Def, Dumb And Blondie*: 'Brite Side', the bass-driven 'Sweet And Low' and 'Maybe For Sure'. Although none of these scored anything resembling a hit, 'Brite Side' was given additional exposure when Deborah performed the number on TV crime drama *Wiseguy*, as part of her short run in the role of faded rock star Diana Price. "I had two different sets of lyrics for it when the producers called up to tell me about the character," she recalled. "Chris and I knew that one set of lyrics to 'Brite Side' fit who she was – a down-and-out singer who is trying to pull her life together."

As had so often been the case with Blondie's albums, *Def, Dumb And Blonde* sold in greater volume outside the US following its autumn 1989 release. In addition to making the Top 10 in both Australia and New Zealand, the disc spent seven weeks on the UK album chart, peaking at number 12. Back home, it failed to crack the *Billboard* Top 100. In part, this was due to Warners-owned Sire focusing on the most commercially viable end of its roster. "I didn't get a fair shake. Some of the problems I had were with Warner Bros Records, because Madonna and I were with the same company." asserted Debbie. "When I did *Def, Dumb and Blonde* she immediately came out with the 'Blonde Ambition' tour. Unfortunately

I was on the same label, so I was definitely shoved to the back to avoid any confusion."

The enduring nature of the Blondie persona also proved problematic. "I don't think anybody knew how to market me or what to do with me. I was like a fish out of water," Debbie recalls. "It's an industry that's based on youthful output and appearance, and the record company wasn't really interested. I wanted to do a tough, more mature, more aggressive version of Blondie. And they didn't really want that."

The most significant factor about the release of *Def, Dumb And Blonde* was that it was supported by a tour. After a seven-year absence from performing live, Debbie opted to return to gigging in a big way. After a warm-up show at the Stone Pony in Asbury Park, New Jersey on September 25, 1989, she would remain on the road for much of the following 12 months, bouncing between the US and Europe and returning to Australia and New Zealand for the first time in over a decade.

"It's been a real long time since I actually had a firm band and gone out and done organised shows," Debbie stated. "It's been so long I don't want to say! I think the last tour was in the late summer of 1982. This time around I want to do some club dates."

When it came to putting a band together for the tour, the first person Debbie turned to was Chris. "Working together happens," she enthused. "It's very easy for us." The line-up was initially rounded out by bassist Leigh Foxx (who played on *Def, Dumb And Blonde* having hooked up with Debbie after stints with Iggy Pop, Patti Smith and Yoko Ono), drummer Jimmy Clarke, former Ashford & Simpson keyboard player Valerie Ghent and guitarist Carla Olla.

Performing a mixture of new material and Blondie favourites such as 'Dreaming', 'Rapture' and 'Heart Of Glass', the group returned to Britain for a week's residency at London's intimate Borderline venue in early October. While in London, Debbie appeared on primetime BBC chat show *Wogan*, where the eponymous host asked her why she opted to play such a small club. "To build up excitement and interest, and also I wanted to feel really comfortable and close to my audience, but mostly we wanted to find out what was happening — it's been a while since I was on the road," she replied.

(The genial Irishman also asked her why she was now calling herself 'Deborah'. "That's my name," she shot back.)

This initial run of shows finished in Paris on December 16, resuming at the end of January with an American tour that continued until March 1990. The band then flew to New Zealand, where Deborah caused a minor media sensation by making a 40 metre bungee jump wearing nothing but a pair of shorts. After several Australian gigs, Debbie and her group returned to England to visit some larger venues, before spending summer on the 'Escape From New York' package with The Ramones, Jerry Harrison and The Tom Tom Club.

In addition to her appearances as Diana Price in *Wiseguy*, which aired in March 1989, and a small role in the Martin Scorsese-directed segment of the portmanteau movie drama *New York Stories*, which opened the same month, Debbie's acting endeavours were further in evidence when she showed up in a number of roles while touring. Most notable of these was *Tales From The Darkside: The Movie*. Cast as a witch named Betty, Deborah's role provided the links between three separate narrative segments, as a child she has captured for the cooking pot reads the trio of stories to her as a means of prolonging his survival. The movie also features former New York Dolls frontman David Johansen, who played a hitman hired to eliminate a malevolent cat. "Back in 1972, when we were stumbling out of the Mercer Arts Center in our platform shoes after drinking too much Southern Comfort together, who could have known we'd end up in a horror movie together," chuckled Deborah.

On television, Debbie appeared as The Old Woman Who Lived In A Shoe in the children's movie *Mother Goose Rock'n'Rhyme* (which also boasted such diverse musical talents as Little Richard, Cyndi Lauper and Art Garfunkel). She took a small role as a doctor in an episode of the *Monsters* horror anthology, and starred as a murder witness in the thriller *Intimate Stranger* – all of which aired during 1991. Although she had now appeared in more than a dozen acting roles, Debbie still came down on the side of music when asked to compare her two careers.

"Despite the work in films I still see myself above all as a singer, especially because the music still represents my identity and main source of income.," she observed. "It would therefore be very awkward for me to throw my musical ambitions overboard completely and fully concentrate on acting. I'm probably just not good enough for that and I haven't got enough practice to be a professional. Even though I do appreciate taking part in a film I could never completely suppress my inclination towards singing. It's a part of my personality I don't want to put aside. On the other hand, my parts in films have also had a great impact on my musical performance. I've become more confident – in singing as well as on stage."

She returned to touring in June 1991, playing around 20 shows across Europe before making a one-off return to CBGB's for a show in November.

★★★

In 1993, Deborah returned to the small screen – featuring alongside jazz behemoth Dizzy Gillespie in an episode of the drama series *Tribeca*, playing a nurse in the camp horror *Body Bags* and showing up as a neighbour in Nickelodeon's *Pete And Pete*. More significantly, she set to work recording her fourth solo album, *Debravation*, for release in August that year. In contrast to *Rockbird* and *Def, Dumb And Blonde*, the disc was devised with experimentation in mind.

"Our intention was to make an album that was avant-garde and creepy and sort of threatening," said Debbie. Put together by a grand cast of over 30 musicians and vocalists, including Chris, Leigh Foxx, former Art Of Noise keyboardist Anne Dudley and The Grid's Richard Norris, *Debravation* presented a patchwork of diversity. However, the inclusion of such radical elements as a version of Nino Rota's instrumental theme from Federico Fellini's 1963 movie, *8½*, a cover of Led Zeppelin's 'Black Dog' recorded at the Hammersmith Odeon in 1991, Leigh Foxx's ethereal, multilayered ballad 'On A Breath' and the funky, witty rap of 'The Date' proved too much for Chrysalis.

"We were met with rejection from the record company," Deborah recounted. "The big boys wanted something more 'refined' and 'commercial'. Basically, they thought it sucked."

The label excluded the above songs from the official release and rejected the version of 'Standing In My Way' featuring Debbie's duet with Joey Ramone. They also removed H. R. Giger's avant-garde noise 'solo' from the version of 'Dog Star Girl' that appeared on *Debravation*. "The fucking record company didn't have a clue, they didn't even know what the fuck they had," raged Chris. "It's a really brilliant piece of music; it's the ultimate sort of cyber, urban, tribal fucking thing for that period."

"Good records," asserted Debbie, "distinguish themselves through character, individuality and artistic ambition. By involving many contrasting musicians in the project it gains expression, potential and tension. You just mix different styles and methods and get something exciting and new. Of course, it can happen, as in the case of Arthur Baker [who wrote album opener 'I Can See Clearly'] that an outside composition is fully accomplished, but then it still depends on how you interpret and adorn the song to keep your own touch. Pop music is a modern form of telling a fairy-tale. As long as your stories are exciting, people are going to listen."

Chrysalis' refusal to release the version of the album Chris and Debbie had envisioned caused a rift that would end their long association with the label. The following year, Harry and Stein issued the awkwardly titled *Debravation (8½): Producer's (Director's) Cut,* which restored the album to its original state and was sold at concerts.

"It just seems very odd to me. I can go anywhere in the world to perform and draw a great audience. I'm a really good singer and, I think, a really good performer. I can also make records and write songs. Yet people in the corporate world look at me as not being a safe bet. It's just a bizarre position to be in," Deborah observed. "I'm not really worried about it — I play the hand I'm dealt — that's what's pulled me through in life. But don't you think there's something wrong with that picture? I do."

Despite Chrysalis' evisceration of the album, *Debravation* still has its moments. Featuring ambiguously dystopian lyrics by SF author William Gibson, 'Dog Star Girl' is fittingly futuristic. "We melded two of his poems together," explained Debbie. "I think it has to do with Sirius — you know, the star — and there's a tribe in Africa that says that they're from that star system. But with Gibson you never know. Musically it has this throbbing thing going on, this tension, and that worked for me."

The Ramone-free version of 'Standing In My Way' is another highlight, blasting out a nineties take on Blondie's signature sound adorned by organ licks that are very much in the Jimmy Destri style, while Toni Colandreo and Debbie's 'Lip Service' demonstrates great conceptual breadth by welding a Chicago house-influenced groove to lyrics that reference Edgar Allan Poe.

With Debbie and Chris' relationship with Chrysalis at an all-time low, it was unsurprising that the label scarcely put any promotional muscle behind *Debravation.* Despite European and American tours the album failed to sell, reaching number 24 in the UK but scarcely registering elsewhere. The upbeat 'I Can See Clearly Now' also made the UK Top 30, and its Arthur

Baker sequencing combined with Deborah's breathless vocal to ensure the song became a US dance-club hit.

Debbie's final release on Chrysalis was the second single from *Debravation*, 'Strike Me Pink'. This emotive keyboard and sax-infused ballad was promoted by a video depicting Deborah watching a man struggling in a tank of water. With echoes of David Lynch's cinematic style, it was too edgy for the many television channels that refused to air it. "It was based on Houdini's water tank trick," Debbie explains. "I was dating a magician at the time, so there was obviously something going on in the back of my mind."

Since separating from Chris, Debbie had eschewed commitment to a serious relationship. Her personal status proved a constant theme during interviews of the period, with many journalists marvelling at the fact that one of the great beauties of the 20th century remained single. Generally, their enquiries revealed nothing more than that she sporadically dated and was happy to do just that. So the journalistic emphasis often switched to quizzing Deborah as to why she and Chris had never married and raised a family.

"I never really thought marriage was for me. I always thought that relationships were important to me, but the idea of marriage in the traditional sense was almost like some sort of bondage to me – and if you're gonna have bondage, you might as well have a little bit of S&M with it," she giggled. "I thought the marriage vows at that time were very inappropriate for me. I think I was probably ahead of my time, because nowadays people just write their own marriage vows anyway. My thinking was more about today. Many of the things that I was the right age for doing seemed totally inappropriate for me."

Similarly, the hectic nature of Debbie and Chris' co-existence had precluded a stable environment in which they might raise a child. "When I was with Chris, I was too unsettled. I didn't really have very much time to have children. I was working all the time. I think I was very selfish and very career-orientated and I knew I didn't want to hurt a child with my ambition," she explained. "Life was just too insane to contemplate starting a family … I wouldn't put a child through that lifestyle. That would be kind of almost abusive."

Given that the media so often deals in archetypes, it is unsurprising that so many interviewers asked Deborah whether she harboured any regrets – as if attempting to portray her as some kind of post-modern Garbo, 'wanting to be alone' as her memories of former triumphs faded alongside her youth. Given that Debbie has regularly asserted just how little time she has for nostalgia and that her world view looks unerringly forward, it was never going to ring true. As a woman approaching her 50th birthday, Debbie was able to go out and perform new material before large, enthusiastic audiences, record new albums and maintain a viable acting career. There was just too much life in Deborah for her to quietly fade away among her own memorabilia.

One of the key elements that both Debbie and Chris had brought to Blondie was their enthusiasm for a wide range of popular culture. In addition to art, literature, theatre, films and television, their interest in whatever was happening in both the mainstream and the counterculture ensured that there were always new creative avenues to explore. Such questing enthusiasm led Debbie to Max's, CBGB's, Studio 54 and now directed her to the East Village for the 1993 Wigstock Festival.

Established in 1985, the world's first outdoor drag festival was held every Labor Day and attracted an exotic cast drawn from the cream of New York's club scene. By the time Deborah made her festival debut, airing the elegiac 'Communion' for the first time, crowds in excess of 25,000 had gathered for an event that marked the end of summer among the city's thriving gay scene. The following year, when Debbie took part in a staged fight with drag duo The Duelling Bankheads (who slurred their way through a suitably camp rendition of 'Heart Of Glass'), there were another 10,000 present.

Already a gay icon, Debbie's appearances at Wigstock helped cement her continuing popularity among a scene she actively supported through her appearances at AIDS benefits and Gay Pride concerts. "I think that the gay following that we've developed has a lot to do with that icon thing and the imagery," she observed. "I think what it boils down to is an understanding and a compassion but also, getting down to basics, the people I hung around with and had a lot of fun with and really hit it off with, a lot of them were and are gay men. You know, I still go to what I think are gay clubs, but it's hard to know whether they're strictly gay any more. I suppose there are only a couple of exclusively gay clubs these days ... One of my favourite places to go in New York is Mr Black ... You'll find naked men just wandering around in there."

Although Debbie had always presented an apolitical front to the media, her activism was inspired by the US Government's de-prioritising of AIDS research and the way in which reactionary elements had used the disease as a means of marginalising homosexuals. "It's infuriating. They put billions of dollars into the arms race, then put a thousandth of that into medical research for AIDS," she declared. "It's not just limited to homosexuals, it's a heterosexual disease. So everyone has to realise that. Personal attitudes and tastes don't concern me."

By 1994, the creative wanderlust that consistently drove Debbie to seek out new sounds and styles now urged her toward jazz. There had been hints of this on *Autoamerican* and the more recent *Debravation* – both 'Strike Me Pink' and 'Mood Ring' contained jazzy elements. However, when she was invited to sing a song entitled 'Dog In Sand' for New York ensemble The Jazz Passengers' sixth album, *In Love*, Debbie initiated a process that would further extend her musical scope. Jazz Passengers saxophonist Roy Nathanson had previously been a member of The Lounge Lizards and had hung around the CBGB's scene during the seventies. Although he was remotely acquainted with Deborah, it was only when producer and former *Saturday Night Live* music supervisor Hal Willner suggested she would be perfect for the song that Nathanson considered her voice in the context of jazz. "I had written this song called 'Dog In Sand' and she sang it great," he recalled. "After that, I thought, 'Well, maybe she wants to work with us,' so I just asked her."

Debbie duly agreed, and joined the group live for the first time at The Knitting Factory in New York on November 19. By June 1995, she had joined the group as a full-time vocalist and took part in their European tour, the highlight of which was an appearance at London's annual Meltdown Festival where they were joined on stage by that year's event curator, Elvis Costello.

"It's much more about real singing, which is definitely what I'm more adept at," Debbie observed. "I work very hard to be a good singer and I study, and I've kept working. In my performance I consciously hold back from dancing too much because I know that it's going to affect my singing. I really work to be a musician, and I contribute to the arrangements as much as I'm capable of doing. And that's what I love. I get joy from that."

Initially, Debbie's new direction confused her established fanbase. "I knew with Debbie involved we'd get bigger audiences, but I didn't really know what that meant," recounted Nathanson. "A ton of people would come to the gigs – like fanatic fans – and they weren't really there to listen to The

Jazz Passengers at all. So that was difficult, but she was so great with us and she was so cool, we kept doing it."

"I think the Jazz Passengers thing was really good for Debbie," asserted Glenn O'Brien. "It enabled her to make music and even improve her skills while taking the spotlight off her and just being one of the boys in the band. That was a situation she was never in before. And I think she's more one of the boys in Blondie now than she was in the beginning. She's not playing up the glamour part so much as just being a great entertainer."

"It was a relief to be part of this thing – to be visible and invisible at the same time," Deborah explained. "I think being an icon is like being stuck in a character role. Some actors in films are stuck in hero roles and it's very hard to get out of them. It takes a lot of age and endurance for Al Pacino to go from being a young lead to other great roles."

Debbie continued to gig with The Jazz Passengers throughout the next two years, recording an album with the group, *Individually Twisted*, in 1996. Credited to 'The Jazz Passengers featuring Deborah Harry', the 13-track disc included a reworking of 'The Tide Is High' and a duet with Elvis Costello, 'Doncha Go 'Way Mad'. She also appeared on the group's 1998 *Live In Spain* album, recorded at the Hotel Cancilla Ayala in the Basque province of Álava. Although Debbie downplayed her contributions as "fake jazz", Craig Leon felt that moving into a new medium had been highly beneficial to her: "In a weird way Debbie has become a lot better than she was … She has gone off into a completely different area and done very well creatively in it. She's become really good at it, to the point where it lights bulbs in my head as to doing a real Debbie Harry jazz album."

While Deborah's collaborations had moved her into a new creative realm, her Blondie persona remained sufficiently marketable to ensure a steady flow of compilation and remix albums were released throughout the nineties. After scoring a gold record with *The Complete Picture* retrospective in 1991, Chrysalis (which also put out the *Once More Into The Bleach* collection three years earlier) evidently believed there was plenty of milk left in the Blondie cash cow, issuing the 47-track *Platinum Collection* in 1994, followed up the next year by *Beautiful – The Remix Album* and *Remixed Remade Remodeled – The Remix Project*, both released within a month of one another.

Although these anthologies and the rolling programme of CD re-releases of Blondie's six studio albums helped to dig Chris and Debbie out of debt, the sense that their legacy was being strip-mined by a label they were no longer signed with rankled. "That shit is based on the fact that record companies realised they could have more than one hit with the same record," blasts Chris. "That shit is appalling, we had such a shitty deal with Chrysalis that they could do that to our songs. Remixes have nothing to do with someone wanting to do something better – or at least not in our case. It has to do with record companies wanting to make more money. It's not creative, but at the same time there is an audience for it. I like house and rap music, and we did reach a younger club audience, so there might be some good coming from it. But we could have done the remixes ourselves, taken a different approach. My problem with it is that someone can take a vocal off an existing track, put any rhythm they like underneath it and call it Blondie."

During her tenure with The Jazz Passengers Debbie maintained her acting career, appearing in the sixties thriller *Dead Beat* before scoring the more substantial role of Delores, a down-at-heel waitress, in *Heavy* – the directorial debut of James Mangold, who subsequently helmed the 2005 Johnny Cash biopic *Walk The Line*. The movie cast Deborah alongside Hollywood heavyweight Shelley Winters, as well as Liv Tyler – the daughter of Aerosmith frontman Steven – and model-turned-singer Bebe Buell. "I got involved through Bebe Buell, Liv's mother and an old friend of mine from the CBGB's days," explained Debbie. "Liv and Bebe were excited about it because it was a sensitive – not commercial – thing. Liv's very serious about acting and doesn't want to be another flip of the page."

Initially uncertain about casting Deborah, Mangold was sufficiently impressed by her down-to-earth nature and took the plunge. "If Debbie was going to be in the movie, I knew people were going to be looking at her with an extra set of ammo, thinking, 'Oh, it's just stunt casting,'" remembered the director. "My feeling was she had to do something so human, so reserved, so tender that she shut them up for good. And she did. Her upstate roots show. In fact, part of her connection to the project is that she once actually worked as a short order waitress in an upstate New York diner. I think she's brilliant in *Heavy*."With many reviews noting the strength of Debbie's performance, it seemed the critics agreed with Mangold, who would recast her in the same role for his big-budget feature *Copland* two years later.

Less significantly, Deborah also starred alongside former singing highwayman Adam Ant in the 1996 music business parody *Drop Dead Rock*. Cast in the role of bizarrely named record company executive Thor Sturmundrang, Debbie imbued the character with generous helpings of evil and mendacity. Asked if she based her portrayal on anybody she may have encountered at Chrysalis, Deborah replied, "No ... Just on everybody I've ever met in the entire industry."

While Debbie was digging into her rock'n'roll past for *Drop Dead Rock*, Chris had decided to part with a small portion of his Blondie heritage by selling unwanted memorabilia. Placing an advertisement in *The Village Voice*, he set in motion a sequence of events that led to a wholly unexpected conclusion. One of those who responded to the advert introduced Chris to veteran tour manager Harry Sandler, who suggested that Blondie reform to record a new album.

"Somebody was talking to Chris about it – not for the first time – and said to him, 'Look, if you don't do it now, you're never going to do it,'" explained Debbie. "So he called me up and said, 'What do you think about putting Blondie back together?' And I laughed! Then he went on and called everybody."

Sandler had been working with promoter and manager Allen Kovac, who shared his belief that a reformation was viable. "He had confidence," said Debbie. "He said he felt he could do it and thought highly of our history and our sales record. Initially, I think he was just going to help us renegotiate our old deal because our old catalogue was still selling."

"Debbie was intrigued that there was the chance that a band could reunite – get the people to heal and really sort out their issues and come back together," recalled Kovac.

But, despite being interested in the possibilities of a Blondie reunion, Debbie remained unconvinced. "I didn't want to get back together. As usual Chris talked me into it. It involves people that basically I feel are vultures picking my bones. That's a very uncomfortable feeling and by then I was doing something that was more meaningful and I preferred to be left alone to do that," she stated. "It was Chris' idea. He felt that if he didn't do it at a time when everybody in the band was still alive, he'd regret it. And he was getting a lot of emails from fans, suggesting the idea. Personally, I would never have thought of it."

After persuading Debbie, Chris contacted Clem who, having long felt that the band should have never split to begin with, readily agreed. Next came Jimmy: "I was in London and my wife called and said, 'Chris Stein called.' And I said, 'Chris never calls. What's it about?' So I called him from London and he was like, 'Let's do it again.' Click. You know, 'click' right after that, so it left me a lot of time to reflect and that's how Chris is. My initial reaction was bewilderment, but happiness too."

Now living in England, Gary Valentine was equally surprised to receive a message from Chris asking him to get in touch. "I hadn't seen or spoken to Chris in 10 years – I call him, and he's ecstatic, 'I want you to come to New York, because I wanna put the band back together.'"

Gary duly flew back in November 1996 to begin rehearsals with Debbie, Chris, Clem and Jimmy. After appearing with Debbie and Chris at a tribute show for William Burroughs in Lawrence, Kansas, the group booked into The Hit Factory to record some demo material. With Debbie committed to touring with The Jazz Passengers in support of their newly released *Individually Twisted* disc in February and March 1997, Valentine – who had been crashing at Chris', then Debbie's apartment before renting a Brooklyn loft with his wife, Ruth – returned to London to prepare songs for the new album.

The reformed quintet reconvened in May, making their first live appearance since 1982 at a private showcase in a midtown studio. "When word got out about the show, the place was packed with a couple of hundred people, and the queue ran down the stairs," recounted Gary. "It was exciting to play again, and with a full band. The crowd loved us and the next day we headed to Washington for our first real gig."

This was the HFStival, which took place on May 31 at the RFK Memorial sports stadium, where Blondie shared a bill headlined by The Prodigy and including another reformed outfit, Echo And The Bunnymen. This was followed by two further festival appearances in Texas and Connecticut. "Those went well," remarked Valentine. "Everyone liked it, we were getting along fine, and the word was, 'OK, work on some songs, and we'll bring you back in a couple of months.'"

As Debbie was in Europe with The Jazz Passengers during the summer, it was December by the time Gary returned to New York to resume working with Blondie. However, when he arrived he was informed by Chris that he didn't think he was right for the live shows. "We tried plugging him in, we did like three shows with him and we tried working with him but he's not a full-time musician, he's a writer," Stein explained. (In addition to penning his rock'n'roll memoir, *New York Rocker*, in 2002, as an author Gary Lachman would write a string of books on the occult, consciousness and assorted esoterica.)

"I left disgusted, but later thought better of it," revealed Valentine. "It was fun doing those shows, but after hanging out with Debbie, Chris and Jimmy again I soon felt that touring wasn't something I wanted to do. Later, I spoke to Chris and said it was fine."

Work on the album that would become *No Exit* began in the summer of 1998. Earlier in the year, Debbie had wrapped up her touring and acting commitments, including a pair of UK shows in late May and her reprisal of the role of Delores for James Mangold's *Copland* — although the bulk of her performance failed to make the final cut. She also had a small part in the TV movie *LA Johns* and a leading role as an overprotective mother in the comedy-crime drama *Six Ways To Sunday*, which also featured Isaac Hayes.

To begin with, work on *No Exit* proved difficult — initial sessions with Mike Chapman were scrapped and a further obstacle was placed in the group's way by Frank Infante and Nigel Harrison, who sued the band in an attempt to prevent use of the name 'Blondie' unless the duo received remuneration. Their lawsuit proved unsuccessful and the group turned to Craig Leon to produce the disc.

"*No Exit* was something that was discussed for a long time in the Nineties as Chris was recovering and, I guess, his personal situation with Debbie was resolved in one way or another and all of that," recalls Craig. "I was always in touch, mostly with Jimmy and Clem. Whenever I went to New York, to the New Music Seminar or those kind of things, we'd go to the bar and say, 'Yeah, we're going to do it, we're going to make a record,' not thinking that it was a comeback record or anything.

"I was going through things with Nigel and even Gary Valentine was in there, going, 'How can it be Blondie without the people from Blondie in it?' I said, 'These guys just hired me to make a record; I don't say who's on it!' Nigel and Frank were secondary musicians as I remember them. They were never full members of the group. Eventually, Clem came over to play on [pocket-sized Take That cutie] Mark Owen's album, which I co-produced with John Leckie at Abbey Road in 1996. I think Simon Cowell was the A&R guy on it. I put the band together for that album, including Dave Gregory from XTC and Louis Jardin. He wanted it to be credible, with a real band with good players. Clem came over to play drums on it, then we started putting the wheels in motion to see if we could get something together. Eventually, Chris was ready to do something by 1998 and they were writing songs. So we made an arrangement with the band to do it, everything was fine and everybody agreed on it. But it was Clem who actually pushed it all through. These days, he's usually the one who gets anything going with the outside world. He was basically the champion of the project.

"They were originally going to make an album with everybody who's ever worked with them as a retrospective reintroduction. Mike was going to do something. I was going to do something. Richie [Gottehrer] was in the doghouse for some unknown reason! This is another thing with Blondie: somebody is always the enemy! As it turned out, the stuff with Mike didn't work so the stuff with me became the whole album. That's how it actually happened."

Chris declared that he was pleased to be working with Leon again. "Clem and Jimmy had both done a little work with him and we didn't have to establish a relationship, we already knew him and he's a very crazy guy and when I finally talked to him, he was very excited and everything he said … seemed like totally the right thing," he enthused. "This is the first record we did digitally and he's a techno guy."

Despite it being more than 30 years since he played a key role in Blondie's eponymous debut album, Craig found the group pretty much as he had left them. "There's always this melting pot of ideas on the same song," he observed. "It can still get pretty violent with everybody fighting for their ideas: Chris wanting it one way, Jimmy wanting something here, Clem wanting something there, and Debbie kind of serenely sitting back and saying, 'When you guys get it together, I'm going to give you the hit melody and vocal.' It's all just because they all have a fabulous sense of pop history."

"They always quarrel, but now they have more informed and amusing quarrels than they used to," said Glenn O'Brien. "During the recording sessions they were having a lot of fun kind of goofing on each other. I think there's a real appreciation that's even been enhanced because of the years where they didn't see each other. It's almost like they never broke up."

"We get on great, but it's like brothers or sisters, or any bunch of people – there's always some conflict," confirmed Chris. "And the doors are always open all of the time, but they never tried to get out. I like that aspect of it, too, because everybody feels like they're stuck together without ever testing the exit sign."

"It was different and it was the same in a way," adds Craig. "As opposed to the loft in The Bowery, it was Chris' basement in this dishevelled place on Greenwich Street in TriBeCa, which had a huge basement and the ground floor up to first floor level filled to the brim with Chris-type memorabilia, like a chair made by Giger that went up almost to the ceiling, which may have been the Captain's seat in *Alien*, skeletons, all this paraphernalia scattered around the floor, dogs and cats and ghosts and whatever, masters for William Burroughs albums that he'd done there and never issued, all this kind of insane stuff. You'd be stepping over original Warhols and the dog would be pissing on them! Basically, on an economy level and because the process of making a Blondie record is quite slow, we started off working in his basement in the Addams Family house!

"We started the same way that we would work in the past; everybody would just sit around and get little bits of ideas, then we'd build them a riff or a verse at a time, or whatever. Jimmy came in with songs that were much more intact, like 'Maria'. The original of 'Maria' was basically a sampled acoustic guitar, him singing in a falsetto voice. It's pretty much the melody line of what it ended up being, with nothing filled in. Most of their songs start in a very rudimentary way like that, and you build them up. Chris' ones usually start out as drum patterns and bass loops. Jimmy's were more pop songs that actually had chords and stuff on them. There was a long, long period of preproduction down there, then we went over to Electric Lady, which again is a place they know from over the years so there's a lot of nostalgia there, and cut the drum tracks and basic tracks there, then went back to his place and finished it and [then took it] up to Chung King Studios. As it came together, it became much faster – by their standards. It still took about a year! They brought in a couple of outside players, who were very good. You could chart it out and they could just play it, once we actually had a song that Chris was happy with. The long part, of course, was getting Chris' guitar solos, which took quite a while."

One of the biggest challenges facing Leon was returning Debbie's now jazz-orientated focus to pop music. "Getting herself comfortable with even singing in a pop style again was hard," he admitted. "She's having fun doing it, it's not like she doesn't enjoy it. It's just totally different to what she's been doing for the past few years, and it's probably musically a little less interesting than the avant-garde things she's recorded."

"If anything, I was impressed with the difference working with Debbie," adds Craig. "She'd become really professional. Her writing was really fast. You'd give her the track and there'd be a little la-la melody line with maybe a couple of hook words. Then she would come back and have all her stuff written and do a couple of takes. If she'd ever want to redo anything after you'd cobbled it together from two or three takes, she might rewrite a couple of words or sing a couple of lines, but that was it. Her things were basically a couple of passes. They're not laboured vocals. The reason that happened was because she got back to what she really loved, which was jazz, so she was now used to singing with pro players and having to come up with things that had shifting tonalities. As a result, I was really interested in developing her solo, helping her branch out; not as opposed to Blondie, but in addition to what she does with Blondie. After we did *No Exit*, I was trying to help her get a jazz thing together. We did get her an offer of a deal, which the management turned down. She did appear on a couple of jazz classical things that I did for Decca on an Italian film project. She was really good, really solid, no nonsense – very helpful in helping other people develop their parts and everything."

In keeping with the ethos that had always underpinned his creativity, Chris was determined that the album was going to be more than just a re-creation of the band's signature tropes. "We wanted to make something that picked up where we left off, doing what we think should be done now. If anything makes it sound like the old stuff it's just that it's the same people, the personal styles involved. We didn't try to repeat ourselves. There's always the approach of taking a lot of the old styles and putting it through a filter to make something new. But we're interested in the new music not the old days," he explained. "It's a lot more minimal than the older stuff. The old records had that Wall of Sound/Phil Spector approach. If there's one major difference about music in the nineties it's the minimalism. Bands like Chic and Talking Heads were ahead of their time."

"The thing about *No Exit* that people missed and part of [if anyone had a negative reaction to] it is they went too far afield in their influences ... stuff like the little Cajun song," Leon observes. "Having said that, that's what they always do. But this time they had more resources and knew them better, it's a little less hybrid. Some of their forays into other genres are actually much closer to those genres and therefore less Blondie. That might be the only fault with their maturity, but they had some darn good songs on that album."

Although individually no strangers to the studio, collectively the group found that developments in production technology over the 17 years since they recorded *The Hunter* added a new aspect. "It's totally different," asserted Chris. We did a real lot of shit in the basement of my house, in my fucking grungy basement. We brought in equipment, I have a little fucked-up recording studio and we brought in extra shit and we did it. It's a big difference. Digital versus tape was a tremendous difference. We did this thing on an Atari Radar, which is a big dedicated 24-track hard drive, basically. The difference with that is, it's very good for capturing inspiration and not having to do something over and over again."

It enabled the band to be more spontaneous in the studio while also allowing them to review recordings with greater flexibility. "It's the difference between not having to repeat yourself because you can cut and paste," Stein explains. "You can do a guitar part and if it came out the right way, I wouldn't have to kill myself trying to play it the same each part of the song, you just move it around and make it in each part of the song. It's kind of like sampling, I mean, it is the same fucking concept. We got to sketch out the whole album beforehand, we demoed the whole record, we got to see the flow of the thing. Even though the record is so eclectic, I think it still has a flow from one thing to the other. We've never been able to do that in the past. We've never been able to hear what the record was going to sound like up front. And then we sort of re-recorded it all."

Thanks in the main to the diverse set of material assembled for the album, *No Exit* fulfilled its brief. Opener 'Screaming Skin' resembled The Specials' 'Gangsters' reworked as a thriller theme. An assertive slice of neon-lit ska, the song has sufficient impact to avoid being derailed by Deborah's not-entirely-successful attempt at a West Indian accent. The group also delved into the box marked 'reggae' for the low-key lovers rock lullaby 'Divine', one of three songs on the album co-written by Go-Go's bassist Kathy Valentine. Blondie also took their relationship with rap into new and exciting territory with the album's title track. Featuring a contribution from Coolio, 'No Exit' is a visit to the Hammer House of Gangsta, as Bach's 'Toccata And Fugue In D Minor' is consumed beneath fierce beats and savage organ stabs. "Initially it was like [Coolio's 1995 smash] 'Gangsta's Paradise', then it became a gothic thing about vampires," explained Chris.

Given the group's history of assimilating elements of reggae and hip hop, it was logical that those forms would be represented. The inclusion of laconic Wild West-style saloon song 'The Dream's Lost On Me' was more unexpected — especially given that fiddles had previously played little part in Blondie compositions. "It's a really great, pretty song," Stein declared. "We had been jamming on 'Tennessee Waltz' and Clem had been wanting to do a song in the 3/4 thing and I had had that together. So it was just more meeting of the minds. Then Romy Ashby, who is a writer and a friend of ours, this is the first bunch of lyrics she'd ever done."

The disc also included a spot of badlands boogie in the shape of the rolling, widescreen 'Under The Gun'. Specifically dedicated to Jeffrey Lee Pierce, the song also pays tribute to the friends Chris has lost along the way. "I probably know close to 200 people, literally, who are dead and out of all of 'em that was the one who particularly shook me up," he revealed. "I think there's going to be a resurgence … I'm hearing talk of Nick Cave and a bunch of people doing a record of his material. He's way overdue, in a way. We have him on there, posthumously. He's singing in the end there and ironically he's singing, 'fixin' to die, fixin' to die.'"

A pair of reflective ballads, 'Double Take' and 'Night Wind Sent', highlight Deborah's vocal mastery — although not to the remarkable extent evident on 'Boom Boom In The Zoom Zoom Room'. Employing a higher vocal register than usual, she delivers the song with precise control, handling tricky time signatures with aplomb to produce one of the album's stand-out moments. The closing 'Dig Up The Conjo' also provides a radical backdrop for Debbie's ever-widening range, as her multi-layered vocals combine with a chanted backing and futuristic blasts from some half-dreamed technological jungle to create a unique miasmic effect.

Amid all this variety, there remain elements that conform to the perceived Blondie archetype — 'Maria' and 'Nothing Is Real But The Girl' sweetly detonate twin blasts of the driving pop with which the band enjoyed huge commercial success, while a new version of 'Out In The Streets' straddles the gulf between the band's past and its present. Originally recorded as a demo more than 20 years earlier, the Ellie Greenwich/Jeff Barry number is given a radical reworking. Orchestral yet minimal, the track gradually gains intensity and would divide opinion among Blondie fans as to whether this, or the 1975 cut, was the better take on the song. "Way back around the first album I didn't want to do 'Out In The Streets,' so maybe they decided to torture me again," says Craig. "I always thought there were better Shangri-Las songs, actually."

Alongside the core quartet, bassist Leigh Foxx and guitarist Paul Carbonara were drafted in to assist with the recording of the album. Chris was appreciative of their contributions to *No Exit* and the duo would subsequently replace Nigel Harrison and Frank Infante when the group took to the road. "We just couldn't have done this without Paul and Leigh," asserted Stein. "It wouldn't have happened with Nigel and Frankie. It wouldn't have happened – it's as simple as that. Leigh, and Paul particularly, is like a brilliant guitar player and really a great guy to work with. A consummate professional and he's like 10 years younger than the rest of us and great. Leigh has been with Debbie and me for like 10 years on all our solo shit."

"It's a miracle that we even got together to do it," insisted Deborah. "It's been difficult to convince people. And the rumour mill is *so* outrageous in the record industry. People actually pay attention to it. It's like reading the *Enquirer* and deciding who to sign, it's madness. But we had a good break with this manager that we got."

"It was F Scott Fitzgerald who said there were no second acts in American life," mused Chris. "But we've kind of proved him wrong about that. And there wouldn't have been any point in just doing the old songs. We didn't want to get stuck in that way. We had to keep on moving forward in the way that Blondie have always been out front. More and more musicians were referencing Blondie, so it seemed the right time to reform."

"It was unfinished business in a way," summarised Debbie. "It felt like we had just gone up in a puff of smoke without a decent conclusion. We left a question mark. It was never really an explosive ending – it just sort of went '*poof*.'"

Chapter Fifteen

The Second Act

"We've always tried to be positive. It's our way of being political. The world is fucked up, so in lieu of actually making political statements we just try to make people feel better. That's a good job."

Chris Stein

With *No Exit* recorded but not due for release until the following year, Blondie travelled to London for rehearsals ahead of their first European gigs since 1980. After an opening show in Stockholm on October 26, 1998 that Chris later described as "dismal", the group quickly hit their stride, shaking off any initial nerves, road rust and technical hassles to delight the sold-out crowds that packed the modestly sized venues. "We're on a tight budget," explained Deborah. "Regardless of all the exposure and all the interest, it's been small halls and not a lot of money. We're doing this in a very traditional fashion."

For those who had waited almost two decades to see the group play live, and others finally getting to see them for the first time, the reunion gigs were hotly anticipated. This time, Blondie didn't have to impress *anyone* – enthusiastically partisan crowds welcomed them back with genuine affection. "It really has been extraordinarily good. I just can't believe it. The audiences have been right there with us. In Scotland, they sang along to everything, except the new songs. And they even tried to sing along to them," beamed Debbie. "They sang over the guitar intro. These guys usually frown at me when I do that, but they let the audience get away with it. But if we never do anything again after this, it'll be fine."

The European tour took up the whole of November, with gigs roughly split between those in Britain and on the continent. Although the new songs were well received, Blondie's set was weighted heavily in favour of crowd-pleasing older material. "We're only doing four new songs," said Chris. "As it goes along week by week, I think everybody's getting much more positive about the whole thing. The last tour Debbie and me did, what'd we do? Two of the fucking hit songs, maybe. And I can remember people leaving and going, 'Well, yeah,' but I had no idea what that was about. Five years ago I wouldn't have wanted to do the old songs, but now I feel real positive and real emotional about doing them. And unless we get heavily bombarded by tomatoes and beer cans, I think it's going to be fine."

"We had a really high energy," recalled Debbie. "And we got such a great response. The most typical comment we got was, 'I never got to see you because I was too young, and I can't believe I'm getting to see you!' I don't know if we satisfied them or not!"

"I just wanted to do this. I knew this was going to be successful, but I had no idea to what extent," Stein declared. "There seems to be a genuine enthusiasm. It's hard to take compliments … When you have a fuckin' roomful of people telling you that you're an icon and a god and all this shit, it's just ridiculous. It's very hard to absorb that shit. It may be my own personal insecurities, but at the same time, it's a little bewildering. Especially because having fucking done nothing for 16 years. Not nothing, you know, I've been active in music, with Debbie's solo shit, but the level, the jump has been so pronounced, the difference between what we've been doing to what's going on now is so severe. It's like leaping off a cliff backwards. It's very odd."

Among those delighted to see Blondie playing live once more was Chris Charlesworth, who had given Debbie her first UK press with his review of The Stillettoes for *Melody Maker* over 20 years earlier. "My wife, Lisa, and I saw the show together, enjoyed the hits and headed for the backstage bar when it was all over," he recalls. "We were leaning against the bar when she came in, as lovely and blonde as ever, and she came straight over to me, ignoring a bunch of heavyweight-looking record company suits with outstretched hands. And she kissed and hugged me too, right in front of everybody, and hardly anyone there even knew who I was. 'This guy,' said Debbie to everyone who'd gathered round, 'was the first man ever to put my picture in a magazine.' It was great. She hadn't forgotten what I'd done for her all those years ago."

In addition to being greeted as returning heroes, the band was also on the receiving end of several media baubles. Most notably, *Q* magazine honoured them with an 'Inspiration' award.

"It was great," Deborah acknowledged. "Very straightforward. They were concentrating on the awards, not making it into a TV show. Unlike the US, where everything is a TV show and it just drags on and on. But this was very down to business. So there was some spontaneity to it." At the London ceremony Debbie demonstrated she could still kick up a sartorial storm, when she took the stage in a dress adorned with razor blades. "I always cut myself when I put on that razor blade dress," she exclaimed. "It's a Michael Schmidt and I love it. He spends hours blunting the razors on a stone, otherwise it would obviously be impossible to wear. The thing that catches you when you put it on is the corners because it's so angular, but once it's on it's great fun to wear. It's terribly comfortable when it's on, very flexible, like wearing a snake's skin. It's very cool."

The band also created a stir when they were invited to receive a cultural award in Lugano, Switzerland. "It was this black-tie fuckin' situation," recounted Chris. "Clem got progressively drunker and drunker and tried to leap over his drums, and he fell on Paul and Leigh in front of this whole crowd of bejewelled courtesans. It was a disaster, but at the same time it was a major existential moment."

"It was like being in a Fellini film," remarked Jimmy. "We did a lip synch, which we're very loath to do as a rule." He pointed at Clem. "For some reason, this idiot decides to hop over the drums. So he hops over his drum kit, doing his middle-aged Keith Moon, and knocks down our bass player, who he picks up by the collar. By now he's in his 1977 'I'm a punk rocker' vibe. So he goes out into the audience, picks up a chair, and starts swinging it above his head. And there's this little Italian guy, who must have been a film producer or something, and he's screaming, 'No, no, no.'"

"I had completely forgotten that I had drunk three bottles of champagne, and also that I had my Anello & Davide Cuban-heel Beatle boots on," Clem explained. "So I go over the drums and next thing I know I'm on the floor on top of Leigh, and then the drums come crashing down in a chain reaction, and all you hear is 500 people going, 'Oh my God' – in Italian, of course."

"By the way," chirped Chris, "the award was a really beautiful thing with a marble base and silver shit and a fuckin' gold mask, whereas our fuckin' Q award must have cost all of $4."

While Blondie viewed such awards as simply part of the music industry's mechanism of self-promotion, the human response left a lasting impression on the band. "It was heart-warming and wonderful to have fans coming out of the woodwork and to see new fans … The other stuff is the downside," Deborah observed. "It's only now that I sense that I did actually touch people's lives in Blondie. When we were in our heyday, we had a very young audience – little kids almost. Now all those kids are young adults, and sometimes they come up to me with tears in their eyes and say things like, 'Oh, when I was eight years old …' It's funny and I laugh it off, but we've all been there. I find it very, very flattering."

"For me it's been very stress-free as a result of so much acceptance," concluded Chris. "I think Debbie's the most worn out, because I get to sort of phase out, whereas Debbie's level of focus is a lot higher."

"I actually enjoy what I do now more than ever," Deborah revealed. "It's odd, because the pressure is on. Yet the pressure is off. I'm pretty sane about it. I want to harken back, to give people a sense of what we were like in the past. But I like to be comfortable on stage, to forget about everything except the music. I do all that other stuff – style, make-up – beforehand. That's what saves me. Then I can go out and forget about it. In the eighties, I had the lucky break of working with Stephen Sprouse. Stephen schooled me in being prepared, in getting my look together, so I could focus on the important stuff."

After a short visit to Australia to see in the New Year by headlining the Falls Festival (a four-day event split between Lorne, Victoria and Marion Bay, Tasmania), followed by a gig in Sydney, Blondie spent the remainder of January shooting TV spots and making publicity appearances ahead of *No Exit*'s February 23, 1999 release date. The album would be trailed by the single release of 'Maria', which came out at the beginning of the month and went straight to number one in the UK. Almost exactly 20 years after 'Heart Of Glass' had reached that summit, the song became Blondie's sixth British chart-topping single.

'Maria' is four-and-a-half minutes of transcendent pop that, when viewed on the following week's *Top Of The Pops*, aroused genuine feelings of joy in anybody with the faintest regard for the band. For committed fans it was a long-awaited moment of sweet triumph. "What a fabulous moment that was," enthused Debbie. "That kind of approval is unbelievable. 'Maria' was a good song, but for my taste a little too retro-feeling. I'd never have chosen it. So, good thing I wasn't in charge, or nobody would have ever known we were back!"

"Hearing 'Maria' for the first time, it was very moving because I realised that – even thinking about it gets me emotional about it – because I realised that it could be a hit," confessed Chris. "The single is so accessible it's amazing. It's a strange mix of stuff, like some weird Buddy Holly modern dance rap thing that's really easy for people to get. People pick up on it when they hear it for the first time … When I heard the finished thing – when we were working on it, I didn't know – but when I heard the final, finished thing it knocked me out how strong it was."

Less happily, the single only managed to make number 82 in the US, in part due to it being issued on manager Allen Kovac's Beyond Music label, financially unable to compete with the far larger promotional budgets of the majors. "Pop isn't as strong or as big in the States, it's more popular over here," observed Debbie. "I was actually against it as a single in the States, I really wanted one of the more dramatic ballady things to go out, and I was right."

Irrespective of disappointing US sales, the hurricane of affection that had met the band's European shows and their first UK single release since July 1982's 'War Child' validated their decision to reform. "In a way it was providential," Deborah declared. "It went in our favour because people were copying us and there was nothing I could do about it, and then when we came back we had taken on this status as being something legendary, or some ridiculous thing. By then I just felt flattered by it. It's interesting to see what becomes style and what becomes acceptable." By the mid-to-late nineties, the music scene was now awash with wannabe-Blondie figures like Gwen Stefani.

Another factor that made the initial reunion enjoyable was that the group's long-established penchant for internal strife was now tempered with humour, drawn from experience. "We keep using the analogy of us being a dysfunctional family, but I think it's still very *a propos*," asserted

Clem. "It's like any relationship you go back to, be it an old friend or an old lover – you bring a lot of emotional baggage back with you. Sometimes that can work to your advantage. We've all been in therapy over the years, so that's a big help."

"I think we look at each other in a lot funnier light now. We don't take each other as seriously," added Jimmy. "We have a bigger background of getting reamed, so therefore we come with a little more cynicism. And that cynicism does breed a humour of like, 'Oh, don't tell me *that!*' It puts a sort of lump in your throat and paints you a little green with envy when an artist that sells half the records you do is living in a mansion in Highgate. But then, some kids my age went to Vietnam and didn't come home."

The release of *No Exit* returned Blondie to the American Top 20 and charted across Europe, reaching number three in the UK. "Someone asked me if we anticipated great success with this record," recounted Chris. "And I said that, for me, success was that we'd made the record. I mean that sincerely. That we actually got back together and made the record. So we already are a success."

"We asked ourselves how we would go about being a band again," stated Clem. "We were never interested in being purely a nostalgia act. Yes, we play our hits, but we needed to make the *No Exit* album before touring. It put the focus on being a band. *No Exit* is simply the next Blondie record. It just took 16 years to make, that's all. And we're very fortunate to have Debbie here to convey the whole thing."

Despite not being signed to a label that could provide enormous advances or large tour budgets, Chris was delighted to escape the Chrysalis/EMI corporate labyrinth. "Our new label gives us a much better deal. This is the first time we've done the cover art for example. The music industry is changing. Our manager is making a lot of enemies by coming out and saying that record companies won't exist for much longer because of the Internet, and he actually runs our record company as well."

The deal with Beyond also gave Blondie greater control over when they toured and how they were presented, both of which had proven contentious during the group's original incarnation. "It's a lot different – it's not as insane as it used to be," Stein explained. "Everybody's like mellowed out a lot and people know their place and the guys aren't as jealous of Debbie. In the old days, we'd be doing the photo session and the photographer would say, 'OK, can I just take some pictures of Debbie?' and all the guys would start complaining. At this point it's, 'Oh, great, I don't have to pose.'"

"We all know who's who and what's what, what our specific roles are," observed Deborah. "It's much clearer. If you have the wisdom to accept who you are, then you might as well accept who everyone else is and make the best of a situation. Being bashed over the head a little bit when you're younger gives you a kind of perspective."

After several one-off shows in March and April, Blondie set out on the US leg of their reunion tour in mid-May 1999. Again, the band was warmly received, although perhaps not with the same sense of abandon as in Europe. "I don't think it's quite Blondiemania any more," Debbie remarked. "It's been a nice reintroduction to our audience and our friends and the music business, but it hasn't quite reached manic proportions. Cher coming back with 'Believe' was much more manic. I think our little musical input or position is a bit more complex than that."

"I think they come a lot based on their memories and stuff like that," observed Chris. "I mean, songs have a lot to do with what they evoke in the listener and what the associations are. It's partially that, maybe, for the older people … There's always been a do-it-yourself quality to Blondie. I mean, everybody really knows that we weren't the product of stylists and all those other kinds of junk. It's always been a home-made thing, so I think people like that."

A second run of US gigs took place in August and September, after the group had spent the early summer on the European festival circuit. Blondie would wrap up their touring commitments with a return to the UK in November. "The only place we've had a difficult time was in Spain," reflected Debbie. "We played in these bullrings with awful acoustics and bloodstains everywhere. It was like the old days – I felt we really had to go out and get 'em!"

As the group dispersed at the end of 1999, there was little question that their reunion had been a success. Although the single release of 'Nothing Is Real But The Girl' had failed to match 'Maria', there was a feeling of certainty that they would continue. "It's as permanent as it gets," assured Chris. "We'll do another record."

Throughout the reunion period Debbie had continued to act, taking another role as a waitress in 1999 comedy thriller *Zoo* and playing 'Ezmeralda the Psychic' in *Red Lipstick* (2000), a comedy about two criminal drag queens. She also appeared in *The Fluffer* (2001) – a comedy-drama set in the sex industry. "I play a lesbian strip club owner. Isn't it obvious they would want me for that?" teased Debbie. "I make a small appearance in a very funny little movie. It's sort of like a soap opera, but naked – and dirty!"

In November 2000, Deborah returned to the theatre, taking one of the four pivotal roles in a Greenwich Village production of *Crave*, a one-act chamber piece by English playwright Sarah Kane, who had committed suicide the previous year. "I can't really describe *Crave*," admitted Debbie. "It's not a play that's plot driven. It's about emotion. It's about inner turmoil and personality. In a way, I guess it's about madness."

Although the play received mixed reviews and only ran until the end of December, critics regularly singled out Deborah's performance for specific praise. Writing in the *New York Times*, reviewer Ben Brantley noted her "subtle, pitch-perfect performance", concluding, "Only Ms. Harry seems to have found this elusive tone. As the lead singer for Blondie, she managed both to send up and trade on her platinum-edged sex appeal without resorting to cheap quotation marks. Here her performance has a corresponding depth of irony, a tension between soul and surface that is never merely glib. There is pathos and a stylish brittleness in her intonations, and her thin, papery voice matches a phrase used by her character: 'the stain of a scream'. The last words she speaks, 'Glorious. Glorious,' are delivered with a mixture of weary acceptance and girlish anticipation. It is the sound of a woman hugging the possibility of ceasing to exist."

For Deborah, being in *Crave* represented the realisation of another youthful ambition. "It was like a dream come true. When I was in high school I used to take the bus into New York City and walk around the West Village and just fantasise about being on stage. Then one night recently I was walking to the theatre, through the West Village, and it all came flooding back. I thought, 'Wow, my dream came true; this is actually happening.'"

In the four decades since Debbie had made those first exploratory trips into New York from Hawthorne, the city had changed considerably. During the eighties, Ronald Reagan's administration slashed funding to many art projects but the downtown scene continued to thrive. Early in the decade, hip hop was still fresh, graffiti was still evident on subway trains, Madonna had just left her Danceteria elevator post and electronic dance music was starting to point towards the house revolution. But, with Wall Street on the up, the decade was most notable for the subtle changes that seemed to be under way, as the city that had been almost a no-go area 10 years earlier started attracting young upwardly mobile professionals. Consequently, rents rose as formerly abandoned areas such as SoHo started gaining boutiques, restaurants and condominiums. Although the crime rate was still lethal, Times Square remained sleazy and the East Village was spectacularly bombed-out, old timers from the downtown scene started moving elsewhere, either lamenting the loss of the buzz or simply priced out of the neighbourhood.

By 1990, the changes to New York were manifest – hip hop became dominated by pantomime gangstas and Avenue A was now negotiable without too much street hassle. Most tragically, the gay community that had driven the city's subterranean currents was decimated by AIDS. Disco was no longer merely a celebratory soundtrack but the music of the doomed, its symbolic death knell marked by the closing of The Paradise Garage in September 1987.

By 1993, the city's conservative mayor, Rudolph Giuliani, had adopted policies aimed at reducing minor crime. While the actual impact of his licensing restrictions, denial of protest rights and crackdown on graffiti artists or subway turnstile jumpers remains hotly debated, his concept of 'zero tolerance' became a rallying call for the Right and served to sanitise New York. Every subsequent return visit to Manhattan was notable for the sprucing up of previously bleak streets and, although it was now possible to venture deep into the East Village without risking a gun in the back, the funk seemed to be draining out of the place. That intangible buzz was no longer coursing under the sidewalk.

Most artists lamented the erosion of the downtown sense of community. While CBGB's traded on past glories by presenting unknown out-of-towners, underground clubs still managed to exist. The cheaper rents, meanwhile, were now to be found over the bridge in Brooklyn. This systematic clean-up of the New York streets and the subsequent influx of outsiders, accompanied by skyrocketing rents and artistic flight, crushed the spirit that spawned so many cultural movements. The rotting Bowery lofts which had housed and nurtured Blondie now sold for upward of a million dollars. This would continue as New York turned into just another city.

"It certainly doesn't have the funk appeal it once had, and I miss that," reflected Debbie. "It's all very tidy since Giuliani went down on his knees with a little toothbrush and cleaned it all up. The entertainment is too 'general public'. Now that all the strip clubs like Billy's Topless are closed, these places on 42nd Street that kinda had the girls doing their thing are illegal. So you get all these strippers in mainstream Broadway shows … it's not even under the radar, it's just not sexy. It's lascivious, but it's not real horny, y'know? People pretend it's funny like they're going along with a joke, but they won't admit they're getting turned on. It's fake-wholesome, like the movie *Chicago.*"

"I hate the fucking clean-up," asserted Chris. "It's not good for the arts, what's going on there. Young kids can't afford to live there. When I lived there, I had a fuckin' $100 apartment. You can't expect to have to make a $1,000 a week to survive and still have a band, it just doesn't work like that. I think urban areas are supposed to be dirty and dangerous, I don't think it's supposed to be fuckin' Disneyland. So on one level it's really grotesque what's going on there now and the police are uptight and a lot of it is very surface what's happening, too. It's just all done for the tourist trade and shit."

Although Debbie continued to live downtown, Chris would leave the city in 2002. "I had a really nice loft on Greenwich Street, but we were right in the fucking thing when the Trade Center blew up. We were right in the front lines there. I had like a 4,000 square-foot loft with a street entrance. It was like a thousand bucks for 10 years, and then it went up to 5,000 bucks. It was like ridiculous. That was the end of it."

Reflecting upon the 2001 World Trade Center atrocity that changed the city's landscape and impacted profoundly on the lives of many New York residents, Debbie found herself missing the innocence of the early CBGB's era. "When the Trade Center went down it hit me hard and I wished it was 1975 again. That was an exciting time to be starting off. The attacks made me realise what an important time that was for me … I'm always amazed that outsiders think New York is an unfriendly place. I think people were very supportive of one another after it happened."

At that time, Blondie had almost completed recording a follow-up to *No Exit* at a studio close to the Trade Center. "We had the stuff stockpiled and were working in a studio in Manhattan," explains Craig Leon. "At that point there were business problems with their management/record company going bankrupt. Allen Kovac's record company compounded my situation because they owed me royalties on *No Exit*. It also compounded making the record difficult because they weren't paying the studio. During one of the periods I went back to the UK to mix a classical project we had recorded in New York for Decca. I would have to be there for three weeks or something. I had copies of the files and the studio had copies, so we'd have them in two different places. I was in the UK, then 9/11 happened, which made it very difficult to transport back and forth. In between all of that, everything kind of went into limbo because they couldn't get the tapes out of the studio to work on them, because they hadn't paid the bill."

While plans for the new album were being reformulated, Blondie set out on a 30-date summer tour, following it up with a shorter 'Greatest Hits' tour in November 2002 – before crossing the Atlantic for a string of arena dates in the UK and Ireland the following month. Although the very nature of a tour based around the group's greatest hits compelled them to emphasise their older material, many songs were given a makeover. "It's refreshing for us," enthused Debbie, "we've done all the other material for so many years. Most of the songs, we've taken and tried to revamp them, and make them interesting for ourselves, as well as to make them more contemporary. So when we bring in something new and start to play it, it's really exciting for us. Also, I noticed in the last three shows, the audiences were really listening to the new material and really paying attention, it was great."

As with the gigs that followed *No Exit*'s release, these shows were celebratory affairs. There appeared to be little dissent between Blondie's principal quartet, an indication of the way maturity had mellowed that often fraught dynamic. "Our last tour was the most fun I ever had on the road," enthused Debbie. "When we did it all first time around, there were always so many tensions and insecurities. Now we feel we can relax. Because we're more comfortable with each other and what we're doing, I think the band sounds better than it ever has."

However, despite the fact that Debbie, Chris, Clem and Jimmy were hardly in their dotage, she was aware that, as the years rolled by, the physical demands of playing live would become increasingly difficult to endure: "It's important to tour now, as we'll have less energy in 10 years. One day, I won't feel like going on the road. But we love what we're doing – so why stop?"

Blondie duly flew south for the summer festival season, playing dates in Australia, New Zealand and Japan. However, Chris had to rush home during the Australian leg of the tour on account of the birth of his daughter,

Akira. In 1999, a decade after he and Debbie broke up as a couple, Chris had married actress Barbara Sicuranza – with whom he would also have a second daughter, Valentina, two years later.

"The pregnancy was a tense time for me, as well as for my wife, because of all the drugs I've done over the years," he explained. "You can't help but wonder what effect that might have. Blessedly, though, our baby is absolutely fine, and very alert and bright. To have a first child at my age is like a gift from above. Suddenly, you find yourself looking forwards rather than back. It's given me a whole new lease of life. And that we should have a little girl is just the icing on the cake. The world needs all the female energy it can get."

Given the enduring nature of his relationship with Deborah, Chris was aware that there were possibilities for feelings of awkwardness and jealousy on all sides. "We've been a hard act to follow. It's always been tough for the women I've been involved with after Debbie, but Barbara and I have worked all of that out. My wife's a great woman, really talented and smart, and I enjoy her company immensely. I think we're very good for each other."

"I think early on in my relationship, I was intimidated and less secure and sort of wondering about this woman, his partner, and they are *so* close," recalled Barbara. "They have love and it was hard for me a little. But I have a different relationship with him and have a different relationship with her. I respect what they have because why would I want to deny people that I love, love for one another?"

Deborah, who would be godmother to both Akira and Valentina, admitted that it took her and Barbara "a little while to build up any kind of relationship ... we had to figure out where we stood with each other and where each of us stood with Chris. We definitely worked at it. But my relationship with Chris was the longest I've ever had and also very important. I think he's a terrific person and I guess he thinks I'm OK, too, as we're still very good friends."

"It's 30 years now since we first met, and we've been closer than close ever since," asserted Chris. "I honestly don't know how to explain our connection. It's so deep that I sometimes think we must have been linked in a former life. And despite all that we've been through, separately and together, it continues to go from strength to strength. It's almost like we're telepathic. We know what each other is thinking, even without asking. It's quicker for me to read Debbie's body language, and she mine, than it is for us to speak."

"We may not be a couple any more, but Chris hasn't stopped being the dearest person in the world to me. He's still the person who best understands how to control my paranoia," revealed Debbie, who continued Blondie's Antipodean tour alongside Clem, Jimmy, Leigh and Paul.

Sadly, while the group were in Australia Deborah received the news that her adoptive father, Richard, had died at home. "Dad had been pretty sick for a while, which was very hard to watch. I imagine I had the same mixed feelings anyone experiences in such circumstances. You hate to lose someone you love, but it's awful to see them suffer. Although we didn't always have a meeting of minds, we'd achieved a real closeness in recent years."

"Both of Debbie's parents have passed away now, and my mother is currently in a pretty bad way," added Chris. "But then, this is the stuff that happens to everyone as they get older. It's the path that all of us are going to have to tread at some time."

Recorded once more with Craig Leon, Blondie's eighth studio album was pieced together from elements of the initial recordings complemented by material laid down by individual band members working alone. "Things have changed quite a lot, because on this record people brought in work they had done in their home studios, but there's still some of the same aspects to recording," explained Clem.

It was prefaced by the September 2003 release of 'Good Boys', a hi-energy hands-in-the-air chunk of sequenced pop, topped by an ethereal vocal. The single, which was not issued in the US, made number 12 in Britain and cracked the Australian Top 40. Written by Debbie and musician/producer Kevin Griffin, 'Good Boys' also cited Queen guitarist Brian May among the writing credits on account of a lyric section that referenced Queen's 1977 hit, 'We Will Rock You'.

One month later, the album appeared under the semi-ironic title *The Curse Of Blondie*. "The 'Curse of Blondie' has been an ongoing refrain for us and when anything bad happened or untoward or surprising, you say 'ah, the curse of Blondie'. I always think of it as being funny and melodramatic and sort of tongue in cheek," explained Debbie.

"I might be the curse of Blondie to Chris, and Chris might be the curse of Blondie to me," laughed Clem. "Part of the curse is being in the band, right? There's the camaraderie and the love, and there's also the backbiting."

"Part of the curse is we finally have achieved some kind of success in the record business, which is going through a drastic transformation now," said Chris. "I think this era of charts and rigidity is going to be over because of the internet. And part of our appeal is that our approach to making music is naturalistic. We do stuff on our own terms."

The 14 tracks that make up *The Curse Of Blondie* contemporise Blondie's signature sound while expanding it into new areas. Numbers such as 'Golden Rod' (part of the band's live set since the 2002 UK tour), the glamtronic bump'n'grind of 'End To End', and Jimmy's urgent 'Last One In The World' are all indicative of the group in 'modern rock' mode. The pop aspects of Blondie's sonic heritage are represented by the perky but hard-edged 'Undone' and 'Shakedown' – which, after a surprisingly visceral opening featuring Debbie's most savage rap to date, takes us on a lyrical journey down the New Jersey Turnpike, before unfurling a cloying R&B chorus.

"There was always this great debate within the band," recalls Leon. "Chris in his writing is very loop-oriented and, like, late seventies/early eighties primitive electronic-oriented in what he does, whereas Jimmy and Clem and just about everybody else were saying that they wanted to do things that were more live.

"Jimmy was kind of locked out on material for it. There was definitely an acrimonious situation between Jimmy and the rest of the group. They were having problems with him. Chris was actually vetoing a lot of things that were Jimmy's. You've got material that lends itself more towards Debbie's solo work that Chris was involved in, rather than an actual Blondie record. It's kind of a Chris and Debbie record. And again, looking for material, there's a lot of filler, written by the bass player and things like that, but it was sounding pretty decent and we were doing it.

"Jimmy was really angry because he didn't have a lot of material on the album. Arguably, he did write or co-wrote quite a lot of their hits. He very much brought in street pop, New York pop and classic pop. The classic pop elements were him and Clem more than anything else – not that Chris and Debbie didn't know them and like them, [but] they were always more into the leftfield influences. You've got to remember they were the people who were into hip hop when it was really underground and all of that. They'd be listening to Cuban salsa music or something."

Ultimately, Craig Leon was prevented from completing his work on *The Curse Of Blondie*. "Like a lot of Blondie events, it ended up with a manager yelling at people and them yelling at each other and yelling at me," he explains. "Quite honestly, I didn't have time to bother with it because of all the other things I was doing, so I was actually quite relieved when Allen Kovac gave me this big long speech where he just kind of sacked me from the record, which I think was unbeknownst to the band as well. I also think he had this viewpoint where he wanted to make them more contemporary, meaning disco 1981 as opposed to classic rock'n'roll 1967 or 1977. I don't even know who finished off those songs. They certainly weren't people I recognised. It's sad because, even though it isn't a classic Blondie album or anything, the original way it was heading would have been much better."

Alongside the big guitars and insistent rhythms that underpin many of *The Curse*'s songs, the album also includes several more restrained moments that are largely Jimmy's work. Described by Destri as "the greatest love story I've ever written", 'Rules For Living' is a wistful ballad that floats atop layers of processed rhythms and synthesized melody. Debbie supplies a reserved vocal that reaches an expertly controlled higher pitch during the chorus, delivering the lyric evocatively as instruments drop out of the mix. Co-written by Jimmy and Debbie, 'Background Melody (The Only One)' is a crystalline shard of sweet pop that drops Latin horn breaks, backwards guitar and sparse trip-hop rhythms into a song that pitches the vocal somewhere in the fragile range. A further Harry/Destri collaboration, 'Diamond Bridge,' begins in a laconically understated manner before developing force and momentum and then returning to the start of its sonic cycle.

In terms of unpredictability, it's difficult to top the band inexorably linked with the sounds and attitude of New York City covering a traditional Japanese folk song. 'Magic (Asadoya Yunta)' originated in Okinawa and recounts the tale of a woman named Asadoya nu Kuyama, who was brave enough to reject a wedding proposal from a government official. Blondie's rendition features understated electronics and guitar supporting multi-tracked choral vocals. A similar world music vibe suffuses 'Hello Joe', a track written in memory of Joey Ramone, who died of lymphoma in April 2001.

"It's a tribute, about witnessing Joey down the years, and saying his memory will never die," Debbie stated. "He'll always be alive for me. I always loved that band and thought Joey was a nice person." 'Hello Joe' emerges as a Latin shuffle that includes the referential lyric, "Hey, hola Joe," and something that sounds remarkably like a processed accordion in the bridge section.

But *The Curse Of Blondie*'s most radically exciting inclusion is the remarkable 'Desire Brings Me Back'. Written by saxophonist Gretchen Langheld and guitarist Carla Olla, the song begins with a maelstrom of discordant jazz, before lurching into Birthday Party mode to assail the listener with a primal, sultry sex beat, topped by such conflicted lyrics as, "How can I feel so free when I'm so bound to you?"

"This record is one of our most eclectic," declared Jimmy. "The interesting thing about the band is that the influences that come from within the band are all over the place and they all kind of come together and assimilate into making what Blondie sounds like."

"I think it's more sophisticated. It's about today. I don't think that we're trying to create a Blondie album that would just live on our reputation from the past. We try to make a record that was part of our thinking and lives today. I think that we're probably all much more capable at what we do in all aspects, so the songs are better, the performances are better," Deborah asserted. "I thoroughly enjoyed doing it. And I feel that since other things in my life have become focused, that I've been able to focus better. It's funny though because the other day I was thinking that Blondie was sort of like a late bloomer, in terms of all the things that were happening back when. Because we tried to cover a lot of ground and do a lot of different styles, and none of us were really educated musicians. We were all self-taught, so it took us a little longer to get all of that together."

Due to Beyond Music having gone bankrupt, *The Curse Of Blondie* was released by Sony subsidiary Epic in the UK, while in America it emerged on Sanctuary Records. Although the album was supported by a European tour on release, it slipped out without a huge amount of promotion and only hit the Top 40 in Britain.

Throughout 2004 and 2005, Blondie settled down into a pattern of regular tours and recuperative breaks. Although there was no sign of any new album during this period, the group appeared to have achieved a mature status as elder statesmen who regularly appeared at festivals alongside bands to whom they had provided inspiration. However, by 2006 the core quartet's dysfunctional family values sparked into life once again. Jimmy was dismissed from the group on account of his ongoing drug issues.

"I used to do tons of drugs and stuff like that, but I stopped after a while and Jimmy found it harder to pull himself out of all that. Even though he thought he was doing OK, everybody else didn't see eye to eye with him. We all thought he was fucking up more than he did," said Chris.

"What they did to me was pretty bald-faced wrong," insisted Jimmy. "Chris had a very serious drug problem and we helped him through it, I was having some drug problems and I was sort of ostracised for it."

"There is something really wonderful about him, but there's also this complete horror," said Debbie of Jimmy's cocaine abuse. "And when he lives in the horror side – which he tends to do quite a bit – you can't be with him, you can't be around him and you can't work with him."

"I think we go through each other like a hot knife through butter, and I can't see myself ever working with them again. Not on stage. Never again. But what I think they're missing is a hell of a fucking lot," Destri concluded.

"We all had to be reassured about everyone's enthusiasm for the project," states Deborah. "As it worked out, three of us really had the inspiration and the drive to do it, and the fourth person dropped out."

Jimmy's keyboard berth in Blondie was taken by composer and session musician Kevin Patrick – there seemed to be no way he would ever return to the band.

"Jimmy just won't mend fences with Debbie and Clem. There's nothing I can do about it," reveals Chris. "Those guys and him are at odds. It would be up to him to make the overture but he just won't do it."

On March 13, 2006, Jimmy was briefly reunited with his former bandmates when Blondie were inducted into the Rock and Roll Hall of Fame. Given his unhappiness about how he had been ejected from the group and the presence of Frank and Nigel, who were also invited by the organisers, there was plenty of scope for conflict. As it turned out, it was Frankie who generated headlines by publicly pleading with Debbie to allow himself, Jimmy and Nigel to play with Blondie at the awards show.

"Not tonight," she answered. "Can't you see my band is up here?"

"If they'd actually wanted to play they should have called up beforehand, which they didn't do," explained Chris. "We would have needed a rehearsal apart from anything else. The idea that they could have just wandered on stage and played like it was the old days again … I'm afraid life is only like that in the movies. Also, if those guys hadn't sued us we would've maybe considered their request more seriously. To this day people ask us how much we paid Frankie to do that! Everybody thought we were going to be eclipsed by The Sex Pistols no-show, but then the headlines were all 'Blondie Mayhem At The Hall Of Fame!' It was all nothing really, but the media's got to latch on to something. I got more congratulations for that than I did for having a kid, so it sunk in by proxy. You can guess which one means most to me."

Like Chris, Debbie admitted to slight ambivalence about Blondie's induction. "I didn't really care at first. Before it all came up, I just thought, 'So what?' But after we got it, there were total strangers from all walks of life coming up to me in a big way, so I was like, 'Oh, gee.' For some reason people really pay attention to those kinds of things," she observed. "It's an honour and it made me feel good, but I think it's very commercial. It's like any major awards show for any industry."

Ever the rock'n'roll enthusiast, Clem's response was less equivocal. "We were on a sold-out tour in the UK when we got the news. I was in an Internet café with my wife, checking my email, and Yahoo [reported it] … My wife and I began screaming, and all these reserved English folk were looking at us, probably thinking, 'Oh, those nutty Americans.' But I was so happy. It legitimises what Blondie did – and still does. But I'm not sure how punk rock it is to be in the Rock and Roll Hall of Fame."

Given that 2006 was the 30th anniversary of what was subsequently recognised as 'punk rock', there was significant media interest in the scene's origins. But as glossy retrospectives hit the racks, a link with the roots of punk was irrevocably severed when CBGB's closed its graffiti-encrusted shutters for the final time, in October. The venue's final nights featured an acoustic set from Blondie, along with appearances from old hands including The Dictators and Patti Smith.

"At first I didn't really give a flying fuck," recalled Debbie in a retrospective feature on the venue. "But CBGB's was a kind of institution and a worldwide name. So then I did a couple of benefits, in the club itself.

That was great, but in the end it just prolonged the agony. Eventually they got their final notice, so we played the next to last night. We played on Saturday and they closed on Monday. It was very moving, I didn't think I'd feel as nostalgic as I did. But I really did have some great times here, difficult as those times were."

Sadly, CBGB's owner Hilly Kristal would die the following year at the age of 75, due to complications arising from lung cancer. "I'm very sorry that Hilly is gone. He was a big help to Blondie and to the New York music scene for many years. His club was a part of New York lore and rock'n'roll history," said Deborah. "Kudos to Hilly for being such a patron of the underground music scene and being such a father figure in a way. That's not an easy thing to do, but somehow or another he had this weird temperament and he could handle it. I think we were the lucky ones to have a place like that. Really, really lucky."

Chapter Sixteen

Much Better For A Girl Like Me

"Most art is analysed after the fact."

Chris Stein

In June 2007, Debbie Harry took to the road for her first solo tour in almost a decade. Spearheaded by singer and activist Cyndi Lauper, the True Colors tour was devised as a means of promoting human rights with specific emphasis on the civil liberties of the gay community. Visiting 15 cities over a three-week period, the shows featured a diverse range of performers from synth-pop duo Erasure and Brechtian goths The Dresden Dolls to special guests such as The B-52s and Rufus Wainwright.

Deborah became involved in the tour when the organisers contacted her management. "At first I wasn't really sure about doing it," she explained. "They kept asking, 'Well, can't you play "Heart Of Glass"? Can't you play "One Way Or Another", "The Tide Is High", or something?' And I kept saying, 'No, I can't.' I would never do that. I feel like it would be unscrupulous to do that without my guys. So there was a little back and forth about that, but I'm really glad about the way it worked out."

Debbie's set comprised solo material, much of which had never previously been performed live, having been written for her forthcoming album. "It was a little scary sometimes. It's like being an opening band again. But it was good to force myself to do that, to break out of the comfort zone. That's one of the seductions of being in a group that has a great track record. You're comfortable. To break out was stimulating for me ... When I would finish some of the songs, they would be silent for a few seconds, and then suddenly they would erupt in applause. So they were listening. I was surprised."

Deborah's popularity on the gay scene and her support of the American Civil Liberties Union, for whom she had previously appeared in a concert and an advertising campaign, overrode the apolitical nature of her recorded work. "I think I've been more political recently, but not in such a way as writing songs about it," she commented. "I think it is a kind of responsibility, being in a position to make people listen, and I think I can add something. I mean, the more people say about human rights, the better off we all are. I certainly feel that consenting adults should be able to live the life that they choose, and that the law should treat everyone equally. We all pay taxes, so we should all be privy to the same privileges. It's the logical and fair thing – it's as simple as that."

The aftermath of September 11, 2001 had seen the American political mindset move abruptly to the right. The outpouring of grief and anger that followed the atrocity had led to a climate where criticism of the state was often labelled 'un-American'. "The conservative wave in America right now is really dangerous," Debbie subsequently stated. "If you criticise the government too much you get called a traitor, you're not a good American. Part of being a good American is challenging what our rights are according to the constitution. I think people forget that. And this Patriot Act too. Why should they call it that? It has nothing to do with patriotism, it has to do with our basic civil rights. The problem is that smart people aren't running the government. It's really nerve-racking."

The climate of fear brought Debbie's activism to the fore, inspiring her to use her celebrity status to support some form of positive change. "Issues of humanity and what is fair treatment and good treatment of a fellow human being should not really be based on a personal sense of right and wrong or judgement. Morality should have to do with killing people or hurting them or stealing from them, but when it comes to adult choices, I don't see it. Basically, Europeans are laughing at us. We're being laughed at around the world, and it's pathetic ... I feel as powerless as the next person. The best thing I can do is make myself as visible as, say, [actress and liberal activist] Susan Sarandon."

A week after the True Colors tour ended, Debbie was reunited with Blondie for a string of European shows that began at the Bospop Festival in Holland on July 7, 2007. "It was one of our most exciting tours. I don't know exactly why, but it was just so much fun," she declared. "After so many years of playing together, there is a very familial feel. You're travelling with people and it's very intimate, so you're happy when you're with them and miss them when you're apart, and sometimes vice versa. Sometimes you just sort of hate everybody, but you really do have to get along with people. You can't be an asshole. When you're out there on the road if somebody is really a jerk it ruins the whole scene and the whole picture ..."

In September, Debbie's fifth solo album, *Necessary Evil*, was released on Allen Kovac's new Eleven Seven label. The majority of the disc's 17 tracks were written in the studio by Debbie with production duo Charles Nieland and Barb Morrison. "It was a very small team, a little trio. It was great working like that, very close and very quick," she explained. "They happened to be very light-hearted people, and they know how to work. When you're in the studio, every minute counts, every hour counts, and you really want to get it done. There's also all of this technology that you're wrestling with, and you really have to keep it light, and they know how to do that. We had a lot of laughs; it was fun."

In addition to the laconic 'Paradise', written by Jazz Passengers Roy Nathanson and Bill Ware, Debbie teamed up with Chris to create two tracks – 'Jen Jen', which combined African influences with chorus–infused electronica, and the lilting, tribal–techno 'Naked Eye' – which were included on the disc as additional bonuses. "I wanted to work with Chris again, because I've worked with him for so many years and I wanted him to be represented," said Deborah. "I asked him to come up with a couple of tracks. I adore his work."

The album was heralded by the release of its opener, 'Two Times Blue', as a single. "That was the last song we wrote, and it was curious because I woke up with these things running through my head. I was thinking 'two times two' and all these other things associated with the phrase, but then I was booked into the studio one night and when I got there I said I'd had a really interesting idea for the hook of a song," Debbie recounted. "The producer said he'd woken up that day with a song in his head too, so started playing it. I sang the lyrics I'd written along to it, and it all worked. It was very serendipitous."

The immediacy with which 'Two Times Blue' came together reflected the streamlined recording process. "It's simpler not having so many people involved. With Blondie it's usually at least four people that have a vote on how things go. That gets a little cumbersome," Deborah remarked. "It was an effortless thing, it wasn't like I was under any pressure to do it. It was just something I had time for and was interested in … I think now that I've worked like this, I would always like to work like this in the future. I would come in with an idea, a lyric maybe, and some idea of a melody and then we'd work it up in the studio. It was very immediate and Barb and Charlie played all the instruments, except for the drums that we put on later."

In keeping with Debbie's eclecticism, *Necessary Evil* encompasses her customary wide range: from the insistent bittersweet pop of 'Two Times Blue' through 'Charm Alarm' (a lascivious duet with Toilet Böys frontman Miss Guy), the reflective and expansive 'If I Had You' and the sparsely funky 'Love With A Vengeance'. "It's that pop spread that I've always done with Blondie," she explains. "I can't really avoid that because it's just the way that I think and what I'm attracted to. I want to do as many different styles as I feel apply."

Neither *Necessary Evil* nor 'Two Times Blue' sold in sufficient quantities to provide Debbie with a solo hit. However, any disappointment was balanced by the freedom afforded by a smaller label. "I feel very good about just being able to keep everything nice and simple, and decision-wise I'm right there for any type of decisions that have to be made," said Debbie. "And because it's a much simpler operation, I feel very at ease about it. I don't feel like things are happening that are way, way out of control [or] maybe a little bit artistically out of line. I feel like this is really manageable and sort of, 'OK, this is really moving along nicely, and I haven't had a lot of people sort of breathing down my neck about it.' It's very nice."

At this stage of her recording career she was looking beyond chart statistics anyway. "I want people to enjoy it … Why else would I put myself in a public position with my music, if I didn't want some kind of acceptance?" The extent to which Deborah enjoyed the process left her open to further solo outings, irrespective of how sales stacked up. "I don't know about another record just yet, but I don't see any reason why there wouldn't be another soon," she mused. "But then the record industry isn't what it once was, so I don't know how the business end of it all will pan out."

Although she stated she didn't feel that she was fighting the past any more, her solo career provided her with an escape from the boundaries of Blondie. "I think that's partly why I did this album. To express myself. To be a part of today. To be exactly who I am at this moment, not who I was 30 years ago, pretending. Doing too many Blondie shows makes me bilious; and audiences get stuck," she verged on complaining. "Blondie was a characterisation. Now I'm better at what I do. I have a more organised vision of it. There isn't a label for the vision. I just try to communicate emotion and tell stories in music."

Accompanied by a stripped-down trio comprising Tommy Brislin on keyboards, Mark Malone on drums and J.P. Doherty on guitar, Debbie aired her new material across a 21-date tour during November and December 2007. "I had to work kind of quickly, and I hired Tommy Brislin to be the musical director," she explained. "He did all the programming. I relied on a lot of programming this time 'cos I wanted to go out with a small band. Tommy picked J.P. and I had used Mark on the album – so I ended up going on the road with a three-piece male band … Initially, I felt a little strange being on stage with different musicians. Only three musicians as well, usually it's six. I did a little tour and I felt naked and weird, but I quickly got over that."

At the same time, Blondie's back catalogue was represented in a theatrical context as part of a West End musical version of Madonna's early star vehicle movie, *Desperately Seeking Susan*. ("I could see that Madonna saw herself as the new blonde in town when I interviewed her in '83," says co-author Kris, "even down to working with Chic.")

"I was approached with the idea and the script, and my first reaction was 'Eugh,'" admitted Deborah. "I'm not really a big musical theatre fan, it's just not really part of my world very much. I've seen a couple over the years, and one of my all time favourites is *Guys And Dolls*, but for the most part I'm not that knowledgeable. But then when I sat down and read the script and actually thought about the whole thing, with our songs fitting in, I thought, 'Yeah, this is kinda great!' I was really, really surprised at how well it works. It's two great elements coming together and it's just so much fun more than anything."

The show, which officially opened in London on November 15, 2007, was directed by Angus Jackson based upon a concept by writer Peter Michael Marino. "He is a great, great nut. He loves Broadway and he loves musical theatre," said Debbie. "One night he was at home watching *Desperately Seeking Susan*, and he turned the sound off and started playing Blondie songs in different spots and thought, 'Wow, this could really work.' So, he wrote it all up and they got the rights to do it."

Unfortunately, neither the critics – who mauled the production – nor the public shared Marino's vision and the show closed in mid-December, losing an estimated $3.5 million in the process. The following year Blondie's past was represented in a more conventional manner, as the band embarked upon a tour celebrating the 30th anniversary of *Parallel Lines*.

With new member Matt Katz-Bohen on keyboards, recruited from the house band at gay/transvestite hotspot Squeezebox, Blondie played an extended run of summer dates in the US and Europe. In order to properly represent the album, they adjusted their set to the order that it first appeared in on vinyl. "We were doing the same show for like several years now anyway, so we wanted to change it around, just the order of stuff," Chris explained. "You know, we've been opening with the same things, closing with the same things, so at least that enabled to us change. It's also the 25th anniversary of *Thriller* and I'm wondering why he got to fucking cash in at 25 when we had to wait to 30. That's my big question. Because all the radio's going, 'Hey! It's the 25th anniversary of *Thriller*.' I've been hearing that for the last few weeks. But it's partially financial and all that other stuff because the money isn't there for recording for us."

Among the shows on the European leg of the *Parallel Lines* anniversary tour was the Guilfest at Guildford on July 5, 2008. Among the crowd was Debbie's old friend Chris Charlesworth, now the editor at Omnibus Press, who lived nearby. "They got me on some backstage list but it wasn't sufficiently VIP for me to be able to actually have a close encounter with them," he says. "It didn't matter. I had a great time watching from the crowd. They loved them – 'heritage rock' now, I suppose. They could have been a bit more organised. There was a delay when they came on and they were standing around doing nothing, which was a bit of an anticlimax, and delays between numbers spoilt the flow of the set, but it didn't really matter."

Charlesworth was told by someone who knew the organisers that Blondie were paid £25,000 plus expenses. "Nice to see them making some decent money at last," he adds.

Debbie and Chris' next project would be an homage to their biggest fan, the late Jeffrey Lee Pierce, who had died of a brain haemorrhage on March 31, 1996. Although Pierce made some enemies in his short, chaotic life, he had many friends who loved the sensitive side of his personality and the wildly creative beast within. "He was a very sensitive guy, and really loved music," Debbie remembers. "Kind of a manic depressive, I guess. But good sense of humour and very smart. I think we got him when he was pretty much in his original state. Sort of an angst-filled teenager. People seemed to understand his angst [in Europe], and they didn't feel personally threatened by him. But they could relate to the poetry and to his achiness. I think in the United States, there were people that really loved him here. But I think they felt more threatened by him."

The Jeffrey Lee Pierce Project was instigated by Cypress Grove, the blues guitarist who collaborated with Jeff in his later days. In 2008, he started embarking on a tortuously realised labour of love which started when he unearthed a dusty old cassette of early nineties bedroom rehearsals, containing several unreleased songs. These skeletal sketches were fleshed out by Jeff's old friends and acolytes, often using Jeffrey's guitar tracks.

The lavishly presented set, entitled *We Are Only Riders* after an old essay by Jeffrey, was released in January 2010. It boasted a line-up including Lydia Lunch, Mark Lanegan, The Raveonettes, Crippled Black Phoenix, Nick Cave and former Bad Seeds Kid Congo Powers, Mick Harvey and Barry Adamson. Cave duets with Debbie on haunting country ballad 'Free To Walk', also adding gentle piano to her astonishing performance of 'Lucky Jim', a desolate ballad from the last Gun Club album in 1993. Underpinned by Chris' Moog guitar, Debbie's voice has rarely been as unadorned and soulful, conveying a genuine sense of grief as she sings words written by her former fan club president, so enamoured with Debbie that he copied her sloppily bleached hairstyle.

"I was surprised about that but, of course, sort of flattered," she recalls. "He just really felt a need to communicate, and his intentions were good. I guess he felt some kind of kinship. And it's kind of really special, that kind of thing. I don't know whether I want to encourage people to hang out in front of my apartment, but that was a long time ago, and I guess it was some kind of real visible link between us."

The vinyl's gatefold sleeve includes a photo of Chris and Debbie, sporting her Gun Club T-shirt. "It's a great project," enthuses Chris. "Jeffrey would have been great to have around now. His legacy has gradually been building up over the years. It's a shame. I was always annoyed that a lot of his followers encouraged his drinking and self-destructive behaviour. The people who were with him should have fucking helped him, put him away or some shit. He came to my house. People I never even knew brought him back to my house because he'd passed out in the street somewhere."

We Are Only Riders went down sufficiently well to merit a further set, *The Journey Is Long*, due to appear in April 2012 after three years in the making, over three continents. It's another unique labour of love, featuring Cave, Harvey, Lunch, Barry Adamson, Youth's Vertical Smile, The Jim Jones Revue, Steve Wynn, Mark Lanegan & Isobel Campbell, Tav Falco – and even Kris Needs, paying homage with his missus, Michelle. Cave and Debbie duet again, this time on a sweeping version of 'The Breaking Hands' (the album's only previously released song, originally appearing on 1987's *Mother Juno*), with accompanists including Chris. After Blondie's punishing summer touring schedule, Debbie's contribution was the last thing recorded for the set, to honour their old friend's memory.

As the first decade of the 21st century entered its final years, the fragmented recording industry was struggling to adapt to the way in which technological developments had changed how people obtained and listened to music. It played a part in ensuring it would not be until three years after the *Parallel Lines* anniversary tour that any new Blondie album emerged. However, although the group were regulars on the summer festival circuits both at home and in Europe, their personal commitments were also now pitched against the demands of playing live and recording new material.

"I took time out to be with my family," says Chris Stein. "I had two kids who are now six and seven, so I sort of stumbled into a full-time dad situation, and that's taken a while. Also, it can be difficult for us because of our age. Touring can be physically exhausting compared to how it used to be. When we started out we were in our twenties and no one our age now was doing anything, but now Bob Dylan's just turned 70 and is still out there doing stuff, and we're still here."

Consistent with their newly sensible work/life balance, Blondie's ninth studio album, *Panic Of Girls*, was recorded at a more measured pace than had previously been the case. Sessions took place in two parts – first at the end of 2009 and then in May the following year. "We recorded in upstate New York, where Chris lives, as well as recording in New York and Hoboken," recalls Debbie. "We tried to make a classic Blondie album. We've always been concerned about producing good songs, and Chris and Matt are prolific songwriters. Our lyrics have sociological things in them, mixed up with romantic ideas and New York City hipness."

"We recorded up here, upstate near Woodstock; a local studio called Applehead because it's easier and cheaper than going to the city," explains Chris. "It's a nice room. We worked with this guy Jeff Saltzman, who did The Killers and Fischer-Spooner and different things. Jeff really worked hard. For him it was a real big project and he really wanted to make it great. He's our age and a big fan. The understanding of the band that he brings adds a whole new dimension."

The bulk of the album was produced by Saltzman, who had initially been contacted by Matt Katz-Bohen. "Chris and I talked about production style and the songs. Debbie was always involved," he explained. "We sent songs back and forth for about six months before going in the studio. There, the room was set up so the band could go in and play live, and they finished working on the songs that way. Instead of going into a rehearsal space to do pre-production, we got everything mic'ed up in the studio, recorded the rehearsals and used pieces of them to build on."

"I wasn't really in full-on writing and production mode when I was working on *No Exit* and *The Curse*," says Chris. "It took me a while to get back in a real fluid mode, because I had the kids and they were still stabilising themselves. For the last two years, I've felt a lot more able to plough ahead and feel really productive now. I worked much harder on this album. The last two years I've really been listening to stuff much more than I had been. There was a period prior to that where I was completely out of all kinds of music. Lately, I've been in more like an avid fan place as far as listening to music goes."

Unusually, Stein only co-wrote three tracks, all of which bore testament to his eclecticism. The sultry 'Wipe Off My Sweat' has Debbie giving her Spanish an airing, while the Latino-infused backing indicated Chris' latest avenue of discovery. "I've been listening to tons of stuff, all different styles. There's so many great Latin things coming out of South America," he observes. "Latinos make up one sixth of the population here now, so it's only natural that Latino music is heard more. There are still a lot of great bands coming out of urban areas, but it's hard for them to sustain things compared to when we were starting out now because the rents are so high. But in terms of listening, I get much more turned on these days listening to Spanish language radio stations."

Written by Chris and Gilles Riberolles and featuring Debbie's vocal in crystalline French, 'Le Bleu' evokes the sound of a Parisian boulevard. "It's aiming for a Gainsbourg feel," Stein explained. "Gilles Riberolles is a friend and I produced a record for his band Casino Music, all in French, back in the eighties, for ZE Records. I sent him this and asked him to write lyrics."

Chris and Debbie's emotive closer 'China Shoes' veers surprisingly toward alt-country, while lyrically conflating its themes of loss, regret and the Chinese practice of foot binding. Chris' lifelong love of reggae is referenced by the band's restrained covers of Sophia George's 1985 hit 'Girlie Girlie' and indie-folk combo Beirut's 'Sunday Smile'. "We did a bunch of cover songs that people will know," he acknowledges. "We were always talking about doing a covers record. We started working on a cover of [Suicide's] 'Ghost Rider', which was going to have a sample of them in but we never finished it."

A further nod to reggae is provided by the rolling pop shuffle of 'The End The End'. "That was a collaborative effort with this guy Ben Phillips and he had this idea about finding someone that you wanted to be with until the very end," Deborah recounted. "So I guess that is a very romantic idea. He gave me this idea of what it was about and then we fleshed out the lyrics."

Phillips' writing partner, Kato Khandwala, contributed to the song, which he also produced. "I was involved with 'Mother' and 'The End The End'," said Khandwala. "Both were recorded in the same sessions, and the band was great to work with. I had no idea what to expect when we entered the studio, but from the moment music started coming out of the speakers, everything else went away; the presentation of the songs and the performance were the only focus."

Released a week before its parent album was available to download, 'Mother' was the first single from *Panic Of Girls*. An up-tempo, multilayered rocker with an uplifting chorus, the song's title and reflective lyrics owe their provenance to one of Debbie's favourite New York nightspots.

"Mother was a club in the Meatpacking District where you could go and explore your fetishes and freaky side," she enthused. "It was awesome and I truly really miss it. People think that as you get older you are going to be content sitting in bed with your rollers in your hair. But I was a child of the sixties, and once you have unlocked your wild side it is very hard to get that genie back in the bottle. Mother was hetero, it was gay, it was bi – it was crazy. [The song 'Mother'] has underlying feelings about searching for motherhood, but I don't necessarily apply it to me."

Like *The Curse Of Blondie*, *Panic Of Girls* opens with a bang. The frantic beats and processed vocals of 'D-Day' expand into a richly textured chorus that sets the tone for tracks such as Matt and Lauren Katz-Bohen's twin contributions: 'What I Heard' – the album's second single – and 'Love Doesn't Frighten Me', both of which possess an immediacy and accessibility that conforms to the group's pop canon.

"I think it's a very strong album," asserted Debbie. "It keeps the spirit of Blondie. I'm happy with it. It's taken us quite a while to get it out – there were moments when we wondered if we would – so I'm glad we're getting good reactions to it."

"I think this record is a little more pointed than the last one," says Chris. "I think it'll do some damage out there. It's less chaotic and crazy in the studio now. In fact, it was very musician-like this time. We just want to get on with stuff. There wasn't any fighting or anything going on! Debbie's lyrics are fucking terrific. I think she keeps getting better with that shit. I'm always amazed at the stuff she's coming up with. She's writing about everything: time, love, romance, this, that, all the usual stuff! This record is more straightforward and hard-edged than the last one: pop-rock with some electronica thrown in. There's still some weird stuff on there. Some of it's really great, the best we've done. I hate to say that, but it really might be. We were just further along with a lot of aspects of what we're doing. I really think this is the most solid album of this period. It's way superior [to] the last record."

Rather than being issued in the established manner, *Panic Of Girls* seeped into public view in stages. After being put back from its original 2010 release date, it was made available as a UK download through Eleven Seven on May 30, 2011. In June, it received a physical British release as a limited edition collector's pack that included a 132-page magazine tribute to Blondie alongside the disc, with a regular version appearing a month later. In Germany, both standard and deluxe double CD editions came out through EMI in July, while the same label made *Panic Of Girls* available in the US on September 13.

Those who opted to buy the album digitally missed out on the full impact of Dutch artist Chris Berens' impressionistic sleeve illustration. "Chris Berens is a wonderful artist," declared Deborah. "He works with fantasies. It has to do with the environment, it's about getting involved with saving all those creatures. I know they're fantastical creatures but they're evocative of real animals. Everybody in the band is concerned about environmental issues, saving these species. In one of the songs I have a line equating the human race with an endangered species. So ultimately that's where we're going with that."

The release of Blondie's first album in five years, and the European and North American tours that followed in its wake, generated considerable interest in the band – particularly in Britain, where Debbie and the group were featured across a wide range of television and radio programmes and in the printed media. As part of her promotional duties, Deborah appeared on the long-running BBC radio show *Desert Island Discs* – which has featured such notable guests as Ivor Novello, Alfred Hitchcock, Louis Armstrong, Margaret Thatcher, James Stewart and Tony Blair during its 69-year history. The programme works in an interview format that requires guests to nominate their favourite songs and a book, as well as a luxury item, to provide consolation in their imagined desert-island solitude.

Despite the heavyweight roster of guests that had appeared on the show, host Kirsty Young seemed genuinely awestruck by Debbie. "It's a strange feeling to be sitting opposite an icon," admitted the forty-something blonde. "When I was younger, I wasted 10 years wanting to be Debbie Harry." Deborah chose music from such diverse artists as The Gossip and Nina Simone, selecting an endless supply of paper and paint as her luxury. During the interview, Debbie was asked for her thoughts on getting older: "As far as ageing goes, it's rough. I'm trying my best now. I'm healthy and I exercise like a fiend and do all that stuff that recovered drug addicts do."

By the time *Panic Of Girls* became available, both Deborah and Chris were in their sixties. Blondie had now existed across five decades. The band's fractious history is such that Debbie is often asked whether she has any regrets. "Of course I have regrets," she confessed. "But I don't wander around moaning about them. Or live in my 'regret area'! I just go, 'Aw, shit,' and then go on, y'know? Of course we regret that we had business problems back then. And also I regret not buying a lot of ATT stock or whatever. Regrets are silly stuff when you get right down to it. Chris and I have talked about this — was it about making money or was it about making art and expressing ourselves? And it was never about just one thing. As humans, and artists, we have a lot of different needs to satisfy."

It's hard to contradict Debbie's assertion that she has "had a fucking interesting life so far". Everything she has personally and professionally experienced has afforded her no shortage of insight and, ultimately, has enabled her to enjoy a balanced existence. "I am happier today than I was 40 years ago," she observed. "I know who I am and I'm more in control. I love what I do and I love how I live. I mix with amazing people, I get to play music on tour, I perform at festivals and my life is never boring. Getting older is hard on your looks, but on stage people sometimes see you as you were, which is nice."

For Debbie, the cliché that age is simply a number rings true — she maintains an energetic lifestyle that many much younger people would find difficult to keep up with and, although Max's, CBGB's and Studio 54 have been consigned to memory, she still enjoys New York's nightlife. "I love to dance," she said. "It's easy for me to go to clubs in New York and be anonymous and have a nice time. I listen to music and dance a few dances."

Unlike Chris, Deborah remains reluctant to leave the city both she and her band are synonymous with. "I travel so much that I feel like I see a lot of different places anyway. New York is where a lot of my friends are, and I have small family ties on the East Coast. The world is a small place now, travel is not really a big deal. But I guess if I was to fall madly in love with some Spaniard I would consider moving to Spain. You never know, right?"

The idea of an artist, previously been feted as one of the world's most beautiful women, now living alone in a modest Manhattan apartment with a succession of small dogs (and the occasional cat) for company is often represented by the media in a negative way — as if Deborah Harry were some *grande dame* from a forgotten golden age. It fails to take into account her fiercely independent nature. In the same way that, during the peak of Blondie's popularity, she only ever assumed the role of frontwoman on her own terms, her lifestyle is a product of this same independence. "

"You know, in the UK when people think of an old woman walking her dog, they think she's sad and pathetic, living a lonely life," she declared. "But people are much more open over here [in Manhattan]. They use the dog as an excuse to chat you up."

As somebody who has lived the majority of her adult life in the public eye, Deborah concedes, "my private life is pretty much my public life. My downtime I spend with friends. Occasionally I have a date, which I really don't like to admit to."

In terms of relationships, Debbie maintains a *laissez-faire* outlook, neither desperately seeking nor avoiding any form of long-term commitment. "I have a complete life. I honestly don't feel the lack of anything. And maybe that makes me too self-sufficient now for it ever to happen to me again. I hope not, but I really don't know," she remarked. "I've tried most things, most ways … I can certainly live with people; it just depends on who the person is."

While Deborah concedes that her public image makes her appear a challenging proposition to some prospective suitors, she claims the perception is wholly superficial. "I'm not a real high-maintenance person," she declares. "If they only knew what a *mushnik* I am! It makes me laugh and it teaches me a lesson. When I meet people who I admire and who are really famous, I'm just like that. And then I think, 'Oh God, I see people responding to me like that.' It's not the way to go, not the way to handle it."

For all her self-confidence, Debbie does not insist on being the dominant half of a relationship. "Men like to take the lead. I don't mind a man taking the lead, but I'm used to doing things. So it takes a person who is very sure of himself, very comfortable, not offended and not uptight. Men are so fragile in that area. About power. It's funny."

Essentially, it seems she has no great sense of need. "I have friends who are so systematic about picking up boys," she explained. "I'm not that systematic. I don't feel I have to have somebody every single night but I do have friends who are like that, who go out every single night specifically to meet people and have sex. I'm a little bit careful about that. I think I have to be. I was a little bit like that when I was younger and sometimes it backfired on me. At this stage in my life, I think with the notoriety and the fame I have, it would be problematic."

Chance often plays a huge part in the formation of personal relationships, and for Debbie it may simply be a matter of encountering the right person at the right time. "I like people who are complicated – that intrigues me. I like a challenge. It's the adventure in me. I'd like to go to parts of the earth that haven't been explored yet. But I don't know about dangerous emotional terrain, because it depends how bad the boy is. I don't have much tolerance for a person who's truly, truly bad. It would depend on how secure I felt within myself, I suppose. I would like to think I could give a person a lot of freedom, because I need a lot of freedom myself."

In any event, the interpersonal chemistry would need to be suitably matched. "I think what I learnt from having this relationship with Chris is that you can evolve from one thing into another to make it work," she explained. "We balanced each other out so well, so one would only hope that if you wanted it enough, anything is possible to balance the other person out."

As to the media's recurring question of why she and Chris never married or had children, these are two forms of commitment that Debbie remains open-minded about. "Marriage might be nice. I grew up in an era when marriage vows were very limited, so I just thought that the whole thing was a bad deal. I barely obeyed my parents – why would I have wanted to obey a husband?"

As Debbie has reached the age where it is now biologically impossible for her to bear children, adoption seems her only likely route to becoming a parent. As an adoptee herself she remains aware of the possibility, but has preferred to help children via involvement in a number of philanthropic schemes. "I've thought of adoption, which I think I'd be really good at. Now that this terrible [March 2011 earthquake] has happened in Japan, there will be a lot of children needing homes. I spread myself around a lot of causes – I'm concerned about the environment and clean water, and being carbon-free. I also support diabetes [research]," she revealed. "These things are really important to me now. I applaud people like Elton John who have used their position to do so much good and I felt it was something I should do too."

As the comedian George Burns once observed, "You can't help getting older, but you don't have to get old." While this certainly applies to Debbie, the fact that her image once adorned thousands of bedroom walls has ensured an ongoing fascination with how she continues to look good despite the ageing process. "Some people I talk to in Britain, women in particular, won't let up on the topic – to the point where I want to scream," she asserts. "While I can understand the motivation, I can't help thinking it makes very gruesome sport. The art of growing old gracefully is not much championed in today's society, and most especially not in the entertainment industry. I find that really sad. But am I going to let it stop me getting on with my life? Very definitely I am not. In areas other than pop, you continue to be valued for as long as you have inspiration and the ability. Longevity is actually prized, rather than seen as a liability. It's not all about being young and pretty, or the Next Big Thing."

Typically forthright, Deborah has never attempted to disguise how she had cosmetic surgery and employs a personal trainer to help keep her weight down. "I've done everything and will probably continue to do everything," she insisted. "I think Joan Rivers has the right idea and I think Cher looks great. We all try to look as good as we can, but I do have moments when I slob around – I don't wear make-up every day and I'll just put on some shades when I go out. I did go through a period when I let myself go, but I got sick of the way I looked in clothes, so I started working out again. It's important to me and to the business I'm in that I take care of myself. I guess a lot of what I've traded on over the years has been my looks, but I do feel better when I look good."

"Ageism is one of the most serious prejudices that people face," Debbie also opined. "When I was younger I felt the same way like, 'OK you old fart, get outta the fucking way, it's my turn now!' I certainly understand that. It's a survival mechanism. But now that I'm in that dangerous position, I think I have something to offer because I've got much better at what I do than I ever was. I think experience really counts. Coming from that punk world, having a stubborn attitude and being a punk, as it were, that definitely works in my favour because I have that attitude of, 'You fuck, just try it!' I have a rebellious attitude and nature. That's part of my make-up."

Sadly, one aspect of ageing that even Debbie can do little about is the way in which, as the years pass, old friends disappear forever. "Unfortunately, a lot of the old gang is dead now. I come from an era when people were taking a lot of drugs and there wasn't much knowledge about them; I would say at least 60 per cent of the people I came up with in New York are dead: Johnny Thunders, Jerry [Nolan] from The Dolls. And then a lot of the people who surrounded the bands are gone. I have been to a lot of funerals."

Given that this fate could so easily have befallen Chris, it is heartening to find him now in good shape and settled into family life, while still maintaining the enthusiasm for music and popular culture that defined his creative output. "My biggest regret is smoking pot constantly for 10 or 15 years, because it definitely takes away your edge," he observed. "It's like the guys in *South Park* say: it makes being bored seem like an OK thing."

Like many of his peers from the blank generation, Chris finds that while good, groundbreaking music is still being made, rock'n'roll isn't what it used to be. "It doesn't have the same kind of cachet. It's not an outsider thing any more; it's so mainstream. That's why Lady Gaga is so popular now. Part of her success comes from her freakiness because people are attracted to that. But we are in a weird place today. On one hand, you have to struggle to get in with a record company who is going to give you $100,000-$200,000 to make a record. At the same time, two kids with a computer can make a record in their basement for $3,000. I don't know if that's better or not. There is something to be said about working hard versus just throwing something down made out of loops. You have to weed through the shit but I do hear a lot of great stuff like Fever Ray, which sounds like it's all done on the computer. It's fantastic."

"I'm glad we came from the era we did," observed Debbie. "Fame today is very different. Back then we felt like pioneers. It was amazing being a woman in a band and there were others, from Patti Smith to Siouxsie Sioux, who were changing the way women in bands were seen. Now music has become showbiz; it's all one big celebrity blob. There is so much pressure on kids today. I don't know how well I would have fared under such an intense microscope."

Reflecting on her own contribution to the status of women in rock, Deborah admits to hoping she made a positive difference. "I would like to think that because I have actually done something to change the way things are, it might inspire other people to do the same. I hate to use the word 'struggles', but I have had a few over the years. I've had as many problems in my own life as other people have had in theirs."

"All the things that Debbie got rapped for are really commonplace now," declared Clem. "To be a beautiful woman, and to play rock music, and to use her sexuality like that – people really came down hard on her. I remember there was one picture of Debbie with her tongue sticking out, licking a record. That caused so much trouble."

"I don't know that I was really trying to do anything, except learn how to do what I do," mused Deborah. "People have a great fondness for the music from that time, I know. The essence of punk rock lingers on, carries on. But maybe not everyone's aware of the historic importance, the real changes that occurred then. I mean, you had the Women's Lib movement. And also Gay Lib. That's two pretty major sexual revolutions that happened in quick succession. As a frontperson was I subversive? I don't know if I was that in control of everything. I was searching, trying to express myself. To discover where I fitted into this whole picture. It was pretty confusing then, more than it is now, to be a woman or girl in front of a band. A lot of people were really against it – they hated it."

"It's a weird paradox in a way: we've had more number one records in the States than a lot of other bands, but we're not really in the mainstream," said Clem. "We've kept our artistic integrity while having some commercial success. It's a very Andy Warholish thing, having success the way we have. What Andy was doing in the art world was very influential for all of us. What does pop art mean? It's to create something within popular culture that's almost throwaway or trashy, which has a lot to do with the aesthetic of Blondie in the early days, especially when you think of B-movies; when we were writing about giant ants from space and things like that, it was all tongue-in-cheek. But as we grew in popularity and the culture progressed, a lot of things we thought were private property became mainstream."

Clem's comparison of Blondie and the Warhol aesthetic seems particularly valid – the band brought aspects of underground culture and art into the mainstream in such a way that they were reproduced across the media. It could be said that this confluence of art and commerce had its nexus in the New York City that both band and artist came to represent.

"If you ever read back over all the old press, Chris and I really promoted that New York scene," stated Deborah. "Chris spoke articulately about CBGB's, and we valued our friends' bands as much as we valued Blondie! We really flew the flag ... My art teacher told me in high school – it's 50 per cent talent and 50 per cent promotion. You write what you write but can you make it available to commerce? There are some genius creators and composers in this world who can't sell themselves. We could. We were popular, but we worked hard at it. It doesn't happen as if by magic."

Despite the recognition Blondie have received, Deborah shies away from the kind of grandiose terms that are bandied around too readily. "The word 'iconic' is used too frequently," she insists. "An icon is a statue carved in wood. It was shocking at first, when I got that reference. It was a responsibility, and it's impossible to live up to – you're supposed to be dead, for one thing. I'm

316

still sort of a cult figure. I'm not J-Lo, I'm not in the gossip mags and *USA Today*. Sometimes I'm in the *New York Post*."

Likewise, she retains a sense of perspective when it comes to the period from which Blondie originated. "Nostalgia is a drag. But it's also enough to make you want to fight for your individuality and make a statement that's not contained within the selling of a product. When we were coming up it was such an open period for art and music, and I was so lucky to have had that experience. It was wonderful to be in love, doing what I was doing. It was something that happens only once in a lifetime. It was my period of innocence, and just great to have had my freedom."

"I've had a lot of really extraordinary things happen to me," Deborah further recalled. "We survived. I survived. Blondie survived. I hope something more than the short, concise, literal version survives, because that would make no sense at all. It's not just about the soundbites, it's about the layers."

Dig beneath those layers to the core of Blondie and you will find one consistent element – the partnership of Debbie and Chris, which endures to this day. "I just love Chris very, very much. He's got a great sense of humour, a great talent. I think we were really lucky to meet each other and have this great adventure. We've certainly had a lot of help from other people. But basically we've stuck it out," Deborah declared. "I don't know if I would have been able to make it in music to the degree that I did without Chris. He was so nonchalant … I never expected anything like this. I was never one to read fan magazines. I didn't know what the music business was about. I just had this vague idea that I wanted to express myself. And I did it. Weird, huh?"

It seems likely that Blondie will continue for as long as Debbie and Chris are able and willing. "I always admire people with longevity. It's the most valuable asset of any of the arts," asserted Deborah. "The dust that collects around you is what you are. For us it's the songs. We wrote a lot of songs; from 'Heart Of Glass' to 'Sunday Girl' … People tell us they still sound fresh and they stand up. On top of that we bring in something new. I think we play better, sing better, perform better than we ever did. Artists have to grow."

"Popular culture has aged, and we've aged along with it," remarked Clem. "It has to do with the generation we're from. People still have an interest in art and music, and it carries through at more of a mass level than before.

We're all interested in many different aspects of the media. This enables us to keep going. Now, Blondie is a home base for all of us. I wish we would've seen it that way before."

"It's good," asserts Chris. "After this, I'm still working and really enjoying stuff. I really enjoy working with the computers, digital stuff, still working on songs. Computers make things faster and more flexible. We'll see what happens because we're going to keep doing stuff and it's easier to make music now."

As for Debbie, her enthusiasm for the band formed amidst the squalor of The Bowery all those years ago remains undimmed. "I'm just loving it, really – working with great people and doing the thing I adore. When you're alive and you like life, you have to go out there and live it to the fullest. You may not be happy about going to your end, but hey, at least I flogged it while I had it."

Acknowledgements

There have been several books about Blondie over the years but, curiously, never one which tells the whole remarkable story. As editor of Blondie's most fervent press champion, *Zigzag*, I interviewed and befriended them to the extent I'd be summoned to hang out when they were in town, witness tour rehearsals in a space the size of a living room, or flee with them on the bus as Blondie-mania raged all around like a scene from *A Hard Day's Night* – once stopping traffic in Kensington High Street, when 3,000 fans turned up for an in-store signing. During Blondie's initial five-year supernova, the need to chronicle this phenomenon was glaringly evident but never got further than the pages of my magazine. I knew that Debbie and Chris were planning their own book, so I didn't want to tread on their toes.

With Blondie back in action recently, it seemed appropriate to finally tell their story once and for all. When Dick Porter conceived this tome, I knew it was time to throw caution to the wind and finally realise the project that had been brewing for over 30 years. We'd worked together before, so I knew he was the only man for the job – that vital foil who would make sure all the bases were covered and blanks filled in. Not only would it be fun to relive experiences which now seem downright surreal, but the group – particularly Debbie, Chris and the mighty Clem Burke – would receive the balanced account they deserve. Without Dick's sterling efforts and crucial wisdom, I'd probably still be stuck probing some old Bowery back alley in 1975.

So I have to thank Debbie and Chris for inviting me onto the Blondie roller coaster which, despite their relentless verbal abuse, provided some of

the most amazing memories of my life. Hopefully, we've emerged with one of the great rock'n'roll stories and a riveting New York tale — although, as Debbie likes to say, "It's still going on!"
KRIS NEEDS, February 2012

Kris Needs and Dick Porter would like to thank the following, without whom writing the book you now hold would have been impossible:

Craig Leon, Blondie's producer, for his crucial input; Marty Thau, the Red Star producer who was first to take Blondie seriously; Elda Stilletto, Debbie's early bandmate; Chris Charlesworth, for his help and advice; Paul Woods, our editor; Clem Burke; Pete Frame; Victor Bockris; Jimmy Destri; Nigel Harrison; Frank Infante; Nile Rodgers; Roberta Bayley; Jayne County; John Peel; Andy Dunkley; David Barraclough; Alan Betrock; Annette Bullock; Eddie 'Ant Man' Duggan; Sheik Hassan; David Stopps; John Tobler; Mike O'Connor and Friars Aylesbury; Cypress Grove, for The Jeffrey Lee Pierce Project.

Bibliography

Books

Bangs, Lester *Blondie*, Omnibus Press (1980)

Beeber, Steven Lee *The Heebie Jeebies At CBGB's*, Chicago Review Press (2006)

Bockris, Victor *Making Tracks: The Rise Of Blondie*, Elm Tree (1982)

_____ *Warhol: The Biography*, Da Capo (2003)

Che, Cathay *Deborah Harry: Platinum Blonde*, André Deutsch (1999)

Colegrave, Stephen and Sullivan, Chris (editors) *Punk*, Cassell (2001)

Easlea, Daryl *Everybody Dance: Chic & The Politics Of Dancing*, Helter Skelter (2004)

Falk, Gaby (editor) *H.R. Giger ARh+*, Taschen (2001)

Fletcher, Tony *All Hopped Up And Ready To Go*, Omnibus Press (2010)

Frame, Pete *The Complete Rock Family Trees*, Omnibus Press (1993)

Grundy, Stuart and Tobler, John *The Record Producers*, St Martin's Press (1982)

Hackett, Pat (editor) *The Andy Warhol Diaries*, Penguin (2010)

Heylin, Clinton *From The Velvets To The Voidoids*, Helter Skelter (1993)

Kasher, Steven *Max's Kansas City: Art, Glamour, Rock And Roll*, Abrams Image (2010)

Kristal, Hilly *CBGB & OMFUG*, Harry N. Abrams (2005)

McNeil, Legs and McCain, Gillian *Please Kill Me*, Grove Press (1996)

Schruers, Fred *Blondie*, WH Allen (1980)

Valentine, Gary *New York Rocker*, Sidgwick and Jackson (2002)

321

Magazines and Newspapers (with authors of articles accredited)
The Age (25/12/98), Patrick Donovan
Attitude (06/2001), Will Stokes
Attitude (12/2002), Paul Flynn
Attitude (10/2003), Simon Gage
Attitude (10/2007), Simon Gage
Beat (23/12/98), Cameron Adams
Beat Instrumental (03/1980), Tony Horkins
Belfast Telegraph (09/08/07), Barry Egan
Billboard (18/03/06), Michael Paoletta
Blitz (12/1983), Simon Garfield
Boulevards (02/1981), Robert Camuto
Cheap Date (09/2000), Anita Pallenberg
Cosmopolitan (12/1978), Bart Mills
Creem (05/1977), Toby Goldstein
Creem (06/1979), Nick Tosches
Creem (02/1980), Dave DiMartino
Creem (12/1981), Chris Salewicz
Creem (08/1982), Toby Goldstein
Daily Express (2000), Barney Hoskyns
Daily Express (20/09/03), Marie Keating
Daily Mail (22/05/04), Alan Jackson
Daily Mail (08/07/11), Adrian Thrills
Daily Mail (11/07/11), Lina Das
Daily Mirror (07/11/03), Gavin Martin
Daily Telegraph (22/05/11), Roya Nikkhah
Dazed and Confused (12/1998), Rachel Newsome
Details (08/1997), Stephen Saban
Details (10/1993), Brantley Bardin
Discoveries (09/1999), Ralph Heibutzki
Diva (06/2004), Joanna Walters
Eastern Daily Press (22/09/07), Andy Welch
Elle (10/2003), Kate Finnegan
Film Review (02/1984), James Cameron-Wilson
Flaunt (05/2004), Jonathan Palmer
Forum (10/1980), unaccredited
GQ (10/2003), Michael Bracewell

Genre (10/1996), Peter McQuaid
The Guardian (23/01/99), Paul Burston
The Guardian (15/09/07), Emma Brockes
The Guardian (23/05/11), Caroline Sullivan
Heavy Metal (12/1981), Chris Stein
The Herald (09/07/11), Neil Cooper
High Times (06/1977), Neil Barlowe
High Times (11/1979), Liz Derringer
Hit Parader (06/1981), Roy Trakin
Hit Parader (12/1981), Roy Trakin
Hot Press (28/04/78), Bill Graham
i-D (12/2003), J.T. Leroy
Icon (09/2007), Stephen Unwin
In Los Angeles (31/05/05), Jackie Beat
The Independent (19/09/03), Nick Hasted
The Independent (13/07/06), David Sinclair
InterView (06/1979), Glenn O'Brien
InterView (03/2004), Tim Blanks
InterView (06/2006), Ana Matronic
International Musician (09/1981), Roy Trakin
The Irish Independent (29/11/02), John Meagher
Jack (10/2003), Michael Holden
Jewish Chronicle (30/06/11), Paul Lester
LAM (06/2004), Gareth Gorman
Lear's (03/1994), Pamela Des Barres
Mail On Sunday (27/11/05), Rebecca Hardy
Mail On Sunday (05/12/10), Louise Gannon
Marie-Claire (06/2007), Janet Street–Porter
Mean (08/2007), Chloë Sevigny
Melody Maker (06/07/74), Chris Charlesworth
Melody Maker (09/09/78), Harry Doherty
Melody Maker (03/03/79), Harry Doherty
Melody Maker (22/12/79), Davitt Sigerson
Melody Maker (05/06/82), Paul Simper
Mojo (02/1999), Barney Hoskyns
Mojo (03/2002), Jenny Bulley
Mojo (11/2002), Edward Helmore

Mojo (11/2003), Mark Paytress
Mojo (12/2005), David Fricke
Mojo (10/2007), Lucy O'Brien
Music Express (05/1990), Kerry Doole
The National (11/06/11), Michael Odell
New Music News (24/05/80), Victor Bockris
New Musical Express (09/04/77), Roy Carr
New Musical Express (04/02/78), Tony Parsons
New Musical Express (02/09/78), Paul Morley
New Musical Express (29/09/79), Roy Carr
New Musical Express (18/12/82), Cynthia Rose
New Musical Express (19/11/83), Cynthia Rose
New Musical Express (11/01/86), Cynthia Rose
New Musical Express (21/02/87), William Leith
New York Rocker (05/1976), Craig Gholson
New York Rocker (09/1978), Diane Harvey
New York Rocker (09/1978), Harold Bronson
New York Rocker (06/1981), Andy Schwartz
New York Woman (06/1990), Lawrence O'Toole
Next (03/11/00), Robert Kent
Next (26/03/04), Rob Roth
Now (21/04/04), Jay Bowers
NY Talk (01/1987), Barbara O'Dair
The Observer (22/07/07), Tim Adams
Origivation (07/2010), Danny Alonso
Penthouse (02/1980), Debra Rae Cohen
People (08/05/90), unaccredited
Performing Songwriter (10/2007), Chris Neal
Photoplay (03/1984), Ken Ferguson
Post Plus (05/03/06), Bernard Bales
Preview (13/02/05), Peter Ross
Preview (13/02/05), Guy Blackman
Prevue (04/1983), Jim Steranko
Q (10/1990), Mat Snow
Q (08/1993), Tom Hibbert
Q (08/1996), Johnny Black
Real Groove (06/1998), Marty Duda

Record Mirror (09/09/78), Barry Cain
Record Mirror (18/11/78), Barry Cain
Record Mirror (28/04/79), Mark Cooper
Record Mirror (30/06/79), Ronnie Gurr
Record Mirror (02/02/80), Rosalind Russell
Record Mirror (22/08/81), Sunie
Record Mirror (08/12/83), Julian Simmonds
Record Mirror (08/11/86), Nancy Culp
Record Mirror (23/09/89), Chris Roberts
Rhythm (12/2003), Jon Cohan
Rock World (07/1993), Marcel Anders
Rolling Stone (28/06/79), Jamie James
Rolling Stone (29/04/04), Austin Scaggs
Scene (01/02/90), Judy Black
Smash Hits (09/03/80), Steve Clarke
Sound International (10/1980), Robin Mackie
Sound On Sound (06/2008), Richard Buskin
Sounds (16/04/77), Richard Cromelin
Sounds (04/02/78), Jane Suck
Sounds (08/07/78), Dave Fudger
Sounds (12/01/80), Garry Bushell
Spin (08/1986), Glenn O'Brien
Spiral Scratch (02/1990), unaccredited
Splash (02/1989), Thomas Beller
Steppin' Out (12/09/07), Chauncé Hayden
The Stool Pigeon (20/06/11), John Doran
Sunday Herald (04/02/01), Jim Shelley
The Sunday Telegraph Magazine (06/08/78), George Feifer
The Sunday Times (21/09/03), Chrissie Iley
The Sunday Times (14/10/07), Tim Cooper
The Sunday Times Magazine (20/03/11), Lynn Barber
The Times (28/04/07), Stephen Dalton
The Times Magazine (17/06/95), Alan Jackson
Tokion (09/2003), Jeremy Jay Massacret
Trouser Press (11/1977), Ira Robbins
Trouser Press (06/1981), Scott Isler
Trouser Press (09/1982), Jim Green

TV Times (24/01/81), Anthea Disney
Uncut (08/2003); Chris Roberts
Us (07/05/1984); George Carpozi Jr.
Vanity Fair (07/1989), Gerri Hirshey
Venice (10/2007), Melanie Kirschbaum
Village Voice (26/06/08), Rob Trucks
The Weekend Australian (01/12/02), Phillip Norman
Who (24/01/05), Di Webster
You (11/07/93), Chrissie Iley

Internet

There are innumerable online fan sites and resources devoted to Blondie. The authors recommend the official Blondie website at www.blondie.net, Debbie's pages at www.deborah-harry.com, Chris' site at www.rednight.net, and also www.rip-her-to-shreds.com.

Selected Discography

BLONDIE

Singles

X-Offender/In The Sun	Private Stock (US)	1976
In The Flesh/Man Overboard	Private Stock (US)	1976
Rip Her To Shreds/In The Flesh/X-Offender	Chrysalis (UK)	1977
Denis/Contact In Red Square/Kung Fu Girls	Chrysalis (UK)	1978
(I'm Always Touched By Your) Presence Dear/		
Poets Problem/Detroit 442	Chrysalis (UK)	1978
Picture This/Fade Away And Radiate	Chrysalis (UK)	1978
I'm Gonna Love You Too/Just Go Away	Chrysalis (US)	1978
Hanging On The Telephone/	Chrysalis (UK)	1978
Will Anything Happen?		
Heart Of Glass/Rifle Range	Chrysalis (UK)	1979
Sunday Girl/I Know But I Don't Know	Chrysalis (UK)	1979
One Way Or Another/Just Go Away	Chrysalis (US)	1979
Dreaming/Sound-A-Sleep	Chrysalis (UK)	1979
Union City Blue/Living In The Real World	Chrysalis (UK)	1979
The Hardest Part/Sound-A-Sleep	Chrysalis (US)	1980
Atomic/Die Young, Stay Pretty	Chrysalis (UK)	1980
Call Me/Call Me (Instrumental)	Chrysalis (US)	1980
The Tide Is High/Suzy & Jeffrey	Chrysalis (UK)	1980
Rapture/Walk Like Me	Chrysalis (US)	1981

Island Of Lost Souls/Dragonfly	Chrysalis (UK)	1982
War Child/Little Caesar	Chrysalis (UK)	1982
Maria (Radio Edit)/Maria (Soul Solution Remix)/		
Maria (Talvin Singh Remix)	Beyond (UK)	1999

Nothing Is Real But The Girl (Boilerhouse Mix)/
Nothing Is Real But The Girl
(Danny Tengalia Club Mix)/
Nothing Is Real But The Girl
(Danny Tenaglia Instradub)   Beyond (UK) 1999

No Exit (Loud Rock Remix)/
No Exit (Infamous Hip Rock Version)/
No Exit (Album Version)   Beyond (UK) 1999

Good Boys (Album Version)/
Good Boys
(Giorgio Moroder Extended Long Version)   Epic/Sony (UK) 2003

Mother [download only]   Eleven Seven 2011

Albums

Blondie (Private Stock, 1976)
X-Offender/Little Girl Lies/In The Flesh/Look Good In Blue/In The
Sun/A Shark In Jet's Clothing/Man Overboard/Rip Her To Shreds/Rifle
Range/Kung Fu Girls/The Attack Of The Giant Ants

Plastic Letters (Chrysalis, 1978)
Fan Mail/Denis/Bermuda Triangle Blues (Flight 45)/Youth Nabbed As
Sniper/Contact In Red Square/(I'm Always Touched By Your) Presence
Dear/I'm On E/I Didn't Have The Nerve To Say No/Love At The Pier/
No Imagination/Kidnapper/Detroit 442/Cautious Lip

Parallel Lines (Chrysalis, 1978)
Hanging On The Telephone/One Way Or Another/Picture This/Fade
Away And Radiate/Pretty Baby/I Know But I Don't Know/11:59/Will

Anything Happen?/Sunday Girl/Heart Of Glass/I'm Gonna Love You Too/Just Go Away

Eat To The Beat (Chrysalis, 1979)
Dreaming/The Hardest Part/Union City Blue/Shayla/Eat To The Beat/ Accidents Never Happen/Die Young, Stay Pretty/Slow Motion/Atomic/ Sound-A-Sleep/Victor/Living In The Real World

Autoamerican (Chrysalis, 1980)
Europa/Live It Up/Here's Looking At You/The Tide Is High/Angels On The Balcony/Go Through It/Do The Dark/Rapture/Faces/T-Birds/Walk Like Me/Follow Me

The Hunter (Chrysalis, 1982)
Orchid Club/Island Of Lost Souls/Dragonfly/Four Your Eyes Only/The Beast/War Child/Little Caesar/Danceway/(Can I) Find The Right Words (To Say)/English Boys/The Hunter Gets Captured By The Game

No Exit (Beyond Music, 1999)
Screaming Skin/Forgive And Forget/Maria/No Exit/Double Take/ Nothing Is Real But The Girl/Boom Boom In The Zoom Zoom Room/ Night Wind Sent/Under The Gun (For Jeffrey Lee Pierce)/Out In The Streets/Happy Dog (For Caggy)/The Dream's Lost On Me/Divine/Dig Up The Conjo

The Curse Of Blondie (Sanctuary [US]/Epic [UK], 2003)
Shakedown/Good Boys/Undone/Golden Rod/Rules For Living/ Background Melody (The Only One)/Magic (Asadoya Yunta)/End To End/Hello Joe/The Tingler/Last One In The World/Diamond Bridge/ Desire Brings Me Back/Songs Of Love (For Richard)

Panic Of Girls (Eleven Seven/EMI, 2011)
D-Day/What I Heard/Mother/The End, The End/Girlie Girlie/Love Doesn't Frighten Me/Words In My Mouth/Sunday Smile/Wipe Off My Sweat/Le Bleu/China Shoes

DEBORAH HARRY

Singles

Backfired/Military Rap	Chrysalis (UK)	1981
The Jam Was Moving/Chrome	Chrysalis (US)	1981
Rush Rush/Rush Rush (Dub Version)	Chrysalis (UK)	1984
Feel The Spin/Feel The Spin (Dub Version)	Warner/Geffen (US)	1985
French Kissin'/Rockbird	Geffen (UK)	1986
Free To Fall/Feel The Spin	Chrysalis (UK)	1987
In Love With Love/In Love With Love (London Mix)	Geffen (US)	1987
Liar Liar/		
Queen of Voudou [The Voodooist Corporation]	Reprise (US)	1988
I Want That Man/Bike Boy	Sire (US)	1989
Brite Side/Bugeye	Chrysalis (UK)	1989
Sweet And Low/Lovelight	Chrysalis (UK)	1990
Maybe For Sure/Get Your Way	Chrysalis (UK)	1990
★Well Did You Evah	Chrysalis (UK)	1990
I Can See Clearly/		
I Can See Clearly (Album Version)	Sire/Reprise (US)	1993
Strike Me Pink/On A Breath/		
Sweet And Low (Phil Harding Mix)	Chrysalis (UK)	1993
Two Times Blue	Eleven Seven	2007
Fit Right In/Heat Of The Moment	Eleven Seven	2008

★ *With Iggy Pop. The b-side features a Thompson Twins version of 'Who Wants To Be A Millionaire?'*

Albums

KooKoo (Chrysalis, 1981)
Jump Jump/The Jam Was Moving/Chrome/Surrender/Inner City Spillover/Backfired/Now I Know You Know/Under Arrest/Military Rap/Oasis

Rockbird (Geffen, 1986)
I Want You/French Kissin'/Buckle Up/In Love With Love/You Got Me In Trouble/Free To Fall/Rockbird/Secret Life/Beyond The Limit

Def, Dumb and Blonde (Sire [US]/Chrysalis [UK], 1989)
I Want That Man/Lovelight/Kiss It Better/Maybe For Sure/Calmarie/
Get Your Way/Sweet And Low/He Is So/Brite Side/Bugeye/End Of The
Run

Debravation (Sire/Reprise [US]/Chrysalis [UK], 1993)
I Can See Clearly/Stability/Strike Me Pink/Rain/Communion/Lip
Service/Mood Ring/Keep On Going/Dancing Down The Moon/
Standing In My Way/The Fugitive/Dog Star Girl

Necessary Evil (Eleven Seven, 2007)
Two Times Blue/School For Scandal/If I Had You/Deep End/Love With
A Vengeance/Necessary Evil/Charm Redux/You're Too Hot/Dirty And
Deep/What Is Love/Whiteout/Needless To Say/Heart Of The Moment/
Charm Alarm/Jen Jen/Naked Eye/Paradise

The Jazz Passengers

Albums

Individually Twisted (32 Records, 1996)
Babble A La Roy/Maybe I'm Lost/L'il Darlin'/Angel Eyes/Pork Chop/
Aubergine/Olé/Imitation Of A Kiss/Jive Samba (Part II)/Doncha Go
'Way Mad/The Tide Is High/It Came From Outer Space/Star Dust

'Live' In Spain (Les Disques Du Crépuscle, 1998)
Intro/Fathouse/Lady Butter/When The Fog Lifts/Dog In Sand/Samba
Uber Alles/Wednesday Afternoon/Maybe I'm Lost/Bullmoose Boulevard

CHRIS STEIN

Singles

★★Wild Style Rap No. 1/Wild Style Rap No. 2   Chrysalis (Japan) 1983

★★*With Grandmaster Caz.*

Index